Ernst Denert Award for Software Engineering 2020

Michael Felderer • Wilhelm Hasselbring •
Heiko Koziolek • Florian Matthes • Lutz Prechelt •
Ralf Reussner • Bernhard Rumpe • Ina Schaefer
Editors

Ernst Denert Award for Software Engineering 2020

Practice Meets Foundations

 Springer

Editors
Michael Felderer
Department of Computer Science
University of Innsbruck
Innsbruck, Austria

Wilhelm Hasselbring
Department of Computer Science
Kiel University
Kiel, Germany

Heiko Koziolek
Corporate Research
ABB
Ladenburg, Germany

Florian Matthes
Institute of Computer Science
Technical University Munich
Garching, Germany

Lutz Prechelt
Department of Mathematics
and Computer Science
Freie Universität Berlin
Berlin, Germany

Ralf Reussner
Program Structures and Data Organization
Karlsruhe Institute of Technology
Karlsruhe, Germany

Bernhard Rumpe
Software Engineering
RWTH Aachen University
Aachen, Germany

Ina Schaefer
Software Engineering and Automotive
Informatics
Technische Universität Braunschweig
Braunschweig, Germany

ISBN 978-3-030-83130-1   ISBN 978-3-030-83128-8   (eBook)
https://doi.org/10.1007/978-3-030-83128-8

This Springer imprint is published by the registered company Springer Nature Switzerland AG.
The registered company address is: Gewerbestrasse 11, 6330 Cham, Switzerland

Contents

Ernst Denert Software Engineering Award 2020

Michael Felderer, Wilhelm Hasselbring, Heiko Koziolek, Florian Matthes, Lutz Prechelt, Ralf Reussner, Bernhard Rumpe, and Ina Schaefer

Abstract This is the introductory chapter of the book on the Ernst Denert Software Engineering Award 2020. It provides an overview of the 11 nominated PhD theses, the work of the award winner, and the structure of the book.

1 Introduction

Software-based products, systems, or services are influencing all areas of our daily life. They are the basis and central driver for digitization and all kinds of innovation. This makes software engineering a core discipline to drive technical and societal

M. Felderer (✉)
Department of Computer Science, University of Innsbruck, Innsbruck, Austria

W. Hasselbring
Department of Computer Science, Kiel University, Kiel, Germany

H. Koziolek
Corporate Research, ABB, Ladenburg, Germany

F. Matthes
Institute of Computer Science, Technical University Munich, Garching, Germany

L. Prechelt
Department of Mathematics and Computer Science, Freie Universität Berlin, Berlin, Germany

R. Reussner
Program Structures and Data Organization, Karlsruhe Institute of Technology, Karlsruhe, Germany

B. Rumpe
Software Engineering, RWTH Aachen University, Aachen, Germany

I. Schaefer
Software Engineering and Automotive Informatics, Technische Universität Braunschweig, Braunschweig, Germany

M. Felderer et al. (eds.), *Ernst Denert Award for Software Engineering 2020*,
https://doi.org/10.1007/978-3-030-83128-8_1

innovations in the age of digitization [4]. The IEEE Standard Glossary of Software Engineering Terminology [5] defines software engineering as follows:

1. The application of a systematic, disciplined, quantifiable approach to the development, operation, and maintenance of software; that is, the application of engineering to software
2. The study of approaches as in (1)

It defines software engineering as an engineering discipline ("application of engineering to software") with its own methodology ("systematic, disciplined, quantifiable approach") applied to all phases of the software life cycle ("development, operation, and maintenance of software"). The two-part structure of the definition of software engineering also makes the tight integration of software engineering (1) and software engineering research (2) explicit.

Therefore, the Ernst Denert Software Engineering Award specifically rewards researchers who value the practical impact of their work and aim to improve current software engineering practices [3]. Creating tighter feedback loops between professional practitioners and academic researchers is essential to make research ideas ready for industry adoption. Researchers who demonstrate their proposed methods and tools on nontrivial systems under real-world conditions in various phases of the software lifecycle shall be supported, so that the gap between research and practice can be decreased.

Overall, 11 PhD theses that were defended between September 1, 2019, and October 31, 2020, were nominated and finally presented during the Software Engineering Conference SE 2021.

All submissions fulfill the ambitious selection criteria of the award defined in detail in the book for the Ernst Denert Software Engineering Award 2019 [2]. These criteria include, among others, practical applicability, usefulness via tools, theoretical or empirical insights, currentness, and contribution to the field. In a nutshell, "The best submissions are those that will be viewed as important steps forward even 15 years from now" [3].

This book includes a chapter on the jury decision process (chapter "Some Patterns of Convincing Software Engineering Research, or: How to Win the Ernst Denert Software Engineering Award 2020"), which might help future candidates to shape the presentation of their work for the Ernst Denert Software Engineering Award and beyond.

In this introductory chapter we give an overview of the nominated 11 PhD theses, present the work of the award winner, and outline the structure of the book.

2   Overview of the Nominated PhD Theses

As mentioned before, 11 PhD theses were nominated for the Ernst Denert Software Engineering Award 2020. They cover the broad range of software engineering research; show the wide spectrum and liveliness of the field with respect to different application domains (covering information systems, embedded systems, and IoT systems in different application contexts) and research methods (covering formal methods, design science, as well as quantitative and qualitative empirical methods); and address software lifecycle activities (covering analysis, design, programming, testing, deployment, operation, and maintenance). In the following, we present a short overview of the nominee's PhD theses (alphabetically sorted by the nominee's names) by a short summary of the chapters on the respective theses contributed to this book.

The chapter by Jonathan Immanuel Brachthäuser entitled **"What You See Is What You Get: Practical Effect Handlers in Capability-Passing Style"** aims to bring effect handlers in programming languages closer to the software engineering practice by developing capability passing as an implementation technique for effect handlers. Capability passing provides the basis for the integration of effect handlers into mainstream object-oriented programming languages and thereby unlocks novel modularization strategies.

The chapter by Mojdeh Golagha entitled **"How to Effectively Reduce Failure Analysis Time?"** proposes methodologies and techniques supporting developers in knowing which data they need for further analysis, in being able to group failures based on their root causes, and in being able to find more information about the root causes of each failing group.

The chapter by Nikolay Harutyunyan entitled **"Open Source Software Governance: Distilling and Applying Industry Best Practices"** develops and evaluates a theory of industry best practices which captures how more than 20 experts from 15 companies worldwide govern their corporate use of open source software. Furthermore, the theory is operationalized via a handbook for open source governance that enables practitioners from various domains to apply the findings in their companies.

The chapter by Dominic Henze entitled **"Dynamically Scalable Fog Architectures"** provides a framework called xFog (Extension for Fog Computing) that models fog architectures based on set theory and graphs. It contains parts to establish the set-theoretical foundations to enable dynamic and scalable fog architectures to dynamically add new components or layers, and to provide a view concept which allows stakeholders to focus on different levels of abstraction.

The chapter by Anne Hess entitled **"Crossing Disciplinary Borders to Improve Requirements Communication"** investigates role-specific views in software requirements specifications. Based on a series of empirical studies that served as a baseline for a secondary analysis role-specific views are defined and evaluated. Moreover, a proof-of-concept implementation is realized that is capable of generating role-specific views.

The chapter by István Koren entitled **"DevOpsUse: A Community-Oriented Methodology for Societal Software Engineering"** introduces the DevOpsUse methodology, which extends DevOps by additionally fostering a stronger involvement of end user communities in software development by including them in the process of infrastructuring, that is, the appropriation of infrastructure during its usage. The developed DevOpsUse methodology and support tools are validated by the transitions between three generations of technologies: near-real-time peer-to-peer web architectures, edge computing, and IoT systems.

The chapter by Yannic Noller entitled **"Hybrid Differential Software Testing"** proposes the concept of Hybrid Differential Software Testing (HyDiff) as a hybrid analysis technique to generate difference-revealing inputs. HyDiff consists of two components that operate in a parallel setup, that is, a search-based technique that inexpensively generates inputs and a systematic exploration technique to also exercise deeper program behaviors. HyDiff is based on differential fuzzing directed by differential heuristics and differential dynamic symbolic execution that allows to incorporate concrete inputs in its analysis.

The chapter by Dominic Steinhöfel entitled **"Ever Change a Running System: Structured Software Reengineering Using Automatically Proven-Correct Transformation Rules"** proposes the concept of structured software reengineering replacing the ad hoc forward engineering part of a reengineering process with the application of behavior-preserving, proven-correct transformations improving nonfunctional program properties. Furthermore, a specification and verification framework for statement-based program transformation rules on Java programs building on symbolic execution is presented. It is applied to code refactoring, cost analysis of program transformations, and transformations reshaping programs for the application of parallel design patterns. Finally, a workbench for modeling and proving statement-level Java transformation rules is provided.

The chapter by Peter Wägemann entitled **"Static Worst-Case Analyses and Their Validation Techniques for Safety-Critical Systems"** provides a novel program analysis approach for worst-case energy consumption bounds, which accounts for temporarily power-consuming devices, scheduling with fixed real-time priorities, synchronous task activations, and asynchronous interrupt service routines. Regarding the validation of worst-case tools, a technique for automatically generating benchmark programs is provided. The generator combines program patterns so that the worst-case resource consumption is available along with the generated benchmark. Knowledge about the actual worst-case resource demand then serves as the baseline for evaluating and validating program analysis tools. The benchmark generator helped to reveal previously undiscovered software bugs in a widespread worst-case execution time tool for safety-critical systems.

The chapter by Michael von Wenckstern entitled **"Improving the Model-Based Systems Engineering Process"** provides approaches and tools for supporting the automotive software engineer with automatic consistency checks of large component and connector models, automatic verification of these models against design decisions, tracing and navigating between design and implementation models, finding structural inconsistencies during model evolution, defining different extra-functional properties for component and connector models, and formalizing constraints on these models for extra-functional properties for automatic consistency checks.

Finally, the chapter by Franz Zieris entitled **"Understanding How Pair Programming Actually Works in Industry: Mechanisms, Patterns, and Dynamics"** is aimed at understanding how pair programming actually works by uncovering the underlying mechanisms and in order to ultimately formulate practical advice for developers by following a grounded theory methodology. Franz Zieris is the winner of the Ernst Denert Software Engineering Award 2020, and we present his work in more detail in the next section.

3 The Work of the Award Winner

We congratulate *Franz Zieris*, his advisor *Lutz Prechelt*, and his Alma Mater Freie Universität Berlin for winning the Ernst Denert Software Engineering Award 2020 for the PhD thesis "Qualitative analysis of knowledge transfer in pair programming."

Dr. Franz Zieris used qualitative research methods to break down the actual work process involved in pair programming (PP). There has been a lot of research on PP in the last 20 years, but it provided remarkably little insight overall:

- In controlled experiments, PP is usually faster than solo programming, but sometimes not (and almost never twice as fast). The results are often better with respect to design quality or reliability than with solo programming, but sometimes they are not.
- The subject of the experiments was almost always toy programs. The results' generalizability to realistic code bases is completely unknown.
- Explanations for the considerable variations between experiments are almost nonexistent.

The work of Franz Zieris has now conceptualized what is going on in the pair programming process in an industrial context:

1. Zieris found a number of behavioral patterns and anti-patterns that can explain why the previous quantitative results have varied so much. For example, the much-investigated differences in programming experience play a much smaller role than whether the developers manage to build and maintain a common mental model of the software system.
2. These patterns provide professional pair programmers and developers who do not like pair programming so far with an opportunity to reflect on their behavior and avoid inefficient behaviors.
3. Zieris found an overall dynamic of PP sessions that makes it clear that the previous experiments completely lack the central element of professional PP sessions, namely the alignment and acquisition of system understanding; thus, the realism of previous experiments is very low.
4. From these findings it is derived which pair constellations are helpful which can help teams to use PP wisely.
5. Both advantages, that is, (2) and (4), were validated with professional developers.

The spectacular thing about Franz Zieris' work is the enormous generality of the improvements, because the results are applicable in any application domain and with any technology, and they are also timeless. The work of Franz Zieris is presented in more detail in chapter "Understanding How Pair Programming Actually Works in Industry: Mechanisms, Patterns, and Dynamics" of this book.

4   Structure of the Book

The remainder of the book is structured as follows. In the next chapter Lutz Prechelt describes the jury's decision process, which might help future candidates to shape the presentation of their work for the Ernst Denert Software Engineering Award and beyond.

This is followed by 11 chapters, one for the work of each nominee listed above. Each nominee presents in his or her chapter

- An overview and the key findings of the work
- Its relevance and applicability to practice and industrial software engineering projects
- Additional information and findings that have only been discovered afterward, for example, when applying the results in industry or when continuing research.

The chapters of the nominees are based on their PhD theses and arranged in alphabetic order.

As already highlighted in the introductory book chapter of the last year's award [3] and by Prof. Denert's reflection on the field [1], software engineering is teamwork. Outstanding research with high impact is also always teamwork, which somewhat conflicts with the requirement that a doctoral thesis must be the work of a single author. Still, the respective chapters are written by the nominees only.

Thanks

We gratefully thank Professor Ernst Denert for all his help in the process and the *Gerlind & Ernst Denert-Stiftung* for the kind donation of the price and the overall support. We thank the organization team of the Software Engineering Conference SE 2021 that was virtually organized by the Technical University of Braunschweig to host the presentations of the nominees and the award ceremony. Finally, we thank the German, Austrian, and Swiss computer science societies, that is, the GI, the OCG, and the SI, respectively, for their support in making the Ernst Denert Software Engineering Award 2020 a success.

References

1. Denert, E.: Software engineering. In: Ernst Denert Award for Software Engineering 2019, pp. 11–17. Springer, Berlin (2020)
2. Felderer, M., Hasselbring, W., Koziolek, H., Matthes, F., Prechelt, L., Reussner, R., Rumpe, B., Schaefer, I.: Ernst Denert Award for Software Engineering 2019: Practice Meets Foundations (2020)

3. Felderer, M., Hasselbring, W., Koziolek, H., Matthes, F., Prechelt, L., Reussner, R., Rumpe, B., Schaefer, I.: Ernst Denert software engineering awards 2019. In: Ernst Denert Award for Software Engineering 2019, pp. 1–10, Springer, Berlin (2020)
4. Felderer, M., Reussner, R., Rumpe, B.: Software engineering and software-engineering Forschung im Zeitalter der Digitalisierung. Inform. Spektrum **44**(2), 82–94 (2021)
5. IEEE: IEEE standard glossary of software engineering terminology. IEEE Std 610.12-1990 pp. 1–84 (1990)

Some Patterns of Convincing Software Engineering Research, or: How to Win the Ernst Denert Software Engineering Award 2020

Lutz Prechelt

Abstract We explain what properties the jury looked for to identify strong contributions and why they are important. They are formulated as seven pieces of advice: (1) Be in scope, (2) Enumerate your assumptions, (3) Delineate your contribution, (4) Honestly discuss limitations, (5) Show usefulness and practical applicability, (6) Have a well-prepared nutshell, and (7) Be timeless.

1 Introduction

This chapter is going to give some insight into the jury's decision process: What we found convincing or not so convincing, and why.

We write this up as much for the benefit of those who want to win this award in the future ("you") as for our own. It helps us to reflect:

- How do our award criteria work out?
- What is the nature of the limitations of works that do not come out victoriously?

It helps you and ourselves getting an idea of some of the relevant psychological dynamics of the jury work.

We write it as a list of separate pieces of advice, formulated as properties that good work should have. The first three we found by counter-examples, the other two by positive examples. We do not name the respective works, but you may be able to identify them by looking at the rest of the book.

We may or may not refine the list in the coming years, for example, by sharpening the terminology used herein.

Each of the remaining sections covers one piece of advice. Please consider them as a proposer or when you prepare your presentation.

L. Prechelt (✉)
Freie Universität Berlin, Berlin, Germany
e-mail: prechelt@inf.fu-berlin.de

© The Author(s) 2022
M. Felderer et al. (eds.), *Ernst Denert Award for Software Engineering 2020*,
https://doi.org/10.1007/978-3-030-83128-8_2

2 Be in Scope

Obviously, to appeal to the jury of a software engineering award, your work must look and feel like software engineering.

In this year's list of 11 works, there was one that we liked *a lot* in many respects, but we felt was too far removed from the technical work in software development. Another, also with some definite strengths, we classified as work in an application domain, not in software engineering as such. Both of these were removed from our consideration quickly.

3 Enumerate Your Assumptions

Make sure you explain carefully where the ideas and techniques you describe will apply, will likely apply, may apply, and will likely or surely not apply.

The jury is allergic to overselling, to claiming something that is not true. So if we spot a case or area where your techniques do not apply or where we expect they will likely not apply, yet perceive you as claiming they do, we will view your work much more critically.

Therefore, make sure you spell out your assumptions regarding aspects such as

- The target application domain(s) of the software your techniques help building (e.g., hard real-time systems), or the nature of those domains (e.g., regarding the possible precision of specifications)
- The specific technologies that software must be using (e.g., Java), or the nature of those technologies (e.g., statically typed languages)
- The software development process (team sizes, qualification of the people involved, roles, specific practices used or not used, etc.)

The above list is horribly poor and the software engineering community has not yet developed taxonomies that could be used as checklists, so you will have to think yourself what relevant assumptions are underlying your work and shortly explain them to the jury. The characterization can be made positively ("applies if") or negatively ("applies unless").

For several of this year's candidate works, the jury was unsure in its discussion where the work might or might not apply. Such uncertainty will stifle the enthusiasm your work must spark in the jury in order to win.

Works with broad applicability are of course great. Works with narrower applicability can often create much larger improvements—also great. Works with unsure applicability, however, are less likely to convince the jury, and several of this year's contributions had a lot of room for improvement in this regard.

4 Delineate Your Contribution

You will, of course, point out what your research contribution is: how your work advances the state of the art. But the flip side of this is also helpful: By pointing out what is *not* part of your contribution (because it was already there before your work), you will often make it a lot easier for the jury to understand what the contribution really is, and appreciate it.

We had at least two submissions where different members of the jury viewed the amount of originality in the work *very* differently. I suspect the ones with the more negative view recognized some aspects they believed were previously known, perceived them as being claimed to be part of the contribution, and then overlooked or underappreciated what was really new. Such situations damage your chances.

5 Honestly Discuss Limitations

We value intellectual honesty. The more you bring of that, the better. Even within the realm of applicability outlined by your assumptions, there will be areas where your techniques work well and others where they work not so well, including cases where they do not work at all. Where the assumptions describe the macro level of applicability, these limitations describe the micro level.

The same advice applies as for assumptions: If the jury spots a limitation you did not mention, our opinion of your work will be damaged a lot more than the limitation itself ever could. Make sure you state all relevant limitations of your work.

6 Show Usefulness and Practical Applicability

One reason why the Ernst Denert Award even exists is that Ernst Denert feels academic software engineering work is often overly academic and neglects usefulness, practical applicability, or both. Therefore, a good candidate work will cater for these aspects and argue why the contribution is strong in this respect.

Ideally, it will report in detail on extensive field use and calculate return-on-invest. However, this is almost always unrealistic.

The next best thing would be widely spread pick-up of a tool: If dozens of teams decide the tool is worth using and keep up use over some time, this is also strong evidence that the tool is useful and applicable. This variant is likely applicable only to tools, not to other types of contribution.

The third-best possibility would be a limited field trial describing what about the contribution worked easily or well and what made problems or showed limitations. Such an approach should present initial evidence that the technique in question is indeed useful and the benefits exceed the costs and downsides. Subjective statements of various participants may be the best you can get, but if done right, they can be convincing.

For contributions that apply to artifacts, applying them in the laboratory to a broad corpus of such artifacts can sometimes be an alternative.

But even that may be impossible: Your work may be groundwork that is not directly applicable. Or it may be insufficiently far developed to overcome many of the practical hurdles against using it in real software development settings. In such cases you need to resort to argumentation: Explain a scenario of how your contribution can be developed into something that is useful and applicable in practice. It will be a lot harder to convince the jury in this way, but if you have done a good job with respect to explaining delineation, assumptions, and limitations, it should be possible.

7 Have a Well-Prepared Nutshell

The importance of the presentation you give to the jury can hardly be overestimated.

Two thousand pages of dissertation text is not something the average (or indeed any) jury member is going to read, let alone understand and remember. One hundred pages of expertises and submitters' rationales are more manageable for a jury member in principle, but are difficult to digest and keep in memory for so many candidates when one is not familiar with the individual works and many of their topic areas. Do not assume any jury member has read any of this material. They may have. But more likely than not, have not.

Therefore, the short presentation you are going to give essentially has to do it all: motivate your work, explain its techniques, explain its results and their contribution, and address the concerns discussed above to overcome the jury members' diverse biases, preferences, and pet peeves.

It is a super-difficult task. While trying to find a solution, keep in mind the following:

- We are a more generalist audience than the collection of experts and semi-experts you encounter in a typical conference session. Therefore:
- Avoid losing us by explaining technical detail we cannot understand because we lack some of the foundations.
- Avoid losing us by going too fast wherever *any* concepts are involved that some of us do not encounter often.
- Under these circumstances, "telling a story" is the approach most likely to work. If you have never tried this, learn it now; it is highly effective in many situations, in research and beyond.
- On the other hand, you do not need to convince us that you "know your stuff." We know all of the works are very good and their authors very capable.

8 Be Timeless

Imagine a time 20 years into the future: What will the role be of your contribution of today in the software engineering knowledge of tomorrow?

- Will it be something that had its 15 minutes of fame 20 years ago but has long become completely irrelevant?
- Will it have been surpassed by improved solutions that address the same problem, but build on your contribution?
- Will it have become a classical tool, hardly changed, but still somewhat useful (like *make*)?
- Will it be a well-known piece of method knowledge, long considered obvious and self-understood (like *refactoring*)?

If your contribution has aspects that you expect to last long, make sure you explain to the jury what those are and why you think so. We appreciate it.

What You See Is What You Get: Practical Effect Handlers In Capability-Passing Style

Jonathan Immanuel Brachthäuser

Abstract Structuring control flow is an essential task almost every programmer faces on a daily basis. At the same time, the control flow of software applications is becoming increasingly complicated, motivating languages to include more and more features like asynchronous programming and generators. Effect handlers are a promising alternative since they can express many of these features as libraries. To bring effect handlers closer to the software engineering practice, we present *capability passing* as an implementation technique for effect handlers. Capability passing provides the basis for the integration of effect handlers into mainstream object-oriented programming languages and thereby unlocks novel modularization strategies. It also enables programmers to apply lexical reasoning about effects and gives rise to a new form of effect polymorphism. Finally, it paves the path for efficient compilation strategies of control effects.

1 Introduction

Structuring control flow is an essential task almost every programmer faces on a daily basis. The control-flow mechanisms offered by modern programming languages range from simple local control-flow mechanisms, such as conditional branching and loops, to more complex constructs that enable non-local control flow transfers, such as exceptions, asynchronous programming, generators, fibers, and many more.

Some programs require combining various of the aforementioned mechanisms to structure control flow. As an example, take the following JavaScript program.

```
async function* readFiles(files) {
  for (const file of files) {
    const contents = await read(file);
```

J. I. Brachthäuser (✉)
EPFL, Lausanne, Switzerland
e-mail: jonathan.brachthauser@epfl.ch

© The Author(s) 2022
M. Felderer et al. (eds.), *Ernst Denert Award for Software Engineering 2020*,
https://doi.org/10.1007/978-3-030-83128-8_3

15

```
    if (!contents) { throw "empty file" }
    else { yield contents }
  }
}
```

The example structures the local program flow using for and if. It also uses exceptions (e.g., throw), generators (e.g., yield), and asynchronous programming (e.g., async / await). Integrating and combining all of those mechanisms in one language (like JavaScript) come with significant challenges.

Programmers struggle to understand programs that combine the various features [41]. Does calling the above function result in a promise containing a generator, or a generator of promises? Where will the exception "empty file" be caught? At the call site of readFiles? When awaiting the promise? When requesting the next result from the generator? At the same time, mechanisms like async/await turn structuring control flow from an implementation detail to a cross-cutting concern, having a negative impact on modularity and modular reasoning.

Language designers have to establish the correctness of the individual features *and* their interaction. Interestingly, generators and async/await have been added individually to ECMAScript in versions 2016 and 2017. The combination (i.e., asynchronous generator functions) however was only considered in ES2018. Most languages that incorporate features like exceptions, generators, or asynchronous programming lack a static type- and effect system that guarantees that all exceptions are handled and that, for example, generators yield values of the correct type. Establishing effect safety without sacrificing flexible use and program understanding appears as a particular challenge for language designers.

Compiler engineers have to optimize the runtime performance of every single construct. This is particularly challenging on platforms with just-in-time (JIT) compilation like JavaScript and Java, since in those languages the features need to be implemented in both the interpreter and the compiler. This affects both the correctness and the performance of the various features and their interaction, which needs to be considered in interpreter *and* compiler.

Algebraic effects and handlers [46–48] (in this chapter we refer to them as *effect handlers*) are a promising solution to many of the aforementioned problems. Originally presented as a mathematical theory to model the semantics of computational effects (like exceptions), they can now be found as a program structuring principle in languages like Koka [33], Frank [40], Multicore OCaml [20], Helium [5], and Effekt [8]. It has been shown that effect handlers can express many of the aforementioned features as libraries. This includes exceptions [34], asynchronous programming [1, 36], generators [7, 34], cooperative multitasking [18, 21], and many more. Expressing those mechanisms as libraries instead of building them into a language has multiple advantages: Programmers only need to learn and understand one language feature instead of a multitude of different features. Modeling language features in terms of effect handlers allows programmers to use the same conceptual framework to understand the features and their interaction. Instead of having to deal with a combinatorial explosion, language designers only need to prove soundness of a single feature, once and for all. By implementing language features as libraries, their composition is automatically well defined. Also compiler engineers are only concerned with implementing and optimizing a single feature. Improving the performance of a single feature automatically impacts the performance of all control structures, which are implemented as libraries in terms of this one feature.

Effect handlers solve many of the aforementioned problems and are constantly gaining traction in the programming languages community. So why have they not been adopted by existing mainstream general purpose programming languages, yet? To prepare them for practical use and facilitate a widespread adoption, we can identify three challenges and corresponding areas of research:

1. Effect handlers have been conceived in the realm of functional programming languages. In consequence, many implementations of effect handlers can be found in functional programming languages. They are either built into the language, like in Eff [3], Koka [33], Frank [40], Multicore OCaml [17], Links [27], and Helium [5]. Or they are implemented as a libraries for Haskell [29, 31, 55], OCaml [29, 32], or Idris [13]. Studying how the paradigm of effect handling can be integrated into other paradigms such as *object-oriented programming* (OOP) could positively impact adoption by OO languages such as Java or Scala.
2. Effect handlers provide a unifying semantic framework to reason about programs. However, just like with exceptions [59], reasoning about the control flow of programs that make extensive use of handlers can remain challenging—in particular in the presence of higher-order functions [39]. Effect systems, as a static approximation of the runtime semantics, often help but easily become complicated to reason about themselves [8]. We believe that being able to *reason lexically* (that is just from the program text) about where an effect is handled could significantly improve program understanding.
3. Effect handlers are general enough to express many control flow mechanisms. This generality comes with a price: *runtime performance*. While great improvements are being made [35, 49, 53], we believe that further improving runtime performance is important to facilitate a widespread adoption. Programmers should not be forced to choose between the right abstraction and efficiency.

After providing an introduction to effect handlers, in this chapter, we present the current state of the art in the above three research areas. In particular, we discuss how the implementation technique of *capability passing* can contribute to improve on the abovementioned problems.

Effect Signature:

```
effect Gen {
  def yield(value: Int): Boolean
}
```

Effectful Program:

```
def range(from: Int, to: Int) =
  if (from ≤ to && yield(from)) {
    range(from + 1, to)
  }
```

Effect Handler:

```
try {
  range(0, 10)
} with Gen {
  def yield(value: Int) = {
    println(value);
    resume(true)
  }
}
```

Fig. 1 Effect handlers generalize exception handlers. They allow resuming the computation at the call site. Examples of an effect signature, an effectful program, and an effect handler in the programming language Effekt

2   Effect Handlers

Here we offer a brief introduction into programming with effects and handlers. The examples in this section use our language Effekt[1] [8], but (unless pointed out) the underlying principles apply to most languages with support for effect handling, such as Koka [37] or Multicore OCaml [21].

Effect handlers can be thought of as a generalization of the simpler and widely known control-flow construct *exceptions*. Similar to exceptions, programs using effect handlers are conceptually split into three parts: effect operations, effectful functions, and effect handlers. All three components are illustrated in Fig. 1.

Effect operations.   Compared with exceptions, *effect operations* correspond to throw as found in languages like Java [25]. However, instead of being built in, effect operations are user defined. One can define operations like yield to output elements of a (push-based) stream, getHttp to send (asynchronous) http-requests, or suspend to (cooperatively) transfer control to a scheduler [34]. In contrast to exceptional control flow with throw, effect operations can potentially return results. The effect operation yield in Fig. 1 takes integer values and returns a boolean value.

Effectful programs.   Programs are *effectful* [3, 29] if they call effect operations. This can occur either directly or indirectly via other effectful programs. Like checked exceptions in Java, some implementations of effect handlers track the effects used by an effectful program in its type. This allows the type checker to distinguish effectful programs from *pure programs* (i.e., programs using no effects) and to assert that all effects are eventually handled. The effectful program range uses the yield operation to yield values between *from* and *to*. Its inferred type is Unit / { Gen }, that is, it does return a value of type Unit

---

[1] The language implementation, further documentation, and a programming environment are available online (https://effekt-lang.org).

(similar to `void` in Java) and uses the `Gen` effect. In general, we can read types like T / { E_1, E_2, ...} as: the computation returns a value of type T and requires handling of effects E_1, E_2, and so forth.

Effect handlers. Effect handlers are generalized exception handlers [2, 17]. They implement the effect operations, specifying what it means for example to yield, send http-requests, or suspend. Like exception handlers delimit the scope with `try { ... }`, effect handlers delimit the *dynamic scope* in which effect operations of a particular effect signature are handled by this very handler. In our example, we handle the generator effect of the program `range(0, 10)` by printing the values obtained from the generator. It then resumes the computation at the original call to `yield`, passing the value `true` as the result of the call to `yield`. This possibility to resume the computation equips effect handlers with the additional expressive power over exceptions.

Effect operations are often declared (and grouped) in *effect signatures* (such as `Gen`), which act as an interface between the user of effect operations (i.e., effectful programs) and the implementor of effect operations (i.e., effect handlers). Programming with effect handlers encourages modularity, by separating the declaration of effect operations from their implementation in effect handlers [29].

2.1 Aborting the Computation

Effect handlers can express many different control-flow mechanisms. Maybe the simplest form are exceptions. Simply by *not* calling `resume`, we can abort the computation that called `raise` as illustrated in the following example.

Effect Signature:

```
effect Exc {
  def raise[A](msg: String): A
}
```

Effect Handler:

```
def divideBy(n: Double) =
  try { println(div(4.0, n)) }
  with Exc {
    def raise(msg: String) = {
      println("Error:" ++ msg)
    }
  }
```

Effectful Program:

```
def div(x: Double, y: Double) =
  if (y == 0.0) {
    raise("division by zero")
  } else {
    x / y
  }
```

The type of `raise` promises to return a value of type `A` for every `A`. This is possible since we will never call `resume` and thus never have to provide such a value. In our example, calling `divideBy(2.0)` prints `2.0` whereas calling `divideBy(0.0)` reports an error.

2.2 Dynamic Dependencies

One important usage of effects is to express dependencies to other components or to model configuration [12]. This is illustrated in the following example.

Effect Signature:

```
effect Request {
  def port(): Int
  def path(): String
}
effect Session {
  def user(): User
}
```

Effectful Program:

```
def render() =
  if (path() == "/index") { index() }
  else { ... }

def index() =
  p("Welcome: " ++ user().name)
```

The example declares two effects: `Request` to represent context information about the current request to a webserver and `Session` to express information that is available in the present session.

Expressing dependencies this way has two advantages: First, context information such as the current request do not need to be passed explicitly as arguments. Instead, the function `render` immediately calls the effect operation `path`, and `index` calls `user`. Neither function requires explicit passing of arguments. Second, dependencies are tracked uniformly by the type system. The inferred type of `index` is `Html / { Session }` communicating that it returns `Html` values using the `Session` effect that needs to be handled at the call site. Similarly, `render` has an inferred type of `Html / { Request, Session }` and thus requires handling of both, `Request` and `Session`. Effects allow us to make dependencies explicit in the type, while type- and effect *inference* improves maintainability and, for instance, simplifies adding dependencies without having to change the type signature.

2.3 Advanced Control Flow

So far, we have seen examples where we either did not call the continuation (i.e., resume) to model exceptional control flow or where we immediately called the continuation to express dynamic dependencies. While these are common use cases, in general, effect handlers can express many more control-flow patterns. For

example, cooperative multitasking can be implemented in terms of an effect like
Fiber:

Effect Signature:

```
effect Fiber {
  def fork(): Boolean
  def suspend(): Unit
  def exit(): Unit
}
```

Effectful Program:

```
if (fork()) {
  println("in fork"); suspend(); ...
} else {
  println("in main fiber"); suspend(); ...
}
```

Effect handlers for Fiber can implement scheduling of virtual threads by storing
the continuation in a queue [9, 21] and resuming them at a later point. Similarly,
control-flow mechanisms for asynchronous programming [36] and generators [34]
can be expressed. That is, all of the features from the introductory example (Sect. 1)
can be modeled in terms of effect handlers. Effect handlers thus provide a unifying
semantic framework to program with complex control flow.

In the remainder of this chapter, we present the implementation technique of
capability-passing style and discuss how different shortcomings of effect handlers
are addressed by it.

3   Effect Handlers and Object-Oriented Programming

Effect handlers have been conceived in the setting of functional programming
languages. Given this heritage, it is not surprising that effect handlers have been
implemented as libraries for functional programming languages like Haskell [29,
31, 55], Idris [13], or OCaml [29, 32]. Similarly, most standalone languages that
support effect handlers are centered around the functional programming paradigm.
Examples include Eff [3], Koka [33], Frank [40], Links [27], and Helium [4].

Implementations in the realm of object-oriented programming (OOP) are much
more difficult to find. Only few implementations, which we are aware of, explicitly
use OOP features in their APIs. This comes somewhat with a surprise: the way we
introduced effect handlers in earlier sections used vocabulary, which is also often
used to describe object-oriented programming. More than that, Fig. 2 shows that we
can directly map concepts from programming with effect handlers to object-oriented

Effect Handlers	Object-Oriented Programming
Effect Signatures	Interfaces
Effect Operation	Method
Effect Handlers	Implementations (Classes)
Effectful Programs	Interface Users
Effect Capability	Instances / Objects

Fig. 2 Mapping concepts from effect handlers to object-oriented programming

programming—an observation that we made in prior work [6, 7, 9] and that has been made independently by other researchers in the field [28, 60].

Effect signatures as interfaces. Effect signatures list the available effect operations, which are associated with one effect. They only specify the type signatures of effect operations without giving a concrete implementation. Effect signatures thus directly correspond to interfaces in OOP, while effect operations correspond to abstract methods defined in the interface.

Effect handlers as implementing classes. Effect handlers specify what it means to call an effect operation like `yield`. They are implementations of effect signatures and thus directly correspond to classes in OOP. One important difference to traditional classes in OOP is that effect handlers can make use of the continuation `resume` to implement effect operations, allowing them to express advanced patterns of control flow. We refer the interested reader to Zhang et al. [60] for a detailed comparison of the control flow offered by handlers and classes and their connection to OOP.

Capabilities as instances. One OOP concept that traditionally has no direct correspondence in the realm of algebraic effect handlers is the one of objects or instances. To implement algebraic effect handlers as libraries for languages like Scala [6, 9], or Java [7], in prior work, we introduced the notion of a *capability* as an instance of an effect handler. A capability not only holds the implementation of an effect handler but can also be seen as the constructive proof that the holder is entitled to use a particular effect. The concept of capabilities is inspired by the object-capability model for authority control [16, 43, 44].

Directly mapping effect handlers to OOP features has several advantages. Reusing existing concepts to structure effect handlers and effectful programs lets users focus on what is new with effect handlers. At the same time, users can immediately apply their knowledge and intuition about interfaces and classes to structure effect signatures and handlers, correspondingly.

Reusing existing abstractions from OOP allows users to combine the advantages of those abstractions with the abstraction of effect handlers. The combination of effect handlers with object-oriented features enables novel modularization strategies, not only for effectful programs but also for effect handler implementations [7]. For instance, programmers can use standard OOP techniques like inheritance, subtyping, private state, dynamic dispatch, and others to structure and implement effect handlers [11]. By embedding handlers in a language like Scala, programmers can additionally use more advanced features (like mixin composition or abstract type members) to modularly describe effects and handlers.

Language implementors benefit from reusing existing abstractions since this removes the burden of re-implementing very similar abstractions all over again. Having fewer features also potentially reduces the risk of bad feature interaction. To implement the functionality of effect handlers as libraries, reuse is even more essential since it simply might not be possible to add new abstractions to a language without modifying its syntax and semantics. Our design allowed us to implement

effect handlers as libraries for Scala [6] and Java [7] without modifications to the
languages.

The focus of this chapter is on capabilities and capability passing—for a detailed
study of the newly gained extensibility and modularity by combining object-
oriented programming with effect handlers, we refer the interested reader to Chapter
4 of [11].

3.1 Capability Passing

Alongside the concept of a capability as a handler instance, we also developed the
technique of *capability passing*—in variants also known as *handler passing* [58],
evidence passing [56], or *lexically scoped effects* [3, 5]. Here we use *capability
passing* as terminology for the implementation technique and *lexically scoped
effects* to describe the mode of reasoning that comes with it.

We can illustrate capability passing by translating our example from Sect. 2.1
from Effekt to explicit capability-passing style.

Effekt Source Program:

```
def div(x: Double, y: Double): Double / { Exc } =
  if (y == 0.0) { raise("division by zero") }
  else { x / y }
```

Program in Capability-Passing Style:

```
def div(x: Double, y: Double, exc: Exc ): Double =
  if (y == 0.0) { exc .raise("division by zero") }
  else { x / y }
```

Importantly, the function `div` now takes an additional argument `exc`—the capability for the exception effect. The call to effect operation `raise` becomes a method
call on the capability. In general, for each effect that is (transitively) used by an
effectful function (like `div`), the function needs to take the corresponding capability
as an additional parameter. At the call site, those capabilities have to be explicitly
passed along, motivating the terminology of *capability passing*.

We developed capability-passing style as a technique to support effect handlers
in the form of libraries in existing OOP languages like Scala or Java [7, 10]. Since
then, capability-passing style evolved into a generic implementation technique for
effect handlers independent of object-oriented programming languages [8]. Much
like a continuation-passing (CPS) transformation makes the evaluation order of a
program explicit [24, 50], an intermediate representation in capability-passing style
makes it explicit where an effect is handled, or in other words, where an effect is
bound. In the remainder of this chapter, we will see how capability passing can
improve reasoning about effectful programs and significantly speed up the runtime
performance.

4 Lexically Scoped Effect Handlers: What You See Is What You Get

Effect handlers are not only syntactically reminiscent of exception handlers; also their semantics is a generalization of exception handlers. One particular aspect of this relationship is that, like exceptions, effects are traditionally handled by the *dynamically* closest handler. We also say, they are *dynamically scoped*.

4.1 Dynamically Scoped Effect Handlers

Let us revisit dynamically scoped handling by analogy to exception handling. Figure 3 shows a JavaScript example that uses exception handling. The code in the left column calls a function `eachLine` with a filename and a callback, which is supposed to be called with each line of the file contents. On encounter of an empty line it throws an exception that is supposed to be caught by the *lexically* (i.e., in the surrounding program text) enclosing exception handler in the same column.

However, the function `eachLine` might be implemented as found in the right column. It could internally use exceptions to signal error conditions and trigger aborting and closing of the file. At runtime, when `throw "Empty"` is evaluated, the stack is dynamically searched by unwinding frames until an exception handler is found. Since the handler in the right column has most recently been installed, it will be used to handle the exception. This is very similar to *dynamically scoped bindings* in a language like LISP [42]. Handlers follow a stack discipline: the handler installed last at runtime is the first to be considered—it *shadows* all previous handlers.

This semantics based on searching the stack carries over from exception handlers to effect handlers. Since the inception of effect handlers [47, 48], most languages that implement effect handlers are based on a dynamic search for the corresponding handler. Examples of such languages include Koka [37], Frank [40], and Multicore OCaml [21]. Dynamic scoping of exception handlers comes with a well-known

```
try {                                   function eachLine(filename, block) {
  eachLine(someFile, line => {            const fh = open(filename);
    if (line == "") throw "Empty";        try {
    else ...                                ... block(fh.read) ...
  })                                      } catch (err) {
} catch (err) {                             console.log("closing file");
  console.log("empty line")                 fh.close()
}                                         }
                                        }
```

Fig. 3 Example of exception handling in JavaScript. An exception is always handled by the *dynamically* closest exception handler. Here, an empty line would lead to the file being closed

set of problems [59] that also immediately apply to the generalized form of effect handlers.

Reasoning. As illustrated in the example in Fig. 4, dynamic handler search makes it difficult to reason about which exception is handled by which handler. In general, the combination of effects (such as exceptions) with higher-order functions (like `eachLine`) can easily lead to *accidental handling* [59]. That is, like in our example in Fig. 3, an exception is handled by a handler other than the expected one. The problem not only pertains to functional programming languages. Quite the contrary, in object-oriented programming, almost every method that takes another object as parameter is higher order in this sense.

Performance. Since it can only be known at runtime which effect is handled by which handler, standard optimizations such as *inlining* of handlers are not easily applicable.

Both aspects are aggravated by the fact that effects (as opposed to exceptions) are proposed as a primitive program structuring technique, not only to be used in an exceptional case, but pervasively throughout the codebase. As such, we believe that addressing the aforementioned problems is essential in order to scale effects and handlers to practical languages.

4.2 Dynamic vs. Lexical Scoping

Much like variables can be scoped lexically or dynamically, the same applies to effect handlers. However, before we go into detail of dynamically vs. lexically scoped effect handlers, let us revisit dynamic scoping in the context of variable bindings. To illustrate, let us assume a hypothetical extension of JavaScript that also includes dynamically scoped variables [38], written ?*x*. The example in Fig. 4 rephrases our running example by replacing the use of exception handlers with a

Dynamic Scoping:
```
function eachLine(block) {
  let ?exc = "closing file";
  block("")
}

let ?exc = "empty line";
eachLine(line ⇒ {
  if (line == "")
    console.log( ?exc )
})
// prints "closing file"
```

Lexical Scoping:
```
function eachLine(block) {
  let exc = "closing file";
  block("")
}

let exc = "empty line";
eachLine(line ⇒ {
  if (line == "")
    console.log( exc )
})
// prints "empty line"
```

Fig. 4 Example illustrating the difference between dynamic and lexical scoping. Dynamically scoped variables are both bound and referenced with ?exc

variable binding `exc`—the overall structure of the example remains the same. The example illustrates the difference between dynamic scoping and lexical scoping. In the case of dynamic scoping (on the left), the use of a variable and its binding are largely disconnected and might arbitrarily change at runtime. In our example, calling `eachLine` shadows the binding of `?exc` and rebinds it to `"closing file"`. Like with exceptions, dynamic binding resolves to the latest (or dynamically closest) binder at runtime. In contrast, in the case of lexical scoping (on the right), the use of the variable and its binding are connected lexically. That is, we can determine the binding site simply by inspecting the source text: starting from the use-site and expanding our search outward until we discover the first binder for `exc`. In our example, we can determine that `exc` is bound immediately before the call to `eachLine`, regardless of implementation details of `eachLine`. While dynamic binding can be useful to describe extension points and model configuration, code using it can be difficult to understand and maintain [38].

4.3   Lexically Scoped Effect Handlers

Capability passing is at the core of languages like Effekt [8] and provides the basis for *lexical scoping of effects* [5]. To see how capability passing enables lexical scoping, we can once more manually perform the steps of the Effekt compiler and translate an Effekt program into explicit capability-passing style. As before, the core idea is to explicitly pass handler instances, that is capabilities, instead of performing a dynamic search at runtime.

As a first step, the left column of Fig. 5 expresses our running example in the Effekt language. The example makes use of the previously defined exception effect. The syntax slightly differs from the JavaScript example. In particular, Effekt introduces the concept of *block arguments* such as `{ line ⇒ ... }`. For our purposes, block arguments can be understood as function arguments, binding the parameter (e.g., `line`) in the body that follows.

Effekt Source Program:
```
try {
  eachLine(someFile) { line ⇒
    if (line == "") raise("Empty")
    else ...
  }
} with Exc {
  def raise(msg: String) =
    println("empty line")
}
```

Program in Capability-Passing Style:
```
try { exc ⇒
  eachLine(someFile) { line ⇒
    if (line == "") exc .raise("Empty")
    else ...
  }
} with Exc {
  def raise(msg: String) =
    println("empty line")
}
```

Fig. 5 Translation to explicit capability-passing style. As part of the language implementation, the Effekt program on the left is translated to an explicit form of capability passing on the right

As a second step, the right column of Fig. 5 gives the translation of the program into explicit capability-passing style. We can see that handling an effect like `Exc` introduces a capability and binds it to the term variable `exc` highlighted in gray. Calling effect operations simply translates to calling methods on the capability (in our case `exc.raise(...)`). Explicit capability passing is essential to establish a lexical connection between an effect handler and the operations it handles. In particular, here we can see that the block passed to `eachLine` now simply *closes* over the capabilities that are in scope at its definition site. Closing over capabilities avoids accidental handling. Our exception will be handled by the correct handler, regardless of the implementation details of `eachLine`.

4.3.1 Effect Types Carry Meaning

In the Effekt language, the translation to capability-passing style is directed by the effect types. That is, whether or not a capability is bound (or passed) is determined exclusively by the involved static types. In consequence, the meaning of our example program depends on the type signature of `eachLine`. The translation in Fig. 5 assumes the following signature:

```
def eachLine(file: File)
        { block: String ⇒ Unit / {} }: Unit / {}
```

where types of block parameters (like `block`) are enclosed in braces[2]. That is, given a filename of type `File` and a block that lets us observe no effects (i.e., the first empty effect set `{}`), we produce a value of type `Unit` while also requiring no effects to be handled (i.e., the second empty effect set `{}`). From the perspective of an implementor of `eachLine`, the empty effect set `{}` in type of `block`

```
block: String ⇒ Unit / {}
```

informs us that it does not allow us to handle any effects it might use. All effects used by `block`, such as the exception `Exc`, need to be handled at the call site of `eachLine`. This is also made explicit by the capability-passing transformation (Fig. 5, right column). The block closes over the exception capability, bound at the call site.

To obtain the capturing behavior of the original JavaScript program, we can change the signature of `eachLine` to:

```
def eachLine(file: File)
        { block: String ⇒ Unit / { Exc } }: Unit / {}
```

---

[2] Enclosing the type of block parameters in braces mimics the syntax at the call site.

The changed type of block now communicates that eachLine is able to handle Exc effects. As a direct consequence of this change, the translation of our user code changes to:

```
try { exc ⇒
  eachLine(someFile) { line ⇒ exc ⇒
    if (line == "") exc .raise("Empty")
    else ...
  }
} with Exc {
  def raise(msg: String) = println("empty line")
}
```

This illustrates how changing the type signature in Effekt influences the meaning of programs. While in the translation of Fig. 5, the exception effect is handled by the lexically enclosing handler, it now is handled by eachLine, which introduces another binding of exc that shadows the outer binding.

4.4 Effect Parametricity

Capability passing provides the necessary operational semantics guaranteeing that effect handlers are *abstraction safe* [58]. Handlers can only handle those effects, which are visible in the static effect types of a program. This also directly enables *effect parametric reasoning* [5, 58]. In general, parametricity [51, 54] allows us to use types (and effects) to reason about the dynamic semantics of programs and obtain program equivalences that can be used, for instance, to carry out semantics preserving refactorings. In our example, only by inspecting the type of eachLine, we can know whether or not it can handle (and hence influence the semantics) of the Exc effect. If its type does not mention the Exc effect, there is no way it can accidentally, or purposefully, handle this effect. The effects in our signature thus enable us to reason about possible implementations

Capability passing furthermore enables *lexical reasoning*: To determine where an effect is being handled, or *bound* in the jargon of variable binders, we simply have to inspect the static effect types in the lexical context of the call site.

Effekt Source Programs:

```
def outer(): Unit / {} = {        def outer(): Unit / { Exc } = {
  def inner(): Unit / { Exc } =     def inner(): Unit / {} =
    raise("error!")                   raise("error!")

  try {                             try {
    inner()                           inner()
  } with Exc { ... }                } with Exc { ... }
}                                 }
```

In the first example, by inspecting the types, we know that `raise` is handled at the *call site* of `inner`, that is, by the handler that follows the definition of `inner`. In the second example, `inner` is annotated with an empty effect set. In consequence, all effects have to be handled at its definition site, that is, at the call site of `outer`.

Admittedly, effect types that influence the operational semantics can be confusing at first. However, following the types and translating the programs to capability-passing style can help in building up some intuition.

Programs in Capability-Passing Style:

```
def outer(): Unit = {                    def outer( exc: Exc ): Unit = {
  def inner( exc: Exc ): Unit =            def inner(): Unit =
    exc .raise("error!")                      exc .raise("error!")

  try { exc ⇒                             try { exc ⇒
    inner( exc )                            inner()
  } with Exc { ... }                      } with Exc { ... }
}                                         }
```

Again, in the translation we can see that for every effect in an effect set, an additional argument is introduced. On the left-hand side `inner` takes an additional argument, while on the right-hand side it closes over `exc` capability in the outer lexical scope.

In consequence, we can conclude that the handler in the right column has no influence on the meaning of our program. Since it does not handle anything, we can refactor it and safely remove the handler to arrive at the semantically equivalent program of

```
def outer(): Unit / { Exc } = {
  def inner(): Unit / {} = raise("error!")
  inner()
}
```

which we can simplify further to the equivalent:

```
def outer(): Unit / { Exc } = raise("error!")
```

Note that this is not the case for the program in the left column. Here, the handler is meaningful since it handles the effects of `inner`, as indicated by the type of `inner`.

4.5 Effect Polymorphism

Explicit capability-passing style not only enables reasoning with effect parametricity [58] and lexical scoped effects [5], but also gives rise to a novel form of effect polymorphism, which we call *contextual effect polymorphism* [8]. In languages with effect systems, effectful functions generally have a type like $\alpha \rightarrow \beta / \varepsilon$, where α and

β are meta-variables representing types, and ε is a meta-variable that represents a collection of effects. We identify two possible readings of such a type signature.

The Traditional Reading.   Traditionally, the signature would be read as follows: *Given a value of type* α, *the function produces a value of type* β *and has effects* ε. Effects are often seen as a *side effect* or additional "output" of a function. In particular, an empty ε implies that the function cannot have effects—it is *pure*. In contrast, a non-empty ε suggests that a function is *effectful*.

The Contextual Reading.   In our design of the Effekt language, we propose a novel reading of the types of effectful functions given above, inspired by Osvald et al. [45]. *Given a value of type* α, *the function produces a value of type* β *and requires the calling context to handle effects* ε. We interpret effects as a *requirement* to the caller or additional "input" to a function. In particular, an empty ε implies that the function does not impose any requirements on its caller—it is *contextually pure*. Contextual purity does not imply purity; a contextually pure function may be side-effecting, but those effects are handled *elsewhere*. In contrast, a non-empty ε suggests that the function is contextually effectful, meaning that the context is responsible for handling the effects.

To better understand the nuances and implications of the different readings, let us inspect the signature of our running example eachLine.

4.5.1   The Traditional Reading

In an effect language that uses the traditional reading (we use Koka [37] here for illustration), a conceivable signature would be this:

```
eachLine : (file, string → <> ()) → <> ()
```

The type of the function parameter has an empty effect row <>, which means it cannot have any effects. Under this type signature our example would not type check, since we pass an anonymous function (block) that throws exceptions and thus *does* have an effect. We could change the signature of eachLine to indicate that the function parameter may throw exceptions. Since eachLine calls its function parameter, we have to adapt the resulting effect type as well:

```
eachLine : (file, string → <exc> ()) → <exc> ()
```

Specializing signatures of higher-order functions to every use-site is practically not feasible and so Koka offers support for *parametric effect polymorphism*.

```
eachLine : forall<e> (file, string → e ()) → e ()
```

This signature expresses that at the call site we can pick an arbitrary collection of effects (called e here). Calling eachLine will have the same effects as the block passed to it.

4.5.2   The Contextual Reading

Clearly, demanding the parameter of eachLine to be pure is too strict, as the example illustrates. Extending the signature for a particular use case is not a modular solution. Parametric effect polymorphism comes with its own set of problems, which we discuss in a moment. In any case, the traditional reading does not allow to express that the parameter of eachLine should be *contextually pure*, which is expressed as follows in Effekt:

```
def eachLine(file: File) { f: String ⇒ Unit / {} }: Unit / {}
```

Effects provided by eachLine   Effects required by eachLine

Applying the contextual reading, the return type of eachLine communicates that it does not require handling of any effects. In consequence, we can call eachLine in any context. More interestingly, the type of the block parameter f also mentions no effects. The function f is contextually pure: While the caller of f might *observe* additional effects (for instance through mutable state), it cannot *handle* them. Instead, all effects that are used by f have to be handled at the call site of eachLine. In our example, the Exc effect, which used to signal empty lines, is handled at the call site.

4.5.3   Parametric *vs.* Contextual Effect Polymorphism

Effect polymorphism means that programmers can reuse eachLine with different function arguments, potentially using different effects. In languages like Koka, with support for *parametric* effect polymorphism, this amounts to instantiating the effect variable e to the effects of choice (i.e., exc in our example). With parametric effect polymorphism, signatures of functions make it *explicit*, which effects they do not care about, which might seem counterintuitive. Parametric effect polymorphism complicates function signatures, and care must be taken to avoid accidental capture [58] and to guarantee encapsulation [14]. We agree with Lindley et al. [40], who state that users should not be confronted with the details of effect polymorphism

> In designing Frank we have sought to maintain the benefits of effect polymorphism whilst avoiding the need to write effect variables in source code.

and with Leijen [37], who states that

> In practice though we wish to simplify the types more and leave out "obvious" polymorphism.

Languages, like Koka and Frank, attempt to hide the details of parametric effect polymorphism behind syntactic sugar. However, once programs get sufficiently complicated, the syntactic abstraction breaks down and effect polymorphism becomes visible to the user (for instance in error messages). To the best of our knowledge, all languages with support for effects and handlers and static effect-typing support this *parametric* form of effect polymorphism.

4.5.4   Contextual Effect Polymorphism

In contrast, Effekt offers *contextual effect polymorphism*. Effekt does not have
language constructs for type-level effect variables or quantification over effects.
Still, it supports effect polymorphic reuse of functions and guarantees effect safety.
We say that effect polymorphism in Effekt is *contextual*. Users never have to deal
with parametric effect polymorphism as the feature simply does not exist.

4.6   What You See Is What You Get

The implementation technique of capability passing truly supports the mantra of
"what you see is what you get." It provides the necessary foundation for lexically
scoped effects—inspecting the lexical scope is enough to determine where an effect
is bound; it enables reasoning with effect parametricity—handlers can only handle
effects that are visible in the static effect types; and it gives rise to a novel form of
effect polymorphism—we only have to consider the visible effects, and all others are
handled elsewhere. While effect handlers do no magically remove the complexity
of programs as the introductory one in Sect. 1, static type and effect systems and a
lexical reasoning principle provide a powerful way of statically approximating the
runtime semantics of programs with complex control flow patterns.

5   Improving the Performance of Effect Handlers

Effect handlers allow high-level, user-definable, and composable control abstractions. However, typically a significant runtime cost is associated with searching the
correct handlers and capturing the continuation. There exist two lines of related
work with the goal to minimize the performance overhead of the abstraction of
effect handlers: runtime optimizations and compile-time optimizations.

Runtime optimizations.   Some languages limit the expressivity of effect handlers to allow more efficient implementation strategies in the language runtime.
For example, Multicore OCaml originally only allowed continuations to be
called once to support efficient (and destructive) stack switching [19, 20].
Other languages detect usage patterns of the continuation, which then can be
supported more efficiently. In the Koka implementation, Leijen [35] syntactically
recognizes that the continuation is only used once in tail position to optimize
capture/resume sequences.

Compile-time optimizations.   Leijen [37] uses effect types to distinguish pure
from effectful computations and only applies a CPS transformation to the latter.
Pretnar et al. [49] explore compile-time source-to-source transformation rules to
implement an optimizing compiler for the language Eff. The idea is to repeatedly
apply rewrite rules in order to specialize effectful programs to their handlers [49].

In general, existing implementation techniques for control effects often try to avoid performance penalties for programs that do *not* use control effects. In 〰〰〰〰〰〰〰〰, these implementations often sacrifice the performance of continuation capture [30].

We believe that effect usage should be the norm rather than the exception. Programmers should not need to trade-off modularity with performance. Efficient implementations of effect handlers would enable programmers to develop many general-purpose or domain-specific control flow constructs as libraries without sacrificing performance. Taking an *effects first* approach, in various lines of work, we studied how capability passing can help improve the performance of programs that make heavy use of effect handlers and control effects.

Capability-passing style allows us to separate two concerns of handling effects: (1) finding the correct handler implementation and (2) capturing the continuation. Both aspects are traditionally associated with additional runtime overhead. In Sect. 5.1, we will see how capability passing offers improvements for the former concern. The subsequent Sect. 5.2 illustrates how capability passing paves the way to optimizations regarding the latter concern.

5.1 Optimizing Handler Search

Traditionally, calling an effect operation triggers a dynamic search for the corresponding handler on the runtime stack. Searching for the correct handler is not only costly but also hinders optimizations across effect calls. Searching the handler implementation is entangled with traversing the call stack and capturing the continuation. In contrast, with capability passing, functions can simply close over capabilities, opening up many standard optimizations performed by compilers and language runtimes [7, 35], such as inlining. To illustrate, how capability passing offers improvements over dynamic handler search, in the following we discuss one common optimization in more detail.

5.1.1 Optimizing Tail Resumptions

In many use cases, the continuation does not need to be captured. This includes most examples that use effects to model dynamic dependencies, as in Sect. 2.2. One such special case can be seen in our example of Fig. 1:

```
try { range(0, 10) } with Gen {
  def yield(value: Int) = {
    println(value);  resume(true)
  }
}
```

Here, the last statement in the handler for Gen is calling resume. Leijen [35] refers to continuations that are called exactly once in tail position as *tail resumptions*.

Observing the control flow of these examples, we can notice that the continuation is being captured and removed from the runtime stack, just to be reinstalled after evaluating the effect operation. Depending on the underlying implementation, capturing and reinstalling of the continuation can come with a significant performance impact. While it is desirable to prevent the unnecessary capture of the continuation, just omitting it does not necessarily preserve semantics. To see why, let us inspect the following extended example:

Original Program:

```
try {
    try { ... yield(42) ... } with Exc { ... }
} with Gen {
    def yield(value: Int) = {
        raise(value); resume(true)
    }
}
```

The handler in this example uses an exception effect that is handled outside of the program. Additionally, the call to the effect operation yield occurs under an exception handler. Importantly, this exception handler should *not* handle the exception used by the handler of yield. Naively optimizing the continuation capture would amount to rewriting the example to:

Optimized Program (Wrong):

```
def yieldImpl(value: Int): Boolean / { Exc } = {
    raise(value); return true
}
try { ... yieldImpl(42) ... } with Exc { ... }
```

That is, we replaced the call to the effect operation yield with a call to the function yieldImpl. Instead of resuming, the function immediately returns true. However, the implementation itself makes use of another effect Exc. As the signature of yieldImpl communicates, this effect is handled at the call site! In consequence, by performing the optimization, we modified the meaning of our program. While in the original program, the exception will be handled at the definition site of the handler, in the optimized program the exception will be handled at the call site of the function.

The problem of our wrong optimization becomes immediate when translating our program to capability-passing style.

Optimized Program in Capability Passing (Wrong):

```
def yieldImpl (value: Int, exc: Exc ): Boolean = {
    exc. false(value), return true
}
try { exc ⇒ ... yieldImpl (42, exc ) ... } with Exc { ... }
```

The exception effect is accidentally handled by the nested exception handler.

To allow such optimizations, while at the same time being semantics preserving, languages that are based on dynamic handler search have to resort to complicated workarounds that amount to remembering where on the runtime stack the effect operation should conceptually be evaluated [35].

In contrast, in languages that establish a lexical scoping of effects, like Effekt does by capability passing, it is very easy to implement such an optimization while also preserving the semantics. In Effekt, we simply have to change the annotated type of `yieldImpl` to express the correct semantics:

Optimized Program (Correct):

```
def yieldImpl (value: Int): Boolean / {} = {
    raise(value); return true
}
try { ... yieldImpl (42) ... } with Exc { ... }
```

As discussed in Sect. 4.3.1, this small change in the type signature means that effects used in the implementation should not be handled at the call site of `yieldImpl`, but at its definition site! Capability passing thus allows us to replace tail-resumptive effect calls by a simple dynamic dispatch [7, 56].

Passing capabilities explicitly enables a unified treatment of capability binders and other variable binders in the language. In particular, under certain conditions, capability passing can be performed *at compile time*, effectively inlining the handler at the call to the effect operation [53]. Similarly, just-in-time compilers can easily specialize effectful functions with respect to concrete handler implementations simply by inlining capabilities [6, 7].

5.2 Optimizing Continuation Capture

In a second line of work, we explore an alternative strategy to efficiently compile control effects and optimize continuation capture. Our compilation strategy rests on the following observations: In general, the semantics of a program with control effects depends on and potentially modifies the call stack. Effect handlers allow capturing parts of the call stack as a continuation—resuming reinstalls the captured continuation onto the call stack. The concrete stack can only be known at runtime. But, what if certain information about the stack can be determined statically, that is, at compile time? Traditionally, in languages that are built on a dynamic handler search, the stack carries both, the effect handler implementations as well as markers delimiting the extent to which a continuation should be captured. If some of this information would be available at compile time, can we use it to partially evaluate (i.e., specialize) the program? We can distinguish the following two classes of potentially static information:

Handler implementation.   We might know the concrete handler implementation that will be present on the stack when evaluating a particular part of the program. This allows us to inline the handler implementations at the call site of the effect operation. Inlining the handlers not only removes the runtime search for the handler implementation, but also potentially opens up further local optimizations.

Stack shape.   We might know in which *order* effect handlers will be present on the stack, when evaluating a part of the program. We refer to this information as the *shape* of the stack. Statically knowing the order in which effect handlers appear allows us to specialize the control flow and continuation capture.

In recent work [52, 53], we explored how to use this static information to efficiently compile control effects.[3]

To make the additional information explicit, we present a language (called λ_{Cap}) that has two distinguishing features [53]. First, similar to our presentation in Sect. 3.1, programs in λ_{Cap} are written in explicit capability-passing style. Second, λ_{Cap} is equipped with a specialized type system that tracks the *stack shape* of an effectful computation: a list of types corresponding to the types expected by enclosing handlers. For example, let us assume the following computation:

```
try {
    val res = try { prog() > 1 } with Gen { ... };
    println(res)
} with Exc { ... }
```

In λ_{Cap} the function prog would be assigned the type:

```
prog : () ⇒ Int [ Unit, Boolean ]
```

It computes an integer value and is required to be run in a context with two surrounding effect handlers. The outer handler is delimited at type Unit (in our example, the Exc effect), and the inner handler is delimited at type Boolean (in our example, the Gen effect). Guided by the stack shape, we implement control effects in λ_{Cap} by performing an iterated CPS translation [15, 52]. That is, for every handler that occurs in the type of a program, our translation performs one CPS transformation. Each iteration of the CPS transformation adds an extra continuation argument to functions. Our example function prog would thus be CPS translated twice, once for each entry in the stack shape.

---

[3] Here we only sketch the highlevel ideas, for a detailed presentation, soundness proofs, and performance evaluation, we direct the interested reader to the full paper [53].

	Time in ms (Standard Deviation)			
Benchmark	Baseline	λ_{Cap}	λ_{Cap}	Native
Koka				
Triple	2504.1 ±19.3	66.2 ±2.2	23.9 ±0.6	6.2 +0.2
Queens (18)	403.4 ±9.3	170.8 ±1.7	171.4 ±1.2	161.9 ±4.1
Count (2K)	56.0 ±1.8	0.4 ±0.0	0.2 ±0.0	0.0 ±0.0
Generator (1K)	43.9 ±1.8	0.4 ±0.0	0.1 ±0.0	0.0 ±0.0
Chez Scheme				
Triple	68.6 ±1.1	3.7 ±0.1	3.7 ±0.1	1.8 ±0.0
Queens (18)	93.7 ±3.5	89.6 ±0.6	88.1 ±1.0	89.5 ±1.2
Count (1M)	445.2 ±27.2	10.5 ±0.6	10.5 ±0.8	1.9 ±0.0
Generator (1M)	664.2 ±14.6	17.6 ±0.5	17.7 ±0.5	2.1 ±0.0
Multicore OCaml				
Triple	25.0 ±2.4	4.5 ±0.1	2.4 ±0.1	2.0 ±0.1
Queens (18)	57.9 ±2.2	33.1 ±0.7	33.7 ±0.6	34.8 ±2.7
Count (1M)	72.5 ±0.9	19.4 ±0.5	7.5 ±0.2	2.8 ±0.0
Generator (1M)	93.9 ±1.3	18.3 ±0.5	10.3 ±0.3	3.9 ±0.1
Primes (1K)	32.2 ±0.6	29.0 ±0.6	22.8 ±0.4	N/A
Chameneos	26.7 ±0.6	32.7 ±1.0	28.7 ±0.9	N/A

Fig. 6 Comparing the performance of λ_{Cap} and λ_{Cap} with Koka 1, Multicore OCaml, and Chez Scheme (from Schuster et al. [53])

5.3 Full Elimination of Control Abstractions

While λ_{Cap} only makes capability passing and stack shapes explicit, in a second language (which we call λ_{Cap}), we make use of this additional information. In particular, λ_{Cap} has the same operational semantics as λ_{Cap} but refines the type system and restricts the class of programs expressible in λ_{Cap} as a sub-language of λ_{Cap} for which we always *statically know* handler implementations.

Statically knowing both the handler for each effect operation and the stack shape allows us to perform capability passing at compile time to effectively inline effect handlers. This way we can fully reduce all abstractions related to effect handlers at compile time.

5.4 Performance Evaluation

To evaluate the performance gains, in our benchmarks (Fig. 6, [53]) we compare code generated from λ_{Cap} and λ_{Cap} with Koka 1 [37], Multicore OCaml [20], and Chez Scheme [22]. The benchmarks indicate that our translation offers significant speedups (of up to 409x) for examples, which heavily use effects and handlers, and shows competitive performance for examples with only simple uses of effect handlers.

Interestingly, on Chez Scheme we cannot observe a significant difference between λ_{Cap} and the fully optimizing λ_{Cap}. It appears that the information, made explicit through our approach, is enough for optimizing compilers (like Chez Scheme) to perform inlining. In particular, by using the stack shape to guide our iterated CPS translation, the control flow and context of effectful function calls are made fully explicit. Similarly, by capability passing, we make explicit which effect is handled by which effect handler.

6   Related Work

Here we offer a brief comparison of our approach of capability-passing style for effect handlers with other closely related techniques.

Object Capabilities
The general idea of explicitly representing the ability to perform an effect operation in a capability that can be passed to other components is not new. To reason about access privileges and authority control, the object-capability model represents security critical resources as *capabilities* [16, 43, 44]. Only the holder to such a capability can perform operations on such resources. It is this line of work that inspired us to use the name *capability* for instances of effect handlers. Object capabilities enable a similar style of lexical reasoning as described in Sect. 4.4. We are not aware of any prior work that combined object capabilities with effect handlers.

(Generalized) Evidence Passing
Xie et al. [56] explore how languages with support for effect handlers can be implemented efficiently by performing *evidence passing*. In contrast to our work, where each handler introduces separate capabilities, Xie et al. pass all currently available handlers in an *evidence vector*. Every effectful function is modified to receive this evidence vector as an additional argument. They develop evidence passing as an implementation technique for traditional languages with effect handlers and parametric effect polymorphism [56, 57]. In consequence, they purposefully do not close over evidence and thus do not establish lexical scoping of effect handlers.

Lexical Effect Handlers
In terms of enabling lexical reasoning for effect handlers, our work is closely related to the one by Zhang et al. [58, 60] as well as the one by Biernacki et al. [5].

Zhang et al. [60] show how passing handlers (what we refer to as "capabilities") can enable effect parametricity. Like in our own prior work [6], their handler instances H^ℓ are pairs of handler implementations H and prompt markers ℓ. While our own prior work focuses on embedding effect handlers into existing languages like Scala [6] or Java [7], they present a standalone calculus, prove it sound, and show important properties such as effect abstraction. In particular, they show that no manual lifting annotations [4, 14, 39] are required to avoid accidental capture.

Biernacki et al. [5] show how effect handlers can be seen as binders for effect operations. They present two variants of operational semantics. First, an "open semantics" where effect handlers are directly treated as binders and reduction is performed under such binders. Second, a "generative semantics," where reducing an effect handlers generates a fresh runtime label, which is then substituted. The treatment of effect handlers as binders is morally equivalent to how effect handlers in our work introduce and *bind* capabilities. Most of our own prior work of effect handlers [6–9] is based on multi-prompt delimited control [23, 26] and thus closer to the generative semantics.

Both lines of work offer striking similarity to our approach of capability passing. Both show that passing effect handlers (or treating them as binders) enables some form of lexical reasoning and prevents accidental capture. However, to the best of our knowledge, we are the first to fully embrace this mode of lexical reasoning by replacing parametric effect polymorphism with contextual effect polymorphism.

7 Conclusion and Future Directions

Originally developed as an implementation technique to embed effect handlers into object-oriented programming languages, capability passing has proved to be an interesting basis for practical implementations of effect handlers. Building on capability passing, we developed library implementations for Scala and Java, as well as a new standalone language "Effekt."

Capability passing immediately gives rise to lexical scoping of effect handlers, allowing programmers to apply the same reasoning principles for effects that they are used to from reasoning about variable bindings. Basing the operational semantics of effect handlers on capability passing, instead of dynamic handler search, also casts a different light on type and effect systems. It gives rise to reasoning with effect parametricity and motivates a novel form of effect polymorphism: contextual effect polymorphism. Furthermore, problems such as accidental capturing of effects and effect encapsulation [14, 39] are ruled out by design.

Capability passing also helps to significantly improve the performance of programs with effect handlers and complex control flow. By replacing dynamic handler search with capability passing, optimizations like tail resumptions and inlining of handlers are facilitated. Combining capability-passing style with explicitly tracking the stack of the runtime stack in the types of programs, we were able to fully eliminate all abstractions associated with effect handlers. While capability passing offers an interesting semantic foundation for new languages, also existing languages (like Koka) can benefit from it. However, since the semantics of capability passing differs from traditional handler search, it is necessary to establish a semantic correspondence between programs in capability-passing style and programs using dynamic handler search. Xie et al. [56] provide an important first step into this direction by identifying a subset of Koka programs that can safely be expressed in a variant of capability-passing style[4] called *evidence passing*. By doing so, the work by Xie et al. provides one foundational basis for version 2 of Microsoft's language Koka.

7.1 Future Directions

To further prepare effects and handlers as a tool for practical software engineering, we can identify the following future directions of research.

- We established that capability passing allows for an efficient compilation under certain conditions [53]. However, in particular both, the order of handlers and the concrete handler implementation do not necessarily need to be statically known. While we believe it is important to make the conditions explicit under which optimal compilation is possible, more research is necessary to also support programs with only partially static knowledge.
- One concrete avenue we plan to pursue is to develop a just-in-time compiler with dedicated support for control effects. A JIT compiler can use recorded traces to generate versions of effectful function, specialized to their calling context. In this way, we could gather information about the stack shape and used effect handlers to apply the above-described optimizations.
- Capability passing enables lexical reasoning about effects and contextual effect polymorphism. It would be interesting to perform user studies to validate the claim that this improves program understanding and maintainability.
- The concrete implementation of contextual effect polymorphism in the Effekt language comes with the restriction that no first-class functions are supported. That is, functions can only be passed as arguments, but cannot be returned or stored in data structures. In ongoing work we are lifting this restriction, while carefully trading off expressivity with understandability.

We are excited to see how effect handlers, and capability-passing style, can shape the future practice of software engineering.

Acknowledgments I would like to thank all my collaborators and coauthors for significantly contributing to all of the papers, which this chapter is directly or indirectly based upon [6–9, 12, 52, 53, 56].

---

[4] There exist a few significant differences between evidence and capabilities. In particular, capabilities are passed individually, while evidence is provided in form of a vector [56]. While this has subtle implications on aspects such as effect polymorphism, from the perspective of this chapter, both achieve similar goals.

References

1. Ahman, D., Pretnar, M.: Asynchronous effects. Proc. ACM Program. Lang. **5**(POPL) (2021). https://doi.org/10.1145/3434305

2. Bauer, A., Pretnar, M.: An effect system for algebraic effects and handlers. In: International Conference on Algebra and Coalgebra in Computer Science, pp. 1–16. Springer, Berlin, Heidelberg (2013)

3. Bauer, A., Pretnar, M.: Programming with algebraic effects and handlers. J. Logical Algebraic Methods Program. **84**(1), 108–123 (2015)

4. Biernacki, D., Piróg, M., Polesiuk, P., Sieczkowski, F.: Abstracting algebraic effects. Proc. ACM Program. Lang. **3**(POPL), 6:1–6:28 (2019)

5. Biernacki, D., Piróg, M., Polesiuk, P., Sieczkowski, F.: Binders by day, labels by night: effect instances via lexically scoped handlers. Proc. ACM Program. Lang. **4**(POPL) (2019). https://doi.org/10.1145/3371116

6. Brachthäuser, J.I., Schuster, P.: Effekt: Extensible algebraic effects in Scala (short paper). In: Proceedings of the International Symposium on Scala. ACM, New York (2017). https://doi.org/10.1145/3136000.3136007

7. Brachthäuser, J.I., Schuster, P., Ostermann, K.: Effect handlers for the masses. Proc. ACM Program. Lang. **2**(OOPSLA), 111:1–111:27 (2018). https://doi.org/10.1145/3276481

8. Brachthäuser, J.I., Schuster, P., Ostermann, K.: Effects as capabilities: effect handlers and lightweight effect polymorphism. Proc. ACM Program. Lang. **4**(OOPSLA) (2020). https://doi.org/10.1145/3428194

9. Brachthäuser, J.I., Schuster, P., Ostermann, K.: Effekt: capability-passing style for type- and effect-safe, extensible effect handlers in Scala. J. Funct. Program. (2020). https://doi.org/10.1017/S0956796820000027

10. Brachthäuser, J.I.: Towards naturalistic EDSLs using algebraic effects (2017). Presentation at Domain-Specific Language Design and Implementation (DSLDI)

11. Brachthäuser, J.I.: Design and implementation of effect handlers for object-oriented programming languages. Ph.D. Thesis, University of Tübingen, Germany (2020). https://doi.org/10.15496/publikation-43400

12. Brachthäuser, J.I., Leijen, D.: Programming with implicit values, functions, and control. Tech. Rep. MSR-TR-2019-7, Microsoft Research (2019)

13. Brady, E.: Programming and reasoning with algebraic effects and dependent types. In: Proceedings of the International Conference on Functional Programming, pp. 133–144. ACM, New York (2013)

14. Convent, L., Lindley, S., McBride, C., McLaughlin, C.: Doo bee doo bee doo. J. Funct. Program. **30**, c9 (2020). https://doi.org/10.1017/S0956796820000039

15. Danvy, O., Filinski, A.: Abstracting control. In: Proceedings of the Conference on LISP and Functional Programming, pp. 151–160. ACM, New York (1990)

16. Dennis, J.B., Van Horn, E.C.: Programming semantics for multiprogrammed computations. Commun. ACM **9**(3), 143–155 (1966)

17. Dolan, S., Eliopoulos, S., Hillerström, D., Madhavapeddy, A., Sivaramakrishnan, K., White, L.: Concurrent system programming with effect handlers. In: Proceedings of the Symposium on Trends in Functional Programming. Springer LNCS 10788 (2017)

18. Dolan, S., Eliopoulos, S., Hillerström, D., Madhavapeddy, A., Sivaramakrishnan, K., White, L.: Effectively tackling the awkward squad. In: ML Workshop (2017)

19. Dolan, S., Muralidharan, S., Gregg, D.: Compiler support for lightweight context switching. ACM Trans. Archit. Code Optim. **9**(4), 36:1–36:25 (2013)

20. Dolan, S., White, L., Madhavapeddy, A.: Multicore OCaml. In: OCaml Workshop (2014)

21. Dolan, S., White, L., Sivaramakrishnan, K., Yallop, J., Madhavapeddy, A.: Effective concurrency through algebraic effects. In: OCaml Workshop (2015)

22. Dybvig, R.K.: The development of chez scheme. In: Proceedings of the Eleventh ACM SIGPLAN International Conference on Functional Programming, ICFP '06, pp. 1–12. ACM, New York (2006). https://doi.org/10.1145/1159803.1159805

23. Dybvig, R.K., Peyton Jones, S.L., Sabry, A.: A monadic framework for delimited continuations. J. Funct. Program. **17**(6), 687–730 (2007)
24. Fischer, M.J.: Lambda calculus schemata. In: Proceedings of ACM Conference on Proving Assertions About Programs, pp. 104–109. ACM, New York (1972)
25. Gosling, J., Joy, B., Steele, G.L.: The Java Language Specification. Addison-Wesley Publishing, Boston (1996)
26. Gunter, C.A., Rémy, D., Riecke, J.G.: A generalization of exceptions and control in ML-like languages. In: Proceedings of the Conference on Functional Programming Languages and Computer Architecture, pp. 12–23. ACM, New York (1995)
27. Hillerström, D., Lindley, S., Atkey, B., Sivaramakrishnan, K.: Continuation passing style for effect handlers. In: Formal Structures for Computation and Deduction, *LIPIcs*, vol. 84. Schloss Dagstuhl–Leibniz-Zentrum für Informatik (2017)
28. Inostroza, P., van der Storm, T.: JEff: Objects for effect. In: Proceedings of the 2018 ACM SIGPLAN International Symposium on New Ideas, New Paradigms, and Reflections on Programming and Software, Onward! 2018. ACM, New York (2018)
29. Kammar, O., Lindley, S., Oury, N.: Handlers in action. In: Proceedings of the International Conference on Functional Programming, pp. 145–158. ACM, New York (2013)
30. Kiselyov, O.: Delimited control in OCaml, abstractly and concretely. Theor. Comput. Sci. **435**, 56–76 (2012)
31. Kiselyov, O., Sabry, A., Swords, C.: Extensible effects: an alternative to monad transformers. In: Proceedings of the Haskell Symposium, pp. 59–70. ACM, New York (2013)
32. Kiselyov, O., Sivaramakrishnan, K.: Eff directly in OCaml. In: ML Workshop (2016)
33. Leijen, D.: Koka: Programming with row polymorphic effect types. In: Proceedings of the Workshop on Mathematically Structured Functional Programming (2014)
34. Leijen, D.: Algebraic effects for functional programming. Tech. rep., MSR-TR-2016-29. Microsoft Research technical report (2016)
35. Leijen, D.: Implementing algebraic effects in C. In: Proceedings of the Asian Symposium on Programming Languages and Systems, pp. 339–363. Springer, Cham (2017)
36. Leijen, D.: Structured asynchrony with algebraic effects. In: Proceedings of the Workshop on Type-Driven Development, pp. 16–29. ACM, New York (2017)
37. Leijen, D.: Type directed compilation of row-typed algebraic effects. In: Proceedings of the Symposium on Principles of Programming Languages, pp. 486–499. ACM, New York (2017)
38. Lewis, J.R., Launchbury, J., Meijer, E., Shields, M.B.: Implicit parameters: dynamic scoping with static types. In: Proceedings of the Symposium on Principles of Programming Languages, pp. 108–118. ACM, New York (2000)
39. Lindley, S.: Encapsulating effects. Dagstuhl Rep. **8**(4), 114–118 (2018)
40. Lindley, S., McBride, C., McLaughlin, C.: Do be do be do. In: Proceedings of the Symposium on Principles of Programming Languages, pp. 500–514. ACM, New York (2017)
41. Madsen, M., Lhoták, O., Tip, F.: A model for reasoning about javascript promises. Proc. ACM Program. Lang. **1**(OOPSLA) (2017). https://doi.org/10.1145/3133910
42. McCarthy, J.: Recursive functions of symbolic expressions and their computation by machine, Part I. Commun. ACM **3**(4), 184–195 (1960). https://doi.org/10.1145/367177.367199
43. Melicher, D., Shi, Y., Potanin, A., Aldrich, J.: A capability-based module system for authority control. In: 31st European Conference on Object-Oriented Programming (ECOOP 2017). Schloss Dagstuhl-Leibniz-Zentrum fuer Informatik (2017)
44. Miller, M.S.: Robust composition: Towards a unified approach to access control and concurrency control. Ph.D. Thesis, Johns Hopkins University, Baltimore, Maryland, USA (2006). AAI3245526
45. Osvald, L., Essertel, G., Wu, X., Alayón, L.I.G., Rompf, T.: Gentrification gone too far? affordable 2nd-class values for fun and (co-) effect. In: Proceedings of the Conference on Object-Oriented Programming, Systems, Languages and Applications, pp. 234–251. ACM, New York (2016)
46. Plotkin, G., Power, J.: Algebraic operations and generic effects. Appl. Categorical Struct. **11**(1), 69–94 (2003)

47. Plotkin, G., Pretnar, M.: Handlers of algebraic effects. In: European Symposium on Programming, pp. 80–94. Springer, Berlin (2009)
48. Plotkin, G.D., Pretnar, M.: Handling algebraic effects. Logical Methods Comput. Sci. **9**(4), ⊫⟍⎮⟋⎕⎮⟍⎸
49. Pretnar, M., Saleh, A.H.S., Faes, A., Schrijvers, T.: Efficient compilation of algebraic effects and handlers. Tech. rep., Department of Computer Science, KU Leuven; Leuven, Belgium (2017)
50. Reynolds, J.C.: Definitional interpreters for higher-order programming languages. In: Proceedings of the ACM Annual Conference, pp. 717–740. ACM, New York (1972)
51. Reynolds, J.C.: Types, abstraction and parametric polymorphism. In: Proceedings of the IFIP World Computer Congress, pp. 513–523. Elsevier (North-Holland), Amsterdam (1983)
52. Schuster, P., Brachthäuser, J.I.: Typing, representing, and abstracting control. In: Proceedings of the Workshop on Type-Driven Development, pp. 14–24. ACM, New York (2018). https://doi.org/10.1145/3240719.3241788
53. Schuster, P., Brachthäuser, J.I., Ostermann, K.: Compiling effect handlers in capability-passing style. Proc. ACM Program. Lang. **4**(ICFP) (2020). https://doi.org/10.1145/3408975
54. Wadler, P.: Theorems for free! In: Proceedings of the Conference on Functional Programming Languages and Computer Architecture, pp. 347–359. ACM, New York (1989)
55. Wu, N., Schrijvers, T.: Fusion for free—efficient algebraic effect handlers. In: Proceedings of the Conference on Mathematics of Program Construction. Springer LNCS 9129 (2015)
56. Xie, N., Brachthäuser, J.I., Hillerström, D., Schuster, P., Leijen, D.: Effect handlers, evidently. Proc. ACM Program. Lang. **4**(ICFP) (2020). https://doi.org/10.1145/3408981
57. Xie, N., Leijen, D.: Generalized evidence passing for effect handlers. Tech. Rep. MSR-TR-2021-5, Microsoft (2021). https://www.microsoft.com/en-us/research/publication/generalized-evidence-passing-for-effect-handlers/. V2, 2021-04-24
58. Zhang, Y., Myers, A.C.: Abstraction-safe effect handlers via tunneling. Proc. ACM Program. Lang. **3**(POPL), 5:1–5:29 (2019)
59. Zhang, Y., Salvaneschi, G., Beightol, Q., Liskov, B., Myers, A.C.: Accepting blame for safe tunneled exceptions. In: Proceedings of the Conference on Programming Language Design and Implementation, pp. 281–295. ACM, New York (2016)
60. Zhang, Y., Salvaneschi, G., Myers, A.C.: Handling bidirectional control flow. Proc. ACM Program. Lang. **4**(OOPSLA) (2020). https://doi.org/10.1145/3428207

How to Effectively Reduce Failure Analysis Time?

Mojdeh Golagha

Abstract Debugging is one of the most expensive and challenging phases in the software development life-cycle. One important cost factor in the debugging process is the time required to analyze failures and find underlying faults. Two types of techniques that can help developers to reduce this analysis time are Failure Clustering and Automated Fault Localization. Although there is a plethora of these techniques in the literature, there are still some gaps that prevent their operationalization in real-world contexts. Besides, the abundance of these techniques confuses the developers in selecting a suitable method for their specific domain. In order to help developers in reducing analysis time, we propose methodologies and techniques that can be used standalone or in a form of a tool-chain. Utilizing this tool-chain, developers (1) know which data they need for further analysis, (2) are able to group failures based on their root causes, and (3) are able to find more information about the root causes of each failing group. Our tool-chain was initially developed based on state-of-the-art failure diagnosis techniques. We implemented and evaluated existing techniques. We built on and improved them where the results were promising and proposed new solutions where needed. The overarching goal of this study has been the applicability of techniques in practice.

1 Introduction

We are in the era of software intensive systems. The complexity of systems is growing as they are being increasingly used in safety critical applications. These new applications have raised the need for intensive testing to assure the reliability of the systems.

M. Golagha (✉)
fortiss, München, Germany
e-mail: golagha@fortiss.org

© The Author(s) 2022
M. Felderer et al. (eds.), *Ernst Denert Award for Software Engineering 2020*,
https://doi.org/10.1007/978-3-030-83128-8_4

These changes have consequently influenced software debugging endeavors. From the increase in the number of tests and the fast pace of delivering software have emerged the need for more automated debugging techniques. Automated diagnosis techniques can reduce the effort spent on manual debugging, which shortens the test-diagnose-repair cycle, and can therefore be expected to lead to more reliable systems, and a shorter time-to-market. Software debugging has always been recognized as a time-consuming, tiresome, and expensive task that cost billions for economies every year [35].

In our terminology, a *failure* is the deviation of actual run-time behavior from intended behavior, and a *fault* is the reason for the deviation [36]. In other words, a fault is the program element that needs to be changed in order to remove the failure. The essence of failure diagnosis is to trace back a failure to the fault or faults [11].

Developers usually get quick and yet preliminary test results from huge amounts of test runs and use this information to attack problems such as locating faults. Such a quick feedback approach may lower the development cost but puts a lot of pressure on developers. In practice, the time resource allocated for each debugging session is usually limited and predetermined. Therefore, developers need an assisting tool which increases their productivity and reduces failure analysis time. We focused on automated diagnosis techniques and tried to improve them to make them applicable in practice. We recognized two general categories of techniques for addressing reducing failure diagnosis time: *failure clustering* and *automated fault localization*.

Failure clustering methods attempt to group failing tests with respect to the faults that caused them [30]. If there are several failing test cases (TC) as the result of test execution, these failing TCs may be clustered such that tests which are in the same cluster would have failed due to the same hypothesized fault. Then, in an ideal world, testers investigate only one representative TC from each cluster to discover all the underlying faults. This process eliminates the need for analyzing each failing TC individually. Thus, there would be a significant reduction in analysis time[9].

Automated fault localization techniques aim to "identify some program event(s) or state(s) or element(s) that cause or correlate with the failure to provide the developer with a report that will aid fault repair" [21]. The debugging process is usually predicated on the developer's ability to find and repair faults. While both steps in the debugging process (fault localization and fault repair) are time-consuming in their own right, fault localization is considered more critical, as it is a prerequisite for fault repair [21]. Furthermore, Kochhar et al. have found that there is a large demand for fault localization solutions among developers [17]. Therefore, over the past ten years, a lot of research has gone into developing automated techniques for fault localization in order to help speed up the process [38].

There is a plethora of failure clustering and automated fault localization techniques in the literature [28]. Although developers find these methods worthwhile and essential [17], these techniques are not adopted in practice yet.

2 Failure Clustering

Clustering failures is effective in reducing failure analysis time [9]. The advantages are threefold:

1. It eliminates the need to analyze each failing test individually. To achieve this goal, it is enough to select one representative for each cluster and analyze only the representatives to find all the underlying faults in case of multiple faults [9].

   In an industrial environment, usually several dozens of TCs are executed each night as regressions happen, and several hundred every weekend, which together usually lead to large numbers of failures. Developers must analyze the failing tests and find all the root causes in the short time they have before the software release. The complexity of the analysis process makes the failure diagnosis process tough and time-consuming. Since in practice, a single fault usually leads to the failure of multiple TCs, analyzing only the representative TCs helps developers to find more faults in a shorter time.

2. It provides the opportunity for debugging in parallel [13].
3. It gives an estimation of the number of faults causing the failures. Fault localization, while there are several faults in the code, is more challenging than when there is only one fault in the code. When a program fails, the number of faults is, in general, unknown, and certain faults may mask or obfuscate other faults [13].

Jones et al. [13] introduced a parallel debugging process as an alternative to sequential debugging. They suggest that in the presence of multiple faults in a program, clustering failing tests based on their underlying faults, and assigning clusters to different developers for simultaneous debugging, reduce the total debugging cost and time. They propose two clustering techniques. Using the first technique, they cluster failures based on execution profiles and fault localization results. They start the clustering process by using execution profile similarities and complete it using fault localization results. Their second technique suggests to only use the results of fault localization.

Hoegerle et al. [12] introduced another parallel debugging method which is based on integer linear programming [25]. They applied the above-mentioned second clustering technique of Jones et al. to compare it with their own debugging approach. Their results show that this clustering technique of Jones et al. is not so effective. But the first technique is effective if it is adapted to the context.

Parallel debugging reduces the analysis time. However, it does not remove the need for analyzing all the failing tests one by one. It provides segregation between faults to facilitate fault localization. But it does not provide segregation between failing tests.

Another shortcoming in this area of research is the lack of a methodology for adapting this idea to different industrial domains.

Moreover, the other similar existing approaches in the literature are either based on coverage data or use context-specific data [31]. Therefore, there is a need for other sources of noncoverage data for the cases that the source code or execution profile is not available.

To close the above-mentioned gaps, we propose a clustering approach. In the following, first we describe our general clustering approach. Then, we explain two different techniques based on available data.

2.1 Clustering Approach

Our general approach consists of usual steps of any clustering solution: First, we run TCs and collect relevant data to use for clustering. Second, we apply hierarchical clustering [32] on data. Third, we use some metrics to choose the best number of clusters and finalize clusters. In an ideal solution, there is one cluster for each underlying fault. Therefore, the number of clusters equals the number of faults. Intuitively, we are not aware of this number beforehand. Fourth, we select one (or k) representative for each cluster to start the debugging process. To implement this clustering approach, one might need to adapt some steps based on available data. In the following, we explain two failure clustering techniques that can be utilized in different settings and at different levels of testing.

2.1.1 Failure Clustering with Coverage

In this approach, we use *test coverage profiles* as data for clustering. First, we run a test suite and extract an execution profile for each TC. Second, utilizing agglomerative hierarchical clustering, we build a tree of failing tests based on the similarity of execution traces. In order to cut this tree into clusters we need to know the best number of clusters. In the third step, we hence utilize fault localization techniques to decide on the best number of clusters. Then, we cut the tree into the found number of clusters. Finally, in the fourth step, we calculate the centers of the clusters and choose the failures which are closest to the centers as representative tests.

Step 1: Running Tests and Profiling Executions

The first step is to run the tests and profile executions. To profile TC executions, we instrument the code. Executing a program while instrumenting the code results in a report about which lines of code have been executed. We developed Aletheia [10] to instrument the code and prepare data for clustering.

Step 2: Generating Failure Tree

We use hierarchical clustering since it enables users to retrieve an arbitrary number of clusters without the need to re-execute the clustering algorithm. This is especially useful in practice since in a real-world scenario, it will not limit the users to a single suggested number of clusters. Users will be able to explore multiple alternatives without the need to wait for the re-execution of the clustering tool. We utilize hierarchical clustering to generate a dendrogram of failing tests. We use execution profiles generated in the previous step, as our feature sets for clustering.

Step 3: Cutting the Failure Tree by Fault Localization

Like any other clustering application, the next question is regarding the best number of clusters. In our case, in an ideal solution, the number of clusters equals the number of underlying fault which we do not know a priori. Therefore, we need a strategy to predict the number of clusters. We use Spectrum-Based Fault Localization (SBFL) (see Sect. 3) to find the best number of clusters k, or the cutting point, of the dendrogram. Liu and Han [19] as well as Jones et al. [13] suggest that if the failures in two clusters identify the same entities as faulty entities, they most likely failed due to the same reason and should be merged into one cluster.

This process can be considered in a top-down manner. This technique computes the *fault localization rank* for the children of a parent to decide whether the parent is a better cluster or it should be divided into its two children. The result of fault localization is a ranked list of entities from the most to the least suspicious. To check similarity between ranked lists, we use Jaccard [24] set similarity as suggested by [13], defined on two sets A and B as follows.

$$Similarity(A, B) = \frac{|A \cap B|}{|A \cup B|} \tag{1}$$

If the similarity of the fault localization rank of two children is smaller than a predefined threshold, they are (likely) pointing to different faults. They are dissimilar and should not be merged. Thus, the parent cluster is not a good stopping point and should be divided into its children. Otherwise, the parent is a better cluster and this is the stopping point for clustering. According to Fig. 1, the first step is to decide whether dashed line 1 is a better cutting point or dashed line 2. To answer this question, the fault localization rank at cluster c2 is compared to fault localization rank at cluster c3. If the similarity between these two sets is larger than the predefined threshold, they are similar and the parent c1 is a better clustering than dividing it into two clusters c2 and c3. As the result, line 1 is the cutting point. If line 1 is not the cutting point, the process continues to the point that no more division is needed. Because of the good results in our large-scale experiments [9], we propose 0.85 as the similarity threshold.

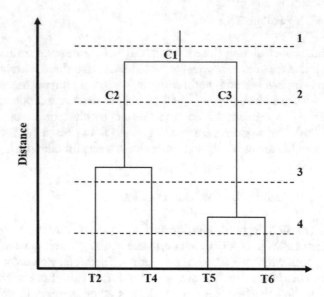

Fig. 1 Hierarchical clustering of four failing tests

Step 4: Selecting Representative TCs

We have already grouped TCs based on their hypothesized root causes by generating the failure tree and cutting it into clusters. Now, we need to suggest a representative for each cluster. Developers investigate only the representatives to find all the faults. Since it is likely that clustering is imperfect, the selection of representatives for a cluster has a great importance: We are aware that clusters are unlikely to be 100% pure [5]. We require our solution to make the representatives reliable. To avoid selecting an outlier (a failure which does not belong to the fault class that has the majority in the cluster) as a representative in clustering, we hence calculate the center of the cluster and find the k-nearest neighbors (KNN) [3] to the center. These KNNs are selected as representatives of the respective cluster. KNN search finds the nearest neighbors in a set of data for each data point. Based on discussion with test engineers, we suggest $k = 1$.

2.1.2 Failure Clustering Without Coverage

In previous section, we explained our first clustering approach that uses the coverage profile of tests as the input for clustering. However, it is not always possible to use this kind of data in practice due to three reasons. First, the source code is not always accessible (e.g., in the case of Hardware-in-Loop tests). Second, in this approach, collecting coverage information when running passing tests is also needed. Sometimes, this requirement imposes extra work on the system.

Third, instrumenting very large projects when running integration tests can be very expensive and time-consuming. In this section, we propose a clustering technique to group failing tests based on noncoverage data, retrieved from three different sources. These data sources make the clustering approach applicable in different stages of testing and other purposes such as test prioritization.

In this approach, first, we collect the data from different non-code-based sources, for example, Jira tickets to make a feature vector for each TC. We binarize all of them to prepare them for hierarchical clustering. Second, utilizing agglomerative clustering, we build a tree of failing tests based on the similarity of their feature vectors. Third, using a regression model on the number of failing tests in previous test runs, we predict the number of clusters. Finally, in the fourth step, we calculate the centers of the clusters and choose the failing tests which are closest to the centers as the representative tests. The developers receive the list of representatives to investigate them. If the suggested number of clusters appears to the developers to be inaccurate, they can immediately adjust the number of clusters on the user interface and get new representatives. Steps two and four are similar to the first clustering approach. In the following, we describe all the steps in detail.

Step 1: Collecting the Input Data

Two main input data sources are: the database of test results that includes several thousand test results from the previous test runs, and the repository of the TCs, providing the source files for the tests. We can extract three sets of features (variables in a data set) using these two data sources. Since the primary objective is to cluster failing tests, these data are extracted only for failing tests. In case of test selection or prioritization, they can be extracted for all tests. Typically, multiple projects (e.g., weekly, daily, nightly) are used to test a unit in an industrial setting (e.g., a single ECU in a car company). Each test run is usually called a *build*. All the feature values are extracted individually for each build. We explain each set of features in the following.

General Features The following features can be extracted from the database [18]: general information about the test; that is, its source file, component, domain, and the hardware that executes the test (if any).

If features are of categorical nature and do not follow an ordinal scale, we transform them into binary data.

Jira History We use the Jira tickets to extract the next feature set which is based on the faults assigned to the previously analyzed failed tests. The idea is that tests which frequently shared the same cause in the past are also likely to fail due to the same cause in the future [18]. Table 1 shows an example. Each "cause" is a Jira ticket ID that has been assigned to the failing test. One ticket may be assigned to several failing tests if the manual analysis shows that these tests are failing because of the same reason. Similar to the previous feature sets, this table should change to a binary form as shown in Table 2.

Table 1 Jira history [18]

Test	Project	Build	Cause
TC 1	Project 1	Build 1	Cause x
TC 2	Project 1	Build 1	Cause x
TC 3	Project 1	Build 1	Cause y
TC 1	Project 1	Build 2	Cause z

Table 2 Binary Jira History

Test	Build1CauseX	Build1CauseY	Build2CauseZ
TC 1	1	0	1
TC 2	1	0	0
TC 3	0	1	0

Test Case Similarity The files used to generate TCs are usually maintained in SVN repositories. These repositories are referenced to define the source files needed to generate the desired test series. Our hypothesis is that the likelihood that two tests failed due to the same cause increases with the similarity of their underlying source files [18]. To facilitate the calculation of similarity between two files, we compare the high level steps taken in each test.

Input Feature Weights We extract three set of features as input for clustering. These three sets lead to the generation of three different data sets. We measure the distance between TCs using all these three sets. Then, to have an aggregated distance value, we assign weights to each group and sum up the distance values. Based on our experience [7], test similarity, general features, and Jira history are almost equally important and therefore can be assigned similar weights, as shown in the following equation:

$$d_{aggregate}(x, y) = 0.31 * d_{general}(x, y) + 0.35 * d_{jira}(x, y) + 0.34 * d_{testFile}(x, y)$$
(2)

Step 2: Generating Failure Tree

Similar to the first approach, we apply hierarchical clustering on collected data.

Step 3: Cutting the Failure Tree by Fitting a Regression Model

In this approach, since we do not have coverage profile of tests, we cannot utilize FL to predict the number of clusters. Therefore, we propose using polynomial regression [16] to examine the relationship between the number of failing tests and the cutting distance on the hierarchical tree which basically shows the number of clusters. To this end, we extract the real number of faults in the previous analyzed builds from the database. Then, we calculate the cutting distances of the respective trees. Finally, we fit the regression model to predict the cutting distance based on the number of failing tests. Figure 2 illustrates an example. However, a model should be fitted for each individue case

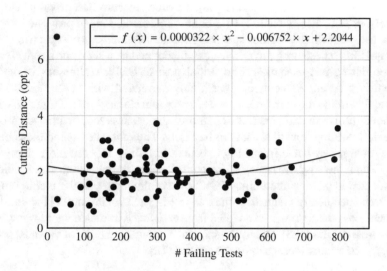

Fig. 2 Polynomial regression model for cutting distance[18]

Step 4: Selecting Representative TCs

Similar to the first approach, the nearest neighbor to the center of the cluster is considered as the representative of the cluster. Since we want the developers to be able to change the number of the cluster in real time, we pre-compute the representatives for all the clusters considering all possible cutting distances.

2.2 Industry Impact

Our large-scale evaluations in [9] and [7] show that using first and second clustering approaches, we are able to reduce more than 80% and 60% of the failure analysis time, respectively. Analyzing only the representative tests, we discovered all the underlying faults in the first approach and more than 80% of the faults using the second approach. These numbers show that our clustering approach is an effective way to reduce failure diagnosis time in an industrial setting.

The second takeaway is that if the source code is available and the highest accuracy is required, one can use approach one; if short response time is important and some level of inaccuracy is tolerable, one can use approach two.

3   Fault Localization

One of the most popular subsets of automated FL techniques is spectrum-based fault localization, known as SBFL [38]. In order to correlate program elements with failing TCs, these techniques are built upon abstractions of program execution traces, also known as program spectra, executable statement hit spectra, or code coverage [38]. These program spectra can be defined as a set of program elements covered during test execution. The initial goal of SBFL techniques is therefore to identify program elements that are highly correlated with failing tests [21]. In order to determine the correlation between program elements and TC results, SBFL techniques utilize ranking metrics to pair a suspiciousness score with each program element, indicating how likely it is to be faulty. The rationale behind these metrics is that program elements frequently executed in failing TCs are more likely to be faulty. Thus, the suspiciousness score considers the frequency at which elements are executed in passing and failing TCs. Some of the more popular ranking metrics have been specifically created for the use in FL, such as Tarantula [14] and DStar [37], whereas others have been adapted from areas such as molecular biology, which is the case for Ochiai [23]. DStar, Ochiai, and Tarantula are three of the most popular and best-performing metrics in recent studies [28].

$$DStar = \frac{(N_{CF})^*}{N_{UF} + N_{CS}},$$

$$Tarantula = \frac{\frac{N_{CF}}{N_f}}{\frac{N_{CF}}{N_F} + \frac{N_{CS}}{N_S}},$$

$$Ochiai = \frac{N_{CF}}{\sqrt{N_F * (N_{CF} + N_{CS})}},$$

where N_F is the number of failing tests, N_S is the number of passing tests, N_{CF} is the number of failing tests that cover the element, N_{CS} is the number of passing tests that cover the element, N_{UF} is the number of failing tests that do not cover the element. DStar metric takes a parameter *. The nominator is then taken to the power of *. There is no significant difference between these metrics [28].

An example of a hit spectrum is shown in Table 3. Each • in the table means that the respective element "e" (can be at different levels of granularity, e.g., statement, method, basic block, etc.) was hit in the respective test run "t". Table 4 shows the suspiciousness scores and ranks of program elements in Table 3 using Ochiai metric. As the ranks indicate, element $e4$ is the most suspicious element.

A study on developers' expectations on automated FL [17] shows that most of the studied developers view FL process as successful only if it:

- Can localize faults in the Top-10 positions
- Is able to process programs of size 100,000 LOC
- Completes its processing in less than a minute
- Provides rationales of why program elements are marked as potentially faulty

Table 3 A hypothetical hit spectrum

Element	Test cases					
	t1	t2	t3	t4	t5	t6
e1		•	•	•	•	•
e2		•	•	•	•	
e3		•	•	•	•	
e4	•	•			•	•
e5		•				
Verdict	F	P	P	P	P	F

Table 4 Ochiai suspiciousness scores

Element	Suspiciousness	
	Score	Rank
e1	0.577	2
e2	0	3
e3	0	3
e4	0.707	1
e5	0	3

Considering these expectations, real-world evaluations [28] show that SBFL techniques are not yet applicable in practice. They are able to process large-size programs, but are not always able to locate the faults in top positions. This might be the consequence of considering the correlation, not causation. Although the goal of any FL technique is "to identify the code that caused the failure and not just any code that correlated with it" [21], SBFL techniques measure the correlation between program elements and test failures to compute suspiciousness scores. Thus, they do not control potential confounding bias [27]. Confounding bias is a distortion that modifies an association between an exposure (execution of a program element) and an outcome (program failure) because a factor is independently associated with the exposure and the outcome (see Sect. 3.2).

In addition, for SBFL techniques, the granularity of the program elements in the program spectra is important, not only to the effectiveness of the system but also to the preferences of developers [17]. Kochhar et al. found that among surveyed developers, method, followed by statement and basic block were the most preferred granularities. But when it comes to the effectiveness of the system, the method and statement granularities may be too coarse- or fine-grained, respectively, to properly locate the faulty program elements [21, 26]. Unfortunately, there is no golden rule to say which granularity is the best for all contexts.

Despite ongoing research and improvements, the real-world evaluations show that FL techniques are not always effective. Considering above-mentioned gaps, we suggest the following improvements on SBFL.

3.1 Syntactic Block Granularity

As mentioned previously, the two main program spectra granularities used by practitioners are statement and method [17]. Unfortunately, neither of these options are perfect, as they both have their limitations.

Due to its fine-grained nature, the statement granularity has a number of drawbacks. First, simple profile elements like statements cannot properly characterize and reveal nontrivial faults. Statements might be too simple to describe some complex faults, such as those that are induced by a particular sequence of statements [21]. In the Defects4J data set [15], which is the largest available database of Java faults, also the most used one for FL studies, the median size of a fault is four lines, with 244 bugs having faults spread across multiple locations in the program [33]. Furthermore, due to the nature of the statement granularity, it is incapable of locating bugs due to missing code, known as a fault of omission [38]. For example, of the 395 bugs in the Defects4J data set, only 228 can be localized by the granularity of statements.

Unfortunately, it is unclear whether developers can actually determine the faulty nature of a statement by simply looking at it, without any additional information [26, 38]. As a possible solution to the drawbacks of the statement granularity, Masri suggests the usage of more-complex profiling types with higher granularity [21]. Previous empirical studies have shown that the effectiveness of SBFL techniques improves when the granularity of the program elements is increased [21]. For that reason, among others, many practitioners prefer to use the method granularity.

However, due to its coarse-grained nature, the method granularity has a handful of drawbacks when used for calculating SBFL scores. Sohn and Yoo suggest two drawbacks to the method granularity due to the nature of methods themselves [34]. First, methods on a single call chain can share the same spectrum values, resulting in tied SBFL scores. Second, if there are TCs that only execute non-faulty parts of a faulty method, they will decrease the overall suspiciousness score of the given method. Furthermore, when given a list of methods ranked by their suspiciousness, a programmer would still have to walk through all the statements in each method while looking for the bug, which can result in a lot of wasted effort, especially if the methods are large. Finally, the method granularity also lacks any sort of context and may not provide any further information to the developer. For instance, if there are failing TCs that focus on testing one specific method, such as a unit test, the developer will already know that the fault is contained within the failing method, so the method granularity results are of no additional help.

As both the statement and method granularities exhibit drawbacks, there is a clear need for a new granularity level that has a higher granularity than statements, without the added wasted effort and lack of context of methods. As a possible solution, we propose the usage of the *syntactic block granularity*. Based on different syntactic components found in the program's source code (see Table 8 for syntactic blocks in Java), it considers a wide range of program elements in an effort to provide more context to the developer with minimal added cost.

Fig. 3 Faulty *mid()* method.
Each syntactic block is
⫿⫿⫿ ⫿⫿⫿ ⫿ ⫿⫿ ⫿ ⫿⫿⫿

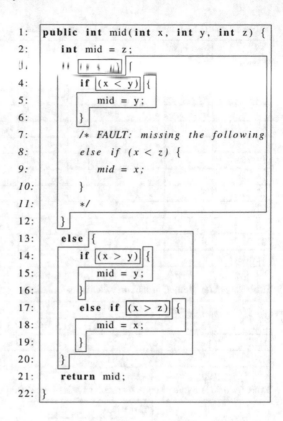

```
1:   public int mid(int x, int y, int z) {
2:       int mid = z;
3:       if (y < z) {
4:           if (x < y) {
5:               mid = y;
6:           }
7:           /* FAULT: missing the following
8:           else if (x < z) {
9:               mid = x;
10:          }
11:          */
12:      }
13:      else {
14:          if (x > y) {
15:              mid = y;
16:          }
17:          else if (x > z) {
18:              mid = x;
19:          }
20:      }
21:      return mid;
22:  }
```

To illustrate the drawbacks of the statement and method granularities, as well as highlight the benefits of the syntactic block granularity, consider the sample program in Fig. 3. The method *mid()* takes as input three integers and outputs the median value. The method contains a fault of omission, where the proper implementation should include the else-if block from lines 8–10. Tables 5, 6, and 7 contain the coverage information from a test suite containing six different TCs for each of the three different granularities. In each table, each TC corresponds to a column, with the top of the column corresponding to the inputs, the black dots corresponding to coverage, and the status of the test at the bottom of the column. To the right of the test case columns are the Ochiai score [1] and the corresponding rank for each element.

As mentioned previously, it is not possible to localize a fault of omission using the statement granularity. Therefore, no SBFL technique using the statement granularity will be able to localize the fault in the *mid()* method.

To localize the fault using the method granularity, the only information provided to the developer is that the fault is contained in the *mid()* method (see Table 6). However, due to the unit test nature of the TCs, this fact is obvious. A developer would still have to go through all the statements in the method to find the fault.

Table 5 *mid*() Statement granularity Ochiai calculations

Line #	Test cases						Ochiai	Rank
	3,3,5	1,2,3	3,2,1	5,5,5	5,3,4	2,1,3		
1	•	•	•	•	•	•	0.577	2
2	•	•	•	•	•	•	0.577	2
3	•	•	•	•	•	•	0.577	2
4	•	•			•	•	0.707	1
5		•					0	6
13			•	•			0	6
14			•	•			0	6
15			•				0	6
17				•			0	6
18							0	6
21	•	•	•	•	•	•	0.577	2
Verdict	F	P	P	P	P	F		

Table 6 *mid*() Method granularity Ochiai calculations

Line #'s	Test cases						Ochiai	Rank
	3,3,5	1,2,3	3,2,1	5,5,5	5,3,4	2,1,3		
1–22	•	•	•	•	•	•	0.577	1
Status	F	P	P	P	P	F		

Table 7 *mid*() Syntactic block granularity Ochiai calculations

Block type	Line #'s	Test cases						Ochiai	Rank
		3,3,5	1,2,3	3,2,1	5,5,5	5,3,4	2,1,3		
MD	1–22	•	•	•	•	•	•	0.577	3
ICS	3	•	•	•	•	•	•	0.577	3
ITB	3–12	•	•			•	•	0.707	1
ICS	4	•	•			•	•	0.707	1
ITB	4–6		•					0	5
IEB	13–20			•	•			0	5
ICS	14				•	•		0	5
ITB	14–16			•				0	5
ICS	17					•		0	5
ITB	17–19							0	5
Verdict		F	P	P	P	P	F		

As seen in Table 7, when using the syntactic block granularity, the fault is localized to the then block of the if statement (*ITB* block) from lines 3–12 with a rank of 1. As an improvement over the method granularity result, the developer would only have to look through one portion of the method to find the fault. Furthermore, the developer would have a further intuition as to the location/type of fault that exists. Due to the average depth of faults within the program elements of the syntactic block granularity, the developer would expect the fault to likely be an issue with the direct children elements of the block, or the block itself. In this case, the faulty missing element would in fact be a direct child of the top ranked *ITB* block from lines 3–12. Furthermore, due to the 0 suspiciousness score of the *ITB* block from lines 4–6, the developer can infer that the fault is either with the if statement conditional at line 4 or is a fault of omission.

This added information provided by the syntactic block granularity, as well as the reduced number of statements required to search through to localize the fault, helps illustrate the benefits of the syntactic block granularity over the other two granularities.

Extracting Syntactic Blocks

Each syntactic block consists of a set of statements that syntactically belong together to form a program element. For instance, every statement in a method declaration belongs together, as whenever the method is called, the contained statements may be run. Furthermore, each element may further be broken into multiple sub-elements. For example, an if statement has three components: the *condition statement*, the *then block*, and the *else block*. Each of these sub-elements may be run separately from each other. For instance, the *condition statement* will always be executed, but depending on the Boolean value of the conditional, either the *then block* or the *else block* will be executed. As a result, for Java programs, the syntactic block granularity consists of the 18 different types of program elements found in Table 8. For ease of use, each syntactic block type has an ID associated with it. An example of each type of syntactic block can be found in bold in the last column in Table 8.

Like the method granularity, for each syntactic block, if any of the contained statements are executed, the syntactic block is also marked as executed. Originally, *Class*, *Interface*, and *Enum* declarations were also considered as types of syntactic blocks. However, due to their average size compared to all other types of blocks, the added benefit of encompassing class level faults (such as missing method declarations or incorrect class variables) was outweighed by the overall added wasted effort associated with inspecting whole classes for a fault.

Due to the hierarchical nature of syntactic blocks, it is possible for one block to completely encapsulate another. For example, in Fig. 3 the *ITB* block from lines 3–12 encapsulates the *ICS* block at line 4 and the *ITB* block from lines 4–6. Because of this, sections of code will appear multiple times as a programmer walks through the ranked list of elements. In order to prevent unnecessary work, any block completely encapsulated by another block with a higher suspiciousness score can be ignored and removed from the final ranking.

While our work focused on faults in Java programs, the concept would be similar for other programming languages with similar syntax, for example, C, C++, C#, Go, PHP, and Swift.

Table 8 Java syntactic block types

Base program element	Syntactic block type	Type ID	Example
–	Constructor declaration	CND	`class X { X() { ... } }`
–	Method declaration	MD	`public int foo() { ... }`
–	Initializer declaration	IND	`static { a = 3; }`
–	Do statement	DS	`do { ... } while (a == 0);`
Foreach statement	Condition statement	FECS	`for (Object o : objects) { foo(); }`
	Body block	FEBB	`for (Object o : objects) { foo(); }`
For statement	Condition statement	FCS	`for (int a = 3; a <10; a++) { foo(); }`
	Body block	FBB	`for (int a = 3; a <10; a++) { foo(); }`
If statement	Condition statement	ICS	`if (a == 5) foo() else bar();`
	Then block	ITB	`if (a == 5) foo() else bar();`
	Else block	IEB	`if (a == 5) foo() else bar();`
Switch statement	Statement	SS	`switch(a) { ... }`
	Entry statement	SES	`case 1: foo(); break;`
Try-catch statement	Try block	TCTB	`try { foo(); } catch (Exception e) { bar(); } finally { x = 0; }`
	Catch block	TCCB	`try { foo(); } catch (Exception e) { bar(); } finally { x = 0; }`
	Finally block	TCFB	`try { foo(); } catch (Exception e) { bar(); } finally { x = 0; }`
While statement	Condition statement	WCS	`while (a > 0) { bar(); }`
	Body block	WBB	`while (a > 0) { bar(); }`

3.2 Re-ranking Program Elements

Using Fig. 4, we explain an example of confounding bias in SBFL results. The code snippet indicates a hypothetical faulty program. Assume that a fault in method F1 propagates only through the left branch where method F2 is triggered, while the right branch, where method F3 is called, executes correctly. Put differently, although F1 contains a fault, only those tests taking the left branch are failing. In this case, an SBFL technique gives the highest suspiciousness score to the method F2, since it is executed more frequently in failing executions and less frequently in passing executions (F1: 1 failing, 1 passing, F2: 1 failing, and F3: 1 passing). However, method F1 is the faulty element.

```
public void F1(int i) {
  if (i < 0) {
    ... // Faulty
    F2(x);
  } else {
    ...
    F3(x);
  }
}
```

Fig. 4 A hypothetical faulty method with two branches

"Confounding bias happens when a seeming causal impact of an event on a failure may be in fact due to another unknown confounding variable, which causes both the event and the failure" [21]. Given a program and a test suite, assume that all failing TCs induce dependence chain (chain of executed program elements in our case) $e_1 \rightarrow e_2 \rightarrow e_{bug} \rightarrow e_3 \rightarrow e_4 \rightarrow e_{fail}$ and all passing TCs induce $e_1 \rightarrow e_2$ only, where e_{bug} indicates the execution of faulty element and e_{fail} indicates a failure. A correlation-based approach such as SBFL would assign the same suspiciousness score to any of e_{bug}, e_3, or e_4, thus resulting in two false positives, whereas a causation-based approach that considers dependencies to have causal effect would assign e_4 the lowest suspiciousness score and e_{bug} the highest suspiciousness score. This means, when computing the suspiciousness scores, the confounding bias to consider for e_4 would involve e_3 and e_{bug}, for e_3 it would involve e_{bug}, and no confounding is involved when computing the suspiciousness score of e_{bug} [21].

In our analysis on SBFL results, we observed that often if the most suspicious element s* does not contain a fault, one of its parents or grandparents contains a fault, as shown in Fig. 4. Method F2 is the most suspicious element, while its parent F1 contains a fault. To improve SBFL effectiveness, we propose a re-ranking strategy based on this observation.

In this approach, we augment SBFL with a combined dynamic call and data-dependency graphs of failing tests. First, using any similarity metric such as DStar, we find the most suspicious method s* of the program. It has rank 1 on the suspiciousness ranking list. We locate it on the combined dynamic call graph of the failing tests and list all of its parents and grandparents. Then, we inject this list between rank 1 and 2 of the ranking list and re-rank all the elements accordingly. The re-ranking approach gives the second rank to the parents (if exists) of s* and the third to its grandparents. We start inspecting the suspicious elements based on the newly ranked list. Visual representation of call graph while highlighting the most

📄 src/main/java/org/apache/commons/lang3/time/FastDateFormat.java [CHANGED]

```
          @@ -817,7 +817,7 @@ public String format(long millis) {
817   817        * @return the formatted string
818   818        */
819   819       public String format(Date date) {
820       -           Calendar c = new GregorianCalendar(mTimeZone);
      820 +           Calendar c = new GregorianCalendar(mTimeZone, mLocale);
821   821           c.setTime(date);
822   822           return applyRules(c, new StringBuffer(mMaxLengthEstimate)).toString();
823   823       }
```

Fig. 5 Human patch to fix Lang-26 [4]

suspicious elements on it aids users in better understanding the problem. In the following, we use a real fault, Lang-26, from Defects4J database as our motivating example to explain each step. This bug is a wrong method reference that causes one test to fail [33] (Fig. 5).

Step 1: Finding the Most Suspicious Method(s) Using SBFL
As mentioned earlier, we arbitrarily use DStar (*=4) to find the most suspicious method in the first step. DStar calculations on Lang-26 spectrum places "lang3.time.FastDateFormat-TextField-1171" and "lang3.time.FastDateFormat-StringLiteral-1130" methods at rank **1**, as the most suspicious methods. Method "lang3.time.FastDateFormat-820" which is the faulty method gets rank **17**.

Step 2: Locating the Most Suspicious Method(s) on the Dynamic Call and/or Data-Dependency Graph
In the second step, we generate a graph which includes dynamic method calls and/or explicit data-dependencies of all failing tests. A dynamic call graph is generated at runtime by monitoring the program execution. The graph contains nodes that indicate the executed methods and edges between methods that represent method calls. We consider dynamic call graph to inspect real, not potential (as is the case in static call graphs), dependencies. An explicit data-dependency graph indicates dependencies between program elements introduced by a common variable used in multiple program elements. A data-dependency exists when two program elements exchange data using a variable. This happens when one program element writes to a field, and another element reads that field later. The result is a data-dependency between the first and second elements.

Considering Fig. 6, a call graph contains only the solid lines. A data-dependency graph contains only the dashed line. A combined graph can be helpful in SBFL. If method *compute* is faulty, method *getResult* will also return a wrong result. Thus, it will be labeled as a suspect. Looking into the combined graph, one can improve the labeling by adjusting for the confounder.

Figure 7 shows the call graph of Lang-26 failing test. Due to space constraints, it is only depicting the left branch. Thick red boundaries highlight the most suspicious methods. All nodes are annotated with their ranks.

Fig. 6 Combined
call/data-dependency graph

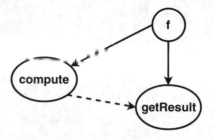

Step 3: Re-ranking Program Methods

In step 3, we find the parents and grandparents of the DStar's most suspicious methods. Then, we inject them between rank 1 and rank 2 and change all the ranks accordingly. Parents get rank 2 and grandparents get rank 3. In our example, "lang3.time.FastDateFormat-888" is the parent and "lang3.time.FastDateFormat-820" is the grandparent. Thus, in our new list, we place them right after ranked 1 methods and change their ranks to 2 and 3, respectively. Users get the new ranking list. As annotations on Fig. 7 show, the rank of faulty method "lang3.time.FastDateFormat-820" changes from **17** to **3** which is a considerable improvement.

3.3 Evaluation

Our evaluation results in [6] show that using our proposed re-ranking techniques, we can improve the average effectiveness of SBFL to 73.5% when it comes to locating faulty elements in Top-10 ranks. This means, in 75.3% of the cases, SBFL with re-ranking listed the faulty element in top ten ranks.

In addition, using syntactic blocks, we add context to SBFL results, provide additional insight into the possible location of the fault, and cover more types of faults than both popular statement and method granularities. Syntactic block granularity exhibits ranking behavior similar to the method granularity, while having a wasted effort (# lines that have to be inspected before finding the fault) equivalent to, if not better than, the statement granularity. Finally, when compared to the method granularity, it exhibits up to a 92.48% improvement when it comes to the locality of the program elements to the fault, a characteristic that provides the user with a better insight into the possible location of the faults. When inspecting program elements containing multiple statements, it is important to be able to have some insight as to which statements are more suspicious than others. For example, when inspecting a method for a fault, it would be helpful for the user to know where to start looking for the fault, instead of having to walk through each statement one-by-one. By knowing certain characteristics of the program elements in each granularity, a user may be able to localize the fault easier. One possible characteristic to consider would be the proximity of the most suspicious faulty program element

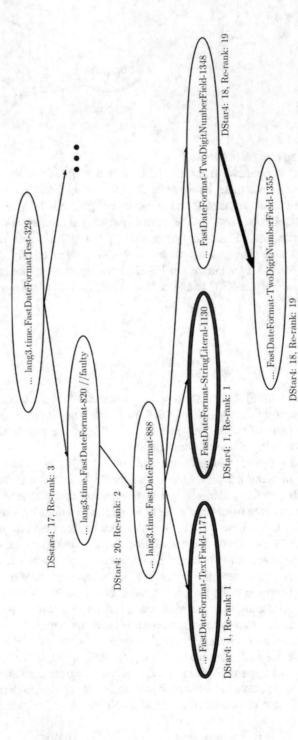

Fig. 7 Left branch of Lang-26 call graph. Numbers in the nodes indicate the line numbers of methods in the source code

e* to the fault itself. If the average depth of the fault in the abstract syntax tree (AST) in the program element e* is low, it will be easier to find the fault, as the user could work their way down the AST, giving higher priority to the shallower elements.

However, we observed an issue when it comes to its application in industrial domains: the effectiveness of SBFL varies from case to case. It is not clear for a user whether using SBFL would help in reducing analysis time or waste time. Therefore, to continue our endeavor in developing practical solutions, first we need to understand what is the reason behind this observation. Why is the effectiveness of these techniques so unpredictable? What are the factors that influence the effectiveness of fault localization? Can we accurately predict fault localization effectiveness? Answering these questions can help in two ways: (1) We would know how to improve the code to facilitate SBFL. (2) We would be able to predict the effectiveness of SBFL. This helps users in deciding where and when to use it to avoid wasting time and money.

3.4 Predicting the Quality of SBFL

We tried to shed light on the observations above and understand what factors explain such variations. Knowing influencing factors and being able to predict the effectiveness of SBFL can improve the user's trust. If SBFL is expected to be bad, we don't use it—and the other way around. Doing this will not always help programmers, but it doesn't frustrate them either with bad predictions of the fault location.

To learn the aspects of the projects with the strongest influence on fault localization effectiveness, we investigated a large number of potential factors affecting SBFL effectiveness and built models, using standard machine learning techniques and a set of carefully selected metrics, to predict effectiveness. We wanted to determine whether we can build a model, using collected metrics as features, that is accurate enough to be used for SBFL effectiveness predictions in practice.

We grouped metrics into three groups according to the source of information they are based on. Metrics were considered potentially relevant when we had a hypothesis about why they could influence SBFL effectiveness. Considering code metrics, a metric had to be actionable as well, meaning that a developer could, using an appropriate programming style, improve its value. Static metrics measure the static aspects of the whole source code. Dynamic metrics measure the dynamic aspects considering the test runs. Test suite metrics are correlated to the test suite. In total, we collected 46 metrics and computed them for the buggy versions of five Defects4J projects. Tables 9, 10, and 11 illustrate the collected metrics.

Based on the metrics defined above, we need to predict if SBFL is effective and define class labels to predict. To define effectiveness, we relied on method-level Ochiai results. If the rank of the faulty method was between 1 and 10, we labeled SBFL as "effective" or "1", otherwise "ineffective" or "0". Using collected metrics as variables or features and SBFL effectiveness as labels, we formed a data set. We

Table 9 Static metrics

ID	Metric	Definition
S1	PML	% of methods with LoC>30
S2	PHFS	% of files with LoC>750
S3	PMFS	% of files with 300<LoC<750
S4	PHND	% of methods with nesting depth>5
S5	PMND	% of methods with 3<=nesting depth<=5
S6	CC	Mean cyclomatic complexity [22]
S7	MCC	# of methods with 10<CC<20
S8	AFFC	Mean afferent coupling [2]
S9	EFFC	Mean efferent coupling [2]
S10	ABKD	Mean block depth
S11	ADIH	Mean depth of inheritance hierarchy
S12	ALOCPM	Mean # of LoC per method
S13	ANOCPT	Mean # of constructors per type
S14	ANOFPT	Mean # of fields per type
S15	ANOMPT	Mean # of methods per type

applied regression analysis and classification algorithms on the data set with the goal to find the most relevant and influential metrics. A model generated using influential metrics helps decide whether or not to proceed with fault localization, thus avoiding misleading recommendations and waste of time.

Our evaluation results in [8] show that the best model is based on random forest; combines 15 static code, dynamic execution, and test suite metrics; and shows an excellent discrimination power (AUC = 0.88). The most influential metrics are: four static metrics (% Methods with LoC>30, % Methods with Nesting Depth>5, % Methods with 3<=Nesting Depth<=5, Mean # of Fields per Type), four dynamic metrics (Mean Node Degree, Max. Node Out-Degree, Graph Diameter, Response for Class), and two test metrics (% Method Coverage, % Methods Covered in Failing Tests). A slightly less accurate model (AUC = 0.87), based on only 10 metrics, relies on logistic regression. There is a considerable overlap of eight metrics which yield an AUC of 0.86 when using logistic regression and 0.87 when using random forest. These prediction models can be used in two ways: (1) to decide whether or not to proceed with fault localization and (2) to guide improvements in code quality and test suites.

4 Contribution and Limitation

We make the following contributions:

- **A failure clustering methodology**. We propose a failure clustering technique and a methodology for adapting the idea of debugging in parallel to a real context.

Table 10 Dynamic metrics

ID	Metric	Definition[a]
D1	VC	# of Nodes in call graph
D2	E	# of Edges in call graph
D3	MAXVD	Max. node degree
D4	MVD	Mean node degree
D5	MAXVI	Max. node in-degree
D6	MVI	Mean node in-degree
D7	MAXVO	Max node out-degree
D8	MVO	Mean node out-degree
D9	MSND	Avg. start node degree
D10	GD	Graph diameter
D11	GR	Graph radius
D12	MGD	Mean geodesic distance
D13	VCON	Node connectivity
D14	ECON	Edge connectivity
D15	ClCo	Mean clustering coefficient [20]
D16	SCOV	% of statement coverage
D17	CBO	Coupling between objects [2]
D18	RFC	Response for class [2]

[a]D1: # methods. D2: # method calls. D3: max. # edges connected to a node. D5: max. # edges entering a node. D7: max. # edges leaving a node. D10: greatest distance between any two nodes. D11: min. distance between any two nodes. D12: # edges in a shortest path between any two nodes. D13: min. # nodes that must be removed to break all paths between two nodes. D14: min. # edges that must be removed to break all paths between two nodes. D15: measures degree to which nodes in a graph tend to cluster

Table 11 Test suite metrics

ID	Metric	Definition
T1	T	# of tests
T2	M	# of methods
T3	PPT	% of passing tests
T4	PFT	% of failing tests
T5	D	Density [29]
T6	G	Diversity [29]
T7	U	Uniqueness [29]
T8	DDU	Density × diversity × uniqueness [29]
T9	MatSpar	Matrix sparsity
T10	MetCov	% of method coverage
T11	COVPT	% of methods covered in passing tests
T12	COVFT	% of methods covered in failing tests
T13	AVGMV	Mean covered methods per test

- **A collection of data sources for failure clustering**. We introduce a list of coverage and noncoverage data that are useful in the clustering of failing tests.
- **A new data granularity for failure diagnosis**. We propose a new granularity for program spectra called the syntactic block granularity which considers 18 different types of program elements.
- **A new ranking strategy**. We propose a ranking approach for SBFL techniques which leverages dynamic call and data-dependency graphs of failing executions.
- **A model to predict the effectiveness of SBFL**. We introduce a set of metrics which influence the effectiveness of SBFL. Using these metrics, we build a model to predict the effectiveness of SBFL. This model can be helpful in facilitating fault localization as well.
- **A tool-chain for failure diagnosis**. We introduce a tool-chain for failure diagnosis which puts failure clustering and fault localization in a pipeline.

However, we are aware that our work has its limitations. The difficulty of gathering data for evaluation prevented us from reporting on several case studies. We evaluated our solution ideas on either C++ programs or Java programs. However, a comprehensive evaluation should contain benchmarks from both languages. Comparing the results, finding similarities, and understanding dissimilarities can help us better understand the important factors in general and in each category.

In our fault localization evaluations, we assumed that each buggy version contains only one bug. However, this is not the case in practice. Although we suggest that before any fault localization attempt, one should do clustering on failing tests to segregate between faults, a comprehensive evaluation should also consider cases with multiple bugs.

5   Summary and Outlook

We proposed techniques and enhancements to facilitate failure diagnosis experience for developers. The proposed techniques can be used stand-alone or form a tool-chain; applying SBFL on fault-focused clusters yields more accurate results. The following is how developers and testers can benefit from using our proposed approaches.

Tester X is responsible for the quality of software development and deployment. She is involved in performing automated and manual tests to ensure the software created by developers is fit for purpose. Every week, she runs 1000 scheduled tests. Test runs take about 2 days. While running tests she collects coverage information. She has also provided a database of relevant data to measure the similarity between TCs.

After each test run, developers have two days to analyze failures, find bugs, repair them, and mark the analyzed failed tests as ready for the next test run. Thus, tester X collects failing tests and clusters them. The clustering results include a prediction of the numbers of bugs, groups of failing tests that are failing because of the same reason, and one representative test for each cluster of failing tests. Tester X, then, assigns each group of failures to one developer and asks them to analyze the representative failing tests to find the reasons behind failures as soon as possible.

Developers Y and Z use SBFL prediction model. Developer Y receives promising results. She continues using SBFL techniques to get some insight regarding the fault in her code. Developer Z, on the other hand, does not receive promising results. She continues the debugging process without using SBFL. However, later she uses the model to improve the quality of her code to facilitate fault localization.

Note Automated failure diagnosis techniques can be very helpful in reducing failure analysis time regardless of the programming language. However, a minimum code and test quality is needed. If software is of poor quality, not only our tool-chain but any other tool or technique cannot be highly effective on it. Thus, there is a prerequisite for using such tools and techniques.

References

1. Abreu, R., Zoeteweij, P., Van Gemund, A.J.C.: On the accuracy of spectrum-based fault localization. In: Proceedings—Testing: Academic and Industrial Conference Practice and Research Techniques, TAIC PART-Mutation 2007 (2007)
2. Bundschuh Manfred, D.C.: Object-Oriented Metrics, pp. 241–255. Springer, Berlin (2008)
3. Cover, T., Hart, P.: Nearest neighbor pattern classification. IEEE Trans. Inform. Theory **13**(1), 21–27 (1967)
4. Defects4J Dissection. http://program-repair.org/defects4j-dissection/#!/bug/Lang/26. Accessed: 2021-10-05
5. DiGiuseppe, N., Jones, J.A.: Fault density, fault types, and spectra-based fault localization. Empir. Softw. Eng. **20**, 928–967 (2015)
6. Golagha, M.: A framework for failure diagnosis. Ph.D. Thesis, Technical University of Munich, Germany (2020)
7. Golagha, M., Lehnhoff, C., Pretschner, A., Ilmberger, H.: Failure clustering without coverage. In: Proceedings of the 28th ACM SIGSOFT International Symposium on Software Testing and Analysis, ISSTA 2019 (2019)
8. Golagha, M., Pretschner, A., Briand, L.: Can we predict the quality of spectrum-based fault localization? pp. 4–15 (2020)
9. Golagha, M., Pretschner, A., Fisch, D., Nagy, R.: Reducing failure analysis time: an industrial evaluation. In: Proceedings of the 39th International Conference on Software Engineering: Software Engineering in Practice Track, ICSE-SEIP '17, pp. 293–302. IEEE Press, Piscataway (2017)
10. Golagha, M., Raisuddin, A.M., Mittag, L., Hellhake, D., Pretschner, A.: Aletheia: a failure diagnosis toolchain. In: 2018 IEEE/ACM 40th International Conference on Software Engineering Companion (2018)
11. Hatton, L.: Characterising the diagnosis of software failure. IEEE Software—SOFTWARE (2008)
12. Hogerle, W., Steimann, F., Frenkel, M.: More debugging in parallel. In: Proceedings—International Symposium on Software Reliability Engineering, ISSRE, pp. 133–143 (2014)
13. Jones, J.A., Bowring, J.F., Harrold, M.J.: Debugging in parallel. In: Proceedings of the 2007 International Symposium on Software Testing and Analysis—ISSTA '07, p. 16 (2007)

14. Jones, J.A., Harrold, M.J.: Empirical evaluation of the tarantula automatic fault-localization technique. In: Proceedings of the 20th IEEE/ACM International Conference on Automated Software Engineering, ASE '05, pp. 273–282. ACM, New York (2005)
15. Just, R., Jalali, D., Inozemtseva, L., Ernst, M.D., Holmes, R., Fraser, G.: Are mutants a valid substitute for real faults in software testing? In: Proceedings of the 22nd ACM SIGSOFT International Symposium on Foundations of Software Engineering—FSE 2014, pp. 654–665 (2014)
16. Khuri, A.I.: Introduction to Linear Regression Analysis, 5th edn. In: Montgomery, D.C., Peck, E.A., Vining, G.G. (eds.) International Statistical Review (2013)
17. Kochhar, P.S., Xia, X., Lo, D., Li, S.: Practitioners' expectations on automated fault localization. In: Proceedings of the 25th International Symposium on Software Testing and Analysis, ISSTA 2016, pp. 165–176. ACM, New York (2016)
18. Lehnhoff, C.: Reducing failure analysis time: a data-driven approach. Master's Thesis, Technical University of Munich (2019)
19. Liu, C., Han, J.: Failure proximity: a fault localization-based approach. In: Proceedings of the 14th ACM SIGSOFT International Symposium on Foundations of Software Engineering, SIGSOFT '06/FSE-14, pp. 46–56. ACM, New York (2006)
20. Luce, R.D., Perry, A.D.: A method of matrix analysis of group structure. Psychometrika **14**(2), 95–116 (1949)
21. Masri, W.: Chapter three—automated fault localization: advances and challenges, pp. 103–156. Elsevier, Amsterdam (2015)
22. McCabe, T.J.: A complexity measure. IEEE Trans. Softw. Eng. **SE-2**(4), 308–320 (1976)
23. Ochiai, A.: Zoogeographical studies on the soleoid fishes found in Japan and its neighbouring regions-II. Nippon Suisan Gakkaishi **22**, 526–530 (1957)
24. Pang-Ning, T., Steinbach, M., Kumar, V.: Introduction to Data Mining (2006)
25. Papadimitriou, C.H., Steiglitz, K.: Combinatorial Optimization: Algorithms and Complexity. Prentice-Hall, Upper Saddle River (1982)
26. Parnin, C., Orso, A.: Are automated debugging techniques actually helping programmers? In: Proceedings of the 2011 International Symposium on Software Testing and Analysis, ISSTA '11, pp. 199–209. ACM, New York (2011)
27. Pearl, J.: Causality: Models, Reasoning, and Inference. Cambridge University Press, Cambridge (2000)
28. Pearson, S., Campos, J., Just, R., Fraser, G., Abreu, R., Ernst, M.D., Pang, D., Keller, B.: Evaluating and improving fault localization. In: Proceedings of the 39th International Conference on Software Engineering (2017)
29. Perez, A., Abreu, R., van Deursen, A.: A test-suite diagnosability metric for spectrum-based fault localization approaches. In: 2017 IEEE/ACM 39th International Conference on Software Engineering (ICSE), pp. 654–664 (2017)
30. Podgurski, A., Leon, D., Francis, P., Masri, W., Minch, M., Sun, J.S.J., Wang, B.W.B.: Automated support for classifying software failure reports. In: 25th International Conference on Software Engineering, 2003. Proceedings, vol. 6, pp. 465–475 (2003)
31. Rogstad, E., Briand, L.C.: Clustering deviations for black box regression testing of database applications. IEEE Trans. Reliab. **65**(1), 4–18 (2016)
32. Rokach, L., Maimon, O.: Chapter 15—Clustering Methods. The Data Mining and Knowledge Discovery Handbook, p. 32 (2010)
33. Sobreira, V., Durieux, T., Delfim, F.M., Monperrus, M., de Almeida Maia, M.: Dissection of a bug dataset: anatomy of 395 patches from defects4j. CoRR abs/1801.06393 (2018)
34. Sohn, J., Yoo, S.: Fluccs: using code and change metrics to improve fault localization. In: Proceedings of the 26th ACM SIGSOFT International Symposium on Software Testing and Analysis, ISSTA 2017, pp. 273–283. ACM, New York (2017)
35. Trembly, A.C.: Software bugs cost billions annually. Nat. Underwriter/Life Health Financ. Serv. **106**(31), 43 (2002)
36. Utting, M., Legeard, B., Pretschner, A.: A taxonomy of model-based testing. Softw. Testing Verif. Reliab. **22**(April) (2006)

37. Wong, W.E., Debroy, V., Gao, R., Li, Y.: The DStar method for effective software fault localization. IEEE Trans. Reliab. **63**(1), 290–308 (2014)
38. Wong W.E., Gao, R., Li, Y., Abreu, R., Wotawa, F.: A survey on software fault localization. IEEE Trans. Softw. Eng. **PP**(99) (2016)

Open Source Software Governance: Distilling and Applying Industry Best Practices

Nikolay Harutyunyan

Abstract Modern software architectures are becoming increasingly complex and interdependent. The days of exclusive in-house software development by companies are over. A key force contributing to this shift is the abundant use of open source frameworks, components, and libraries in software development. Over 90% of all software products include open source components. Being efficient, robust, and affordable, they often cover the non-differentiating product requirements companies have. However, the uncontrolled use of open source software in products comes with legal, engineering, and business risks stemming from incorrect software licensing, copyright issues, and supply chain vulnerabilities. While recognized by a handful of companies, this topic remains largely ignored by the industry and little studied by the academia. To address this relevant and novel topic, we undertook a 3-year research project into open source governance in companies, which resulted in a doctoral dissertation. The key results of our work include a theory of industry best practices, where we captured how more than 20 experts from 15 companies worldwide govern their corporate use of open source software. Acknowledging the broad industry relevance of our topic, we developed a handbook for open source governance that enabled practitioners from various domains to apply our findings in their companies. We conducted three evaluation case studies, where more than 40 employees at three Germany-based multinational companies applied our proposed best practices. This chapter presents the highlights of building and implementing the open source governance handbook.

1 Introduction

Traditionally, companies tended to develop large parts of their software products internally with the occasional outsourcing or supplier code. However, modern software development requires the use of free/libre and open source software

N. Harutyunyan (✉)
Friedrich-Alexander-Universität, Erlangen-Nürnberg, Germany
e-mail: nikolay.harutyunyan@fau.de

(FLOSS) components. Major software infrastructures are built using Linux servers; many projects rely on open source libraries in Python, web browsers, and database management systems; and much more are critically dependent on the use of open source software. Moreover, many successful companies embrace open source software development and contribute their own software as open source projects including TensorFlow,[1] a library for machine learning developed by Google; React,[2] a front end library for building user interfaces or UI components; Android; Angular; and Chromium just to name a few. While these and many other FLOSS components are used daily by companies, few of them know about the associated risks of such unstructured use.

When not properly managed, incorporating open source software in a company product can have unforeseen legal, technical, and business consequences. A common example is the unintended use of an open source component licensed under a GPL (GNU General Public License) license,[3] which requires the user of the code to in turn open source their software under the same license. If an unaware developer uses a piece of GPL-licensed code in a company product, the company will eventually be forced to either open source the whole product (which might not make business sense) or replace the incorporated open source component. Over the years, companies have been dealing with copyright and licensing violations [1, 2], issues with complex licensing [3, 4], technical issues due to the dependency on other open source projects [5, 6] and low quality documentation [7, 8], and other risks [9–11].

Another major challenge of the uncontrolled FLOSS use are the software supply chain vulnerabilities. A recent 2021 story by Alex Birsan[4] outlines a remarkably simple software supply chain attack, which affected PayPal, Apple, Microsoft, and many other companies. In a nutshell, a developer analyzed several companies' commonly used software components that were developed internally by these companies. He then created public open source packages on GitHub with matching names but unintended functionalities. Surprisingly, many developers from these companies started using his public libraries instead, a confusion that can easily happen when open source software development is highly integrated with in-house development. This led to bugs and supply chain vulnerabilities across the board,

---

[1] TensorFlow is a free and open-source software library for machine learning maintained by Google and community—https://www.tensorflow.org/.

[2] React is an open-source, front end, JavaScript library for building user interfaces or UI components. It is maintained by Facebook and a community of individual developers and companies—https://reactjs.org/.

[3] The GNU General Public License is a series of widely used free software licenses that guarantee end users the freedom to run, study, share, and modify the software—http://www.gnu.org/licenses/gpl-3.0.en.html.

[4] An article by Alex Birsan titled "Dependency Confusion: How I Hacked into Apple, Microsoft and Dozens of Other Companies"—https://medium.com/@alex.birsan/dependency-confusion-4a5d60fec610.

demonstrating that even successful industry players sometimes lack comprehensive open source governance.

What causes the above-mentioned risks and problems when using open source components in companies?

We aimed to answer this question in the first phase of our study. The answer essentially was the lack of open source software governance. Companies that did not have a structured and explicit approach for dealing with open source related questions were bound to have such problems. Among the companies we studied, some employees claimed that the use of open source software in their products was not allowed. However, even in such cases, developers used open source libraries and components simply without authorization or any checks, thus exacerbating the problem.

We then set out to find the recommendations for comprehensive open source governance. On the one hand, while many researchers recognized the issue [12–14], the academic literature with actual FLOSS governance guidelines were scarce and often limited to the "hot" topics, such as licensing [3, 15]. On the other hand, practitioners were filling the gap with their own experience reports [10, 16], which, however, did not follow rigorous or scientific methods for the elicitation of the recommended practices.

Seeing the industry relevance and need for this research, as well as acknowledging its potential business impact, we set out to study open source governance at companies with an advanced understanding of the topic. Based on the state-of-the-art literature and our preliminary industry interviews, we identified four key subtopics: getting started with open source governance, inbound governance, supply chain management, and outbound governance. Accordingly, we asked the following research questions:

- RQ1: How should companies using open source components in their products get started with open source governance based on existent industry best practice?
- RQ2: How should companies using open source components in their products govern the inbound aspects of the FLOSS use?
- RQ3: How should companies using open source components in their products govern their software supply chains?
- RQ4: How should companies using open source components in their products govern the outbound aspects of the FLOSS use?

Our goal was to gather expert knowledge from the industry through interviews, observations, and primary materials analysis, in order to distill and propose a set of industry best practices for open source software governance.

This phase of our study took about two years and resulted in more than 80 recommended industry best practices for different aspects of FLOSS governance, including:

- Transition toward open source governance
- IP-at-risk analysis
- Component search

- Component approval
- Component reuse
- Bill of materials management
- License compliance and more

Following the qualitative survey method by Jansen [17], we collected and analyzed data from more than 20 expert interviews at 15 companies, primary materials, and observation notes. This resulted in a proposed theory of industry best practices for corporate open source governance.

From an academic view, we built a theory, but we wanted to go beyond that and see our findings actually used by companies. To do this, we cast our theory as a practical handbook for open source governance that can be easily customized and used by practitioners in their companies. In each subsection of this chapter, we present best practice subsets from the handbook.

We concluded our study by conducting three evaluation case studies at large, multinational companies based in Germany. We followed the multiple-case case study method by Yin [18]. The collaboration with the selected companies was essential for the successful evaluation of our proposed best practices. We worked for over two years with the case study companies to implement parts of our open source governance handbook at different production projects. Over time, we observed how these companies with little to no previous understanding of FLOSS governance were able to establish internal processes and tools to efficiently and comprehensively manage their open source use. In the course of the implementation, we identified the lacking aspects of our theory and addressed them. At the same time, we helped these companies take their first steps toward FLOSS governance, which increased their benefits from using open source components while limiting the potential risks. In the following subsections, we couple the proposed best practices with their implementation reports at the case study companies.

Observing the actual industry impact of our research work was very rewarding, and we are happy to share our experience in this chapter, which is structured as follows. Section 2 focuses on the discovery and capture of industry best practices for open source governance including subsections on getting started with FLOSS governance, supply chain management. Section 3 goes on to describe the case studies where the proposed best practices were applied. Section 4 concludes the paper outlining the potential directions for future research.

2 Distilling Industry Best Practices

In the first phase of our study we developed a theory of industry best practices for corporate open source governance based on expert interviews, primary materials, and observations we conducted at 15 companies worldwide. These companies all had an advanced understanding of open source governance, included a form of open source program office responsible for establishing and executing open source governance processes, and were willing to be interviewed for our study. We selected these companies from a larger sample of 140 companies in our professional network. We first classified these companies using different predefined criteria such as the size of the company, product types, business models, and more. We aimed for a point theoretical sampling that would result in companies with different profiles and from different industries. As a result we had a mix of small, medium, and large companies from varying domains such as automotive, consulting, and enterprise software. The details of the sampling and method description can be found in the dissertation [19].

After analyzing the collected data following Jansen's qualitative survey method [17] and using qualitative data analysis tools such as MAXQDA,[5] we distilled the frequent best practices highlighted by experts. Figure 1 illustrates the hierarchical structure of the distilled best practice categories and subcategories.

Answering the research questions RQ1-RQ4 we addressed the main concepts of open source governance proposing subsets of industry best practices for each category. As an example, we can consider the Supply Chain Management (SCM) category in Fig. 1. Answering RQ3, we analyzed how expert companies established their SCM policy and processes focused on presenting governance and corrective governance. The former would include among other things recommendations for supplier selection with open source governance aspects in mind. The latter would focus on assessing the risks of supplier vulnerabilities and mitigating potential risks. Each subcategory (leaf in the tree) would then include individual best practices presented in the following subsections. An example of a best practice covering the choice of the right supplier as a preventive SCM measure is presented in Table 1.

Together all the best practices we identified form a handbook that can be modified and applied by any company that has software as part of their products. Additionally, to make the handbook more applicable for practitioners, we constructed workflows of interconnected best practices. Customizing and then following such a workflow would make the application of the handbook at a company easier. A sample page from the handbook is presented in Fig. 2.

2.1 Getting Started with FLOSS Governance

Answering the research question RQ1, we addressed a common problem companies have when faced with the issue of open source software governance: where does one start. The first part of our handbook is devoted to getting started with corporate open source governance.

In this "Getting Started" category, we identified the following best practices:

- Product Analysis (OSGOV-GETSTA-PROANA)—eight best practices
- IP-at-Risk Analysis (OSGOV-GETSTA-IPRISK)—nine best practices

---

[5] MAXQDA is a software program designed for computer-assisted qualitative and mixed methods data, text, and multimedia analysis—https://www.maxqda.com/.

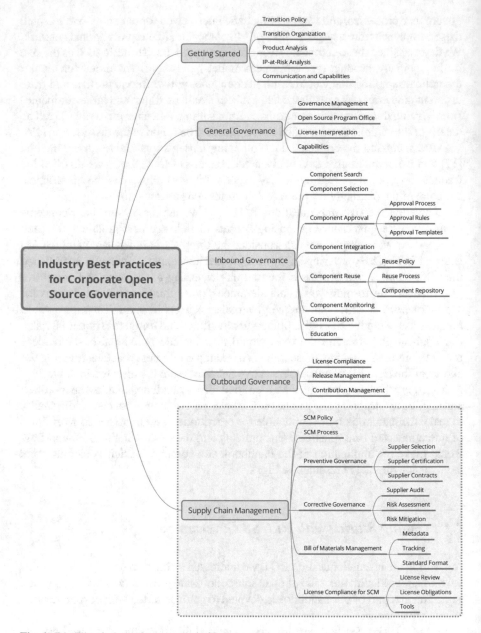

Fig. 1 Distilling industry best practices: Key concepts

- Transition Policy (OSGOV-GETSTA-TRAPOL)—three best practices
- Transition Organization (OSGOV-GETSTA-TRAORG)—eight best practices
- Communication and Capabilities (OSGOV-GETSTA-COMCAP)—five best practices

Table 1 OSGOV-SUCHMA-PREGOV-1. Choose the right supplier

Name	Choose the right supplier
Actor	Supply chain management responsibles, IT department, procurement department
Context	Virtually all companies use supplied software components as part of their products. Not all suppliers are the same in terms of open source governance and compliance. Choosing a supplier without open source governance consideration can result in functionally superior software with open source components that are not compliant with the company's license use case pairs
Problem	If supplied code causes open source governance and compliance risks, you will have to either change your supplier or address the risks in cooperation with the supplier after the delivery. How can such situations be prevented?
Solution	To prevent potential issues with FLOSS governance and compliance you should choose the right suppliers that are aware and mature in terms of governance and compliance, as well as experienced in using open source components in their products. To do this, you need to → *assess open source governance and compliance awareness and maturity* which can be done by → requesting supplier certification or self-certification from potential suppliers. To establish a consistent approach for preventive governance → *design supplier contracts with open source governance aspects in mind* and use the governance related clauses in case of license non-compliance by a supplier. The latter can be used for corrective governance, namely to → *trigger supplier contract clauses and get the supplier to take care of the issue*

The Product Analysis subcategory included practices for an initial scanning of the open source components already in use at a company. Even if the company had a policy discouraging the use of open source software, more often than not, there are a considerable number of such components that were previously undetected or undocumented. This cannot be ignored when getting started with FLOSS governance. You need to take stock of the overall FLOSS use before establishing the governance processes.

Once the initial assessment is conducted, companies need to perform an IP-at-Risk Analysis, which covers the assessment of potential licensing issues, copyright violations, or other inconsistencies. The identified risks need to be mitigated at this stage either by complying with the component license or by removing or encapsulating the component.

Afterwards, the company can start the transition from the unstructured use of open source software to basic governance defined in a Transition Policy and operationalized through the proposed Transition Organization best practices. During the whole transition, companies need to pay close attention to communicating the changes to all the stakeholders and building internal capabilities where needed.

An example best practice from the Getting Started category is presented in Table 2, which covers the basic process that the project architect will use for reporting and assessing ongoing additions of open source components during the transition.

A. Process Template for Supplier Management 1

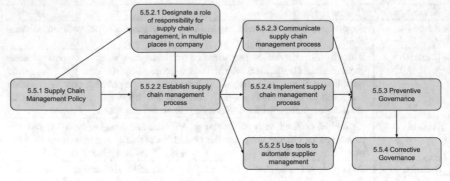

Figure 10. Supplier Management Process

B. Process Template for Supplier Management 2

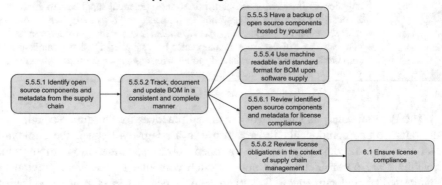

Figure 11. Supplier Management Process

A Best Practices Handbook for Open Source Governance and Compliance
© 2018-2019 Bayave GmbH and FAU, 2019-02-13 – Status: Final.

68

Fig. 2 Distilling industry best practices: Key concepts

All the proposed best practices can be traced to the primary data we analyzed in the first stage of our study. Here is an example of such a trace from Company 14s[6] legal counsel responsible for open source compliance talking about the specifics of establishing a process of continuous reporting and assessment of open source components:

---

[6] Company and interviewee names were anonymized per their request.

Table 2 OSGOV-PROANA-1.2. Establish a process of continuous reporting and assessment

Name	Establish a process of continuous reporting and assessment
Actor	Transition manager and/or project architect
Context	You already → used one mandatory survey for initial assessment. Now you need a process for continuous reporting and assessment of any open source usage during the transition
Problem	The transition needs to prepare the company for fully structured FLOSS governance. However, during the transition how should the process of continuous reporting and assessment look like?

Solution	Establish a process of continuous reporting and assessment that involves defined and easy-to-follow steps for developers when using new open source components during the transition. This can be achieved using a product architecture model (a meta-model for all governance related information such as license information, copyright noticed, export restrictions, etc.), bill of materials documentation, questionnaires or forms, etc. The process should help:
	
	 • Continuously report new use of open source components during transition
	 • Automate this reporting as much as possible, by → *selecting and using governance tools for automation*
	 • Continuously assess new use of open source components during transition
	
	    – Assess license compliance
	    – Assess copyright notices
	    – Assess export restrictions
	    – Assess software supply chains
	
	 • Document the assessment findings
	 • Share the reported use of open source and documented assessment findings

When our developers are reporting the open source via [our internal tool], there is always the main file which is also mentioned in the license file which is also computed by GitHub or by the community behind. And with this scan tooling, we cross-check the whole software, so we definitely see, okay, that's not only the MIT license which is mentioned in the license file but also other licenses, so the GPL files. And, then, we're talking to our developer which is reporting the open source. In most cases, the developer says, no to the GPL files, we don't use it, we only use the MIT file. And, so, they need to cross check what files they use, and what licenses are used by them. – Company 14

More best practices on getting started with open source governance can be found in the dissertation [19] or in our previous paper on the subject [20]. Furthermore, we addressed the research questions RQ2 and RQ3 on inbound and outbound governance in our previous papers [21] and [22], as well as in the dissertation [19].

2.2 Supply Chain Management

Answering the research question RQ2, we focused on the core topic of our research—software supply chain management in the scope of FLOSS governance.

Software supply chains include both proprietary code (developed in-house or supplied) and open source code. Modern software supply chains have multiple tiers where each supplier has multiple suppliers on the deeper tiers. In each instance, open source components are used and integrated into the larger software package that ends up in the software of the end user sold by the OEM (Original Equipment Manufacturer) company. In a nutshell, in case of issues due to poor FLOSS governance down the supplier hierarchy, the whole responsibility can rarely be put on suppliers.

We can consider a car example. The car manufacturer has commissioned a supplier to develop an infotainment system for the car including navigation, music, and other functionalities. The supplier (or their suppliers) uses open source libraries for the graphical interface and a Linux-based operating system, both of which are licensed under the GPL v3 (GNU General Public License version 3) license. This license requires any user of the code to publish it under the same license and to disclose the original copyright holders. If the suppliers fail to mention this to the automotive company and the company does not do its own due diligence in terms of FLOSS governance, a copyright holder of the original software under the GPL license can sue the company for license non-compliance. As a result, the company would face steep legal or operational costs as they would either have to settle or update their software to comply with the license.

In this category we distilled industry best practices for the following subcategories:

- Supply Chain Management Policy (OSGOV-SUCHMA-SCMPOL)—three best practices
- Supply Chain Management Process (OSGOV-SUCHMA-SCMPRO)—five best practices
- Preventive Governance (OSGOV-SUCHMA-PREGOV)—four best practices
- Corrective Governance (OSGOV-SUCHMA-CORGOV)—four best practices
- Bill of Materials Management (OSGOV-SUCHMA-BOMMAN)—four best practices
- License Compliance for Supply Chain (OSGOV-SUCHMA-LICCOM)—two best practices

To go one level deeper, we can consider the specific best practices focused on corrective governance:

- OSGOV-SUCHMA-CORGOV-1. Audit your supply chain
- OSGOV-SUCHMA-CORGOV-2. Mitigate identified risks
- OSGOV-SUCHMA-CORGOV-2.1. Assess risks in accordance to the supply chain management policy
- OSGOV-SUCHMA-CORGOV-2.2. Trigger supplier contract clauses and get the supplier to take care of the issue
- OSGOV-SUCHMA-CORGOV-2.3. Do not run your supplier out of business

An example best practice in this subcategory is presented in Table 3. While somewhat counter-intuitive, we found an industry best practice discouraging an extreme pressure on the suppliers in case of FLOSS governance issues identified too late. If you were to put the whole responsibility on the supplier, you are running a chance of bankrupting the supplier, which could leave your company in a worse situation. As a result, you still have to deal with the litigation but also need to find a different supplier or maintain their code on your own.

Table 3 OSGOV-SUCHMA-CORGOV-2.3. Do not run your supplier out of business

Name	Do not run your supplier out of business
Actor	OSPO (Open Source Program Office), Lawyer/legal counsel
Context	You have identified compliance and governance risks in your supply chain and → *assessed these risks in accordance with the supply chain management policy*. For certain critical risks you → *triggered supplier contract clauses to take care of the issue*
Problem	What actions should you not take when addressing the identified risks of non-compliance by a supplier?
Solution	Most companies have suppliers that are smaller than themselves, thus giving them higher negotiation power over the suppliers. This means that in case of non-compliance with open source licenses in the supplied code, you can easily force your supplier to fix the risk causing software non-compliance. You can even sue your supplier and get compensation. However, you should be careful not to endanger the operation of the supplier company
	If you run your supplier out of business by pressuring them with lawsuits or financial pressure, you can end up with a binary instead of a source code and no ability to maintain or update the software that was causing the non-compliance issue in the first place. Most software is not supplied as source code, but rather as a binary in order to protect the intellectual property of the supplier that makes money by selling a different version of the product that uses its know-how in the form of source code. If a company goes bankrupt, you might have to look for another supplier, which is costly and time consuming. In a nutshell, do not run your supplier out of business, when possible. Alternatively, make sure to get the source code in case of the supplier bankruptcy or before changing the supplier to avoid the above mentioned risk

More practices on the topic of supply chain management can be found in the dissertation [19] or in our previous publication [23].

3 Applying Industry Best Practices

In the second phase of our study we applied our handbook for open source governance at three companies in order to evaluate our findings in a real-life context using the case study methodology by Yin [18]. We identified three Germany-based companies that had little to no experience of open source governance, but had products incorporating software. These companies were willing to learn and implement FLOSS governance processes following our recommendations. On the one hand, this was an opportunity for them to learn from the leading companies in terms of open source use and governance. On the other hand, it was an opportunity for us to have an actual industry impact by having our theory implemented and testing it in real life. The three companies were at different stages in terms of FLOSS governance. Company A had no prior experience of structured open source governance, while Company B and C had some basic experience. Company B, in particular, was dealing with many software suppliers and needed support in that domain.

Further details on the case study company profiles and specifics can be found in the dissertation [19].

3.1 Case Study A

Once the Getting Started part of the handbook was completed, we started the evaluation phase that was running in parallel to the further theory building and handbook extension. We implemented a subset of the proposed Getting Started best practices at Company A, namely at five of their divisions with a focus on Division A.1 (with aerospace products including software systems and components).

In the course of the transition toward open source governance at Division A.1, a newly established open source program office (OSPO)[7] followed our Getting Started best practice *OSGOV-GETSTA-PROANA-3.1. Run open source use analysis in products*. An R&D manager who was part of the OSPO ran an initial analysis of the current FLOSS use at the division using an open source tool called FOSSology[8] [24]. An excerpt from this analysis is presented in Fig. 3. Following the best practice was well worth it, as the OSPO identified a number of problematic components that were previously overlooked or ignored, including but not limited to open source software licensed under GPL and AGPL[9] (GNU Affero General Public License) licenses. These components were later reviewed and analyzed individually.

Case Study A was extensive spanning over 2.5 years and enabled us to run a longitudinal study into the implementation of various parts of our handbook across five different divisions operating in different industries and in different countries including Germany, Mexico, and China. Figure 3 presents only a brief snippet of an evaluation artifact. More artifacts and thorough details can be found in the dissertation [19], including a complete open source governance process that Company A created when customizing our handbook.

---

[7] Open Source Program Office (OSPO) is a typical organization unit responsible for managing the internal and external aspects of corporate open source governance, often composed of software developers, software architects, lawyers, and product managers.

[8] FOSSology is an open source license compliance software system and toolkit that can be used to scan software for license, copyright, and export control issues—https://www.fossology.org/.

[9] GNU Affero General Public License is based on the GPL license but has more restrictive license terms—https://www.gnu.org/licenses/agpl-3.0.en.html.

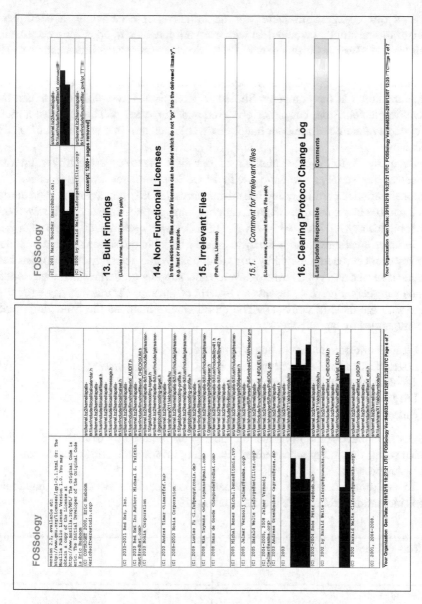

Fig. 3 Applying industry best practices: Initial open source use assessment at Case Study A

3.2 Case Study B

Company B was an enterprise software company operating internationally but based in Germany. With nearly 5000 employees, the company had different approaches for open source governance across different teams and business units. At the time of our engagement, there was an initiative of establishing a centralized organizational unit that would deal with everything related to open source software. This team has been acquiring new FLOSS governance responsibilities and was glad to collaborate with us in the scope of a research project. We introduced a subset of best practices for Supply Chain Management from our handbook and observed their implementation at the company. Similar to Company A, we did not conduct the actual implementation, but rather observed and supported it. This enabled a more unbiased evaluation of how our handbook would perform in a real-life setting of a company.

Company B followed a number of our best practices establishing internal processes for supplier evaluation with FLOSS governance in mind, as well as optional supplier certifications, bill-of-materials (BOM) management, and more. As a notable example, the software supplier manager at Company B followed our best practice *OSGOV-SUCHMA-PREGOV-1.1. Assess open source governance and compliance awareness and maturity* to create a supplier questionnaire that included the key aspects recommended by our handbook. While abstract, the proposed best practices served as a good basis to develop new supplier guidelines that were sent to actual suppliers. Figure 4 presents an excerpt of the supplier questionnaire (its first page with the table of contents). The questionnaire included the following points recommended by our handbook:

- License information (including open source licenses)
- Level of open source awareness
- Technologies used in the development process
- Integration of third party software into supplier code
- Bill-of-materials information

Our best practice did not cover all the aspects required by Company B, so they added points on quality management (including information on ISO certifications), and sales process.

To see more details of our evaluation case studies, as well as handbook implementation artifacts, see the dissertation [19].

Licensor Name	
Name of product	
Version of product	
Is the product white labeled	[_] yes [_] no

Fig. 4 Applying industry best practices: Supplier questionnaire at Case Study B

4   Conclusion

This section concludes the book chapter with the results' highlights from our work on open source software governance in companies. In the first stage of the study, we distilled some best practices used in the industry for open source governance. We captured and presented them as part of a larger handbook for FLOSS governance that focused on getting started with governance, managing the inbound and outbound aspects, as well as supply chain management. The handbook was the practical artifact we developed to make our research results more relevant and applicable for practitioners, who could customize and use our best practices. The handbook consisted of topical categories and subcategories. Individual best practices were arranged into workflows that would enable an easier execution at a company.

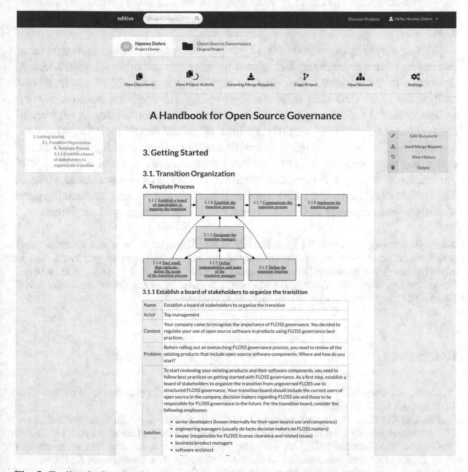

Fig. 5 Tooling for handbook representation and forking: Editive—https://editive.com/en/

In the second stage of the study, we took parts of the handbook to companies in Germany willing to put our findings to test in their production projects. We conducted three case studies, where different best practice subsets were implemented and evaluated in a real-life setting. The case studies demonstrated the pitfalls of some best practices that we later addressed. They also demonstrated the limitations of best practice transferability across companies. As a result, our handbook and its best practices had to be abstract in nature and not specific for one industry domain. Instead, we aimed for broad applicability and customization.

Going beyond the traditional academic work of theory building and working closely with the industry to evaluate our findings, we also faced some setbacks. Namely, Case Study C partially failed due to the misaligned expectations from the project, as well as different visions for the open source governance handbook. We learned that large shifts in company software architectures or processes are no easy feat. They need to be thoroughly prepared and be backed by different stakeholders across the company. And even in such cases, success is not a given. However, we were able to learn from both our successes and failures during the three years of working on this topic.

We see future opportunities for extending the research into other aspects of both open source governance and related topics, such as corporate open sourcing or license compliance. We also want to highlight the potential of the handbook method for other studies in software engineering and computer science. Finally, we see potential tooling support for the handbook that would make it even easier for companies to use and modify the best practices across their organizational complexities. In fact, we collaborated with a startup (Editive—https://editive.com/en/) based on a spin-off project at our university to create a *forkable* prototype of our handbook to present to our industry partners. A screenshot is presented in Fig. 5. The further development of such tools can make introducing and maintaining open source governance easier and more streamlined for any company in the future.

Acknowledgments This was not an individual effort. Throughout the whole research, many people supported me—my family, my friends, my colleagues, and industry partners. I want to especially thank my professor Dirk Riehle and my colleagues Ann Barcomb, Andreas Bauer, Fariba Bensing, Maximilian Capraro, Hannes Dohrn, Michael Dorner, Andreas Kaufmann, Daniel Knogl, and Georg Schwarz for their contributions to this research.

References

1. Ruffin, C., Ebert, C.: Using open source software in product development: a primer. IEEE Softw. **21**(1), 82–86 (2004)
2. Lin, L.C.-H., Shen, N.: Copyleft referring to GPL-3.0 was cited as a defense method in Chinese intellectual property court in Beijing. Int. Free Open Source Softw. Law Rev. **10**(1), 1–7, (2019)
3. German, D.M., Hassan, A.E.: License integration patterns: addressing license mismatches in component-based development. In Proceedings of the 31st International Conference on Software Engineering, pp. 188–198. IEEE Computer Society, Silver Spring (2009)

4. Merilinna, J., Matinlassi, M.: Assessing the role of open source software in the European secondary software sector: a voice from industry. In: 1st International Conference on Open Source Systems (2005)
5. Chen, W., Li, J., Ma, J., Conradi, R., Ji, J., Liu, C.: An empirical study on software development with open source components in the Chinese software industry. Softw. Process Improv. Practice 13(1), 89–100 (2008)
6. Agerfalk, P.J., Deverell, A., Fitzgerald, B., Morgan, L.: State of the art and practice of open source component integration. In: 32nd EUROMICRO Conference on Software Engineering and Advanced Applications (EUROMICRO'06), pp. 170–177. IEEE, Piscataway (2006)
7. Akkanen, J., Demeter, H., Eppel, T., Ivánfi, Z., Nurminen, J.K., Stenman, P.: Reusing an open source application—practical experiences with a mobile CRM pilot. In: IFIP International Conference on Open Source Systems, pp. 217–222. Springer, Berlin (2007)
8. Ayala, C., Hauge, Ø., Conradi, R., Franch, X., Li, J., Velle, K.S.: Challenges of the open source component marketplace in the industry. In: IFIP International Conference on Open Source Systems, pp. 213–224. Springer, Berlin (2009)
9. Stol, K.-J., Ali Babar, M.: Challenges in using open source software in product development: a review of the literature. In: Proceedings of the 3rd International Workshop on Emerging Trends in Free/Libre/Open Source Software Research and Development, pp. 17–22. ACM, New York (2010)
10. Popp, K.M.: Best Practices for commercial use of open source software: business models, processes and tools for managing open source software. BoD–Books on Demand (2015)
11. Helmreich, M.: Best practices of adopting open source software in closed source software products (2011)
12. Kemp, R.: Towards free/libre open source software governance in the organization. IFOSS L. Rev. 1 (2009)
13. Markus, M.L.: The governance of free/open source software projects: monolithic, multidimensional, or configurational? J. Manag. Governance 11(2), 151–163 (2007)
14. Gangadharan, G., D'Andrea, V., De Paoli, S., Weiss, M.: Managing license compliance in free and open source software development. Inform. Syst. Front. 14(2), 143–154 (2012)
15. Alspaugh, T.A., Asuncion, H.U., Scacchi, W.: Analyzing software licenses in open architecture software systems. In: Proceedings of the 2009 ICSE Workshop on Emerging Trends in Free/Libre/Open Source Software Research and Development, pp. 54–57. IEEE, Piscataway (2009)
16. Peters, S.: Best practices for creating an open source policy (2010)
17. Jansen, H.: The logic of qualitative survey research and its position in the field of social research methods. Forum Qualitative Sozialforschung/Forum: Qualitative Social Research 11(2), (2010)
18. Yin, R.K.: Case Study Research and Applications: Design and Methods. Sage Publications, New York (2017)
19. Harutyunyan, N.: Corporate Open Source Governance of Software Supply Chains. doctoralthesis, Friedrich-Alexander-Universität Erlangen-Nürnberg (FAU) (2019)
20. Harutyunyan, N., Riehle, D.: Getting started with floss governance and compliance: a theory of industry best practices. In: Proceedings of the 15th International Symposium on Open Collaboration, Forthcoming, 2019
21. Harutyunyan, N., Riehle, D.: Industry best practices for FLOSS governance and component reuse. In: Proceedings of the 24th European Conference on Pattern Languages of Programs. ACM, New York (2019)
22. Harutyunyan, N., Riehle, D.: Industry best practices for component approval in floss governance. In: Proceedings of the 25th European Conference on Pattern Languages of Programs. ACM, New York (2020)
23. Harutyunyan, N.: Managing your open source supply chain-why and how? Computer 53, 77–81 (2020)
24. Gobeille, R.: The FOSSology project. In: Proceedings of the International Working Conference on Mining Software Repositories, pp. 47–50. ACM, New York (2008)

Dynamically Scalable Fog Architectures

Dominic Henze

Abstract Recent advances in mobile connectivity as well as increased computational power and storage in sensor devices have given rise to a new family of software architectures with challenges for data and communication paths as well as architectural reconfigurability at runtime. Established in 2012, Fog Computing describes one of these software architectures. It lacks a commonly accepted definition, which manifests itself in the missing support for mobile applications as well as dynamically changing runtime configurations. The dissertation "Dynamically Scalable Fog Architectures" provides a framework that formalizes Fog Computing and adds support for dynamic and scalable Fog Architectures.

The framework called xFog (Extension for **Fog** Computing) models Fog Architectures based on set theory and graphs. It consists of three parts: xFogCore, xFogPlus, and xFogStar. xFogCore establishes the set theoretical foundations. xFogPlus enables dynamic and scalable Fog Architectures to dynamically add new components or layers. Additionally, xFogPlus provides a View concept which allows stakeholders to focus on different levels of abstraction.

These formalizations establish the foundation for new concepts in the area of Fog Computing. One such concept, xFogStar, provides a workflow to find the best service configuration based on quality of service parameters.

The xFog framework has been applied in eight case studies to investigate the applicability of dynamic Fog Components, scalable Fog Architectures, and the service provider selection at runtime. The case studies, covering different application domains—ranging from smart environments, health, and metrology to gaming—successfully demonstrated the feasibility of the formalizations provided by xFog, the dynamic change of Fog Architectures by adding new components and layers at runtime, as well as the applicability of a workflow to establish the best service configuration.

D. Henze (✉)
Technical University of Munich, Munich, Germany
e-mail: henzed@mytum.de

© The Author(s) 2022 91
M. Felderer et al. (eds.), *Ernst Denert Award for Software Engineering 2020*,
https://doi.org/10.1007/978-3-030-83128-8_6

1   Introduction

With the constant increase of computational power and available storage, mobile devices get more and more involved in distributed systems, which are "collections of independent computers that appear to be one single system to users" [1]. Nevertheless, mobile devices will always be resource poor in comparison to static hardware, as static hardware is not capped by properties such as heat dissipation or battery life [2, 3]. Therefore, mobile devices will always struggle with the most advanced media and data analysis.

Mobile cloud computing was introduced to bridge this gap and combines mobile computing with cloud computing to leverage the computational power of the cloud for mobile devices [4, 5]. However, clouds are usually distant from the mobile devices and using them creates high latencies, which are insufficient for real-time applications such as augmented reality.

To address this issue, concepts such as Cloudlets, Edge Computing, and Fog Computing emerged. Satyanarayanan et al. described these concepts to utilize resource-rich components near the mobile device to offload computational intense tasks while having "low latency, one-hop, high-bandwidth wireless access" [3]. While Cloudlets use trusted, nearby components with excessive computational power, Edge Computing focuses on the entirety of the network trying to push services as close to the edge as possible [6, 7].

Bonomi et al. introduced Fog Computing as a three-layered software architecture containing a Cloud, Fog, and Edge layer [8]. These layers interact using subscriber models with one layer acting as the provider and the other one as its user. Accordingly, application scenarios such as dynamic vehicles, smart grids, distributed sensor networks, and smart environments can benefit from using Fog Computing.

This loose definition has led to many interpretations of Fog Computing as well as attempts to sharpen the definition. Nevertheless, there is no commonly accepted definition of what Fog Computing or a Fog Node is, and the difference to similar concepts such as Edge Computing is not clearly defined [9].

To address these misunderstandings, the dissertation "Dynamically Scalable Fog Architectures" [10] follows the intent of the paper "Fog horizons—a theoretical concept to enable dynamic fog architectures" [17] to create a formalized definition for Fog Computing based on software architectures and set theory. It is based on the organized and systematic research approach design science established by Hevner and Wieringa [11, 12]. It investigates the following knowledge and technical research goals:

Knowledge Goal 1: Establish Fog Computing as a subclass of software architectures.

Technical Research Goal 1: Define a framework that provides a formalized definition of Fog Computing.

These goals are achieved with xFog, an extension for **Fog** Computing, and xFogCore which defines the foundations of the framework. These foundations are then used to address two additional challenges by formalization: Providing support for dynamic components and addressing the ambiguity of layers, in particular of the Fog.

> **Technical Research Goal 2:** Define an extension to the foundations of Fog Computing that supports components joining and leaving an architecture (*Dynamics*).

> **Technical Research Goal 3:** Define an extension to the foundations of Fog Computing that supports the process of adding and removing layers (*Scalability*).

These goals should be addressed with xFogPlus, one part of xFog that relies on the foundations introduced by xFogCore and formalizes dynamics and scalability in Fog Architectures.

The combination of both, xFogCore and xFogPlus, enables xFog to support a variety of advanced concepts, such as xFogStar. xFogStar is an extension that investigates the selection of service providers which is addressed with the following goal:

> **Technical Research Goal 4:** Enable service provider selection in dynamic scalable Fog Architectures.

Finally, we want to investigate if and how xFog, its parts, and extension describe Fog Computing:

> **Knowledge Goal 2:** Investigate the feasibility of xFog.

> **Knowledge Goal 3:** Investigate the feasibility of xFogStar.

Therefore, we validate three different aspects: *Dynamic Fog Components*, *Scalable Fog Architectures*, and *Service Provider Selection*. Each aspect is addressed by multiple case studies with cases from different domains.

2   xFog: An Extension for Fog Computing

To define an architecture based on the component and connector definitions by Shaw and Garlan, Bass and Kruchten for software architectures [13–15], we have to investigate the components included within an architecture and the connections

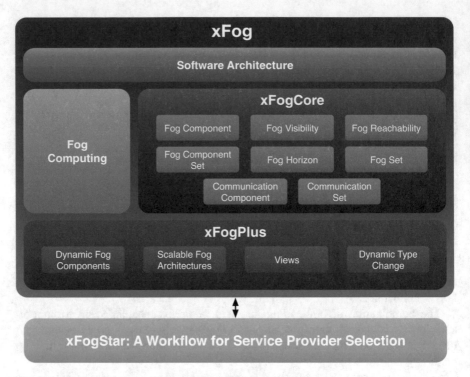

Fig. 1 Overview of the xFog framework highlighting the most important concepts

among them. The framework xFog addresses this goal for Fog Computing and its resulting architectures for the purpose of formalization. The name xFog is short for an e**X**tension for **Fog** Computing and accordingly uses its principles and ideas to provide a formalization which addresses knowledge goal 1 and the technical research goal 1 (Fig. 1).

xFog is separated into two parts: xFogCore and xFogPlus. While xFogCore focuses on the formalization of Fog Computing, xFogPlus extends these formalizations by the concepts of dynamic reconfigurability and scalability. Finally, xFogStar extends xFog with a workflow that supports service consumers with the selection of service providers.

2.1 Fog Component

Fog Computing is defined using three types of components: *Cloud Devices*, *Fog Nodes*, and *Edge Devices*. While Cloud Devices are servers / data centers offering storage, computational power, or specific software, Fog Nodes are devices on the way between the cloud devices and edge devices that could potentially offer services with less computational power but faster response times, location awareness, and mobility [8]. Lastly, Edge Devices are end-user devices that strive to use services offered by cloud devices and/or Fog Nodes.

In order to make the following concepts more type independent and easier to understand, we define a *Fog Component* as a common superclass. This Fog Component shows the direct similarity to the software architecture definitions and allows its comparability. The group of all Fog Components is called Fog Component Set.

2.2 Fog Visibility

The first concept based on the Fog Component definition is the Fog Visibility. The Fog Visibility is the virtual area around a Fog Component including all other Fog Components that can be "seen." This idea is translated to the terminology of software architectures and networking as shown in Definition 1 using received messages without transitivity.

Definition 1: Fog Visibility

FogVisibility$(x) := \{y \mid y$ receives direct messages from $x\}$

with:
$\quad x, y \in FogComponentSet$

Therefore, the Fog Visibility describes a relation on the Fog Component Set which allows us to use and assign properties of sets and relations to it.

One limitation of the Fog Visibility and all following concepts is the communication channel used by the Fog Components. While communication channels such as Wi-Fi, 3G, or 4G can potentially include a large amount of Fog Components, others, such as Bluetooth, might be inherently limited. This aspect will be further investigated in Sect. 2.7.

Figure 2 shows two examples of Fog Visibilities for a Fog Component A. The Fog Visibility on the left describes the self-containing set and the Fog Visibility on the right a more generic example. To show the Fog Visibility in both cases, we display the range in which a Fog Component can send messages as circles. This shape as well as the radius of the Fog Visibility can change substantially depending on the communication channel used.

Also the first example is of less practical use; it describes the edge case of the Fog Visibility definition and answers the question if Fog Components without other communication partners still maintain Fog Visibilities. As we do not exclude the Fog Component itself as a viable communication partner, the Fog Visibility relation is reflexive and, therefore, exists even without other Fog Components in range.

The second example includes Fog Components A - F with Fog Components A - C and E being inside A's Fog Visibility. D and F are outside the circle and therefore excluded.

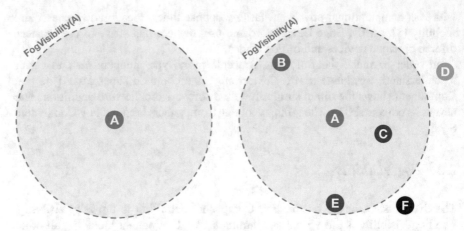

Fig. 2 Example graph of the Fog Visibility

2.3 Fog Horizon

The second concept is called Fog Horizon. Its name is on the one side inspired by the visual line separating the earth from the sky and on the other side by the event horizon of a black hole from which nothing can escape its gravitational field. Transferring those ideas to the area of Fog Components, it describes devices that closely interact with each other, have a certain locality attached, and share a common medium, in our case a communication channel.

This aspect can be described using the introduced Fog Visibility. As shown in Definition 2, the Fog Horizon is the symmetrical closure of the Fog Visibility and contains all Fog Components that can send as well as receive messages from each other, establishing a bidirectional communication. Based on this definition and the property of the Fog Visibility, the Fog Horizon is reflexive as well as symmetric. Accordingly, if one Fog Component A is in the Fog Horizon of Fog Component B, B is also in the Fog Horizon of A.

Definition 2: Fog Horizon

$FogHorizon(x) := FogVisibility(x)^{\leftrightarrow} =$
$FogVisibility(x) \cap FogVisibility(x)^{-} =$
$\{y \mid y \in FogVisibility(x) \land x \in FogVisibility(y)\}$

with:
  $x, y \in FogComponentSet$

Figure 3 shows a Fog Horizon example: As the circle around A does not include any other Fog Components, its Fog Visibility and therefore Fog Horizon only contain the component itself. In the case of Fog Component B, these sets do not match up. While B can "see" D, this is not true the other way around, making the

Fog Visibility of *B* equal to *B* and *D* and the Fog Horizon just *B*. *C* and *D* on the other hand can send messages to each other, including them in each other's Fog Horizons

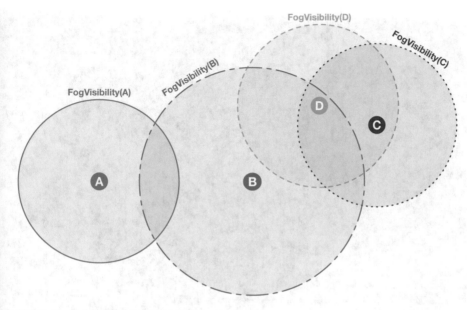

Fig. 3 Example graph for the Fog Horizon

2.4 Fog Reachability

The Fog Reachability describes the maximum outreach a Fog Component can have and therefore addresses the missing indirect communication from the Fog Visibility and Fog Horizon. While these concepts establish small isolated sets, the Fog Reachability also includes Fog Components that can be reached using other Fog Components as hops. Accordingly, as shown in Definition 3, the Fog Reachability is defined as the transitive closure of the Fog Visibility or every Fog Component that can receive direct or indirect messages.

Definition 3: Fog Reachability

$FogReachability(x) := FogVisibility^+(x) =$
$\{y \mid y$ receives direct or indirect messages from $x\}$

with:
  $x, y \in FogComponentSet$

Figure 4 shows an example with four Fog Components *A*, *B*, *C*, and *D*. With *A*'s Fog Visibility containing *B* and *B*'s Fog Visibility containing *C* and *D*, *A*'s Fog

Reachability contains all four Fog Components. B does not contain A, C does not contain any Fog Components and finally D contains B and C.

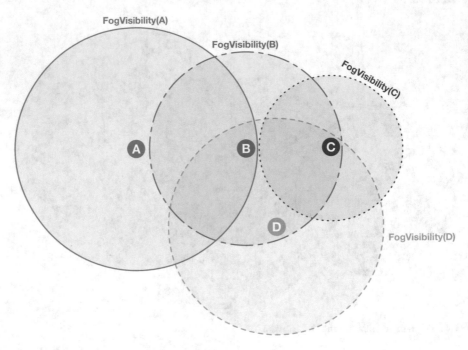

Fig. 4 Example graph for the Fog Reachability

One issue of the Fog Reachability is shown as soon as the Fog Components are not an isolated set, but open to the internet. According to the Fog Reachability's definition, just one open connection would result in a huge part of the internet being included in the Fog Reachability.

2.5 Fog Set

To address this issue, we have to further limit the Fog Components that are included in the set that describes a Fog Architecture, since we would not consider all these Fog Components to be part of a single architecture but rather a superset. Similar to the definition of the Fog Reachability, we use the transitive closure to create a set that is not limited to single hops, but this time for the Fog Horizon instead of the Fog Visibility as shown in Definition 4. This makes the Fog Set reflexive and symmetrical, but also transitive, and allows us to emphasize the close interaction between Fog Components that is described by the Fog Horizon.

Definition 4: Fog Set

$FogSet(x) := FogHorizon^+(x) =$
$\{y \mid y \in FogVisibility^{-1}(x) \land x \in FogVisibility^{-1}(y)\}$

with:
$x, y \in FogComponentSet$

Figure 5 shows an example for such a Fog Set. Since A's Fog Horizon includes B and B's Fog Horizon includes C and D, the Fog Set of A includes all four Fog Components. In fact, this is also the case for the Fog Sets of the other Fog Components.

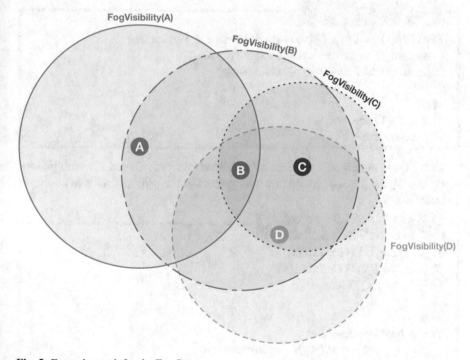

Fig. 5 Example graph for the Fog Set

Since the Fog Set is reflexive, symmetrical, and transitive, it is an equivalence relation and therefore the same and unique set for each involved Fog Component—which is what we would expect from Fog Components in the same Fog Architecture.

2.6 Service Constraints

In addition to the previously introduced concepts, most architectures are limited to specific services which are offered within them. These services are summarized in the *Service Set* as shown in Definition 5.

Definition 5: Service Set

$ServiceSet := \{s \mid s$ is a Service $\}$

To address this, the following three service sets—Provide, Consume, and Interest—create sets based on the Fog Components relation to the given service as defined by their names (Definition 6).

Definition 6: Service Sets

$Provide(s) := \{x \mid x$ *offers and advertises* $s \in ServiceSet\}$
$Consume(s) := \{x \mid x$ *requests* $s \in ServiceSet\}$
$Interest(s) := Provide(s) \cup Consume(s)$

with:
  $x \in FogComponentSet$
  $s \in ServiceSet$

Using these definitions, we define the following sets P, C, and I, which present selections on the given Fog Concept with respect to the provided service as shown in Definition 7.

Definition 7: Service Constraint

$P_s(f(x)) := f(x) \cap Provide(s)$
$C_s(f(x)) := f(x) \cap Consume(s)$
$I_s(f(x)) := f(x) \cap Interest(s)$

with:
  $x \in FogComponentSet$
  $f(x) \in \{ FogVisibility(x),\ FogHorizon(x),$

          $FogReachability(x),\ FogSet(x)\}$
  $s \in ServiceSet$

These sets will be of particular interest in Sect. 3.1 as soon as we establish layers.

2.7 Communication Set

The second set we want to investigate is the *Communication Set*, and therefore the interactions/connectors between the different components of the Fog Set.

While most architectures use the same communication medium for the entire communication, Fog Architectures often involve different communication channels depending on the devices used. These channels can range from close proximity such as NFC or Bluetooth up to long distance communication such as 3G, 4G, or 5G. The following Fig. 6 shows an excerpt of different communication channels which can be found within Fog Architectures.

In the diagram, the channels are placed within a 2×2 grid in which the columns indicate whether the channels are wired or wireless and the rows indicate local and remote proximity. Therefore, the placement within the grid describes a double inheritance of the contained channel to the according superclasses. Additionally, all superclasses are Communication Channels themselves. This set, called *Communication Channel Set*, is defined in Definition 8. It contains all potential communication channels that can be used within a Fog Architecture.

Definition 8: Communication Channel Set

CommunicationChannelSet $= \{c \mid c$ is a communication channel.$\}$

While most communication channels that are used in the context of Fog Architectures are bidirectional, network limitations as well as sensors only providing data can include unidirectional communication channels. To include and address these channels, our definition of Fog Visibility is unidirectional in comparison to the Fog

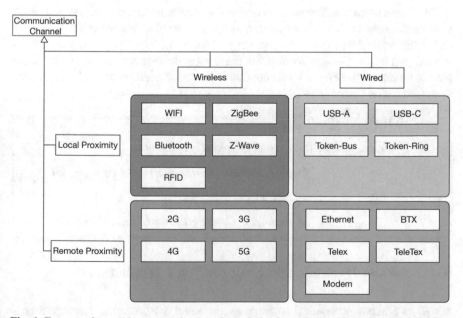

Fig. 6 Excerpt of possible communication channels in the context of Fog Architectures: The channels are divided based on the physical medium that they are using (wired versus wireless), but also the physical distance for which the communication channels can be used

Horizon, and accordingly, the Communication Set can also include unidirectional communication channels.

Bidirectional communication channels can be easily limited to unidirectional communication using software solutions. Channels such as Wi-Fi, Bluetooth, or USB rely on an open bidirectional communication approach. Therefore, encapsulating a certain amount of trust to other participants within the communication structure is essential for Fog Architectures; only trusted instances are described as part of a Fog Architecture.

In addition to the equivalent of a *Component* in the context of a Software Architecture which is the Fog Component and the related sets, we define a *Communication Component* as the equivalent to the *Connector*.

A *Communication Component* is a triple that consists of the source Fog Component, the used *Communication Channel*, and the destination Fog Component as shown in Definition 9. Specifying the source and destination allows to define unidirectional communications.

Definition 9: Communication Component

$CommunicationComponent := \{SourceFogComponent,$

$CommunicationChannel,$

$DestinationFogComponent\}$

All *Communication Components* of one Fog Architecture are grouped within the *Communication Set*. The *Communication Set* is defined as shown in Definition 10 and is the equivalent to the Fog Set. For a *Communication Component* to be considered part of the *Communication Set*, the *source* and *destination* Fog Component have to be part of the Fog Set, and the Communication *channel* has to be part of the *Communication Channel Set*.

Definition 10: Communication Set

$CommunicationSet := \{c : CommunicationComponent =$

$(source, channel, destination) \mid source \in FogSet$

$\wedge\ destination \in FogSet$

$\wedge\ channel \in CommunicationChannelSet\}$

---

3 xFogPlus: Dynamic and Scalable Fog Architectures

xFogPlus addresses technical research goals 2 and 3 to achieve dynamic reconfigurability and scalability of Fog Architectures. This allows the addition of new components to existing Fog Architectures and the addition of layers.

3.1 Dynamic Reconfigurability

ᴡᴏᴛᴛᴜ ᴛᴛᴏᴏᴏ ᴛᴛ ᴏᴛᴛ ᴛᴛᴇ ᴡ ᴛᴛᴛᴏᴘᴏᴏᴏ ᴛᴛᴛ ᴛᴛ ᴛ ᴛᴛᴛ ᴛᴛᴏᴛᴛ ᴇᴛᴛᴏᴘᴛᴏ ᴛᴏ ᴘᴛᴍ simplified based on the overarching mathematical definitions introduced in Sect. 2. Based on those definitions, each component that should be considered part of the Fog Architecture needs to fulfill two requirements. First, the component needs to be part of the Fog Component Set, and second, it needs to be part of the Fog Set: As all concepts introduced in Sect. 2 are based on the Fog Component Set, it is a mathematical necessity for all of them, including the Fog Set, but the Fog Set is only sufficient for the Fog Component Set.

The Fog Component Set itself already poses a problem. Based on the definition shown in Sect. 2.1, the Fog Component Set consists of all potential Fog Components. While Fog Components can be any IoT device on MOF level M0 and M1, the Fog Component itself is an instance of the Fog Type on M3, which in turn has the subclasses Edge Device, Fog Node, and Cloud Device. Although this definition is helpful if different Fog Architectures are available and they should be differentiated between each other, it is the wrong way around if new components should be added: In order to be considered part of the Fog Component Set, the component needs to be a Fog Component, and therefore already part of a Fog Architecture which is not the case for new components.

Therefore, to be able to add components to the Fog Component Set, an alternative definition for a Fog Component is required which solely focuses on properties of the component itself. The first hard requirement is that every Fog Component is necessarily an IoT device. This means that a component needs to have the capability:

1. To be interconnected
2. To have the intention to share information across platforms
3. To be uniquely addressable
4. To have computational capabilities

Soft requirements are that the components:

1. Preferably use wireless communication
2. Have an interest in locality
3. Have general-purpose computational power
4. Which they offer as services to other components

This definition allows us to extend the Fog Component Set by new components which are not involved in any Fog Architecture, yet.

The second requirement is that the component satisfies the definition of a Fog Set and thus can be included in a Fog Architecture. Based on Definition 4, for a *Fog Component* x to be included in a *Fog Set* , the *Fog Component* needs to be in the transitive closure of the *Fog Horizon* of a *Fog Component* within the Fog Architecture that the *Fog Component* should be added to. Accordingly, it is mathematically sufficient for the *Fog Component* to be able to send and receive direct messages to and from any single *Fog Component* in the Fog Architecture.

After adding new components to the Fog Component Set and Fog Set, we have to address the issue on which layer the component is added. In Fog Computing, components can be assigned to three layers: the Edge Layer, the Fog Layer, or the Cloud Layer. While the Edge Layer and Cloud Layer consist of single layers, the Fog Layer can consist of several individual layers.

To indicate that the Fog Layer can consist of several layers, we rename the Fog Layer to *Fog Layer Set* in compliance with the introduced concept of xFogCore. The Fog Layer Set can consist of several Fog Layers itself.

Definition 11: Fog Layer Set

$FogLayerSet := \{l \mid l$ is a Fog Layer$\}$

We present definitions for the different types of layers. Definition 12 shows the properties of a *Fog Component* to be considered part of the *Edge Layer*. Each *Fog Component* x needs to be part of the *Fog Set*, thus, part of the *Fog Architecture*, and does not provide any services to other *Fog Components*, which is represented by not having any service s which makes *Fog Component* x part of its provide set.

Definition 12: Edge Layer

$EdgeLayer := \{x \mid x \in FogSet \land \nexists s \in ServiceSet : x \in Provide(s)\}$

The *Fog Layer* is defined as every *Fog Component* x that is, equal to the *Edge Layer*, part of the *Fog Set* and for which at least two services s_1 and s_2 exist, so that *Fog Component* x consumes one of the services and offers the other one, as shown in Definition 13. This describes the idea that *Fog Components* in the *Fog Layer* bring services of higher layers, for example, the *Cloud Layer*, closer to the *Edge Layer* but also do their own calculations.

Definition 13: Fog Layer

$FogLayer := \{x \mid x \in FogSet \land \exists s_1, s_2 \in ServiceSet :$

$x \in Consume(s_1) \land x \in Provide(s_2)\}$

The *Cloud Layer*, as shown in Definition 14, includes every *Fog Component* that does not consume any service itself.

Definition 14: Cloud Layer

$CloudLayer := \{x \mid x \in FogSet \land \nexists s \in ServiceSet : x \in Consume(s)\}$

Each *Fog Layer* in the Fog Layer Set is defined by a service pair s_i, s_j that is on the one side consumed by the layer and on the other side provided by the layer. If different layers include the same Fog Components although being defined by different service pairs, those layers are fused to one layer consuming or providing several services.

Using the provided definitions for the different layers, the issue of adding Fog Components to specific layers can be reduced to these Fog Components providing or consuming the services that uniquely identify each layer.

Figure 7 shows an example of different Fog Components distributed on three layers: Edge Layer, Fog Layer Set, and Cloud Layer. The Fog Layer Set consists of three layers: Fog Layer 1, Fog Layer 2, and Fog Layer 3.

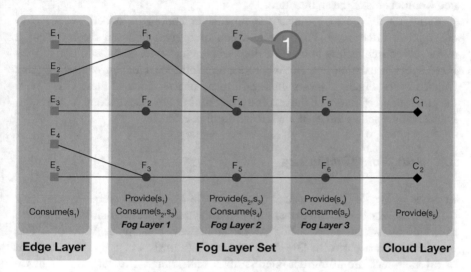

Fig. 7 The graph shows an example for a Fog Architecture which is distributed over the three layers *Edge Layer*, *Fog Layer Set*, and *Cloud Layer*

Although, in this example, all Fog Components in the Edge Layer consume the same service s_1, they could also consume other services as long as they do not offer any services themselves. The first two Fog Layers are examples for multiple consumed or provided services (s_2, s_3). These two layers present an instance of fused Fog Layers as the service pairs s_1, s_2 as well as s_1, s_3 result in the same set of Fog Components and therefore are on the same layer. The third Fog Layer provides service s_4 and consumes s_5 which is provided by the Cloud Layer.

Additionally, the example shows the case that Fog Component F_7 is added to the Fog Architecture. Based on the provided and consumed services s_2, s_3, and s_4, the new Fog Component can be added to the second Fog Layer; although no connections are established, yet.

3.2   Scalability

Adding new layers to existing architectures is one key aspect for making them dynamic and scalable. As most applications nowadays use client-server architectures, it is also essential for the transition from a centralized approach to a decentralized approach using Fog Computing.

With the introduced layer definitions and their service-based nature, the process of adding new layers to a Fog Architecture is simplified to the addition of a new Fog Component that offers and consumes a new pair of services that is used by existing Fog Components of the architecture.

Based on the position where the new layer should be added, we have to differentiate three cases. First, the addition of a layer between the layers of a client server architecture to create a Fog Architecture, second the addition of new Fog Layers in existing Fog Architectures, and third the creation of new Edge or Cloud Layers. Figure 8 shows three examples, one for each of these cases, with the previous architecture on the left and the resulting Fog Architecture on the right. Each example shows the resulting service configuration.

3.3   Handling Complexity

In order to handle the introduced complexity in Fog Architectures by new Fog Components and layers, and to make Fog Architectures more accessible for different stakeholders, we introduce a Fog Architecture view concept. A **View** of a Fog Architecture is a part of a Fog Architecture that consists of a specified amount of layers, which are of current interest for a stakeholder. The definition is based on the view concept introduced in SysML which provides a perspective that spans different abstractions, in our case layers [16]. Our *View* is defined based on a tuple that contains natural numbers which refer to the selected layers of interest.

Definition 15: Fog Architecture: View, Viewpoint, and Abstraction Level

$$View(s) := \bigcup_{i=0}^{|s|-1} Layer(s_i)$$

with:

$s :=$ Tuple containing the numbers referring to the selected layers

$|s| =$ Amount of layers within the View $\leq |FogArchitecture|$

$View \subseteq FogArchitecture$

Figure 9 shows a view example for a Fog Architecture describing a smart city with six layers. The view highlights the Edge Layer and the lowest two Fog Layers.

Looking at the View, one can describe the view as a Fog Architecture itself using the previous introduced layer definitions. Accordingly, Fog Components can take different rolls depending on the current View. For example, Fog Components on the "Street" layer which are on Fog Layer 2 of the entire Fog Architecture act as the Cloud for the highlighted View.

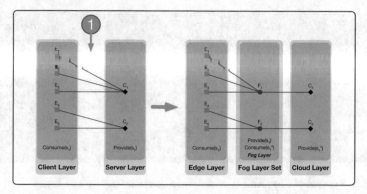

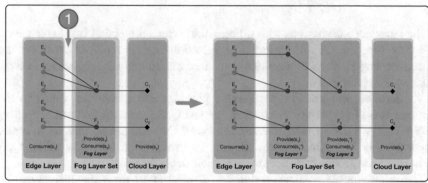

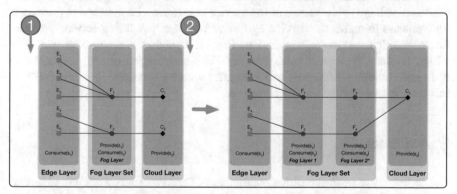

Fig. 8 Three examples of layer additions: the transition to a Fog Architecture, the addition of a new Fog Layer, and the addition of a new Edge/Cloud Layer

4   xFogStar: A Workflow for Service Provider Selection

Based on xFog, and accordingly xFogCore and xFogPlus, many new concepts can be established in dynamically, scalable Fog Architecture. We introduce xFogStar, one such concept, that focuses on the relation between service consumers and service providers, the players suggested by Bonomi et al. [8], to show an application

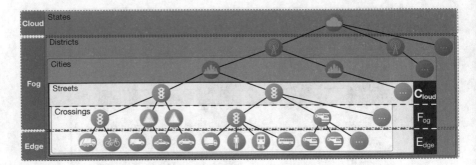

Fig. 9 View example of a Fog Architecture describing a smart city with six layers

of the introduced framework with a Fog Architecture containing two layer views. xFogStar supports the service provider selection in case multiple providers are within the Fog Horizon of a service consumer requesting one service, addressing technical research goal 4.

To describe properties of the service provider and its service, but also the requirements of the service consumers, we use QoS parameters and an according QoS vector. We investigated an extensive list of QoS parameters that are of major importance in Fog Architectures. Figure 10 provides an overview of all QoS parameters and groups them according to their dependencies.

Depending on the application domain, a selection of these parameters can be used to match the requirements of the service consumer with the service providers. This process to match the service consumer with the best fitting service provider for a specified service is depicted in Fig. 11. It shows a seven-step workflow which translates the requirements using availability strategies, limits, comparability strategies, ordering strategies, and weightings into a transparent, ordered list of service providers for the service consumer.

5 Validation

Due to the extent of the empirical validation of the xFog framework and xFogStar addressing *Knowledge Goal 2* and *Knowledge Goal 3*, this section only provides an overview of the conducted validation. Detailed descriptions on each individual case study, including each case study's design, its results, and the discussion, can be found in the dissertation "Dynamically Scalable Fog Architectures" [10].

The validation tries to justify if stakeholder goals would be met if the treatment is implemented in the problem domain's context. It investigates if the requirements for the treatment are addressed within a model of the problem domain. As the validation is part of the design cycle, and thus conducted in a laboratory setting, the implementation of the treatment in the problem domain is not of interest, yet. This results in the validation being independent of the stakeholders, which is the

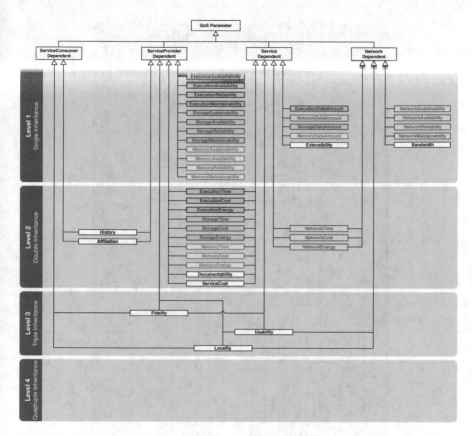

Fig. 10 Overview on QoS parameters for Fog Architectures and their dependencies

main difference between validation and evaluation. Therefore, different research approaches are used such as modeling, simulations, and testing [11].

The validation of xFog was separated into the three aspects of the xFog framework provided by xFogCore, xFogPlus, and xFogStar. Each validation relied on the validation approaches modeling and simulation. First, we introduced the design of the different case studies. We presented the problem domain of the case study, the requirements, and which concepts of xFog or xFogStar were addressed. We selected cases in different domains to support domain-independent conclusions. In total, we addressed six different domains: *Smart Environments*, *Smart Cities*, *Health*, *Continuous Integration*, *Metrology*, and *Gaming*. These domains were used in eight case studies mapped to three validations.

Second, we reported on the results of the validation for the three core concepts: Dynamic Fog Components, Scalable Fog Architecture, and Service Provider Selection. While the formalization of Fog Computing (xFogCore) is used throughout all three concepts, each of the concepts can be assigned to an addition to xFog as shown in Fig. 12. *Dynamic Fog Components* and *Scalable Fog Architectures* are covered

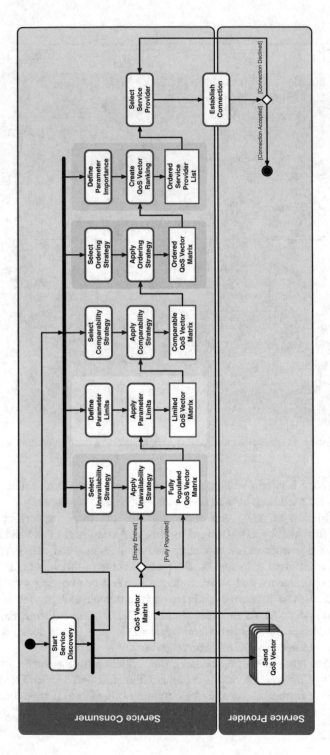

Fig. 11 The workflow for service provider selection (UML Activity Diagram)

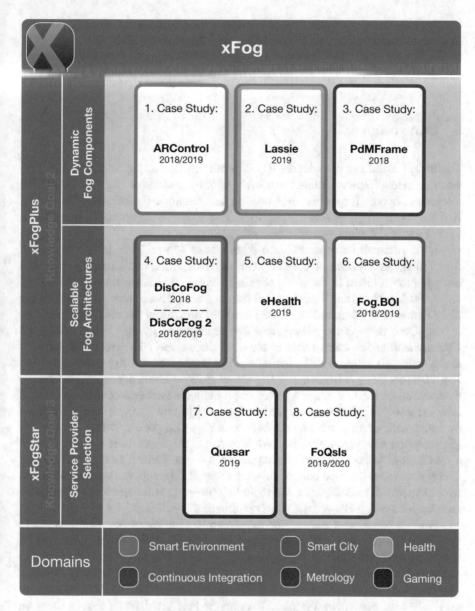

Fig. 12 An overview of the validation design for the xFog framework. Each of the three rows represent a validation with Dynamic Fog Components and Scalable Fog Architectures belonging to concepts related to xFogPlus and the Service Provider Selection belonging to the xFogStar workflow. The coloring of the case studies represents the domains they belong to

in xFogPlus as shown in the first two rows of the diagram. The *Service Provider Selection* uses xFogCore and the workflow introduced by xFogStar.

Third, we discussed the impact of the results for the xFog framework, interpreted the results, and addressed threads to the validity of the validation approach.

6 Conclusion

The main goal of the dissertation "Dynamically Scalable Fog Architectures" [10] was to create a framework that establishes a formalization for Fog Computing and integrates support for mobile applications and dynamic reconfigurability of Fog Architectures. We implemented the formative research approach design science using treatment designs and treatment validations.

The results can be separated into three parts: The problem investigation and description, the creation of the xFog framework and its validation. The problem investigation resulted in the goals shown in Fig. 1, which we translated into use cases and functional and nonfunctional requirements. These were addressed by the xFog Framework which can be divided in xFogCore, xFogPlus, and xFogStar.

xFogCore defined the *Component Set* represented by the Fog Set and the *Communication Set* which relate to the components and connectors of a software architecture. To define the Fog Set, xFogCore introduced the *Fog Component Set*, *Fog Visibility* , *Fog Horizon* , and *Fog Reachability* . These concepts describe the components of a Fog Architecture based on mathematical definitions. We showed how the component sets can be constrained to specific services that are offered or consumed, or that are of interest for a Fog Component, which allows the identification of layers within Fog Architectures. We defined the *Communication Set* as a set of *Communication Components* which are defined by the involved Fog Components and the used communication channel. The sets were put into context by a meta model on MOF level M2 including the basic building blocks of software architectures which allowed the interpretation of the sets as graphs.

xFogPlus introduced support for the dynamic addition of Fog Components to the Fog Architecture at runtime by redefining the idea of Fog Components and by providing definitions for the three layers: *Edge Layer*, *Fog Layer*, and *Cloud Layer*. Second, new layers can be described and added to the Fog Architecture enabling scalability. As the scalability increased the complexity of the Fog Architecture, we established the concept of different *Views* on the Fog Architecture to set a focus on different layers depending on the stakeholder's current interest.

xFogStar defined a workflow for the service provider selection in dynamically scalable Fog Architectures which are described by the concepts of xFogCore and xFogPlus. The workflow is used to select the best fitting service provider for the service consumer's needs. These needs are represented as a vector of QoS parameters which we defined and categorized according to their dependencies. We investigated the different steps of the xFogStar workflow to outline arising problems.

We validated three aspects that use the foundations and formalization of xFog to investigate *Knowledge Goal 2* and *Knowledge Goal 3*: *Dynamic Fog Components* , *Scalable Fog Architectures* , and the *Service Provider Selection*. For each aspect, we used a multiple case study to gather quantitative data on the feasibility of xFog, and thus xFogCore, xFogPlus, and xFogStar. *Dynamic Fog Components* and *Scalable Fog Architectures* related to xFogCore and xFogPlus, while the *Service Provider Selection* addressed the xFogStar workflow.

Each validation compared the expected results with the results provided by xFog. The first validation investigated three cases from different domains to support generalizable conclusions. It demonstrated the feasibility of xFog and in particular xFogPlus by examining the addition of components at runtime. The second validation included three cases to show the feasibility of the scalable concepts of xFogPlus by adding new layers to existing Fog Architectures. The resulting Fog Architectures were used to highlight the applicability of the *View* concept which addresses complexity depending on the stakeholder's current point of interest. The last validation for the *Service Provider Selection* demonstrated the feasibility of the xFogStar workflow in two cases.

Acknowledgments I would like to thank my first and second advisors Prof. Dr. Bruegge and Prof. Dr. Lichter for their valuable insights and feedback. Additionally, I would like to thank all members of the chair for applied software engineering from the Technical University of Munich for the discussions and the students who took part in my case studies.

References

1. Tanenbaum, A., Van Steen, M.: Distributed Systems: Principles and Paradigms. Prentice-Hall, Englewood Cliffs (2013)
2. Ferrer, A.J., Marquès, J.M., Jorba, J.: Towards the decentralised cloud: survey on approaches and challenges for mobile, ad hoc, and edge computing. ACM Comput. Surv. **51**, 111 (2019)
3. Satyanarayanan, M., Bahl, P., Caceres, R., Davies, N.: The case for VM-based cloudlets in mobile computing. IEEE Pervasive Comput. **8**, 14–23 (2009)
4. Dinh, H., Lee, C., Niyato, D., Wang, P.: A survey of mobile cloud computing: architecture, applications, and approaches. Wirel. Commun. Mobile Comput. **13**, 1587–1611 (2013)
5. Qi, H., Gani, A.: Research on mobile cloud computing: review, trend and perspectives. In: 2012 Second International Conference on Digital Information and Communication Technology and it's Applications (DICTAP), pp. 1–6 (2012)
6. Satyanarayanan, M.: The emergence of edge computing. IEEE Comput. **50** 30–39 (2017)
7. Dolui, K., Datta, S. K.: Comparison of edge computing implementations: fog computing, cloudlet and mobile edge computing. In: Global Internet of Things Summit (GIoTS), pp. 1–6 (2017)
8. Bonomi, F., Milito, R., Zhu, J., Addepalli, S.: Fog Computing and its role in the Internet of Things. In: MCC Workshop on Mobile Cloud Computing, vol. 1, pp. 13–16 (2012)
9. Marín-Tordera, E., Masip-Bruin, X., García-Almiñana, J., Jukan, A., Ren, G., Zhu, J.: Do we all really know what a fog node is? Current trends towards an open definition. Comput. Commun. **109**, 117–130 (2017)
10. Henze, D.: Dynamically Scalable Fog Architectures. Technische Universität München, München (2020)

11. Wieringa, R.: Design Science Methodology for Information Systems and Software Engineering. Springer, Berlin (2014)
12. Hevner, A., March, S., Park, J., Ram, S.: Design science in information systems research. MIS Q. **28**(1), 75–105 (2004)
13. Shaw, M., Garlan, D.: Software Architecture. Prentice-Hall, Englewood Cliffs (1996)
14. Bass, L., Clements, P., Kazman, R.: Software Architecture in Practice. Addison-Wesley, Reading (2003)
15. Kruchten, P.: The 4+ 1 view model of architecture. IEEE Softw. **12** 42–50 (1995)
16. ISO: IEC/IEEE systems and software engineering: architecture description. In: ISO/IEC/IEEE 42010: 2011 (E)(Revision of ISO/IEC 42010: 2007 and IEEE Std 1471-2000). IEEE, New York (2011)
17. Henze, D., Schmiedmayer, P., Bruegge, B.: Fog horizons—a theoretical concept to enable dynamic fog architectures. In: IEEE/ACM International Conference on Utility and Cloud Computing, vol. 12, pp. 41–50 (2019)

Crossing Disciplinary Borders to Improve Requirements Communication

Anne Hess

Abstract Software requirements specifications (SRS) serve as an important source of information for a variety of roles involved in software engineering (SE) projects. This situation poses a challenge to requirements engineers: Different information needs have to be addressed, which are strongly dependent on the particular role(s) that SRS stakeholders have within a project. This chapter summarizes the contributions of a thesis that aimed to address and reduce role-specific defects in SRS that negatively influence the efficient usage and acceptance of these documents. To achieve this goal, we collected empirical data about role-specific information needs in a series of empirical studies that served as a baseline for a secondary analysis toward the definition of role-specific views. Moreover, we realized a proof-of-concept implementation that is capable of generating role-specific views on SRS. The results of a case study revealed that role-specific views have the potential to efficiently support SRS consumers during the analysis of a given SRS. Besides conducting further empirical studies in industry, future work aims to foster cross-disciplinary collaboration and requirements communication, especially in agile teams. Thereby, we are exploring synergy potential with best practices from non-SE disciplines.

1 Introduction

Software development is a cooperative and creative process that requires stakeholders from various software engineering (SE) disciplines to collaborate, exchange information, and coordinate their tasks and efforts [1, 2]. In order to make this collaboration successful, a shared understanding of the functional and nonfunctional requirements of a software system is therefore required [3, 4].

A. Hess (✉)
Fraunhofer IESE, Kaiserslautern, Germany
e-mail: Anne.Hess@iese.fraunhofer.de

© The Author(s) 2022
M. Felderer et al. (eds.), *Ernst Denert Award for Software Engineering 2020*,
https://doi.org/10.1007/978-3-030-83128-8_7

A key discipline that supports the detailed analysis and communication of these requirements is requirements engineering (RE) – a systematic and disciplined approach to the elicitation, analysis, specification, and management of requirements [5]. The results of these RE activities are typically documented in various requirements artifacts, which are consolidated and structured in software requirements specifications (SRS). These SRS finally serve as an important information basis for various people involved in SE disciplines such as architecture design, interaction/user interface design, and software testing.

Despite their importance, we have observed that the acceptance of SRS is often limited and that SRS are often neglected in practice. A more detailed investigation of this observation revealed a number of so-called *role-specific requirements defects* that are not sufficiently addressed by today's RE approaches (see Table 2, Sect. 2.2). While these defects can basically be traced to insufficient quality of SRS, as well as the requirements artifacts they contain, they are characterized by an interesting fact: Different SRS consumers might experience these defects individually – depending on their particular discipline-related roles, responsibilities, and tasks within an SE project.

In fact, the occurrence of role-specific defects is critical as they negatively influence the efficient usage and analysis of an SRS from the consumer's viewpoint. This situation can again lead to failures, delays, and frustration in subsequent SE activities and, ultimately, to costly changes and budget or time overruns [6, 10].

Addressing these role-specific defects finally motivated the practical improvement goals of the thesis "Role-Specific Views on SRS: An Empirical Approach" [11], whose contributions are summarized in this chapter. Within the scope of this thesis, we collected empirical data about role-specific information needs in a series of empirical studies, which served as a baseline for a secondary analysis aimed at the definition of role-specific views. Moreover, we realized a proof-of-concept implementation of our envisioned solution that is capable of generating role-specific views on SRS. The results of the case study revealed that role-specific views have the potential to efficiently support SRS consumers during the analysis of a given SRS as well as requirements engineers during specification activities.

Following the thesis work, we continued to further investigate and improve cross-disciplinary collaboration and requirements communication, especially in agile teams. In doing so, we even cross the borders of the field of SE to get inspired by best practices from non-SE disciplines such as criminology, film studies, psychology, and law. The research objectives that we are pursuing in this research context include the identification of synergies with such best practices and their incorporation – as well as adaptation – into innovative methods and techniques to overcome existing challenges.

In the remainder of this chapter, we will first discuss the background and results of the research activities that shaped both the practical and scientific thesis goals in Sect. 2. Then we will provide an overview of the overall solution idea, the research approach, and our thesis contributions in Sect. 3. In Sect. 4, we will share insights and results from our series of empirical studies, which served as a baseline for the definition of role-specific views on SRS. Section 5 introduces current and future research activities that followed the thesis. The chapter concludes with a summary in Sect. 6.

2 Background and Improvement Goals

This section introduces some background information related to the notion and role of requirements artifacts and shares the results of research activities that were conducted to shape the practical and scientific improvement goals of the thesis.

2.1 Requirements Artifacts

A central activity of RE approaches is the documentation of requirements-related information (covering both functional and nonfunctional system aspects, as well as elements of the usage environment) established and worked out during elicitation, validation, and negotiation activities. This documentation typically results in a set of *requirements artifacts*, which we define as "...an object produced or shaped by a human conception or agency in order to externalize requirements-related information" [12].

Requirements artifacts are predominantly written in natural language, both in unstructured common language and in a structured form using templates and forms [13, 14]. Other documentation types include conceptual models (like UML state diagrams or UML activity diagrams) or hybrid documentation combining natural language and conceptual models [5].

In fact, requirements artifacts represent an important factor for the success of a project [15, 16] as they serve as a medium of communication between interdisciplinary project team members with different roles and tasks [17] (see Table 1).

2.2 Practical Improvement Goals

To become a good basis for the various consumers, both the SRS and the requirements artifacts they contain must meet certain quality criteria (such as unambiguity, consistency, or completeness) in order to prevent the occurrence and propagation of requirements defects [7, 17]. Such defects ultimately may lead to major delays, cost overruns, commercial consequences, and even the loss of lives [18].

Despite this major impact that requirements defects have throughout the whole lifecycle of a software product, the data analysis of an industry survey as well as literature reviews revealed that industry is still facing problems and challenges in

Table 1 Consumers of requirements artifacts [5, 15]

Role	Tasks based on requirements artifacts
Project manager	Planning of work packages and milestones for the implementation of the system
Customer	Validation of requirements as part of contract
Software architect	Design of system architecture; analysis of change impacts; validation of requirements as part of quality assurance
Usability expert (Interaction designer)	Design of interactions and user interface; analysis of change impacts; validation of requirements as part of quality assurance
Developer	Implementation of the system; analysis of change impacts
System test engineer	Development of test cases to validate the system; analysis of change impacts; validation of requirements as part of quality assurance
Maintenance engineer	Analysis of defects during system maintenance

addressing quality-related issues when documenting requirements artifacts. As a consequence, the acceptance of SRS is often limited and the documents are often neglected in practice by their consumers.

To better understand and shape the practical problem of the thesis, we conducted expert interviews and performed a literature review with the goal of identifying requirements defects that hinder an efficient use and analysis of SRS from the viewpoint of their readers. This activity resulted in a taxonomy of 14 requirements defect categories [11].

Within the thesis, we focused our research activities on a subset of these defects – so-called *role-specific requirements defects* – which are characterized by an interesting fact: In contrast to "general defects" (such as ambiguity, missing, or lacking traceability), role-specific requirements defects are possibly experienced differently by different readers, depending on the role they have in a project [19]. Hence, we excluded the aforementioned "general defects" from our taxonomy and obtained a list of role-specific defects, which are summarized in Table 2 together with a list of requirements for a suitable solution.

Table 2 Role-specific defects and corresponding solution requirements

Role-specific requirements defect	Requirements for suitable solution
Important information is missing [6–9]	The SRS contains all information that is relevant for a particular role
Superfluous information is specified [6, 8, 9]	The SRS contains only information that is relevant for a particular role
Important information is misplaced [6, 8, 9]	The SRS is appropriately structured so that relevant information can easily be found by a particular role
Requirements artifacts are in an unusable form [6, 8, 9]	Requirements artifacts are specified at the right level of detail using the right notation

As highlighted earlier, the occurrence of role-specific defects negatively influences the efficient usage and analysis of an SRS, as it is time-consuming and/or cognitively difficult for SRS consumers to resolve and reconcile these problems while working with the SRS [6, 8]. This is critical, as it might again lead to failures, delays, and frustration in subsequent SE activities, and ultimately to costly changes and budget or time overruns [6, 10].

Hence, addressing these role-specific problems ultimately constituted the practical improvement goals of the thesis, which are stated as:

Improve the quality of SRS by addressing and reducing role-specific requirements defects in SRS. Resulting from this achievement, we aim to increase the efficiency of SRS analysis and hence the acceptance of an SRS from the viewpoint of its readers.

2.3 Literature Review Activities

To strengthen and isolate the scientific contribution of the thesis, the role-specific defects and corresponding solution requirements in Table 2 were subjected to further literature review activities. The underlying research goal (RG) and related research questions (RQ) of these activities are summarized in Table 3.

Table 3 Research goals and research questions of literature review activities (LRA)

RG_{LRA}: Investigate and analyze the state of the practice/state of the art with regard to existing solutions that particularly address role-specific defects and the corresponding requirements.
RQ_{LRA-1}: To what extent do existing requirements documentation and quality assurance methods, techniques, or guidelines address role-specific defects and corresponding requirements?
RQ_{LRA-2}: To what extent do existing view-based approaches support our overall solution idea of generating role-specific views on requirements documents?

Our literature review activities toward RQ_{LRA-1} revealed several *(normative) references* that highlight and report on good quality characteristics of both individual requirements and SRS [5, 8, 15, 18, 20]. However, we found that all of these references are quite vague when it comes to describing what completeness or minimality means from a role-specific point of view. This issue is also claimed and supported by the work of [17], who argue that some quality criteria (such as completeness) have to be rethought from a quality-in-use perspective. In fact, their ABRE-QM (activity-based RE quality models) concept fits well into the scope of this thesis as our empirical work contributes to the instantiation of their quality models and our tool-based solution represents a concrete implementation of their vision.

Similarly, existing *writing guidelines* [15, 21], *languages, or requirements templates* [5] do not provide any information on the preferred level of detail and notation that is suitable for a particular role. This observation also holds for *standard SRS structures* such as [20, 22], which define an overall structure and corresponding information that should be included in an SRS but do not provide any advice on the suitable level of detail, as well as the right notation that should be used to specify the information in the various sections. Moreover, these references do not address the requirement of "minimality," i.e., they do not hide irrelevant information from the reader.

Requirements *validation techniques* [5, 23–25] seem to be helpful for identifying and resolving role-specific defects [26] but typically happen after the SRS has been created (rather than during the construction of the SRS). Moreover, these activities easily get tedious and cognitively difficult for the inspectors if they have to search for the relevant information that they have to validate from a dedicated perspective. Also, inspection guidelines and checklists have to explicitly contain and address the role-specific information needs that are to be checked with regard to their fulfillment. And this knowledge is often missing.

There also exist a variety of *formal methods* that are capable of automatically detecting and handling quality-related defects such as ambiguities, inconsistencies, or missing traceability [27–29]. However, to the best of our knowledge, none of these approaches is capable of automatically detecting and resolving the role-specific defects that are the focus of the thesis.

Addressing RQ_{LRA-2}, we identified several *view(point)-based solutions* in the context of RE [30–32]. However, the definition and usage of these viewpoints differ between the various solutions. That is, some viewpoints reflect (orthogonal) viewpoints of the system, or process-specific or organizational viewpoints rather than role-specific views. Moreover, from a technical perspective, existing commercial requirements management tools are capable of automatically generating views on SRS that fit role-specific information needs. This is typically realized by applying filter rules to predefined attributes [5]. However, in order to define and instantiate these attributes, detailed knowledge about role-specific information needs is required, which is not available in the tools but rather has to be obtained individually.

We conclude that many good approaches are available that at least partially address the role-specific defects and related requirements stated in Table 2. However, what all of these approaches are lacking is the explicit provision of detailed knowledge about role-specific information needs. That is, to sufficiently address role-specific defects and corresponding requirements – and hence to ultimately address our practical improvement goals – we claim that detailed empirical knowledge about role-specific information needs is required. It is exactly this empirical knowledge that constitutes the core scientific improvement goal of the thesis, stated as:

Investigate role-specific information needs regarding SRS from the viewpoint of different SRS readers

3   Solution Idea and Research Approach

The overall solution idea of the thesis is illustrated in Fig. 1.

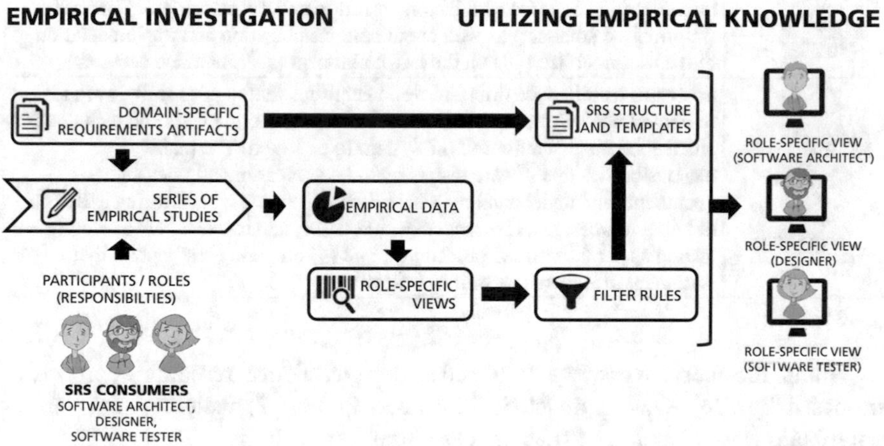

Fig. 1 Solution idea

The approach is based on the idea of conducting *a series of empirical studies* on a given set of *domain-specific requirements artifacts* in order to collect *empirical data* with regard to role-specific information from the perspective of *SRS consumers*. To limit the scope of the thesis, we focused our investigations on three types of SRS consumers: software architects, usability experts in the role of designers, and software testers. We selected these three types because their SE-related activities strongly rely on information documented in SRS. Table 4 briefly summarizes the main responsibilities of the three different roles.

The collected empirical data serves as a baseline for the derivation of *role-specific views* on the investigated requirements artifacts. In this context, a role-specific view comprises a set of requirements artifacts that are relevant for performing role-specific tasks specified at a preferred level of detail using preferred notations.

These role-specific views in turn serve as input to a technical solution that utilizes the empirical knowledge to apply *filter rules* to a given *SRS structure, as well as requirements artifact templates*, in order to ultimately *generate role-specific* views on the specification that meet the role-specific information needs.

Table 4 Roles and responsibilities of selected SRS consumers [33–35]

	**Software architects** are responsible for designing an architectural solution that satisfies expected system functionalities and has a long-lasting impact on major quality attributes of a software-intensive system (like cost, evolution, performance, safety, and security). To achieve this, software architects have to fulfill a variety of complex tasks in order to make, realize, validate, and document design decisions regarding a high-quality software architecture based on a detailed understanding of the expected functionalities and qualities of a software system.
	Designers (usability experts) are responsible for conceptualizing and designing human-system interactions based on documented requirements with the aim of ensuring effectiveness, efficiency, and satisfaction when performing tasks with the system (interaction designer). Moreover, efficient task execution requires suitable organization and structuring of information (information architect) as well as suitable visualization and implementation of the user interface (UI) on the target platform (user interface designer).
	Software testers have different responsibilities that require skills, such as in-depth knowledge about test design and execution methods and techniques and a good understanding of the system to be tested. The main responsibilities of software testers include: (1) reading all relevant documents and understanding what needs to be tested; (2) creating and defining test designs, test processes, test cases, and test data; (3) executing testing as per the defined procedures; and (4) preparing test reports that document procedures as well as test results.

Within the thesis work, we followed a design science research approach as proposed by [36]. Our approach is illustrated in Fig. 2, including the various contributions we elaborated in each phase of the approach.

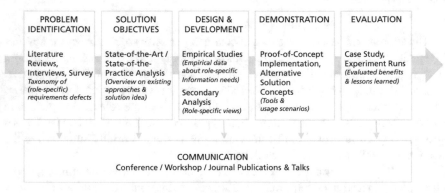

Fig. 2 Research approach and contributions

The previously introduced *taxonomy of (role-specific) requirements defects* (see Sect. 2.2) as well as *the results of the literature review activities* conducted to shape the scientific contributions of the thesis (see Sect. 2.3) were identified and elaborated in the *problem identification phase*, as well as in the *solution objectives phase* of the research approach.

In the subsequent *design and development phase*, we conducted a series of empirical studies to first collect empirical data with respect to *role-specific information needs*, from which *role-specific views* were then derived and defined in a subsequent secondary analysis. A more detailed discussion of the empirical work can be found in Sect. 4.

In the *demonstration phase*, we realized a *proof-of-concept implementation* (and *alternative solution concepts*) that is capable of utilizing the gained empirical knowledge about role-specific views to support *typical usage scenarios* of SRS both from the consumers' and from the requirements engineers' point of view [37].

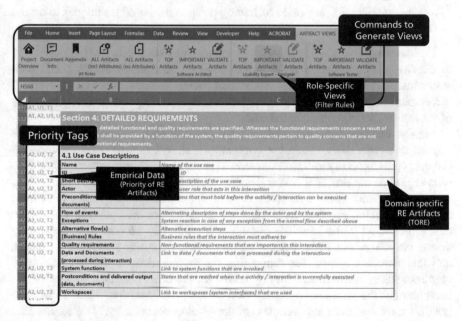

Fig. 3 Proof-of-concept implementation

This technical solution (depicted in Fig. 3) was implemented as an extension of Microsoft Excel®, a common tool often used in practical settings for creating and reading requirements specifications. It comprises an SRS template that defines the overall structure of the SRS as well as a set of domain-specific requirements artifact templates (see Sect. 4.1). The empirical data we collected and analyzed in the series of empirical studies (see Sects. 4.2 and 4.3) was incorporated in the form of priority tags and filter rules (see Sect. 4.3). These filter rules can be applied via commands in the menu bar (see Fig. 3) to generate different views for each of the three roles (software architect, designer, and software tester):

- *TOP Artifacts*: Executing this filter function displays only requirements artifacts and related information details that are of high priority for the corresponding role. Such requirements artifacts include key information for the artifact consumers that is critical for fulfilling their role-specific tasks. Hence, these artifacts and the related information have to be specified timely and precisely.
- *IMPORTANT Artifacts*: Executing this filter function displays requirements artifacts that are rather important, respectively of medium priority. In contrast to high-priority artifacts, these artifacts and the related information are less critical. That is, the artifact stakeholders could also do their tasks based on high-level descriptions of these artifacts.
- *VALIDATE Artifacts*: Executing this filter function displays all requirements artifacts that are of both high and medium priority. This artifact view is intended to support validation activities following perspective-based techniques to assure SRS quality.

Besides these role-specific views, our implementation also offers the possibility to display all requirements artifacts and related information details (both with and without meta-information). Additional views such as "Project Overview," "Document Info," and "Appendix" are intended to further reduce the complexity of the information displayed in the SRS.

Finally, within the *evaluation phase*, the proof-of-concept implementation was applied in a *case study* within the context of a team-based software engineering project at the University of Kaiserslautern. There we investigated several hypotheses with regard to the practical and scientific improvement goals of the thesis. Even though the validity of the case study is limited, the case study revealed promising results. Among the conclusions and lessons learned from the case study, we found that role-specific views have the potential to efficiently support SRS consumers during the analysis of SRS, that the views reflect role-specific information needs, and that they are helpful for supporting the communication and discussion of requirements in software-developing teams. On the other hand, we found that the usefulness of the views strongly depends on the project setting. That is, they are possibly most beneficial in the context of the development of large systems resulting in complex SRS that serve as a major source of requirements-related information.

In addition to the case study, we performed *two trial runs of experimental investigations* with the overall goal of investigating hypotheses that compare the efficiency of SRS analysis with our view-based solution and that of "traditional" SRS. We found that properly designing such experiments is indeed a challenge in terms of ultimately drawing valid conclusions. However, we gained interesting insights and learned lessons from these investigations that will serve as guidelines for future evaluation activities.

We continuously shared and published the results of our research activities with and to research and industry as part of the *communication phase*. The presentations of our results, the feedback we gained from the reviewers, and the fruitful discussions we had at the various conferences and workshops confirmed the relevance of our research for the RE community. The feedback we obtained from both practitioners and researchers helped us to continuously improve and validate our work.

4 Empirical Studies

This section shares some insights into the series of empirical studies we conducted to address the scientific improvement goal of the thesis, which ultimately served as a baseline for the definition of role-specific views. In fact, we consider the results of these studies as well as the underlying methodological approach as a core contribution of the thesis that can be utilized and transferred into different solutions aiming to improve requirements communication in software development.

4.1 Research Goals and Agenda

The overall *research goal* that we aimed to investigate in the empirical studies was to *identify and characterize requirements-related information that downstream development engineers (SRS consumers) seek in an SRS to satisfy their needs and to accomplish their role-specific tasks.*

As outlined in the background section (Sect. 2), requirements-related information is typically specified in the form of requirements artifacts in SRS. Due to the variety of existing requirements artifacts, and to ensure comparability between the different study results, we focused our investigation on well-known requirements artifacts that are typically created when RE is performed within the information systems domain. In particular, we considered artifacts that are created during the application of the Task-oriented Requirements Engineering Framework – or TORE Framework for short [38]. Due to their general nature, these requirements artifacts and thus the results of our investigations can be easily mapped and transferred to other RE approaches that produce requirements artifacts of this kind.

The investigated artifacts comprised:

- *Descriptions of stakeholders* capturing relevant information and characteristics about stakeholders who are to be supported by or have an influence on the system to be built.
- *Descriptions of project goals* that different stakeholders would like to achieve with the system to be built. The project goals include and refine the vision of the system and are considered the rationale for the system's requirements.
- *Descriptions of as-is situations* that illustrate the execution of the tasks/business processes that are to be supported by a system in the current situation, i.e., without the system to be built.
- *Descriptions of to-be situations* that illustrate the execution of tasks/business processes to be supported in the future by the system.

- *Descriptions of the system context* that define the system's environment (e.g., users, external systems), including an overview of functionalities that the system offers to it.
- *Descriptions of interactions* that describe how the system interacts with entities in its environment (e.g., users, external systems).
- *Descriptions of system functions* that specify the input, internal behavior, and output of system functionalities. In contrast to interactions, system functions represent functionalities that are automatically performed by the system.
- *Descriptions of quality requirements* that specify desired qualities (nonfunctional requirements) of the system to be built.
- *Descriptions of technical constraints* that limit the solution space beyond what is necessary for meeting the requirements.

Considering these requirements artifacts, we further refined the above research goal into three research questions and corresponding metrics, which are summarized and stated in Table 5.

Table 5 Research questions (RQ)

Research Question RQ-1$_{EmpStudies}$
What are typical requirements artifacts that should be contained in an SRS from the viewpoint of document stakeholders (SRS consumers) in order to accomplish their role-specific tasks?
Metric RQ-1$_{EmpStudies}$: Importance level of TORE requirements artifacts
Research Question RQ-2$_{EmpStudies}$
At what level of detail should relevant requirements artifacts be specified from the viewpoint of document stakeholders (SRS consumers)?
Metric RQ-2$_{EmpStudies}$: Relevant description items of TORE requirements artifacts
Research Question RQ-3$_{EmpStudies}$
Which notation should be used to specify relevant requirements artifacts from the viewpoint of document stakeholders (SRS consumers)?
Metric RQ-3$_{EmpStudies}$: Preferred notation for documenting TORE requirements artifacts

In order to investigate the research goals and questions above, we designed and conducted a series of four empirical studies as part of our research agenda. These studies comprised:

- *Study #1: An eye-tracking study* conducted with two software architects and two usability experts in the role of designers to investigate the relevance of TORE artifacts ($RQ-1_{EmpStudies}$) as well as the suitable level of detail ($RQ-2_{EmpStudies}$) and the preferred notations ($RQ-3_{EmpStudies}$).
- *Study #2: A survey study (U-KL)* conducted in two practical software engineering courses with a total of 18 participants in the role of software architects. In this study, we retrospectively evaluated the relevance of TORE requirements artifacts for architecture design activities ($RQ-1_{EmpStudies}$).
- Study #3: A *survey study (MUC)* conducted with ten usability experts during a tutorial session that aimed to investigate the relevance of TORE requirements

artifacts ($RQ\text{-}1_{EmpStudies}$), the suitable level of detail ($RQ\text{-}2_{EmpStudies}$), and the preferred notations f($RQ\text{-}3_{EmpStudies}$) for interaction/UI design activities.

- Study #4: A *survey study (FHNW)* conducted in semi-industrial software development projects with a total of 17 participants in the role of software architects, 40 participants in the role of usability experts/designers, and 49 participants in the role of software testers. This study aimed to collect data with regard to the relevance of requirements artifacts for architecture design, interaction/UI design, and testing activities ($RQ\text{-}1_{EmpStudies}$).

Detailed descriptions of the design and the procedures of each of these studies can be found in [11]. The elicited raw data of the studies is publicly accessible via [39].

4.2 Analysis of Individual Studies: Empirical Baseline

Even though the setting and the procedures varied between the four different studies, we asked the participants in each of the studies to rate the importance of various requirements artifacts on a 4-point rating scale with the help of a questionnaire. This rating scale was defined as follows:

- 1 = "This requirements artifact is very important for my task"
- 2 = "This requirements artifact is rather important for my task"
- 3 = "This requirements artifact is rather unimportant for my task"
- 4 = "This requirements artifact is very unimportant for my task"

We decided to use this 4-point scale in order to evoke a decision between (very) important and (rather) unimportant.

4.2.1 Data Analysis Strategy: An Example

In the following, we would like to share some insights into the data analysis strategies we applied on the questionnaire data based on the example of survey study #4. This study was conducted within the scope of a practical project course offered at the University of Applied Sciences and Arts Northwestern Switzerland (FHNW). A first study run (FHNW$_{A\text{-}2013}$) was executed during the autumn term of 2013. We repeated the same study in a second run (FHNW$_{S\text{-}2014}$) in the subsequent spring term of 2014. A third run (FHNW$_{A\text{-}2014}$) was executed during the autumn term of 2014, and the final fourth run (FHNW$_{S\text{-}2015}$) in the subsequent spring term of 2015. At the end of a term (i.e., after the students had completed their role-specific tasks), the coach responsible for the requirements engineering phase distributed our questionnaire, which captured the importance of specified requirements artifacts for role-specific tasks on the 4-point scale introduced above.

Table 6 shows an extract of the results of the application of our data analysis strategy to the questionnaire data we collected from the viewpoint of usability experts in the role of designers in the different study runs at FHNW.

Table 6 Data analysis results of FHNW study (usability experts/designers)

Importance of requirements artifacts[a]

	FHNW A-2013 (N = 13)		FHNW S-2014 (N = 11)		FHNW A-2014 (N = 10)		FHNW S-2015 (N = 6)		FHNW ALL (N = 40)		OS-WSRT (FHNW$_{ALL}$)			KW (N = 40)
	Mdn (M)	Min–Max	Mdn (M)	Min–Max	Mdn (M)	Min–Max	Mdn (M)	Min–Max	Mdn[b] (M)	Min–Max	HMdn	Z	p	p
Descriptions of stakeholders	2 (2.08)	1–4	1 (2.18)	1–4	1.5 (1.50)	1–2	2 (2.00)	1–3	2*** (1.95)	1–4	3	−4.462	<0.001	0.762
Descriptions of goals	4 (3.00)	1–4	1 (2.09)	1–4	1 (1.20)	1–2	1.5 (1.50)	1–2	1 (1.62)	1–4 (N = 27)	3	−4.230	<0.001	**0.012**
Descriptions of as-is situations	4 (3.08)	1–4	1 (2.09)	1–4	1 (1.20)	1–2	1.5 (1.50)	1–2	1*** (1.63)	1–4 (N = 27)	3	−4.230	<0.001	**0.009**
Description of to-be situations	4 (3.00)	1–4	1 (2.09)	1–4	1 (1.20)	1–2	1.5 (1.50)	1–2	1*** (1.63)	1–4 (N = 27)	3	−4.230	<0.001	**0.012**

(continued)

Descriptions of system context	4 (3.08) 1–4	1 (2.09) 1–4	2 (1.90) 1–4	1.5 (1.67) 1–3	3* (2.53) 1–4	2	2.729 0.006	).06
Descriptions of interactions	2 (2.38) 1–4	1 (1.64) 1–4	2 (1.90) 1–4	1 (1.17) 1–2	1*** (1.88) 1–4	3	−4.604 <0.001	0.10
Descriptions of system functions	1 (1.23) 1–2	1 (1.36) 1–4	1 (1.10) 1–2	1 (1.17) 1–2	1*** (1.23) 1–4	3	−5.872 <0.001	0.17
Descriptions of quality reqs.	1 (1.23) 1–2	1 (1.36) 1–4	1 (1.10) 1–2	1 (1.17) 1–2	1*** (1.23) 1–4	3	−5.872 <.001	0.17
Descriptions of technical constraints	1 (1.46) 1–4	1 (1.36) 1–4	1 (1.10) 1–2	1 (1.17) 1–2	1*** (1.30) 1–4	3	−5.762 <0.001	0.91

[a] Response rating scale: 1 = The RA is very important for my task, 2 = The RA is rather important for my task, 3 = The RA is rather unimportant for my task, 4 = The RA is very unimportant for my task

[b] One-sample Wilcoxon signed-rank test:

if Mdn $(x) < 3$: H_0: H-Mdn$(x) = 3$; * $p < 0.05$; ** $p < 0.01$; *** $p < 0.001$

if Mdn $(x) > 2$: H_0: H-Mdn$(x) = 2$; * $p < 0.05$; ** $p < 0.01$; *** $p < 0.001$

To analyze the questionnaire data, we first calculated *descriptive statistics*, particularly the median (Mdn), sample means (M), minimum (Min), and maximum (Max) values, for each requirements artifact in each study run based on the questionnaire data [39]. As all the data sets were not normally distributed (according to the Shapiro–Wilk test), we applied the *Kruskall–Wallis test* (KW) for independent samples in order to determine possible differences in the medians between the four groups ($FHNW_{A-2013}$, $FHNW_{S-2014}$, $FHNW_{A-2014}$, and $FHNW_{S-2015}$) for each of the investigated requirements artifacts. For those variables that did not reveal any significant difference in their median, we calculated the aforementioned descriptive statistics on the *consolidated data set* ($FHNW_{ALL}$). Moreover, we applied the *one-sample Wilcoxon signed-rank test* to check whether the participants shared a meaningful opinion with regard to the relevance of the investigated artifacts. To do so, we verified whether an observed median ($Mdn(x)$) was equal to hypothetical values H-Mdn = 2 (if $Mdn(x) > 2$), respectively H-Mdn = 3 (if $Mdn(x) < 3$). The significance level (p) was set to 0.05 in all tests. We performed all data analysis activities with IBM$^{®}$ SPSS$^{®}$ PASW Statistics 18.

As highlighted in Table 6, we detected significant differences between the samples $FHNW_{A-2013}$ and $FHNW_{A-2014}$ in the case of descriptions of goals, as-is situations, and to-be situations. Due to this significant difference, we decided to exclude the values of sample $FHNW_{A-2013}$ from the consolidation step. This decision was also underpinned by our assumption that the observed difference between the samples might be attributed to a slight difference in the questionnaire design that we used in the $FHNW_{A-2013}$ study. However, we did not yet discard this sample at this point in our analysis but kept the values of $FHNW_{A-2013}$ separately as input to the secondary analysis (see Sect. 4.3).

4.2.2 Data Interpretation

In order to draw a conclusion with regard to the overall importance level of a certain requirements artifact – and hence to contribute to RQ-1$_{EmpStudies}$ – we interpreted the mean values (M) that resulted from the analysis of the descriptive statistics on the consolidated data set. To do so, we applied the following rules:

- If $1.0 \leq M(x) < 1.5$, the RA is very important for role-specific tasks.
- If $1.5 \leq M(x) < 2.5$, the RA is rather important for role-specific tasks.
- If $2.5 \leq M(x) < 3.5$, the RA is rather unimportant for role-specific tasks.
- If $3.5 \leq M(x) \leq 4.0$, the RA is very unimportant for role-specific tasks.

Applying this scheme to the example data presented in Table 6 led to the following conclusions:

From the viewpoint of the participants of the FHNW study in the role of designers, we identified descriptions of system functions and quality requirements as very important requirements artifacts. In order of importance, these were immediately followed by descriptions of goals, as-is situations, to-be situations, interactions, and descriptions of stakeholders, which were all identified as rather important artifacts. Only descriptions of system context were identified as rather unimportant.

All these findings were also underpinned by the application of the one-sample Wilcoxon signed-rank test (see column OS-WSRT, Table 6). This observation proves the existence of a meaningful opinion shared among the participants regarding the importance rating of the investigated requirements artifacts.

We applied the data analysis and interpretation scheme to the questionnaire data of all studies for each role [39]. Ultimately, we consolidated the various interpretations with regard to the importance of the investigated requirements artifacts that we received from these initial data analysis activities.

Table 7 provides an overview of the consolidated findings over all requirements artifacts from each of the investigated viewpoints.

This cross-study comparison of the analysis results revealed interesting findings. We *identified differences between the different studies (and even between different study runs) with respect to the importance rating of the various requirements artifacts.* At this point of our research, it was still unclear whether the observed differences between the different studies are significant or not. This analysis was the subject of the secondary data analysis (see Sect. 4.3) that consolidated the results we gained in the individual studies in order to arrive at final and more fine-grained conclusions with regard to role-specific information needs and implications on role-specific views.

In this fine-grained conclusion, we also aimed to address the following observation: *We identified many requirements artifacts as "rather important" – some of them close to the border to "very important."* In other words, the range underlying our categorization based on the mean value ($1.5 \leq M(x) < 2.5$) was possibly too broad for the definition of role-specific views.

Apart from the differences between the different studies, *we also observed variances within samples of the individual studies.* This was indeed an interesting observation that motivated future research on factors such as personality or individual reading behavior, which might possibly influence the relevance of requirements artifacts from the viewpoint of their consumers (see Sect. 5).

Table 7 Cross-study comparison

Investigated requirements artifacts	Software architect (N = 67)			Usability expert/designer (N = 52)			Software tester (N = 49)
	Eye-Tracking	U-KL	FHNW	Eye-Tracking	MUC	FHNW	FHNW
Descriptions of stakeholders	RI	RI	RU	VI	RI	RI	RU
Descriptions of goals	VI	RI	RI	RI	RI	VU RI	RU
Descriptions of as-is situations	RI	VU RU	RI	RU	RI	VU RI	RU
Descriptions of to-be situations	RI	RI	RI	RI	VI	VU RI	RU
Descriptions of system context	RI	RU	RI	RI	N/A	RU	VU RU
Descriptions of interactions	RI	RI	RI	RI	RI	RI	RI
Descriptions of system functions	RI	VI	VI	RI	RI	VI	RI VI
Descriptions of quality requirements	RI	RI	VI	RI	N/A	VI	RI VI
Descriptions of technical constraints	VI	RI	VI	RU	N/A	VI	RI VI

Very important (VI)	Rather important (RI)	Rather unimportant (RU)	Very unimportant (VU)

4.3 Secondary Data Analysis: Role-Specific Views

Based on the empirical baseline introduced in the previous section, we performed a secondary data analysis. The overall goal of this secondary data analysis was twofold: First, we aimed to compare and consolidate the data we had obtained in the various empirical studies in order to ultimately arrive at a conclusion with regard to the *overall importance level* of the different TORE requirements artifacts from the viewpoint of software architects, designers, and software testers (RQ-1$_{EmpStudies}$).

Second, we aimed to link our findings to our envisioned solution idea (see Sect. 3) and interpret the findings in terms of suitable contents of *role-specific views* for each of the three downstream roles. The latter decision explicitly incorporated the results we obtained from investigating RQ-2$_{EmpStudies}$ and RQ-3$_{EmpStudies}$.

In the following, we will introduce and illustrate our data analysis strategy and interpretation of this secondary data analysis with a concrete example.

4.3.1 Data Analysis Strategy: An Example

The description of the data analysis strategy we followed during the secondary data analysis comprised six analysis steps:

1. For each requirements artifact, we created a table summarizing the final priority ratings of the different samples we derived from the data analysis of the individual studies (see Sect. 4.1).
2. To test whether our data is normally distributed, we applied the *Shapiro–Wilk test*, which led us to assume a non-normal data distribution.
3. Hence, in order to test for possible significant differences between the different study samples, we applied nonparametric tests of independent samples (in particular *Kruskal–Wallis tests*, respectively *Mann–Whitney U tests*) and reported the resulting p-values, which correspond to the asymptotic significance values (for $N \geq 30$) and the exact significance values if $N < 30$.
4. In the case of any significant differences identified in Step 3, we performed a *pairwise comparison* to identify the particular samples that revealed differences and reported the corresponding significance level (p), the observed value (Z), the sample size (N), and the effect size (r).
5. Next, we calculated *descriptive statistics* based on the consolidated sample data sets comprising median (Mdn), mean (M), minimum (Min), and maximum (Max) values and generated a histogram visualizing the frequencies of the importance ratings.
6. Last, we performed a *one-sample Wilcoxon signed-rank test* to check whether a meaningful opinion shared among the participants can be observed with regard to the importance of a particular requirements artifact. To do so, we tested for possible significant differences to a hypothetical median value H-Mdn(x) = 2, respectively H-Mdn(x) = 3. We report the Wilcoxon signed-rank observed value (Z) as well as the significance level (p).

Table 8 illustrates our data analysis scheme for the example of the requirements artifact "Descriptions of as-is situations" from the viewpoint of designers. The columns Sample S1 to Sample S4 summarize the final priority ratings of the different study samples we derived from the data analysis of the individual studies (see Sect. 4.1). The Kruskall–Wallis test applied to the samples S1 to S4 revealed significant differences between the four study groups ($p = 0.006$, $N = 51$). The subsequent pairwise comparison identified significant differences between sample S_3 and sample S_4 ($p = 0.006$, $Z = 3.291$, $N = 40$) with a strong effect size of $r = 0.5$. The fact that this secondary analysis also revealed a significant difference between the FHNW$_{A-2013}$ and other samples supported our previously stated claim that the difference might be attributed to a slight difference in the design of the questionnaire that we used in FHNW$_{A-2013}$ to elicit the importance of requirements analysis. Hence, to mitigate this possible threat, we excluded sample S_3 from the consolidation and the calculated descriptive statistics (see Column ConData$_{S1S2S4}$) and applied the one-sample Wilcoxon signed-rank test to this consolidated data set. The latter revealed a significant difference between the observed median Mdn = 2 and the hypothetical median value H-Mdn = 3 ($p < 0.001$, $N = 38$, $Z = -4.833$). This shows a clear opinion regarding the high relevance of descriptions of as-is situations in the consolidated data set. We also observed minor variances in the consolidated data set, as indicated in the histogram in Fig. 4.

Table 8 Secondary data analysis of "as-is situations" from the designer's viewpoint

Importance of descriptions of as-is situations[a]				
				ConData$_{S1S2S4}$
Sample S_1	Sample S_2	Sample S_3	Sample S_4	($N = 38$)
Eye-tracking ($N = 2$)	MUC$_{2011}$ ($N = 9$)	FHNW$_{A\text{-}2013}$ ($N = 13$)	FHNW$_{ALL}$ ($N = 27$)	
Mdn (M) Min–Max	Mdn (M) Min–Max	Mdn (M) Min–Max	Mdn (M) Min–Max	Mdn[b] (M) Min–Max
3 (2–4)	2 (1.78) 1–2	4 (3.08) 1–4	1 (1.63) 1–4	1*** (1.74) 1–4

[a]Response rating scale: 1 = The RA is very important for IxD/UI design, 2 = The RA is rather important for IxD/UI design, 3 = The RA is rather unimportant for IxD/UI design, 4 = The RA is very unimportant for IxD/UI design
[b]One-sample Wilcoxon signed-rank test H$_0$: H-Mdn (x) = 3; *$p < 0.05$; **$p < 0.01$; ***$p < 0.001$

Fig. 4 Histogram visualizing frequencies of importance ratings

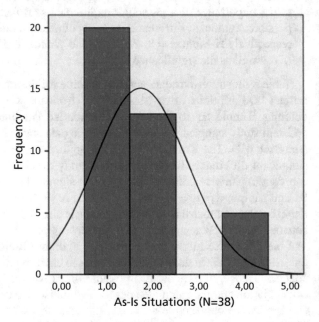

4.3.2 Data Interpretation

In order to draw general conclusions with regard to the *overall importance level* of a certain requirements artifact, we first interpreted the mean values (M) resulting from the analysis of the descriptive statistics on the consolidated data. To do so, we applied the same rules as during the data analysis and interpretation of the individual studies introduced in Sect. 4.2.2.

As highlighted in our conclusions in Sect. 4.2.2, we aimed to introduce a more fine-grained differentiation of the classification of those requirements artifacts that were identified as "rather important." The fine-grained conclusions link our empirical data and knowledge to the *role-specific views* utilized in our envisioned technical solution (see Fig. 3).

As introduced in Sect. 3, we envisioned a role-specific view containing high-level or detailed descriptions of requirements artifacts that are of high priority for a certain role (TOP Artifacts). Besides that, we envisioned a second view (IMPORTANT Artifacts) containing high-level or detailed descriptions of requirements artifacts that are important but less critical than the artifacts contained in the TOP Artifacts view. Requirements artifacts and related descriptions considered as rather unimportant or even very unimportant will not be included in the role-specific views. Based on these concepts, we defined the following interpretation scheme for drawing fine-grained conclusions toward the role-specific views:

- IF ($1.0 \leq M(x) \leq 1.5$), THEN assign detailed descriptions of the requirements artifact to the view TOP Artifacts for the corresponding role.
- IF ($1.5 < M(x) \leq 2.0$), THEN assign detailed descriptions of the requirements artifact to the view IMPORTANT Artifacts for the corresponding role.
- IF ($2.0 < M(x) < 2.5$), THEN assign only high-level descriptions of the requirements artifact to the view IMPORTANT Artifacts for the corresponding role and hide further details in the role-specific views.
- IF ($2.5 \leq M(x) \leq 4.0$), THEN hide descriptions of the requirements artifact in the role-specific views.

The concrete shape and representation of "detailed descriptions" or "high-level descriptions" for each of the requirements artifacts were defined based on the results regarding the suitable level of detail (RQ-2$_{EmpStudies}$) and the preferred notations (RQ-3$_{EmpStudies}$) for relevant requirements artifacts that we investigated in Study #1 (eye-tracking study) and Study #3 (MUC) (see Sect. 4.1).

Referring to our example illustrated in Table 8, the application of our data interpretation scheme led to the following conclusions for descriptions of as-is situations from the viewpoint of designers:

> In general, descriptions of as-is situations are rather important for designers.
> We assign *detailed descriptions* (in particular process models (e.g., in the form
> of UML Activity Diagrams) and detailed activity descriptions) to the view
> *IMPORTANT Artifacts* for designers.

Again, we applied the data analysis and interpretation scheme to all requirements
artifacts from all three viewpoints (software architects, usability experts in the role
of designers, and software testers).

4.3.3 Data Utilization

Table 9 provides an overview of the consolidated results of the secondary data
analysis. For each of the three roles (i.e., software architects, usability expert and
tester), the table reflects the priority as well as the preferred level of detail of the
investigated artifacts based on the interpretation scheme introduced in Sect. 4.3.2
respectively the data utilization introduced in Sect. 4.3.3.

As introduced previously in Sect. 3, our technical solution utilizes our empirical
knowledge about role-specific information needs by applying filter rules on a given
SRS structure and requirements artifact templates that are defined in Microsoft
Excel$^{®}$. These filter rules are based on priority tags that are assigned to each
description item of the artifact templates (see Fig. 3). Thereby, each priority tag
corresponds to the relevance of the investigated requirements artifacts from the
viewpoint of software architects (A), usability experts/designers (U), and software
testers (T). In particular, depending on the preferred level of detail, selected
description items of artifacts that were assigned to the view "TOP Artifacts" were
tagged with priority A1 (respectively U1 and T1), whereas selected description
items of artifacts that were assigned to the view "Important Artifacts" were tagged
with priority A2 (respectively U2 and T2). That is, executing the command "Top
Artifacts" for software architects in the menu bar (see Fig. 3), for instance, applies
a filter rule that displays only requirements artifacts and description items tagged
with priority tag A1.

5   Limitations and Future Work

The empirical work of the thesis is rather complex, and besides interesting observations and lessons learned, we also identified and discussed several threats to validity
that have to be considered when interpreting the results and that motivated future
work. For instance, the majority of subjects were students rather than practitioners
with a different level of expertise. Even though we mitigated this threat by cross-

Table 9 Role-specific views on requirements artifacts

Requirements artifacts	Software architect		Usability expert		Software tester	
	TOP	IMPORTANT	TOP	IMPORTANT	TOP	IMPORTANT
Descriptions of stakeholders	Hidden			Detailed	Hidden	
Descriptions of goals		High-level		Detailed	Hidden	
Descriptions of as-is situations		High-level		Detailed	Hidden	
Descriptions of to-be situations		High-level		Detailed	Hidden	
Descriptions of system context		High-level		High-level	Hidden	
Descriptions of interactions		Detailed		Detailed		Detailed
Descriptions of system functions	Detailed		Detailed		Detailed	
Descriptions of quality requirements	Detailed		Detailed		Detailed	
Descriptions of technical constraints	Detailed		Detailed		Detailed	

checking our results with role-specific information needs reported in the literature, further studies with practitioners are needed to increase the external validity of our empirical results. Moreover, in all of our studies, we observed differences in the ratings of requirements artifacts, both between different studies and even within one sample. Even though these differences were (mostly) not significant, we claim that there exist factors (such as working experience, project scope, or personality) that influence the relevance of requirements artifacts. In the future, we aim to investigate such influencing factors in more detail.

In the thesis, we focused our investigations on requirements artifacts that are typically created when RE is performed within the information systems domain, particularly when following the TORE framework. Due to the widespread use of agile methodologies in industry, we aim to transfer our results to the context of agile project settings, which are characterized by extensive collaboration, e.g., face-to-face communication rather than in-depth documentation. In [40], we presented a research agenda and early results that allowed us to better understand RE-related challenges and their implications as well as the relevance of RE-related agile practices from the viewpoint of different agile team members. We also elaborated first guidelines on the example of user stories that incorporate our findings regarding role-specific information needs.

In fact, improving requirements communication in interdisciplinary teams is a highly interesting and relevant topic that motivates our current and future research activities in the context of "learning from non-SE disciplines." The core objective of this research field is to cross the borders of the SE world and get inspired by best practices from disciplines such as psychology, criminology, film studies, etc. Thereby, we aim to identify synergy potential between these best practices in order to ultimately incorporate and adapt them into new methods.

Currently, we are pursuing the idea of so-called "conspiracy walls," which are typically used by detectives in criminal investigations to visualize any data, information, assumptions, and potential interrelations related to a particular crime. We envision that a similar visualization applied to requirements-related information could bring several benefits [41]. For instance, joint discussions and analysis of the visualized data could foster communication and information exchange in interdisciplinary teams and hence contribute to a better-shared understanding of both the requirements and the information needs and responsibilities of the various team members.

6   Summary

Delivering high-quality SRS that fit the demands of their consumers is a challenging task for requirements engineers, as different information needs and expectations have to be addressed. These information needs and expectations are strongly dependent on the particular role(s) that the SRS consumers have within a project.

Within the context of the thesis "Role-Specific Views on SRS: An Empirical Approach" we aimed to address practical problems experienced and observed by us in industry that can be traced to role-specific requirements defects in SRS. In fact, such problems might have a negative influence on the efficient usage of SRS, as it becomes time-consuming and/or cognitively hard for the document stakeholders to resolve and reconcile these problems while working with the SRS. This is critical as it might in turn lead to failures, delays, and frustration in subsequent SE activities, and ultimately to costly changes and budget or time overruns.

In order to address and reduce these defects, we aimed to empirically investigate role-specific information needs regarding SRS from the viewpoint of different SRS consumers involved in downstream tasks such as architecture design, interaction/UI design, and testing. Following a design science research approach, we achieved various contributions, which are summarized in this chapter. Besides a *taxonomy of role-specific defects* as well as an *overview of existing quality assurance and view-based approaches* in the context of requirements documentation activities, we derived *role-specific views* from a series of empirical studies. These views ultimately served as a baseline for a *proof-of-concept implementation* that is capable of automatically generating role-specific views on SRS by filtering the information in accordance with the empirical knowledge about role-specific information needs. The main purpose of this implementation was to demonstrate our solution idea of generating role-specific views on SRS. Moreover, it was subjected to a *case study* that we conducted to investigate hypotheses with regard to the improvement goals of the thesis. We found that role-specific views have the potential to efficiently support SRS consumers during the analysis of SRS and that they are helpful for supporting the communication of requirements in software-developing teams. However, their usefulness depends on the project setting. That is, they are possibly most beneficial in the context of the development of large systems resulting in complex SRS.

In future work, we aim to conduct further empirical studies in industry contexts in order to increase the external validity of our results. Moreover, we will continue our follow-up activities on improving requirements communication in agile project contexts, thereby exploring synergy potential with best practices from non-SE disciplines, such as psychology, criminology, or film studies.

Acknowledgments I sincerely thank my supervisors Prof. Dieter Rombach, Prof. Barbara Paech, and Prof. Schneider as well as Dr. Jörg Dörr, Dr. Marcus Trapp, and Prof. Norbert Seyff for their continuous support and valuable advice, which helped me a lot to shape the thesis and to align and focus my research activities.

References

1. Zhang, W., Pastel, R.: Interdisciplinary team collaboration between software engineers and technical communicators. Proc. Hum. Factor. Ergon. Soc. Annu. Meet. **59**(1), 1137–1141 (2016)
2. Whitehead, J.: Collaboration in software engineering: a roadmap. In: Future of Software Engineering (FOSE '07), pp. 214–225. IEEE, Piscataway, NJ (2007)

3. Glinz, M., Fricker, S.A.: On shared understanding in software engineering: an essay. Comput. Sci. Res. Dev. **30**(3–4), 363–376 (2015)
4. Bjarnason, E., Sharp, H.: The role of distances in requirements communication: a case study. Requir. Eng. **22**(1), 1–26 (2017)
5. Pohl, K., Rupp, C.: Requirements engineering fundamentals. In: A Study Guide for the Certified Professional for Requirements Engineering Exam, Foundation Level, IREB Compliant. Rocky Nook, Santa Barbara, CA (2015)
6. Firesmith, D.: Common requirements problems, their negative consequences, and the industry best practices to help solve them. J. Obj. Technol. **6**(1), 17–33 (2007)
7. Alshazly, A., Elfatary, A.M., Abougabal, M.S.: Detecting defects in software requirements specification. Alex. Eng. J. **53**(3), 513–527 (2014)
8. Simon, T., Streit, J., Pizka, M.: Practically relevant quality criteria for requirements documents. In: 2008 International Conference on Software Engineering Research & Practice (SERP 2008), pp. 115–121. CSREA Press, Las Vegas (2008)
9. Lopes Margarido, I., Faria, J.P., Vidal, R.M., Vieira, M.: Classification of defect types in requirements specifications: literature review, proposal and assessment. In: 6th Iberian Conference on Information Systems and Technologies, pp. 1–6. IEEE, Piscataway, NJ (2011)
10. Macaulay, L.: Requirements for requirements engineering techniques. In: Proceedings of 2nd International Conference on Requirements Engineering (ICRE'96), pp. 157–164. IEEE, Piscataway, NJ (1996)
11. Hess, A.: Role-specific views on software requirements specifications – an empirical approach. In: PhD theses in experimental software engineering 69. Fraunhofer Verlag, Stuttgart (2020)
12. Adam, S., Riegel, N., Gross, A., Uenalan, O., Darting, S.: A conceptual foundation of requirements engineering for business information systems. In: Enterprise, Business-Process and Information Systems Modeling, pp. 91–106. Springer, Berlin (2012)
13. Mich, L., Franch, M., Novi Inverardi, P.: Market research for requirements analysis using linguistic tools. Requir. Eng. **9**(1), 40–56 (2004)
14. Femmer, H., Unterkalmsteiner, M., Gorschek, T.: Which requirements artifact quality defects are automatically detectable? A case study. In: 2017 IEEE 25th International Requirements Engineering Workshops (REW 2017), pp. 400–406. IEEE, Piscataway, NJ (2017)
15. Sommerville, I.: Software Engineering. Pearson, Boston (2011)
16. Femmer, H., Mund, J., Méndez Fernándes, D.: It's the activities, stupid! A new perspective on RE quality. In: 2nd International Workshop on Requirements Engineering and Testing (RET 2015), pp. 13–19. IEEE, Piscataway, NJ (2015)
17. Femmer, H., Vogelsang, A.: Requirements quality is quality in use. IEEE Software. **36**(3), 83–91 (2018)
18. Firesmith, D.: Specifying good requirements. J. Obj. Technol. **2**(4), 77–87 (2003)
19. Gross, A., Doerr, J.: What you need is what you get! The vision of view-based requirements specifications. In: 2012 IEEE 20th International Requirements Engineering Conference (RE'12), pp. 171–180. IEEE, Piscataway, NJ (2012)
20. IEEE 830-1998.: Recommended Practice for Software Requirements Specifications
21. Sommerville, I., Sawyer, P.: Requirements Engineering. A Good Pratice Guide. Wiley, Chichester (1997)
22. Robertson, J., Robertson, S.: Volere requirements specification template. https://www.reqview.com/blog/2019-02-27-news-volere-requirements-specification-template.html. (2019). Accessed 30 Apr 2021
23. Wiegers, K.E.: Peer Reviews in Software. A Practical Guide. Addison-Wesley, Boston (2002)
24. Gilb, T., Graham, D., Finzi, S.: Software Inspection. Addison-Wesley, Boston (1993)
25. Shull, F., Rus, I., Basili, V.: How perspective-based reading can improve requirements inspections. Computer. **33**(7), 73–79 (2000)
26. Felderer, M., Beer, A.: Using defect taxonomies for requirements validation in industrial projects. In: 2013 IEEE 21st International Requirements Engineering Conference (RE'13), pp. 296–301. IEEE, Piscataway, NJ (2013)

27. Shah, U.S., Jinwala, D.C.: Resolving ambiguities in natural language software requirements: a comprehensive survey. Software Eng. Notes. **40**(5), 1–7 (2015)
28. Thiroul J.H., Herhtvil A,, Junduram, S K Holbrook, E.A., Vadlamudi, S., April, A.: REquirements TRacing On target (RETRO): Improving software maintenance through traceability recovery. Innov. Syst. Software Eng. **3**(3), 193–202 (2007)
29. Nair, S., de La Vara, J.L., Sen, S.: A review of traceability research at the requirements engineering conference@21. In: 2013 21st IEEE International Requirements Engineering Conference (RE'13), pp. 222–229. IEEE, Piscataway, NJ (2013)
30. Kotonya, G.: Practical experience with viewpoint-oriented requirements specification. Requir. Eng. **4**(3), 115–133 (1999)
31. Sommerville, I., Sawyer, P.: Viewpoints: principles, problems and a practical approach to requirements engineering. Ann. Software Eng. **3**, 101–130 (1997)
32. Pohl, K.: The three dimensions of requirements engineering. In: Seminal Contributions to Information Systems Engineering, pp. 63–80. Springer, Berlin (2013)
33. Kruchten, P.: What do software architects really do? J. Syst. Software. **81**(12), 2413–2416 (2008)
34. Fischer, G.: User modeling in human-computer interaction. User Model User Adapt. Interact. **11**(1/2), 65–86 (2001)
35. Meyer, B.: Seven principles of software testing. Computer. **41**(8), 99–101 (2008)
36. Peffers, K., Tuunanen, T., Rothenberger, M.A., Chatterjee, S.: A design science research methodology for information systems research. J. Manag. Inf. Syst. **24**(3), 45–77 (2007)
37. Hess, A., Doerr, J., Seyff, N.: How to make use of empirical knowledge about testers' information needs. In: 2017 IEEE 25th International Requirements Engineering Conference Workshops (REW 2017), pp. 327–330. IEEE, Piscataway, NJ (2017)
38. Adam, S., Riegel, N., Doerr, J.: TORE. A Framework for Systematic Requirements Development in Information Systems. https://re-magazine.ireb.org/articles/tore (2014). Accessed 30 April 2021.
39. Hess, A.: Empirical Baseline for the Investigation of Role-Specific Information Needs. (2021). https://fordatis.fraunhofer.de/handle/fordatis/202
40. Hess, A., Diebold, P., Seyff, N.: Understanding information needs of agile teams to improve requirements communication. J. Ind. Inf. Integr. **14**, 3–15 (2018)
41. Hess, A., Mennig, P., Bartels, N.: Conspiracy walls in requirements engineering - analyzing requirements like a detective. In CEUR Workshop Proceedings Volume 2584. http://ceur-ws.org/Vol-2584/CreaRE-paper1.pdf (2020). Accessed 30 Apr 2021

DevOpsUse: A Community-Oriented Methodology for Societal Software Engineering

István Koren

Abstract The demanded fast innovation cycles of the ongoing digital transformation create an unstable environment in which the demands of heterogeneous professional communities need to be addressed. Moreover, the information systems infrastructure of these professional communities has a strong influence on their practices. However, the evolution of the web as infrastructure is shaped by an interplay of new technologies and innovative applications. It is characterized by contrasts, such as centralized versus peer-to-peer architectures and a large number of end users versus a small number of developers. Therefore, our aim is to stabilize these dichotomies apparent in the web by means of an agile information systems development methodology. The DevOps approach promotes stronger cooperation between development and operations teams. Our DevOpsUse methodology additionally fosters a stronger involvement of end-user communities in software development by including them in the process of infrastructuring, that is, the appropriation of infrastructure during its usage. The developed DevOpsUse methodology and support tools have been successfully validated by the transitions between three generations of technologies: near real-time peer-to-peer web architectures, edge computing, and the Internet of Things. In particular, we were able to demonstrate our methodology's capabilities through longitudinal studies in several large-scale international digitalization projects. Beyond web information systems, the framework and its open-source tools are applicable in further areas like Industry 4.0. Its broad adaptability testifies that DevOpsUse has the potential to unlock capabilities for sustainable innovation.

I. Koren (✉)
Information Systems and Databases, RWTH Aachen University, Aachen, Germany
e-mail: koren@dbis.rwth-aachen.de

© The Author(s) 2022
M. Felderer et al. (eds.), *Ernst Denert Award for Software Engineering 2020*,
https://doi.org/10.1007/978-3-030-83128-8_8

143

1   Introduction

The profound digital transformation of industrial processes is inevitably leading to more software use. The underlying information systems not only need to be initially developed, but they also have to be maintained. Shorter time-to-market processes and far-reaching system integration additionally make it necessary to increase the number of updates. To address this challenge, there have been tremendous advances in software engineering methodologies over the past few decades. While historically the waterfall model has been adopted for the strict process from formal contract to product, it is now being replaced by agile methods. Technology support has also followed this development. Modern frameworks are driving the separation of concerns even further. This has resulted in component-based architectures with microservices on the backend and user interface components on the frontend.

Software development, however, is no longer only object of developers. Instead, it has far-reaching implications into the world of business models and processes, and society in general. Therefore, the question is whether current methodologies can cope with the increased speed and widespread societal involvement. How to incorporate modern aspects such as increased agency of end-user communities and data sovereignty? Especially with regard to the end users, we notice that even in agile methods like Scrum, the users are only at the beginning and at the end, that is, they are largely detached from the actual development. In our research we have thus developed a methodology that explicitly integrates end-user communities. Our solution is characterized by the deep integration of collaboration tools, as well as the application of peer-to-peer architectures. At the same time, contextual forces such as changing technologies need to be stabilized in order to allow a sustainable development process. The evolution of information systems from mainframes to PCs and cloud systems leads us to *societal software*, which increases the responsibility of its users by paying as much attention to the process of creating software as to the software product itself [46]. The implications of the research presented here go beyond the technical aspects and open up new interesting questions that extend into operational and legal perspectives.

This chapter is structured as follows. In the next section, we discuss the motivation behind our research. Section 3 then presents the methodology in detail. Section 4 provides an evaluation of technological and methodological aspects, before discussing implications for societal software development projects. Finally, Sect. 5 concludes this chapter and gives pointers on future work.

2   Motivation

The unrestrained demand for software products together with fast development cycles lead to many challenges. Rapid innovation cycles and changing technology create a disruptive and unstable environment in which the requirements of endless communities must be met. The shift in speed becomes evident when considering the update rates in the newly established app market economies of mobile operating systems. The number of available developers alone cannot satisfy this demand. Research fields such as *End User Development* attempt to solve this dilemma by putting tools in the hands of users to build software themselves [34]. The shift toward societal software development mentioned in the previous section extends this end-user integration and expands it to the entire methodology.

Information infrastructure plays a special role here. The general term *infrastructure* thereby refers to an underlying factor. Information systems infrastructure, while only partially visible and thus hard to grasp, has a strong influence on user and developer practices. Driven by a body of standards, the web has reached significance not only of technological nature but also quite distinctly of a societal dimension. Its proliferation highlights the ubiquitous nature; it is now available everywhere, on various types of hardware. Constantly evolving standards thereby ensure interoperability between manufacturers and devices. Today, smartwatches have built-in browsers, industrial assets are controlled by web interfaces, and even the touchscreen control panels of the latest generation of space capsules work with web technologies like JavaScript and HTML.[1] Conceptually, the web is a graph of linked resources [40]. Open interfaces allow the composition of these linked resources to form distributed services and apps. However, changing interfaces can also make them drift apart. One of the web's key strengths is therefore also among its weaknesses: the continuous context changes do not only increase the web's applicability and adoption, but also require constant retraining of users, developers, and operators in order to handle the new realms.

Figure 1 highlights current dichotomies in web information systems engineering. On the left, we see the everlasting duality between centralized and distributed technologies,[2] plus the combination of those. On top, device innovations create a constant need for software adaptation, frameworks, and even usability considerations. On the right, the imbalance is portrayed between a small number of developers who know *how* to create software versus a large number of end users who as domain experts know *what* they need. Finally, the bottom layer refers to the ongoing changes in workplace settings caused by digitization. Connecting all of these aspects, the challenge is to create a core that holds and links everything together.

2.1 Central Hypothesis

In this field of mutually influencing dichotomies and the underlying infrastructure, several research questions arise. What are the building blocks of community-

---

[1] cf. https://cnet.co/3fiK0V5.

[2] The reader is kindly referred to the history of computers from mainframes to personal computers to the cloud, back to current edge computing efforts.

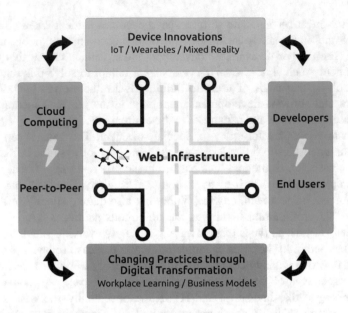

Fig. 1 Dichotomies in web information systems engineering

oriented information systems? How can we enable communities to develop information systems on their specific information systems infrastructure? How to create a sustainable life cycle of the developed information systems? Our central hypothesis is that we can provide a stabilized socio-technical infrastructure on top of the web as open ground. We therefore augment the collaborative notion of DevOps as automation-driven cooperation between developers and operators by the notion of end users. The goal of this extension to DevOpsUse is to make information systems more resilient to technological disruptions by continuously engaging their users. We provide automation of end-user participation via tools for social requirements engineering and service deployment, among many others. Throughout this chapter, we give selected pointers to these tools; for the in-depth discussion and answers to the above questions we refer to the dissertation [26]. As overall methodological research framework, we work along the design-science methodology by Hevner et al. [17]. The seven guidelines tackle the problem-solving process by building and applying an artifact that is later evaluated with due rigor. Instead of a single design artifact, we created multiple particular tools that we then connect in the overarching methodology.

2.2 Research Background

Agile practices in software engineering promote a stronger focus on the social aspects like the development team and the customer. Additionally, the mindset of the

Agile Manifesto acknowledges frequent changes and overall working software [12]. Most popular instantiations include, for instance, *Extreme Programming*, *Scrum*, or *Kanban*. *DevOps*, as a clipped compound of *development* and *operation* teams, is driving a stronger cooperation between these by extensive automation. Recently related concepts have been introduced, like *DevSecOps* that stresses the growing importance of security. We argue, however, that these methodologies do not explicitly integrate users into the development process itself. In Scrum, for example, users appear at the beginning and end of each sprint. Integrating end users, more specifically *Communities of Practice* (CoP) as groups of professionals working toward a common goal [53], helps not only leveraging their domain knowledge but also increasing their agency and involvement, thereby sustaining the development results.

Approaches that integrate end users are categorized as End User Development (EUD) [34]. According to Liberman et al., there are two possible realizations: parametrization of software products and creation from scratch. The research domain of EUD is rather concerned with the second. Numerous ways have been introduced, like macros for automating tasks in office applications and programming-by-example in smart home settings. Yet they all specifically target an application case and do not extend their findings to the methodological core. In our research, we look at the underlying structures supporting information systems: the infrastructure. Generally spoken, an infrastructure is "an underlying base or foundation especially for an organization or system" [1]. In the obvious analogy of traffic infrastructure, road networks connect cities and countries to ports and other continents. With this, we can exemplify the transitory nature of infrastructure: what is infrastructure for one (driver) is the work item for the other (road worker). This transition is intrinsically much faster in software engineering, where today's developer tools render it possible to build a simple application and scale it to thousands of users in the matter of a few days or hours. In information systems literature, the term *Infrastructuring* has been coined [41, 51] to signify the creation and continuous adaptation process. It represents *in situ* design work, respectively *design-in-use* as opposed to *design-before-use* [42]. *To infrastructure* emphasizes the conditional, flexible and open character of the infrastructure design process [51]. Thereby, the creation process is shaped by conventions of practice. At the same time, the demands of professional communities are under constant change, so their designs are expected to evolve with them [5]. This highlights the need for better collaboration between communities and the developers and operators supporting them. Communication is considered an essential part of infrastructuring that acts as a bridge between actors and resources in different contexts and practices [35]. Similarly, the gap between users and designers is one of the major challenges in design [47].

It is costly to put a lot of work in features that are not needed. *Open innovation* tackles the circumstance that ideas are often planned without meeting the real requirements, by opening up the ideation process to external influence [9]. However, the duality between being too closed and too open may harm the original business model of companies. For a sustainable open innovation strategy, we argue that

Fig. 2 The DevOpsUse life
cycle has the DevOps model
at its core, while aspects of
end-user communities are
surrounding and influencing it

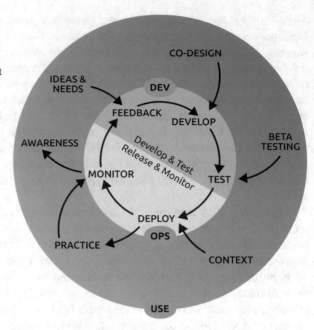

the opening must be well-integrated into the methodological foundation. This is impressively demonstrated by the open-source movement in the software industry, scaling to a massively distributed, open effort. Tuomi therefore sees open innovation to be strongly related to open-source software [52]. In this context, Hippel's *lead users* [18], who stand for domain experts acting as innovators, need to be included.

In this section, we explained the theoretical backgrounds that have significantly influenced our research. In the following, the DevOpsUse methodology is explained in detail.

3   DevOpsUse Methodology

One of the main parameters that influence the velocity in software engineering in the context of frequent changes is the choice of the software development methodology. This area has already seen a great deal of progress in the last decades: The shift from inflexible waterfall models to agile environments has made a significant contribution toward dealing with change. DevOps is a recent concept that furthermore includes operators and thus provides a holistic view on development and deployment [11]. In this approach, automation between these groups plays an important role in resolving the inherent conflict between them. At the core of Fig. 2 we see the simplified life cycle of the cooperation between developers and operators. The arrows represent steps involving automation. Starting from feedback on the top, that is, the requirements engineering phase, the development of software takes place.

The resulting artifacts are then tested. From the testing phase, the software gets delivered and staged to deployment. Finally, its usage is monitored. According to this conception, the points of connection to users become clear: specifically, at the beginning (feedback) and at the end (monitoring) Commonly, this model is characterized by a lack of attention to end users, as they are not explicitly involved in any of the development or operational phases. The software artifacts produced therefore still have a lot of potential to become even more innovative and user-friendly.

As progressive digitization affects more and more parts of our lives, software also plays an increasingly important role therein. The detachment of development practices from societal processes would therefore become even more critical in the future. We therefore propose *DevOpsUse* as a new methodological foundation for societal software engineering. It adds to DevOps the user as a cross-cutting concern across the whole development and operation cycle. As a vehicle to carry out these ideas, our methodology focuses on the underlying information systems infrastructure, upon which development, operation, and usage are happening. The inclusive development process leverages the collective strengths and potential weaknesses of the people involved.

The outer circle of Fig. 2 exemplifies points of user participation in software development. In the following, we highlight these aspects while going around the circle and present the overarching elements that conceptually connect these points. The first aspect is continuous innovation, that is, the influx of new ideas at every development and usage phase. In particular, we showcase the boundary objects connecting the individual tools.

3.1   Continuous Innovation

Requirements engineering (RE) captures the goals of the users and is the basis for all other development activities [43]. However, common issue trackers are not easy enough to be used by end users. Overall, they are very technical and require to specify details, while for users it is often not evident whether it is caused by a backend or frontend bug. Many open-source projects on GitHub additionally require to follow a strict template with developer-specific terms that are hard to understand.

Social requirements engineering aims at collecting requirements in a way that resembles social networks like Facebook and Twitter [45]. It serves both developers and end users; the latter can easily enter new ideas or bug reports and approve existing ones, while the former can start a dialog with the reporting users through comments. Methodologically similar, *CrowdRE* describes automated or semiautomated approaches to integrate a large number of users into RE [14]. However, CrowdRE explicitly discusses pull and push mechanisms as feedback patterns. Contrarily, in DevOpsUse users are part of a community with developers.

Specifically, our Requirements Bazaar[3] web application extends social RE to web scale. It is a continuous innovation tool that allows a social exchange of ideas while making requirements traceable across ideation, conception, and realization phases. Following the design-science methodology, it was developed iteratively with continuous exchange of its users on the very same platform. The web application runs on mobile and desktop browsers. Filtering functionalities allow to filter only the most or least active requirements, for instance. As a conclusion of this section, we deem continuous innovation principles to be important to keep up disruptive capacities of information systems and to create a sustainable long-term development process.

3.2 Collaborative Modeling

Eliciting the mental representation of stakeholders while being as close to the real world as possible is one of the challenging goals of modeling. At the same time, it is a highly social activity. We thus see models as the smallest common denominator between the domains of developers and end users. In our community-driven approach, the mutual engagement of developers and end users within a CoP helps to build better tools. As a starting point, we take a formal description of REST-based APIs available in service repositories on the web. The OpenAPI interface description language (formerly called Swagger) is a well-known format that is widely used for automatic verification and conformance checks [38]. Along with the goals of model-driven software engineering, it allows the type-safe generation of API access layers for frontend applications. We leverage its expressiveness and created a web-based collaboration tool for wiring services together with user interface components. For this reason, we used the *Interaction Flow Modeling Language* (IFML) that is governed by the Object Management Group, the same standardization organization that oversees the *Unified Modeling Language* (UML). It is a visual domain-specific modeling language for creating visual models of user interactions and frontends [7]. The *Direwolf Model Editor* therefore allows the model-driven composition of APIs and UIs [30]. Technically, it translates the data types described in an OpenAPI description into a palette of possible UI elements, like an HTML list for an array or a label for a string. Similarly, object types that are used as input attribute of a service result in an HTML form being generated. Besides the user interface creation, the tool can support other types of collaborative model creation, as we have demonstrated for example with the *iStar 2.0* strategic goal modeling language [30].

The Direwolf Model Editor is a boundary object between end users and developers. It shows how model-driven methods and associated benefits such as generalization and code generation can be leveraged in a community-driven end-

---

[3] cf. https://requirements-bazaar.org.

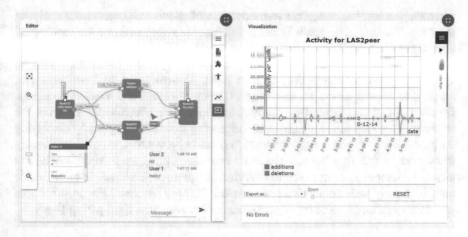

Fig. 3 Screenshot of the SWEVA collaborative visual analytics tool

user development approach. Using generative approaches, repetitive patterns in application creation, like creating input forms based for API inputs, can be scaled to a myriad of users and device types.

3.3 Monitoring

At the intersection of professional communities, the IoT, web services, and peer-to-peer communication between individuals and devices, challenges of analytics are amplified. *Visual Analytics* is the "science of analytical reasoning facilitated by interactive human-machine interfaces" [23]. It facilitates the exploration of large data collections by combining the best of both worlds; computers that can cope with large amounts of data, and humans who can see links and dependencies between two seemingly unrelated datasets.

Since we noticed a lack of open-source or commercial visual analytics tools that are general-purpose, draw on heterogeneous data sources, are community-aware, and can be embedded in community-oriented applications, we developed *Social Web Environment for Visual Analytics* [29]. It visualizes data coming from and flowing between Internet of Things device networks, social (human) networks, and the communication between apps and their components. Its web environment enables a model-driven visual flow design of processing pipelines, which is executed in real time. Thereby, data sources can be anything from real Industry 4.0 machines, body-worn wearable sensors, or input captured on smartphones. Possible methods include, for example, social network analysis like (overlapping) community detection and expert identification.

Figure 3 shows a screenshot of SWEVA. The tool allows different community members to work simultaneously on models and visualizations to support each other. On the left, the collaborative modeling tool allows to design visual analytics pipelines. The underlying data model is a directed acyclic graph, whose topological ordering ensures that the pipeline can be run without conflicts. It highlights broken nodes to enable quick troubleshooting. The nodes represent either data retrieval operations, custom calculations, or user input. Currently, the tool supports text, number, numerical slider, Boolean toggles, enum selection, and fixed value inputs. On the right, the collaborative visualization tool is responsible for showing the results of the visualization pipeline and influencing its interactive parts by displaying the previously configured user input possibilities. In between these parts sits the core framework, which runs the modeled data processing pipeline. It can either be run locally or remotely on an execution service. All parts or the whole is embeddable into third-party web applications via custom HTML elements. For instance, the `<sweva-visualization-container>` integrates the right part of Fig. 3.

3.4 Connecting the DevOpsUse Life Cycle

In the following, we connect the aspects of the previous subsections with the three particular stages of DevOpsUse, development, operations, and usage. We present aspects of industrial state-of-the-art, related research work and, finally, how we tackled the challenges by showing how they contribute to the overall infrastructure.

Development The role of end users in requirements engineering, either directly through focus groups or indirectly via domain experts, is important by definition. In contrast, end-user involvement during actual programming is much more difficult, as the cognitive hurdle in common textual programming languages is much higher. Increased componentization efforts in software engineering have led to higher maintainability and reduced complexity of individual software packages. This applies to user interfaces just as much as to the encapsulation of many basic app functionalities by libraries. On the backend, microservice architectures similarly lead to higher maintainability and better scalability. To ensure that modularization does not come at the expense of complexity, standards are required for the interfaces. On the traditionally client/server-driven web, the standards can be roughly assigned to the frontend, the backend, and the communication in between. The formal background of standards on the web makes them applicable to model-driven technologies like validation, runtime interpretation, and code generation. User interface components in particular are subject to modeling efforts, as they can be effectively abstracted. Additionally, they are very concrete in terms of the cognitive model of end users, as user interfaces provide the entry point to any application.

Numerous research works have utilized this circumstance by providing formal models as interface description languages. Standardized user interface modeling approaches, for instance, include *Abstract Interaction Objects* [4], *ConcurTask-Trees* [39], and *Cameleon* [8], among others. Prototypes like *Swashup* [36] or frameworks like *ServFace Builder* [37] allow to graphically wire together visual representations of components. Similar prototypes exist for connecting functionalities in the Internet of Things, for instance, by *RAML for IoT* [24], the open-source *Node-RED* [22], or the commercial *IFTTT* [21].

Similarly, our Direwolf Model Editor allows the wiring of user interface elements with backend functionality. It builds on the idea that developer and end-user communities can support each other. Our tool allows the community-driven creation of frontends by end users with domain knowledge. We are convinced that by enhancing the collaboration between end users and developers, we finally improve the tooling also for developers. In the end, the creation of context-specific, specialized user interfaces, for example, for filling a database in order processes, could be entirely done by the users themselves. Letting domain experts create their own tools puts a focus on their own mental model and understandings. Based on the established formalized descriptions of service APIs, not only graphical but also voice-based user interfaces can be designed, such as for voice assistants.

Operation After a software system is developed, it gets delivered and finally deployed to be executed and used. On a personal computer, software is downloaded and then put on the local hard disk via an installer. For smartphones, the installation process is even easier, as the app is selected in an appstore and with the click of a button, the download and installation happens, after which the app icon appears on the home screen. In web applications users can simply open up a URL and start using the app; with modern *progressive web applications*, the web applications can even be linked on the home screen, with the look and feel of native apps. On the backend, concerning services, users are left out from the possibility of installing apps. The question is therefore, how to allow community members to deploy services on their own, community-specific infrastructure. For example, a learning community in the construction sector could collect photographs of new building material on an in-house server. For this, we leverage containerized microservices. Microservices, first described by Lewis and Fowler and in a blog article [13], combine several advantages. For instance, the decoupling allows them to be developed independently. Defined interfaces (cf. the last section) make sure their compatibility, as they only have to know their deployment URL to connect. Tooling concerning the operation of microservices allows a high degree of automation. Software containers are packages that bundle services together with their libraries, so that they can be run within a sandbox with defined interfaces. This uniform format allows them to be deployed on any host and even makes it possible to change the underlying provider fast. *Docker* containers have reached mainstream adoptions as particular technology that can be run inside clusters in the cloud (e.g., *Kubernetes*).

Thus, to enable end-user communities of practice to deploy their own services, we conceptualized and implemented the *Layers Box*, a host environment for running Docker services. It is a federated cloud-in-a-box that brings industrial-strength container technology in often inexperienced professional communities. One of the main advantages is that CoPs maintain full control over their data, while keeping the authority to decide which data to share. Its high degree of automation allows it to be deployed on different kinds of hardware, that is, local servers, or within private, public, or hybrid cloud environments. The built-in *Layers Adapter* is a light-weight reverse proxy that accepts incoming service calls over HTTP and forwards them to internally registered services. In the case of a sudden cloud burst, it may also forward requests to previously configured remote Layers Boxes. As additional core part, all Layers Boxes come with a single sign-on solution. For this, we chose the *OpenID Connect* (OIDC) authentication standard, which is built on top of the *OAuth2* authorization framework. OIDC is also supported by a number of online account providers like Google, Auth0, or the German netID. Under the hood, our OIDC server can connect to existing LDAP or Shibboleth user directories.

When deploying services close to professional communities using them, we are entering the field of edge computing [48]. In the literature, typical use cases that leverage the low latency on the edge are analytics [49], machine learning, or visual applications in the area of augmented and virtual reality [15]. Another possibility to reduce latency by offloading applications from the cloud is to use peer-to-peer architectures. Peer-to-peer systems break up the dichotomy of client and server. In use cases where large chunks of data need to be transferred through the network, resources can be saved by directly forwarding data on the shortest topological path. Another advantage is increased privacy, as data does not need to be routed over a central entity that can possibly intercept message content. We developed a number of tools targeted to end-user communities that leverage recent web standards to allow browser-to-browser communication [26]. We were able to show that by providing abstractions in terms of library supported, the increased complexity can be managed well. Besides, advanced standards on the web render service discovery of local Internet of Things devices possible, without the indirection of a cloud. In particular, we connected the ideas of end-user development and the IoT [28].

Usage We conclude the DevOpsUse life cycle by focusing on its usage aspect and, in particular, on analytics functionalities. Gartner reports several commercial tools for analytical reasoning [20], for instance, *RapidMiner* and *Tableau*. *KNIME* is another visual workflow builder for interactive data analytics [3]. There are also tools specialized on visualizing aspects of the Internet of Things, like the *IBM Watson IoT Platform* [19] and the *Bosch IoT Suite* [6]. While DevOps focuses on metrics provided by the host environment that are interesting to developers and operators, DevOpsUse extends the approach to integrate end users by giving them tools for self-monitoring. Through collaboration and awareness functionalities, multifaceted visual analytics with possibly conflicting views about interpretation of results can be carried out. Our SWEVA tool allows to collaboratively design processing pipelines while accessing a variety of community-specific data sources. We thereby leverage visual analytics that combines the power of computer-generated analytics and human interpretation. The approach is universally applicable and easy-to-use and runs on all web platforms, even on constrained devices, as processing can be offloaded to more powerful nodes running microservices. As a use case spanning the mentioned interplay of IoT, human, and services, we demonstrated its usability within the *Immersive Community Learning Analytics* scenario portrayed in Fig. 4. Learning analytics aims to collect, manage, analyze, and exploit data from learners

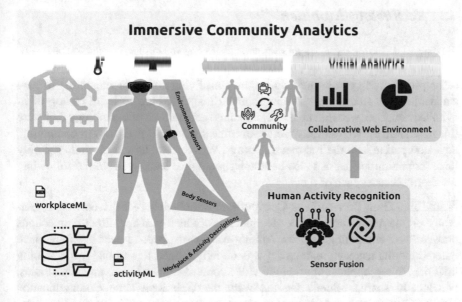

Fig. 4 Immersive community analytics of human activities on the shopfloor

and instructors to facilitate the actual learning process [25]. It connects body-worn sensors described by the ARLEM standard with a data processing infrastructuring running sensor fusion. The results are visualized within the web browser running in the augmented reality headset.

For an in-depth discussion on community-aware analytics capabilities, for example, including the design of community information system success measures, we refer to the dissertation [26]. Generally, our methodology and tool acknowledge the collaboration between involved stakeholders. It is a concern that influences all phases of software engineering. Although it is in the nature of stakeholder collaboration, advanced real-time collaboration capabilities need to be made explicit and integrated into development support tools.

4 Methodological and Technical Evaluation

We evaluate our methodology regarding three aspects. First, we look at three major advancements of the web on a technological level; our framework was not only able to handle but even to support them. We then show how evidences of DevOpsUse tools and processes can be found in a real societal research and development projects and present best practices. Finally, we look at the inherently more complex area of Industry 4.0 and show how DevOpsUse relates to it and provides a path for its continuous innovation.

4.1   Technology Evolution

Starting as a document exchange platform between researchers at CERN, the web has come a long way and is now spreading into more and more areas. The speed of its proliferation can be noticed by the conceiving and implementation of new standards. This frequently changing context makes it hard to build on top of it. With DevOpsUse, we were able to tackle three generations of technology that were integrated into the web's infrastructure over the last decade: peer-to-peer computing, edge computing, and the Internet of Things. We thereby show that we do not only target communities but can also handle technological leaps well. In the following, we shortly discuss each of them.

Near Real-Time Peer-to-Peer Computing The client/server-driven web is generally orthogonal to peer-to-peer technologies, which aim for direct connections between two computing devices. Among consumers, peer-to-peer has long since entered the mainstream, although it was initially tainted due to major file-sharing lawsuits. Today, applications include video conferencing, blockchain technologies, and locally shared folders. On the web, the Web Real-Time Communication (WebRTC) standard made browser-to-browser messages possible around the year 2013 with Google's Chrome browser. In 2017, Apple and Microsoft followed with their own implementations, and only recently, in January 2021, the version 1.0 of the standard was announced by the W3C and IETF organizations. We evaluated the technology early on and were able to cut browser-to-browser roundtrip latency from around 150 ms to around 25 ms in a local network [27]. Specifically, following the methodological core of building upon standards, we were able to replace the connection layer of a collaborative multi-display user interface from a client/server to a peer-to-peer architecture, without touching the user interface source code itself. This enabled new use cases like gaming across browsers.

Edge Computing With the Layers Box, we pioneered self-managed installations of services on-premise. In the meantime, the open-source Kubernetes platform has taken over the market rapidly. Serverless computing is a next evolutionary step in the history of componentization and modularization that microservice architectures pioneered for backend services. They further encapsulation service modules into dedicated functions, each responsible for a single API call. This makes onboarding new developers easier, as no large monolithic technology stack needs to be learned to integrate new functionality. As it is possible to further package these into Docker containers, they can be easily integrated into our Layers Box. The web is currently undergoing another technological transition from resource-oriented to query-based service interfaces. In this evolutionary step, the GraphQL framework for query-based API access gains popularity. In a recent work, we were able to provide automated transformations from the previously used OpenAPI stack to GraphQL [31]. This relatively simple step allows all of our end-user modeling tools to still be used.

Internet of Things The model-based approach of connecting the API description language OpenAPI to IFML as described in Sect. 3.2 can be extended to the Internet of Things as well. For that we can leverage the AsyncAPI documentation convention that describes asynchronous event-based architectures as they are common in the Internet of Things [2]. Again, in our tools, the replacement is a minor step, yet it enables entirely new use cases.

The societal impact of each one of these technological steps is profound. Beyond web information systems, the framework and its open-source tools are applicable in further innovative areas like mixed reality and Industry 4.0.

4.2   Best Practice Guidelines

We were able to demonstrate our methodology's capabilities through longitudinal studies in several large-scale international digitalization projects. Additionally, scalability and involvement aspects were confirmed in entrepreneurial and medical teaching courses. In the former, our student researchers acting as developers (computer scientists) were asked to use and evaluate tools like Requirements Bazaar. In the context of the latter studies, medical students in turn used the end-user-oriented tools. Most of societal research problems require complex information systems that need to be developed. Due to the involvement of our research group in multiple European projects in the area of Technology-Enhanced Learning (TEL), it was obvious to analyze their technology development. The area of lifelong learning in TEL is particularly interesting to aspects of societal software development, as its main subjects are humans and their learning capabilities in changing professional environments. The speed at which new skills are needed as workplaces continue their digital transformation is increasing.

Figure 5 portrays information system design and development activities within the Learning Layers project of the European Commission (Framework Program 7, runtime 2012–2016). They are put into context around the DevOpsUse life cycle. The tool development was partitioned into four co-design teams. The precise team descriptions can be found in a previous publication [33]. Two of them (Bits & Pieces and PANDORA) tackled societal issues in healthcare, while the other two were dealing with the construction sector (CAPTUS and Sharing Turbine). To analyze their processes of information system development, we collected data points like their initial requirements selection. Additionally, we gathered numerous artifacts left behind by the design teams, including various pages created and updated in the project wiki, text documents shared in the collaborative cloud space, as well as photos, videos, and audio recordings distributed within the project. Overall a flow of information (domain knowledge) comes in from the left, while on the right, developed artifacts and material can be seen. For instance, CAPTUS performed a market study. PANDORA worked with interviews of end users and developers. The Sharing Turbine team organized group workshops. Bits & Pieces created user interface mockups and discussed them with researchers.

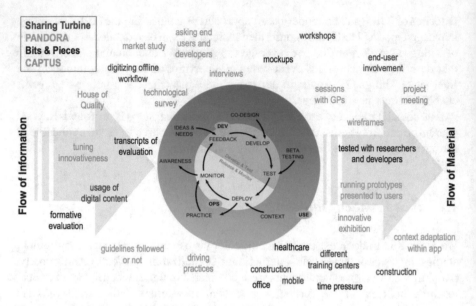

Fig. 5 DevOpsUse case study with four co-design teams

Following our experiences in these and multiple other research projects dealing with societal matters, we distilled best practices and recommendations to tackle common software engineering challenges, which we presented in detail earlier [46]. Here, we shortly outline the main recommendations. Generally, they can be divided into social and technical instruments. Social aspects play a major role in community-driven information systems development. We therefore set up two subcommunities. One is the *developer task force*, a group of developers that regularly meet to tackle everyday issues in software development. The other is a governing body or *architecture board* that decides with wider, often strategic impact on the project.

Concerning the technical setting, we suggest multiple building blocks. The technological development infrastructure needs to be standardized across participating organizations. Following the ideas of open innovation in open-source systems [52] they work best when the pivotal point is institutionalized, that is, central information systems need to be set up and fixed early on. For instance, it includes services for source code management and versioning, continuous integration, continuous delivery, continuous deployment, as well as continuous innovation by tools like Requirements Bazaar. These systems should be interconnected via means of automation, for example, to perform regression tests. The particular software systems need to be decided early on to not hamper the initial development efforts. However, they should not be understood as a fixed entity that cannot change over time and across projects. Recommendations change over time because of the everlasting duality between social and technical development. Pointers to particular software are highly susceptible to changes in the tool environment and licenses. Overall, integration should be a convergent force on three layers. First, social integration should happen with application partners, end users, and domain experts. Second, server-side integration ensures that services are compatible to each other. Third, client-side integration makes it possible to share data across apps.

As a one-stop shop for interested open-source developers, a developer hub should collect all project documentation and resources like libraries. These dedicated websites collecting all of an enterprise's offers for developers or integrators are also pursued by large companies like Google and Amazon. For instance, in our experience, video tutorials with accompanying textual documentation about particular APIs work well as teaching material. Additionally, in our case, we were able to retarget these videos for teaching DevOpsUse in our entrepreneurial lab course [10].

4.3 Application in Industry 4.0

In the last section we discussed the application of DevOpsUse in the realm of large-scale societal development projects. An area that is even harder to manage is the inherently complex Industry 4.0 setting. The term Industry 4.0 refers to the fourth industrial revolution, driven by digital transformation and characterized by data-driven insights [32]. Figure 6 discusses a typical setting in industrial companies today. The environments are divided into the *development*, *production*, and *user*. While in information systems development there are numerous programming languages, integrated development environments, and runtime frameworks, the production (planning) landscape is characterized by an even more diverse set of design and planning software, file formats, product, and runtime specifications. This leads to disruptive and incompatible data exchange. For instance, data and models are only available within proprietary systems and not ready for cross-domain use.

These incompatibilities in information systems can be generally considered less resource-intensive compared to asset-heavy industrial settings. Still, modern production settings heavily rely on software, making particular aspects of DevOpsUse applicable. In the interdisciplinary cluster of excellence *Internet of Production* at RWTH Aachen University that started in 2019, we are currently actively implementing the methodological findings of our research. Here, data plays a much larger role than in the socio-technical systems of TEL that were discussed in Sect. 4.2. First achievements were setting up a large-scale Kubernetes-based server cluster that is able to instantiate services in Docker containers. Within this cluster, we have put in place multiple databases to create a *data lake* [44] that ingests raw data from production and makes it available for later data-driven operations. Following our own recommendations, a central identity provider (Keycloak) is authenticating and authorizing human users, and later industrial assets that want to push data into the data lake. With the help of model-based technologies we want to automatically generate data schemas from SysML descriptions. Machine learning algorithms will then be able to work on the data to generate (real-time) insights to automate processes.

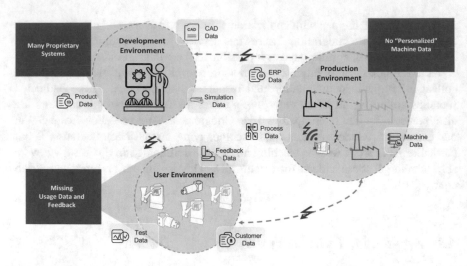

Fig. 6 Challenges of production settings

While this work is still at its infancy, we have already made significant progress setting up open-source web technologies. For instance, we are currently evaluating the use of the new bytecode standard WebAssembly to uniformly target computational use cases on the edge and on the cloud. Another example is the use of GraphQL as the primary access layer to the data lake. Finally, the adoption of further means of the DevOpsUse methodology, like continuous innovation and automation, may unlock the full potential that Industry 4.0 promises in terms of productivity [50].

5 Conclusion

During the dissertation project, the full extent of which we could only touch on here, we developed a methodology and tool support that stabilizes the conflicting aspects evident in the development of information systems. With the advent of societal software, development processes have become much more complex and engineering methods have to consider informal structures of Communities of Practice much more than before. Our community-oriented development life cycle DevOpsUse acknowledges that existing agile methods do not integrate end users to the full extent. Using a digital ethnography approach, where we as researchers took part, we validated our findings in several large-scale societal development projects and their professional communities of practice. Our tools are available and actively enhanced as open-source solutions on GitHub.[4] Lack of interoperability between

---

[4] cf. https://github.com/rwth-acis.

new and existing tools was tackled by relying on standardized, open interfaces from industrial practice. Each software developed features synchronous remote collaboration capabilities to stress the collaborative nature of infrastructuring within communities [16]

Our work is based on the fundamental insight that communities work on their specific but web-based infrastructure. Therefore, we have been guided by infrastructuring theories from information systems and adjusted parameters on top of it, while pushing established boundaries like in the case of peer-to-peer technologies. The artifacts were created and communicated following the phases of the design science in information systems guidelines [17]. For instance, we presented and discussed results at several summer schools in the area of technology-enhanced learning, as well as the open-source community at venues such as FOSDEM. Additionally, we carried out our research together with numerous students of our technical university, for example, in yearly practice-oriented lab projects, where students work together with local high-tech startups.

We validated DevOpsUse with three technological shifts that happened on the web, namely peer-to-peer technologies, edge computing, and the Internet of Things. At the intersection of these, technical improvements such as reduced latency, economical merits, and even privacy aspects can be considered. Beyond the demonstrated technology-enhanced learning projects, our findings can be applied to other societal and industrial aspects of information systems development, such as Industry 4.0. This opens up several interesting new challenges. We are working on implementing the methodology in industry. Here, the impact of web technologies is still small, but is expected to increase significantly, driven by artificial intelligence methods that leverage data-driven technologies. In future, software engineering will likely play an even stronger role in cross-functional teams, integrating mathematical and engineering disciplines. Yet, innovation as quality characteristic heavily relies on feedback from multiple sources, in particular those of end users. Therefore, leveraging web technologies, the analytical cycle for instance of industrial manufacturers will extend into the usage cycle, that is, when produced artifacts are used by their customers.

We are convinced that our methodology is employable for future societal challenges and technological leaps as well. Information system development is best dealt with in a societal context, explicitly integrating all community members while keeping their agency and strengthening their involvement. In the end, the principles of far-reaching automation and end-user integration will pave the way for a sustainable societal software engineering.

Acknowledgments Thanks are due to all those who supported me while I was writing my PhD thesis. In the context of this chapter, I would like to thank my advisors Prof. Dr. Matthias Jarke and PD Dr. Ralf Klamma as well as the reviewers for providing helpful feedback. The thesis project has received funding from the European Commission's FP7 IP "Learning Layers" under grant agreement no. 318209, from the European Union's Horizon 2020 research and innovation program under grant agreements no. 687669 (WEKIT), and from the European Union's Erasmus Plus program, grant agreement 2017-1-NO01-KA203-034192 (AR-FOR-EU). Funded by the Deutsche Forschungsgemeinschaft (DFG, German Research Foundation) under Germany's Excellence Strategy—EXC-2023 Internet of Production—390621612.

References

1. American Heritage Dictionary of the English Language. Houghton Mifflin Harcourt (2018)
2. AsyncAPI: AsyncAPI specification 2.0.0 (2019). https://www.asyncapi.com/docs/specifications/2.0.0/
3. Berthold, M.R., Cebron, N., Dill, F., Gabriel, T.R., Kötter, T., Meinl, T., Ohl, P., Thiel, K., Wiswedel, B.: KNIME—The Konstanz information miner. SIGKDD Explor. Newsl. **11**(1), 26 (2009). https://doi.org/10.1145/1656274.1656280
4. Bodart, F., Vanderdonckt, J.: Widget standardisation through abstract interaction objects. In: In Advances in Applied Ergonomics, pp. 300–305. USA Publishing (1996)
5. Bødker, S., Dindler, C., Iversen, O.S.: Tying Knots: participatory infrastructuring at work. Comput. Supported Coop. Work **26**(1–2), 245–273 (2017). https://doi.org/10.1007/s10606-017-9268-y
6. Bosch: Bosch's IoT platform (2017). https://www.bosch-si.com/de/iot-plattform/bosch-iot-suite/homepage-bosch-iot-suite.html
7. Brambilla, M., Fraternali, P.: Interaction flow modeling language: model-driven UI engineering of web and mobile apps with IFML. The MK/OMG Press. Morgan Kaufmann (2014)
8. Calvary, G., Coutaz, J., Thevenin, D., Limbourg, Q., Bouillon, L., Vanderdonckt, J.: A Unifying Reference Framework for multi-target user interfaces. Interact. Comput. **15**(3), 289–308 (2003). https://doi.org/10.1016/S0953-5438(03)00010-9
9. Chesbrough, H.W.: Open Innovation: The New Imperative for Creating and Profiting from Technology. Harvard Business School Press, Boston (2003)
10. de Lange, P., Nicolaescu, P., Klamma, R., Koren, I.: DevOpsUse for rapid training of agile practices within undergraduate and startup communities. In: Verbert, K., Sharples, M., Klobučar, T. (eds.) Adaptive and Adaptable Learning. Lecture Notes in Computer Science, vol. 9891, pp. 570–574. Springer, Cham (2016). https://doi.org/10.1007/978-3-319-45153-4_65
11. Ebert, C., Gallardo, G., Hernantes, J., Serrano, N.: DevOps. IEEE Softw **33**(3), 94–100 (2016). https://doi.org/10.1109/MS.2016.68
12. Fowler, M., Highsmith, J.: The agile manifesto. Softw. Dev. **9**(8), 28–35 (2001). http://users.jyu.fi/~mieijala/kandimateriaali/Agile-Manifesto.pdf
13. Fowler, M., Lewis, J.: Microservices (2014). http://martinfowler.com/articles/microservices.html
14. Groen, E.C., Doerr, J., Adam, S.: Towards crowd-based requirements engineering a research preview. In: Fricker, S.A., Schneider, K. (eds.) Requirements Engineering: Foundation for Software Quality. Lecture Notes in Computer Science, vol. 9013, pp. 247–253. Springer, Cham (2015). https://doi.org/10.1007/978-3-319-16101-3_16
15. Ha, K., Pillai, P., Richter, W., Abe, Y., Satyanarayanan, M.: Just-in-time provisioning for cyber foraging. In: Proceeding of the 11th Annual International Conference on Mobile Systems, Applications, and Services, pp. 153–166 (2013). https://doi.org/10.1145/2462456.2464451
16. Hanseth, O., Lundberg, N.: Designing work oriented infrastructures. Comput. Supported Cooper. Work **10**(3–4), 347–372 (2001). https://doi.org/10.1023/A:1012727708439
17. Hevner, A.R., March, S.T., Park, J., Ram, S.: Design science in information systems research. MIS Q. **28**(1), 75–105 (2004). http://dl.acm.org/citation.cfm?id=2017212.2017217
18. Hippel, E.V.: Lead users: a source of novel product concepts. Manag. Sci. **32**(7), 791–805 (1986). https://doi.org/10.1287/mnsc.32.7.791
19. IBM: Watson IoT Platform (2017). https://www.ibm.com/internet-of-things/platform/watson-iot-platform/

20. Idoine, C., Krensky, P., Brethenoux, E., Linden, A.: Magic Quadrant for Data Science and Machine Learning Platforms (2019). https://www.gartner.com/doc/reprints?id=1-65WC0O1& ct=190128&st=sb

21. IFTTT Inc.: IFTTT (2018). https://ifttt.com/

22. JS Foundation: Node-RED (2018). https://nodered.org/

23. Keim, D.A., Andrienko, G., Fekete, J.D., Görg, C., Kohlhammer, J., Melançon, G.: Visual analytics: definition, process, and challenges. In: Kerren, A., Stasko, J., Fekete, J.D. North, C. (eds.) Information Visualization. LNCS, vol. 4950, pp. 154–175. Springer, Berlin (2008). https://doi.org/10.1007/978-3-540-70956-5_7

24. Khodadadi, F., Dastjerdi, A.V., Buyya, R.: Simurgh: A framework for effective discovery, programming, and integration of services exposed in IoT. In: 2015 International Conference on Recent Advances in Internet of Things (RIoT), pp. 1–6 (2015). https://doi.org/10.1109/RIOT. 2015.7104910

25. Klamma, R.: Community learning analytics—challenges and opportunities. In: Wang, J.F., Lau, R.W.H. (eds.) Advances in Web-Based Learning: ICWL 2013. Lecture Notes in Computer Science, vol. 8167, pp. 284–293. Springer, Berlin (2013). https://doi.org/10.1007/978-3-642-41175-5_29

26. Koren, I.: DevOpsUse: Community-Driven Continuous Innovation of Web Information Infrastructures. Ph.D. Thesis, RWTH Aachen University (2020). https://doi.org/10.18154/RWTH-2020-06868

27. Koren, I., Bavendiek, J., Klamma, R.: DireWolf goes pack hunting: a peer-to-peer approach for secure low latency widget distribution using WebRTC. In: Casteleyn, S., Rossi, G., Winckler, M. (eds.) Web Engineering. LNCS, pp. 507–510. Springer, Cham (2014). https://doi.org/10. 1007/978-3-319-08245-5_38

28. Koren, I., Klamma, R.: The Direwolf inside you: end user development for heterogeneous web of things appliances. In: Bozzon, A., Cudre-Maroux, P., Pautasso, C. (eds.) Web Engineering. Lecture Notes in Computer Science, vol. 9671, pp. 484–491. Springer, Cham (2016). https:// doi.org/10.1007/978-3-319-38791-8_35

29. Koren, I., Klamma, R.: Enabling visual community learning analytics with Internet of Things devices. Comput. Hum. Behav. **89**, 385–394 (2018). https://doi.org/10.1016/j.chb.2018.07.036

30. Koren, I., Klamma, R., Jarke, M.: Direwolf model academy: an extensible collaborative modeling framework on the web. In: Michael, J., Bork, D. (eds.) Modellierung 2020 Short, Workshop and Tools & Demo Papers, pp. 213–216 (2020). http://ceur-ws.org/Vol-2542/ MOD20-TuD5.pdf

31. Kus, D.A., Koren, I., Klamma, R.: A link generator for increasing the utility of OpenAPI-to-GraphQL translations (2020). https://arxiv.org/abs/2005.08708

32. Lasi, H., Fettke, P., Kemper, H.G., Feld, T., Hoffmann, M.: Industrie 4.0. Wirtschaftsinformatik **56**(4), 261–264 (2014). https://doi.org/10.1007/s11576-014-0424-4

33. Ley, T., Cook, J., Dennerlein, S., Kravcik, M., Kunzmann, C., Pata, K., Purma, J., Sandars, J., Santos, P., Schmidt, A., Al-Smadi, M., Trattner, C.: Scaling informal learning at the workplace: a model and four designs from a large-scale design-based research effort. Br. J. Educational Technol. **45**(6), 1036–1048 (2014). https://doi.org/10.1111/bjet.12197

34. Lieberman, H., Paternò, F., Klann, M., Wulf, V.: End-user development: an emerging paradigm. In: Lieberman, H., Paternò, F., Wulf, V. (eds.) End User Development. Human-Computer Interaction Series, vol. 9, pp. 1–8. Springer, Dordrecht (2006). https://doi.org/10.1007/1-4020-5386-X_1

35. Marttila, S., Botero, A.: Infrastructuring for cultural commons. Comput. Supported Coop. Work **26**(1–2), 97–133 (2017). https://doi.org/10.1007/s10606-017-9273-1

36. Maximilien, E.M., Wilkinson, H., Desai, N., Tai, S.: A domain-specific language for web APIs and services mashups. In: Krämer, B.J., Lin, K.J., Narasimhan, P. (eds.) Service-Oriented Computing—ICSOC. Lecture Notes in Computer Science, vol. 4749, pp. 13–26. Springer, Berlin (2007). https://doi.org/10.1007/978-3-540-74974-5_2.

37. Nestler, T., Feldmann, M., Hübsch, G., Preußner, A., Jugel, U.: The ServFace builder—a WYSIWYG approach for building service-based applications. In: Benatallah, B., Casati, F.,

Kappel, G., Rossi, G. (eds.) Web Engineering. Lecture Notes in Computer Science, vol. 6189, pp. 498–501. Springer, Berlin (2010). https://doi.org/10.1007/978-3-642-13911-6_37

38. OpenAPI Initiative: The OpenAPI Specification: Version 3.0.2 (2018). https://www.openapis. org

39. Paterno, F., Mancini, C., Meniconi, S.: ConcurTaskTrees: A diagrammatic notation for specifying task models. In: Howard, S., Hammond, J., Lindgaard, G. (eds.) Human-Computer Interaction INTERACT '97, pp. 362–369. Springer, Boston (1997). https://doi.org/10.1007/ 978-0-387-35175-9_58

40. Pautasso, C., Zimmermann, O.: The web as a software connector: integration resting on linked resources. IEEE Softw. **35**(1), 93–98 (2017). https://doi.org/10.1109/MS.2017.4541049

41. Pipek, V., Syrjänen, A.L.: Infrastructuring as capturing in-situ design. In: 7th Mediterranean Conference on Information Systems (2006)

42. Pipek, V., Wulf, V.: Infrastructuring: Towards an integrated perspective on the design and use of information technology. J. Assoc. Inform. Syst. **10**(5), 447–473 (2009)

43. Pohl, K.: Requirements Engineering: Fundamentals, Principles, and Techniques. Springer, Heidelberg and New York (2010)

44. Quix, C., Hai, R.: Data lake. In: Sakr, S., Zomaya, A. (eds.) Encyclopedia of Big Data Technologies, pp. 1–8. Springer International Publishing, Cham (2018). https://doi.org/10. 1007/978-3-319-63962-8_7-1

45. Renzel, D., Klamma, R. (eds.): Large-Scale Social Requirements Engineering, vol. 2. IEEE Special Technical Community on Social Networking (IEEE STCSN) (2014)

46. Renzel, D., Koren, I., Klamma, R., Jarke, M.: Preparing research projects for sustainable software engineering in society. In: Proceedings 2017 IEEE/ACM 39th IEEE International Conference on Software Engineering (ICSE) (2017). https://doi.org/10.1109/ICSE-SEIS.2017. 4

47. Sanders, E.B.N., Stappers, P.J.: Co-creation and the new landscapes of design. CoDesign **4**(1), 5–18 (2008). https://doi.org/10.1080/15710880701875068

48. Satyanarayanan, M., Bahl, P., Cáceres, R., Davies, N.: The case for VM-based cloudlets in mobile computing. IEEE Pervasive Comput. **8**(4), 14–23 (2009). https://doi.org/10.1109/ MPRV.2009.82

49. Satyanarayanan, M., Simoens, P., Xiao, Y., Pillai, P., Chen, Z., Ha, K., Hu, W., Amos, B.: Edge analytics in the Internet of Things. IEEE Pervasive Comput. **14**(2), 24–31 (2015). https://doi. org/10.1109/MPRV.2015.32

50. Schuh, G., Potente, T., Wesch-Potente, C., Weber, A.R., Prote, J.P.: Collaboration mechanisms to increase productivity in the context of industrie 4.0. Proc. CIRP **19**, 51–56 (2014). https:// doi.org/10.1016/j.procir.2014.05.016

51. Star, S.L., Bowker, G.C.: How to infrastructure. In: Lievrouw, L.A., Livingstone, S. (eds.) Handbook of New Media: Social Shaping and Consequences of ICTs, pp. 151–162. SAGE Publications, London (2002). https://doi.org/10.4135/9781848608245.n12

52. Tuomi, I.: Internet, innovation, and open source: actors in the network. First Monday **6**(1) (2001). https://doi.org/10.5210/fm.v6i1.824. http://firstmonday.org/ojs/index.php/fm/ article/view/824/733

53. Wenger, E.: Communities of Practice: Learning, Meaning, and Identity. Learning in Doing. Cambridge University Press, Cambridge (1998)

Hybrid Differential Software Testing

Yannic Noller

Abstract Differential software testing is important for software quality assurance as it aims to automatically generate test inputs that reveal behavioral differences in software. Detecting regression bugs in software evolution, analyzing side-channels in programs, maximizing the execution cost of a program over multiple executions, and evaluating the robustness of neural networks are instances of differential software analysis to generate diverging executions of program paths. The key challenge thereby is to simultaneously reason about multiple program paths, often across program variants, in an efficient way. Existing work in differential testing is often not (specifically) directed to reveal a different behavior or is limited to a subset of the search space. This work proposes the concept of Hybrid Differential Software Testing (HYDIFF) as a hybrid analysis technique to generate difference revealing inputs. HYDIFF consists of two components that operate in a parallel setup: (1) a search-based technique that inexpensively generates inputs and (2) a systematic exploration technique to also exercise deeper program behaviors. HYDIFF's search-based component uses differential fuzzing directed by differential heuristics. HYDIFF's systematic exploration component is based on differential dynamic symbolic execution that allows to incorporate concrete inputs in its analysis. HYDIFF is evaluated experimentally with applications specific for differential testing. The results show that HYDIFF is effective in all considered categories and outperforms its components in isolation.

Please note that this book chapter is a condensed version of the original dissertation [1] and the corresponding publications [2–7].

Y. Noller (✉)
National University of Singapore, Singapore, Singapore
e-mail: yannic.noller@acm.org

© The Author(s) 2022
M. Felderer et al. (eds.), *Ernst Denert Award for Software Engineering 2020*,
https://doi.org/10.1007/978-3-030-83128-8_9

167

1 Introduction

Software Engineering (SE) is the "systematic application of scientific and tech-nological knowledge, methods, and experience to the design, implementation, testing, and documentation of software," as defined by the IEEE [8]. A key insight in the community is that "programming-in-the-large" [9] is much more com-plex than "programming-in-the-small", and hence, requires a proper *engineering* approach [10]. The objective of SE *research* is the study of how to develop software (in the large), in order to provide the scientific knowledge and methods to do so. It searches for techniques to improve, simplify, and support software development. A crucial part of software development is *software quality assurance* facilitated by *software testing* [8], as it searches for *errors* in software.

Therefore, software testing is an essential part of software development, which is widely applied by practitioners and is also the focus of numerous research projects [11]. The goal is to provide confidence in the correctness of software by searching for errors in its behavior. The manual creation of test cases can be very expensive and time consuming. Therefore, recent research has focused on *automated test input generation* [11, 12]. Identified errors can be investigated and fixed, and so, software testing contributes to the quality of the software.

A special area in this research field is *differential software testing*, which aims to identify *behavioral differences* in software, that is, differences in the execution behavior of a program. Such differences can be represented by several forms, for example, a difference in the direct output of a program, a difference in the execution time, or also a difference in the covered code fragments. *Differential program analysis* (here also called *differential software testing*) means the analysis of one or multiple programs in order to reveal behavioral differences. In general, the search for behavioral differences can be separated into two categories: It can reveal divergences between two execution paths (1) of different program versions or (2) within the same program. Figure 1 illustrates these two types of differential analysis. Category (1) (on the left side of Fig. 1) searches for input x that leads to a different execution behavior between program P and its successive variant P'. Note that generally P and P' can be completely different programs. Category (2) (on the right side of Fig. 1) searches for two different inputs x and y that lead to a different execution behavior for (the same) program P. Depending on the application it can be interesting how similar the two inputs are. Both analysis categories require multiple program executions, which makes differential software testing a *challenging* problem.

For example, differential testing is often applied in *software maintenance* to perform *regression testing* [13, 14], where the goal is to reveal differences between two successive software versions. Such differences can be observed, for example, along the control-flow or in the actual output of the execution. Other flavors of differential program analysis are used in the area of software security to perform automated *vulnerability detection*, for example, with regard to *worst-case execution paths* [15, 16] or *side channels* [17–19]. For example, *algorithmic complexity vulnerabilities* can be exploited to cause a denial of service attack. *Side-channel*

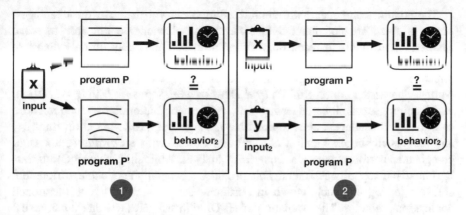

Fig. 1 Two categories of differential software testing

vulnerabilities can be exploited to reveal sensitive information by observing the nonfunctional characteristics of the program behavior, such as the execution time, memory consumption, response size, or network traffic. A novel application of differential analysis is the robustness analysis of *neural networks* [20, 21], which concerns the *software reliability*. This kind of analysis aims to identify two inputs that differ only very slightly, that is, for a human almost imperceptible, but for which the neural network produces a different output (e.g., it results in different classifications) [22]. The differences between such inputs are also called *adversarial perturbations* and represent major safety and security issues.

This work focuses on the above problem of *differential* software testing with its numerous application areas. In particular, it develops concepts and techniques for the automated generation of test inputs that reveal behavioral differences in software. Furthermore, it provides a general framework, which can be applied to all the mentioned analysis types. In summary, differential software testing is investigated in the context of the following applications:

Application Areas

A1 Regression analysis—The search for behavioral differences with the same input in successive program versions.

A2 Worst-case complexity analysis—The search for worst-case triggering inputs that perform significantly *different* than the average case.

A3 Side-channel analysis—The search for side-channel vulnerabilities in security-critical applications, which involves analyzing correlations between resource usages over multiple program paths.

A4 Robustness analysis of neural networks—The search for adversarial behaviors in neural networks, which requires reasoning about multiple network executions.

The existing techniques in differential testing come with their own disadvantages: Many of them are not directed to differential behavior, are not able to solve necessary constraints to reach deep program behavior, or rely on an exhaustive exploration. They are limited in the effectiveness of their analysis. An efficient and effective testing approach asks for a hybrid execution setup [16, 23]. Therefore, this work proposes the concept of **HY***brid* **DIFF***erential Software Testing* (HYDIFF), which combines search-based testing with a systematic exploration technique. More specifically, this concept aims to combine the *speed* of search-based fuzzing [24] and the systematic exploration of symbolic execution in a *parallel* setup. Both components perform their own *differential* analysis, while they exchange (interesting) inputs to support each other. This provides a generally applicable, differential software testing approach, which in particular can be applied to the mentioned application scenarios. The evaluation of HYDIFF investigates whether it can reveal behavioral differences in software and how the hybrid combination performs in contrast to its components in isolation. HYDIFF is evaluated based on a quantitative analysis with benchmarks taken from the above-mentioned application scenarios.

Core Contributions

C1 The **concept of differential fuzzing** that incorporates various differential metrics to provide a general differential analysis. In particular it allows the search for side-channel vulnerabilities because it also uses cost metrics to determine the cost difference of two executions.

C2 The **concept of differential dynamic symbolic execution** as a technique to perform a dynamic symbolic exploration driven by differential heuristics, which allows to incorporate concrete inputs during the analysis. This allows the continuous guidance of the symbolic exploration to interesting program behaviors.

C3 The **concept of a general hybrid approach** in differential program analysis, which combines the strengths of single techniques in this research field. This concept closes a gap in the research of differential program analysis that is currently performed by specialized techniques with their own advantages and disadvantages. The hybrid concept allows to combine their advantages and compensate their disadvantages.

C4 The **concept of a hybrid setup** for applying fuzzing and symbolic execution **in parallel** as an alternative to already existing hybrid approaches in test input generation. The parallel environment allows that both techniques can continue their own powerful differential analysis while being supported by the results of the other component.

2   Hybrid Differential Testing: Assumptions and Concept

Assumptions The overall goal of this work is to generate test inputs that expose behavioral differences. The assumption thereby is that existing tests, like a regression test suite, are not sufficient to expose the behavioral differences. This assumption is valid because existing work has shown that regression test suites need augmentation to cover the changed behavior [25] as well as prioritization or minimization to make its execution feasible [25, 26]. The assumption is also valid for other applications of differential software testing that aim to discover security vulnerabilities or to show robustness issues. They represent *unexpected* behavior that is challenging to avoid [16, 18, 27], and there are usually no existing tests to discover them. Therefore, there is a need to generate these inputs. Furthermore, the proposed techniques in this work are designed to be effective with only one valid seed input that is used to initially execute the application under test. This increases the applicability of the presented techniques because they only make little assumptions about the availability of existing tests for the application.

Concept The concept of **HY***brid* **DIFF***erential Software Testing* (HYDIFF) is to combine powerful techniques to tackle the problem of test input generation to reveal *behavioral differences* in software. Differential software testing approaches a difficult problem because it generally requires to reason about multiple program executions. The existing work on differential analysis does not provide yet any hybrid differential software testing approach. Furthermore, the existing single approaches for a differential analysis have their own limitations. Therefore, this work proposes the usage of a *hybrid* approach, which combines random-based exploration (fuzzing) and systematic exploration (symbolic execution). The hybrid setup includes the exchange of interesting inputs between both single approaches that run in parallel. Both approaches can benefit from each other, and the overall analysis can explore a larger state space, while quickly generating results.

In order to illustrate this idea, Fig. 2 shows the overall concept. By running fuzzing and symbolic execution in parallel, both single techniques can perform their own exploration and can incorporate *interesting* inputs from the other component as well. This supports fuzzing to overcome narrow constraints in the program by importing inputs from symbolic execution, which is a whitebox technique that can analyze and solve these constraints with a constraint solver. Additionally, this hybrid concept also provides guidance for symbolic execution to focus on *interesting* program areas triggered by inputs from the fuzzing component. The term *interesting* depends on the specific type of the differential analysis. For example, in the context of regression analysis, an interesting input exposes a divergence between two program versions, while in the context of worst-case complexity analysis an interesting input maximizes the cost of the program execution. For a hybrid differential analysis, both single techniques need to be able to perform their own differential analysis.

Fig. 2 Conceptual overview
of the parallel hybrid
exploration

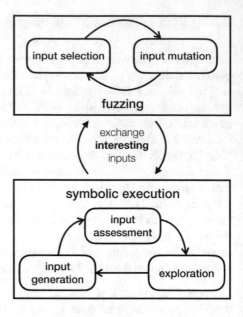

Differential Fuzzing (DF) *Fuzzing* as a representative of inexpensive, random-based exploration techniques [28] can generate a large number of inputs in a short time period due to its low overhead. Therefore, fuzzing is known for its input generation *speed* [24]. However, fuzzing is based on random operators and is usually implemented as blackbox or greybox technique. It lacks the knowledge about the program to go beyond complex constraints that guard deeper program behavior [24].

Similarly to standard fuzzing techniques, the proposed differential fuzzing process consists of a loop between *input selection* and *input mutation* (see the upper box in Fig. 2). The input mutation applies various mutation operators to generate new inputs. The input selection determines which mutated inputs are reported as *interesting* and which are kept for following evolutions. In order to perform a differential analysis, the input selection is driven by *differential heuristics*.

Differential Dynamic Symbolic Execution (DDSE) Existing approaches based on *(dynamic) symbolic execution* [29, 30] provide a systematic exploration of the state space, which can be guided by several heuristics. They have the full knowledge about the program, and hence, can unleash the full spectrum of program analysis techniques, for example, to reach low-probability branches. However, the scope of symbolic execution is usually limited to smaller programs because its systematic exploration encounters the path explosion problem and expensive path constraints solving [24]. Therefore, it does not scale to real-world applications.

The proposed differential (dynamic) symbolic execution consists of a loop between *input assessment*, *exploration*, and *input generation* (see the lower box in Fig. 2). The input assessment performs a concolic execution of concrete inputs, which includes the analysis of the executed branches based on *differential heuristics*.

This analysis results in the identification and ranking of unexplored branches. The highest ranked, unexplored branch is used as starting point for some additional symbolic exploration. The resulting constraints of newly explored paths are extracted and used to generate new concrete inputs. These inputs are again associated with concolic execution, which also reports interesting inputs for the fuzzing component.

3 Differential Fuzzing

Fuzzing Background Fuzzing [28] is a powerful technique to generate inputs that reveal errors (e.g., crashes) in programs. Recent fuzzing research efforts focus on optimizing the search process to find more crashes and cover more code [31, 32]. The metric to select new inputs from the mutated inputs for keeping them in the mutation corpus is only based on the ability to increase the code coverage. Leveraging a fuzzer for differential program analysis appears to be interesting due to the fact that behavioral differences might be triggered by unexpected inputs, which is exactly what fuzzing is made for. Nevertheless, for a differential program analysis the current fuzzing approaches need to be significantly extended. The fuzzer should not only generate inputs for crashes or increased code coverage but should specifically search for difference revealing inputs. In addition to coverage-based fuzzing, there are also efforts on directing fuzzing to specific program areas, for example, with AFLGo [33]. However, such approaches cannot be explicitly targeted to differential behavior. Nevertheless, such guiding capabilities are crucial because, for example, hitting the areas of changed code is a key ability to find regression bugs.

In general, a mutation-based fuzzer can be guided by three parameters: the seed inputs, the applied mutation operators, and the selection mechanism.

Guidance by Seed Inputs Guiding a fuzzer by its *seed inputs* requires existing inputs that already touch interesting areas of the program under test. Although in general an existing test suite can provide good seed inputs, it is a rather strong assumption that there are enough existing test inputs to sufficiently guide fuzzing. Additionally, a fuzzer will likely leave the areas touched by the seed inputs quite fast, based on its random mutation operators. A differential fuzzer should be able to make progress even without good seed inputs and at the same time it should have the possibility to incorporate new seed inputs during its fuzzing process.

Guidance by Mutation Operators Guiding a fuzzer with its mutation operators is already implemented to some extent in the state-of-the-art greybox fuzzers. For example AFL [34] implements mutation operators, which insert "known interesting integers" like 0, 1, or maximum values of data types like `Integer.MAX_VALUE`. Such mutation operators make sense when searching purely for crashes in programs, but might not be as efficient for a differential analysis. In differential analyses we need to guide the fuzzer first in interesting areas of the program, where actually a difference is occurring.

Guidance by Selection Finally, the third option to guide the fuzzing process is the selection mechanism. In evolutionary algorithms, as they are used in fuzzing [31, 34], the mutant selection is the core guidance procedure. The selection procedure determines whether a mutant is kept in the mutation corpus and, hence, is reused for future mutations, or whether a mutant is eliminated. Therefore, a smart selection of mutants significantly helps to guide the fuzzer into interesting program behaviors. Typically, a fuzzer like AFL would identify inputs that produce program crashes, program hangs, or which cover new program branches because the goal is to find exactly these program behaviors. Inputs that produce crashes and hangs are moved into separate output folders and are no longer used for further mutations. Only the inputs that increase the coverage are kept in the mutation corpus. A differential fuzzer has slightly different needs: Inputs that lead to crashes and hangs should be still sorted out and not kept for further mutations. However, they should only be reported if they reveal behavioral differences. On the other hand, not only inputs that increase the branch coverage should be kept in the mutation corpus but also inputs that, for example, get closer to a change, show some output difference, or show some difference in its program exploration. Therefore, a differential fuzzer needs to be *guided* by a various set of differential metrics, like *output difference*, *decision difference*, *cost difference*, and *patch distance*. Additionally, a differential fuzzer should also keep inputs that increase the program coverage, to further guide it into unexplored areas.

Differential Fuzzing (DF) is defined as a method to identify behavioral differences with a guided mutational fuzzing approach.

Approach Overview In order to provide *differential fuzzing*, this work extends coverage-guided fuzzing by modifying the mutant selection mechanism (see Fig. 3). The presented approach uses several differential metrics like output difference, decision difference, cost difference, and patch distance to assess the behavioral properties of the mutated inputs. The focus is on coverage-guided, mutational fuzzing because the related work has shown that such a search-based fuzzing approach is highly effective. Furthermore, it does not make strong assumptions about the existing testing artifacts, for example, test suites or input grammars. Mutation-based fuzzing is built on a genetic algorithm, which belongs to the class of global search algorithms, known to be flexible, that is, being able to overcome local maxima, and to scale up well to larger problems [35]. However, note that the idea of differential fuzzing is not limited to this kind of fuzzing technique.

Figure 3 shows the overview of the proposed differential fuzzing technique. Similar to coverage-based, mutational fuzzing, it starts with some initial seed inputs (see step 1 in Fig. 3). It uses a queue (see step 2 in Fig. 3) to store the current fuzzing corpus. In order to generate new mutants, it first trims the inputs (see step 3) and afterwards applies several mutation operators on the inputs (see step 4). The main difference to standard greybox fuzzing is in the mutation selection mechanism (see step 5), which is specifically designed to select mutants that show new interesting behavior properties. As outlined in step 5 in Fig. 3 it takes an input and parses it to extract the various parameters of the application, which are then used to execute the input on multiple program executions. Finally, the various observations are compared and the differences are determined. Overall, differential fuzzing keeps inputs that show new interesting behaviors for future mutant generation (see step 6).

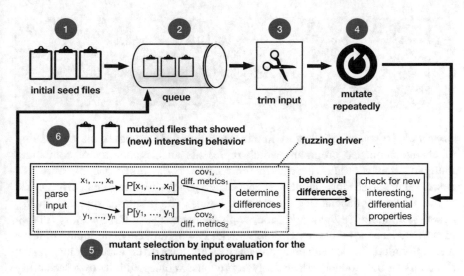

Fig. 3 Conceptual overview of differential fuzzing

4 Differential Dynamic Symbolic Execution

Symbolic Execution Background Symbolic execution [30] is well known for traversing the application in a systematic way. Under some assumption like that constraints can be solved in a reasonable time, or that third-party libraries calls can be analyzed or appropriate models are available, symbolic execution can efficiently generate test inputs to touch interesting program behavior. However, out-of-the-box symbolic execution has the limitation that it focuses on only one software version at once. A differential analysis, like regression analysis, is hence not possible with the standard symbolic execution approach.

In the last decade, a couple of approaches have been proposed to perform some sort of differential analysis with symbolic execution in the area of regression analysis [13, 14, 36, 37]. In summary, the recent advances provide the basis for a general differential testing approach, although none of them provide all necessary aspects. They either perform their analysis only on the new version, rely too much on concrete inputs for its guidance, or suffer from scalability issues, which makes it hard for a practical application. Moreover, all of them focus on regression analysis and not on a general differential analysis. For a scalable, general, and differential analysis, it needs a dynamic approach, to drive the exploration in interesting program areas. Furthermore, the differential analysis should be able to analyze multiple program versions at the same time to simplify constraints and prioritize paths early that show the best chances to reveal divergences. The analysis should allow the guidance by syntactic information about the program changes, so that paths can be pruned efficiently.

> **Differential Dynamic Symbolic Execution** (**DDSE**) is defined as a systematic exploration of the program's input space, characterized by symbolic values, which is specifically focused and guided on generating inputs that reveal behavioral differences.

Approach Overview Shadow symbolic execution [13] proposes the exploration of change-annotated programs, which represents an elegant way of combining multiple versions or allowing multiple *differential* behaviors in one execution. As described in [6], shadow symbolic execution [13] might miss important divergences due to its strong dependence on concrete inputs. The proposed approach in [6], *complete shadow symbolic execution*, explores the usage of the four-way forking idea in standard symbolic execution, without having any concrete inputs to drive the exploration. While such an approach does not miss divergences, as long as the program can be explored exhaustively, it obviously comes with its own scalability issues. Therefore, the proposed solution for *differential dynamic symbolic execution* (DDSE) allows the usage of concrete inputs to drive the exploration, but still uses a complete four-way forking approach to detect all divergences in the search space. Consequently, DDSE is driven by differential expressions introduced by change-annotations inside the program and is further guided by differential metrics like the cost difference and the patch distance. In a hybrid differential analysis setup, DDSE is receptive for guidance based on concrete inputs from the fuzzing component.

Figure 4 shows the overview of the proposed differential dynamic symbolic execution approach, consisting of five phases: (1) import of inputs, (2) input assessment, (3) exploration, (4) input generation, and (5) export of inputs. Note that all symbolic execution variants presented in Fig. 4, that is, concolic execution, trie-guided symbolic execution, and bounded symbolic execution, support the execution of a change-annotated program. All together, denoted with the dashed area in Fig. 4, form the so-called *differential dynamic symbolic execution*.

Central Data Structure: Trie The central data structure in this dynamic symbolic execution is a so-called *trie*, which has been adapted from Yang et al. [37]. A trie represents a subset of the symbolic execution tree, where nodes represent the choices during symbolic execution that include symbolic variables. Therefore, a trie is a simplified variant of a symbolic execution tree, where only the components are included, which are interesting for the analysis and which are necessary to replay specific paths in the tree. In this approach it used to store the current state of the analysis (see step 4 in Fig. 4) and to select a promising point to continue the exploration (see step 3 in Fig. 4).

(1) Input Import The process starts with *importing* initial seed inputs (see step 1 in Fig. 4). Note: The term *importing* inputs refers to the fact that such an import can not only be performed in the beginning of the analysis but also periodically throughout the whole process. This functionality is crucial for the synchronization with another technique in a hybrid setup.

(2) Input Assessment The given inputs are executed concolically, that is, the symbolic execution follows only the path of the concrete values but collects all symbolic information (i.e., the value mapping and the path constraint) along this path (see step 2 in Fig. 4). The execution is mapped to the simplified symbolic execution tree called *trie*. After the concolic execution of the given inputs, each node, which has unexplored branches, represents a potential entry point for further exploration. The nodes are analyzed and ranked with the defined *heuristics*, which is followed by the selection of the most promising node.

(3) Exploration The idea behind the expanded exploration step (see step 3 in Fig. 4) is to discover new, interesting parts of the state space. In order to reach the actual symbolic state at the selected node it starts with a *trie-guided* symbolic execution and switches to a bounded symbolic execution as soon as it hits the selected node.

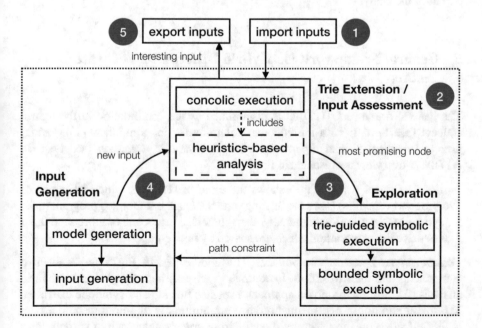

Fig. 4 Conceptual overview of dynamic, heuristic-driven symbolic execution; based on [4]

Trie-guided means that the symbolic execution simply follows the choices stored in the trie without any invocation of a constraint solver. This step is very efficient and builds the symbolic state. As soon as hitting the selected node, the execution switches to a bounded symbolic execution mode, which will perform an exhaustive symbolic execution up to a predefined bound. The exploration step results in a sequence of satisfiable path constraints.

(4) Input Generation In step 4 in Fig. 4 an SMT solver is leveraged to generate a model for each path constraint. Afterwards, these models are used to construct inputs. The input generation is application-specific since the path constraints and their models have no information about the actual input formats and requirements. Note that the inputs have been generated based on the exploration of a promising node determined by heuristics. This means that after the generation the inputs need to be assessed for their actual usefulness for the current analysis. Therefore, they are executed concolically (see step 2 in Fig. 4), and the trie is extended.

Altogether, the steps 2, 3, and 4 form an analysis loop (see dashed area in Fig. 4). The loop can be paused for the import of new inputs (e.g., in the hybrid setup), it can be stopped by a user-specified bound, or it is finished after the complete (i.e., exhaustive) exploration.

(5) Input Export As soon as a generated input is assessed as interesting, that is, it shows some new behavior interesting for the current analysis, it is reported for the export (see step 5 in Fig. 4). In a hybrid setup the exported inputs are made available for the other technique; in a single analysis setup, the exported inputs represent the output of the analysis.

5 General Framework for Hybrid Differential Software Testing

The general framework HYDIFF is instantiated as the combination of the hybrid concept (see Sect. 2) with the concrete solutions for its components *differential fuzzing* (see Sect. 3) and *differential dynamic symbolic execution* (see Sect. 4). HYDIFF's overview is presented in Fig. 5.

Inputs The upper part of Fig. 5 shows the *input* of HYDIFF, which takes one or two program version(s) (used for fuzzing) and the change-annotated program (used for symbolic execution). Additionally, the approach expects one or more seed input files to drive the exploration, which are shared by both components.

Collaborations Between Components The middle part of Fig. 5 shows the two components and their workflow. In contrast to the existing related work on hybrid analysis [24, 38], the proposed approach executes fuzzing and symbolic execution in *parallel* and not in a sequential order. The intuition is that both techniques are highly effective on their own but benefit from some guidance into certain areas

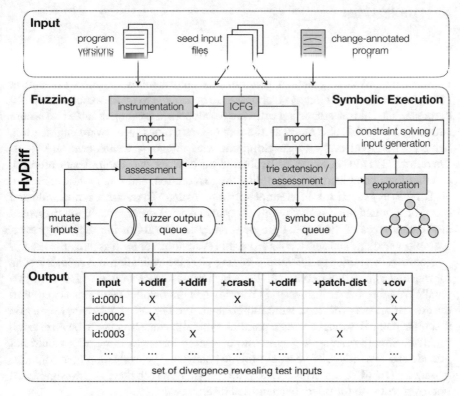

Fig. 5 Overview of HYDIFF's workflow [7]

of the search space. *Conceptually* this is performed by importing the inputs from the other's output queue (see the arrows from the output queues to the assessment nodes in both sides in the middle of Fig. 5). Additionally, both components use the information from the inter-procedural control flow graph (ICFG) to drive/prune their exploration, which is, for example, relevant for regression testing. DF leverages the ICFG to calculate the distance values, which are used to determine whether inputs get closer to the changed location(s), and hence, to guide the DF toward the modification(s). DDSE uses it to prune paths that cannot reach any changed area.

Outputs The lower part of Fig. 5 shows the expected output of the hybrid analysis, which is a list of generated inputs and their characteristics in terms of differential behavior. They are classified according to the differential metrics.

6   Applications

The main research interest in hybrid differential software testing is to expose software bugs related to differential behavior. Finding such bugs is essential to improve the software quality in general. The contributions by this work aim at providing efficient and effective techniques to contribute to this research interest. In particular, they aim at supporting software developers in creating reliable and secure software, and hence, also facilitate the main research idea in software engineering, namely to support software development with methods, techniques, and tools. Therefore, HYDIFF needs to be evaluated on how its two components proceed, whether their combination can amplify the exploration, and finally, how effective HYDIFF is in general for differential software testing. These aspects are evaluated based on a quantitative analysis with experiments and benchmarks in the presented application areas of differential program analysis. The following sections present exemplary insights and summaries from this evaluation for each application area.

Note that in addition to *differential fuzzing* (DF) the evaluation also reports results for *parallel differential fuzzing* (PDF), which represents a variant of DF with two parallel running fuzzer instances. PDF mitigates the parallel nature of HYDIFF in the evaluation and provides a more fair comparison. For DDSE it is hard to provide a similar parallel variant because parallel symbolic execution is its own research problem. Simply running two symbolic execution instances in parallel would not provide any benefit due to its deterministic behavior. The evaluation therefore also included a DDSE variant with double time budget; however, there was no significant improvement with regard to the identified differences.

6.1   Regression Analysis (A1)

Regression analysis is one of the main applications of differential program analysis where the goal is to identify behavioral differences between two successive software versions. The most meaningful semantic different behaviors are differences in the actual output of an application like the result of a calculation or another output message. Unintended behavioral differences are called *regression errors*. Regression analysis is also one of the "most extensively researched areas in [software] testing" [11] and is therefore the major focus of HYDIFF.

Example Listing 1 shows a change-annotated program, combining two versions of the program `calculate`. This program is an artificial example, which shows the strengths and drawbacks of fuzzing and symbolic execution. It processes two integer inputs, `x` and `y`, and calculates a division based on these two values. The large `switch` statement with cases from 0 to 250 (lines 4–7) is a challenge for symbolic execution because there are a lot of branches to explore. In this example it is especially problematic because none of them can be pruned because all of them can reach the changed condition in line 18, and the interesting part is at the

Listing 1 Example program for regression testing with HYDIFF [7]

```
1  int calculate(int m, int y) {
2      int div;
3      switch (x) {
4          case 0: div = y + 1; break;
5          case 1: div = y + 2; break;
6          ...
7          case 250: div = y + 251; break;
8          default:
9              if (x == 123456)
10                 // CHANGE: expression y + 123455 to y + 123456
11                 div = change(y + 123455 , y + 123456);
12             else
13                 div = x + 31;
14     }
15     int result = x / div;
16
17     // CHANGE: added conditional statement
18     if (change(false, result > 0))
19         result = result + 1;
20     return result;
21 }
```

end of the switch statement, which will be reached late in the exploration (when having a deterministic exploration order). In the default case of the switch statement (line 8), there is a check for the value 123456 representing a magic value, which guards the first change in line 11. There the developer changed the right-hand-side expression from y + 123455 to y + 123456, which fixed a division-by-zero error for y=-123455, but introduced another crash for y=-123456. In contrary to symbolic execution, fuzzing is expected to traverse the program quite fast, but it will have problems with handling the magic number. In line 19, the developer added a conditional statement result = result + 1 if result > 0. This influences the output for all positive results. However, it does not directly fix or introduce any crash.

To further illustrate the challenges of each individual component, the following paragraph first discusses the results for running both components in isolation and afterwards together in the hybrid setup. The differential fuzzing component finds its first output difference after 5.07 ($\pm$ 0.99) sec (where the $\pm$ value denotes the 95% confidence interval over 30 runs). In total it finds 1.37 ($\pm$ 0.17) output differences and 1.00 ($\pm$ 0.00) decision differences. The *new* crash is not found within the time bound of 10 min. Therefore, fuzzing is very fast in finding an output difference (less than 5 s), but the narrow constraint at the end is difficult to reach for fuzzing: (x=123456 & y=-123456). In contrast, the differential dynamic symbolic execution component finds its first output difference after 135.27 ($\pm$ 0.66) s. In total, it finds 35.10 ($\pm$ 1.10) output differences and 2.00 ($\pm$ 0.00) decision differences. So it reveals much more output differences than fuzzing within the given time bound.

In fact, the DDSE component can traverse all paths in 5 min. In contrast to fuzzing it also finds the new crash, after 135.80 ($\pm$ 0.64) s. Nonetheless, symbolic execution needs relatively long to find its first output difference. In the hybrid setup, the differential fuzzing and symbolic execution components are started with the same seed input. Both run their analysis in parallel and exchange inputs that are deemed interesting according to the divergence metrics after a prespecified time bound. The experimental results are as follows: first output difference after 4.73 ($\pm$ 0.78) s, in total 35.13 ($\pm$ 1.04) output differences and 2.00 ($\pm$ 0.00) decision differences. The hybrid technique finds the new crash already after 14.43 ($\pm$ 0.30) s. Figure 6 shows the temporal development of the results for the three techniques. Although DDSE and HYDIFF come to similar conclusions after 10 min, HYDIFF is significantly faster in finding the first output differences (as well as the crash). DF is fast in generating first results, but cannot achieve the same numbers as DDSE and HYDIFF within the 10 min time bound.

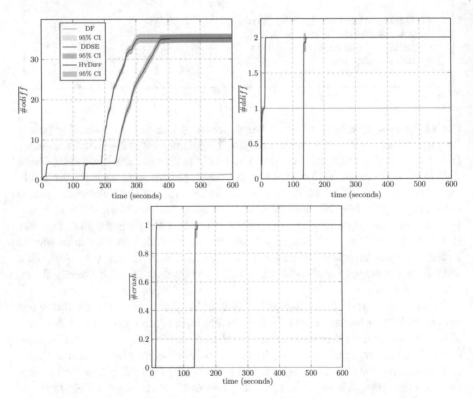

Fig. 6 Results for DF, DDSE, and HYDIFF on hybrid approach sample (lines and bands show averages and 95% confidence intervals across 30 repetitions)

The hybrid approach detects the regression bug more than *nine times faster* than DDSE component in isolation. The DF component (in isolation) times out after

10 min without detecting the regression bug. The hybrid setup can leverage the ꜱᴛⅰ ⅰⅰⅰ ⅼⅼⅼₐ ᴏf ʙₒₜₕ techniques, so that it can get into many more paths by using symbolic execution and qⅰⅰₑₖₗy ⅼₙⅾ ⅰₜₙ ⅰⅰⅰⅰ ⅰⅰⅰⅰⅼⅼⅼₐₜ difference by using fuzzing.

Summary of Evaluation For the evaluation of the application *regression analysis* the subjects are taken from multiple versions of the Traffic Collision Avoidance System (TCAS) [39] as well as subjects from the Defects4J benchmark [40]. Additionally, HYDIFF is evaluated on subjects from Apache Commons CLI library [41]. The conducted experiments indicate that the symbolic execution component of HYDIFF can greatly benefit from the combination with fuzzing and vice versa. The performance of differential fuzzing can be improved by running it in a parallel setup, but still it cannot classify all subjects correctly. In contrast, HYDIFF does classify all subjects correctly, that is, it identifies for all subjects output differences, for which they actually exist. Furthermore, the overall evaluation shows that HYDIFF still outperforms DDSE, DF, and PDF for the presented subjects.

6.2 Worst-Case Complexity Analysis (A2)

Worst-case complexity analysis (WCA) searches for worst-case execution paths, which represent a serious threat to the system under test. The main objective is not to identify the theoretical complexity of an algorithm but to identify inputs that trigger a worst-case execution behavior. Similar to the next application *side-channel analysis*, it is a highly relevant application in the security area because such a characterization of an algorithm's complexity can help, for example, to identify worst-case complexity vulnerabilities [16]. The current need for such techniques is also recognized by the US *Defense Advanced Research Projects Agency* (DARPA), which recently organized the *Space/Time Analysis for Cybersecurity* (STAC) program [42] that supported the development of new analysis techniques to identify algorithmic complexity and side-channel vulnerabilities. Due to the simpler nature of the worst-case complexity analysis (compared to the other application scenarios), this approach is quite straightforward because it does not require the reasoning about multiple execution paths at the same time. The basic goal is to maximize the observed execution cost.

Example Listings 2 shows an implementation of the sorting algorithm *Insertion Sort* taken from JDK 1.5, for which the worst-case execution behavior (in terms of the runtime) is known: N^2, where N denotes the length of the input array. The worst-case would be triggered by a reverse-ordered array.

Table 1 shows the results for applying DF, PDF, DDSE, and HYDIFF on the presented *Insertion Sort* subject. The experiments have been executed for 1 h and repeated for 30 times. The columns in this table show the average maximum cost obtained within the given time bound ($\overline{c}$), the maximum cost value over all runs (c_{max}), and the time in seconds until the first cost improvement with regard to

Listing 2 Sample program for WCA: *Insertion Sort*

```java
1  public static void sort(int[] a) {
2      final int N = a.length;
3      for (int i = 1; i < N; i++) {
4          int j = i - 1;
5          int x = a[i];
6          while ((j >= 0) && (a[j] > x)) {
7              a[j + 1] = a[j];
8              j--;
9          }
10         a[j + 1] = x;
11     }
12 }
```

Table 1 Results for the *Insertion Sort* with $N = 64$ ($t = 3600\,s = 60\,min$, 30 runs). The execution cost c is measured as the number of executed JAVA bytecode instructions

Technique	$\bar{c}$	c_{max}	$t : c > 0$
DF	9048.40 ($\pm$ 85.51)	9567	5.70 ($\pm$ 0.16)
PDF	9355.03 ($\pm$ 41.53)	9571	5.10 ($\pm$ 0.11)
DDSE	1157.00 ($\pm$ 00.00)	1157	2.13 ($\pm$ 0.15)
HYDIFF	9693.77 ($\pm$ 42.44)	9923	2.93 ($\pm$ 0.16)

the cost value of the initial input ($\bar{t} : c > 0$), which had a cost value of 509 bytecode instructions. The numbers in Table 1 show that HYDIFF can generate inputs with significantly higher costs. However, within the 1 h time bound, none of the techniques has been able to identify **the** worst-case input. The maximum cost value generated by HYDIFF was 9923 and the actual worst-case cost value would be 10,526 for a totally reverse-ordered array with $N = 64$. Nonetheless, the input by HYDIFF with 9923 gets very close to this worst-case (see Listing 3). Therefore, HYDIFF achieves on average a *slowdown* of ca. 19.04×, that is, that the identified cost value as 19.04× more expensive than the cost value of the initial input.

Listing 3 HYDIFF's worst-performing input for *Insertion Sort* $N = 64$ ($t = 60\,min$)

```
a=[22, 23, 22, 21, 20, 20, 19, 19, 18, 17, 17, 17, 17, 13, 16,
   16, 16, 15, 13, 14, 16, 16, 15, 13, 14, 15, 12, 12, 12, 11,
    9, 10, 11, 11,  9,  9, 10,  7,  7,  7,  8,  7,  8,  5,  6,
    6,  6,  6,  4,  6,  5,  5,  5,  5,  4,  3,  2,  2,  2,  2,
    2,  2,  1,  0]
```

Parallel differential fuzzing (PDF) takes the second position with a slowdown of 18.38× followed by single differential fuzzing (DF) with a slowdown of 17.78×. Far behind is differential dynamic symbolic execution (DDSE) with a slowdown of 2.27×, which cannot achieve high cost values. However, with regard to the time to the first cost improvement, DDSE is the best followed by HYDIFF. Note that these differences are quite small and also the fuzzing techniques show very similar behavior.

More interesting is the comparison of the techniques over the analysis time run shown in Fig. 7. During the first 2 min DF, PDF, and HYDIFF perform very similar, but afterwards HYDIFF can break away and can generate an average cost value of 9000 executed bytecode instructions within 8.2 min, for which PDF needs 27.5 and DF 54.6 min.

Fig. 7 Results for DF, PDF, DDSE, and HYDIFF on the *Insertion Sort* Example with $N = 64$ (lines and bands show averages and 95% confidence intervals across 30 repetitions)

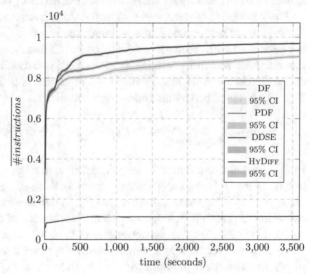

Summary of Evaluation For the evaluation of application *worst-case complexity analysis*, the subjects are chosen based on the evaluation of the approach SLOW-FUZZ [16], since it is the most related work in this context. The data set includes textbook algorithms like Insertion Sort and regular expression matching from the JAVA JDK. It also includes algorithms from the STAC program [42] and real-world applications, for example, APACHE COMMONS COMPRESS [43].

HYDIFF successfully combines the strengths of DDSE and DF. Symbolic execution helps HYDIFF to quickly make progress and fuzzing supports by continuously improving the score. Therefore, in the majority of the cases, HYDIFF is as good as its components or even outperforms them. In particular, HYDIFF's strength is to quickly generate a high cost value, for which the other techniques take quite long.

6.3   Side-Channel Analysis (A3)

Side-channel analysis searches for information leakages that are caused by diverging cost-behaviors within the same application. As already mentioned for **A2**, side-channel analysis is highly relevant with regard to security and is in the focus of recent research projects. The popular *Meltdown* [44] and *Spectre* [45] side-channel attacks also gave it some publicity outside the research community. Side-channel analysis is difficult because it requires the reasoning about multiple execution paths at the same time and additionally involves the handling of cost behaviors.

The key idea for the implementation of side-channel analysis with HYDIFF is to use the idea of self-composition [46] and consider two execution paths, which both are initialized with the same *public* input but different *secret* inputs. The goal is to maximize the cost difference (δ) between these two execution paths. The higher the cost difference can be identified, the more severe is a side-channel vulnerability. This idea is described by the following formula:

$$\underset{pub, sec_1, sec_2}{\text{maximize:}}\ \delta = |c(P[\![pub, sec_1]\!]) - c(P[\![pub, sec_2]\!])|$$

In this formula *pub* denotes the public value, and sec_1 and sec_2 denote the two secret values. $P[\![pub, sec_1]\!]$ denotes the execution of program P with the public value *pub*, and the secret value sec_1. $c(P[\![..]\!])$ denotes the cost measurement of the execution of program P. δ denotes the cost difference of both program executions.

For HYDIFF's fuzzing component this means to fuzz three values: the public value and two secret values. Note that this approach naturally extends to tuples of values. The most important metric to detect the side-channel vulnerability is the cost difference between these two executions, but the fuzzer will also collect the information about decision differences and output differences. They are still important metrics to drive the fuzzing process, although they cannot directly measure the severity of a side-channel vulnerability. For HYDIFF's symbolic execution component, the variation in the secret input can be realized by the usage of change-annotations:

$$secret = change(secret_1, secret_2)$$

The differential dynamic symbolic execution does also require three inputs (one public and two secret values), but does combine the two secret values in one change-annotated expression. This means that for symbolic execution there is only one program execution necessary. Since this change-annotation happens directly in the driver, the program itself does not contain any change-annotation, and hence, the patch distance metric is not relevant for side-channel analysis. Also the control-flow information cannot help to prune any path because the differential expression is introduced straight in the beginning. The primary goal of the symbolic execution in the hybrid setup is to support the fuzzing component by solving complex branching conditions, which are infeasible for fuzzing.

Example To illustrate the analysis approach, consider the *unsafe* password comparison algorithm in Listing 4. The algorithm takes two arrays as parameters, one array for the (public) user input pub and the other for the stored (secret) password sec. It starts with comparing the length of both arrays and will return false if both lengths do not match. As long as both arrays have the same length, the algorithm continues with comparing the passwords byte by byte. As soon as there is a mismatch, the algorithm will return false, and only if all byte values match, the algorithm will finally return true. Therefore, this *unsafe* algorithm has two early-returns, in lines 2 and 4, which are the reason for the vulnerability. In order to avoid the timing side-channel, it would be necessary to iterate over the complete public input without having such early returns.

Listing 4 Side-channel analysis example: an unsafe password checking algorithm

```
1  boolean pwcheck_unsafe(byte[] pub, byte[] sec) {
2      if (pub.length != sec.length) return false;
3      for (int i = 0; i < pub.length; i++)
4          if (pub[i] != sec[i]) return false;
5      return true;
6  }
```

Table 2 shows the experiment results for applying DF, PDF, DDSE, and HYDIFF on the password checking example. The experiments have been executed with a time bound of 5 min and have been repeated 30 times. The number of executed bytecode instructions are used as cost metric, which is an alternative to measure the real runtime of the algorithm. Other processes running on the machine are expected to influence the actual real-time measurement, and hence, counting the executed bytecode instruction is a more robust metric.

Table 2 Results for the unsafe password checking example ($t = 300\,\text{s} = 5\,\text{min}$, 30 runs)

Technique	δ	δ_{max}	$\bar{t} : \delta > 0$
Differential fuzzing (DF)	34.30 (± 3.11)	47	4.20 (± 1.53)
Parallel differential fuzzing (PDF)	40.93 (± 1.84)	47	2.33 (± 0.63)
Differential dynamic symbolic execution (DDSE)	47.00 (± 0.00)	47	13.27 (± 0.24)
HYDIFF	47.00 (± 0.00)	47	4.43 (± 1.00)

Listing 5 Input for maximum cost difference after 5 min

```
  pub= [16, 0, 108, 108, 111, 32, 67, 97, 72, 101, 108, 108, 111, 32, 67, 97]
sec_1= [114, 110, 101, 103, 105, 101, 32, 77, 101, 108, 114, 110, 101, 103,
        105, 101]
sec_2= [16, 0, 108, 108, 111, 32, 67, 97, 72, 101, 108, 108, 111, 32, 67, 97]
```

For this experiment, the maximum input size was set to 16 bytes, which allows a maximum cost difference of 47 bytecode instructions. Listing 5 shows an input, which triggers the maximum cost difference.

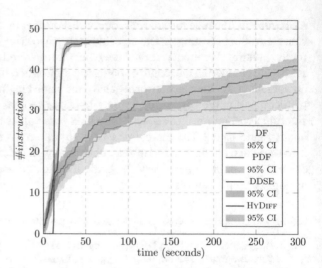

Fig. 8 Results for DF, PDF, DDSE, and HYDIFF on the password checking example (lines and bands show averages and 95% confidence intervals across 30 repetitions)

All of the four experiment setups (DF, PDF, DDSE, and HYDIFF) have been able to reach the maximum value at least once (see δ_{max} column in Table 2). The values in the table also show that DF and PDF cannot reliably generate this maximum value within the time bound of 5 min. However, the fuzzing techniques show a better performance in identifying the first input for an improved δ value (see column $\bar{t} : \delta > 0$). Figure 8 shows the temporal development. DF, PDF, and HYDIFF perform quite similar in the beginning, whereas DDSE takes longer to generate an interesting input. After approximately 13 s, DDSE jumps almost directly to the actual maximum cost difference. HYDIFF follows quickly, whereas DF and PDF take longer to get to this maximum value.

Summary of Evaluation The evaluation of application *side-channel analysis* includes subjects from the evaluation of two state-of-the-art static analysis tools BLAZER [17] and THEMIS [18]. Additionally, the evaluation includes more subjects from the STAC program [42] and the modular exponentiation known from the RSA encryption technique [47].

Although HYDIFF shows some peaks in the evaluation, it is usually not much better than the naive combination of the results from both components. Nevertheless, HYDIFF represents a well-balanced combination. As it combines both techniques, it can identify a cost difference very fast and is able to assess the severity of side-channel vulnerabilities very well because it can quickly identify large δ values. For all subjects HYDIFF and its components can efficiently detect side-channel vulnerabilities. Furthermore, the comparison between differential fuzzing and BLAZER/THEMIS shows that HYDIFF can keep up with state-of-the-art static analysis tools for the detection of side-channel vulnerabilities. Additionally, HYDIFF's fuzzing component has been used to reveal multiple new vulnerabilities, which later got fixed by the developers (as presented in [2]).

6.4 Robustness Analysis of Neural Networks (A4)

Robustness analysis of neural networks is a relatively novel application of differential program analysis where the goal is to identify vulnerabilities in neural networks with regard to their robustness. It requires reasoning about multiple network executions, which makes it very expensive, and hence, serves as a stress testing application of HYDIFF and its components. HYDIFF is specifically used to find adversarial inputs for an image classification network. Since HYDIFF performs the analysis of JAVA bytecode, the first step is to rewrite a given neural network model into a JAVA program [48]. Similarly to the side-channel analysis, the idea for the differential analysis is to allow changes in the input and observe differences in the network's behavior. More precisely, the proposed analysis changes up to $x\%$ of the pixels in the input image and checks whether there can be any difference in the output.

Some preliminary experiments have shown that with HYDIFF in its default setup (i.e., differential fuzzing and differential dynamic symbolic execution start at the same time), both components do not synchronize with each other because they are busy with their own analysis due to the expensive program execution. Therefore, the execution setup for the neural network analysis is different: the experiments start with differential symbolic execution for 10 min. After this time bound the differential fuzzing component is started with the already generated inputs by the differential symbolic execution component as additional seed inputs and both component run in parallel for the remaining time. The 10 min delay provides sufficient time to the DDSE component to generate a first interesting input.

Example Listing 6 shows an extract of the JAVA program, which represents the *transformed* neural network model for the experiments for this case study. The program takes a double array as input, which represents a normalized 28×28 grayscale image. The image is expected to include a handwritten digit and the network has been trained to recognize such digits. Each compartment of this program denotes a layer of the neural network. The final layer shows the final classification of the hand-written digits into the numbers 0–9.

The implemented analysis tries to identify two images that differ only up to a given threshold and that are differently classified by the neural network. In order to illustrate the effect of this approach, consider Fig. 9. It shows two inputs that have been generated by differential fuzzing after 1375 s. The image on the left side is classified as the digit 6 and the image on the right side is classified as the digit 5. The generated images are not necessarily representative as adversarial inputs as they do not fulfill the assumption of the neural network, namely that it expects handwritten digits. Due to the analysis implementation, the search process can change the complete image, and so, these images look randomly generated. Note that this case study is used as stress testing for HYDIFF and its components. Therefore, it is fair enough to identify images that differ slightly and lead to different classifications in order to assess the robustness of the neural network.

Listing 6 Extract of the transformed neural network model as JAVA program

```
1   int runDNN(double[][][] input) { // input image is of shape 28x28x1
2     // layer 0: convolution
3     double[][][] layer0 = new double[26][26][2];
4     for (int i = 0; i < 26; i++)
5       for (int j = 0; j < 26; j++)
6         for (int k = 0; k < 2; k++) {
7           layer0[i][j][k] = biases0[k];
8           for (int I = 0; I < 3; I++)
9             for (int J = 0; J < 3; J++)
10              for (int K = 0; K < 1; K++)
11                layer0[i][j][k] += weights0[I][J][K][k] *
12                    input[i + I][j + J][K];
13        }
14
15    // layer 1: activation
16    double[][][] layer1 = new double[26][26][2];
17    for (int i = 0; i < 26; i++)
18      for (int j = 0; j < 26; j++)
19        for (int k = 0; k < 2; k++)
20          if (layer0[i][j][k] > 0)
21            layer1[i][j][k] = layer0[i][j][k];
22          else
23            layer1[i][j][k] = 0;
24
25    // layer 2: convolution
26    double[][][] layer2 = new double[24][24][4];
27    for (int i = 0; i < 24; i++)
28      for (int j = 0; j < 24; j++)
29        for (int k = 0; k < 4; k++) {
30          layer2[i][j][k] = internal.biases2[k];
31          for (int I = 0; I < 3; I++)
32            for (int J = 0; J < 3; J++)
33              for (int K = 0; K < 2; K++)
34                layer2[i][j][k] += weights2[I][J][K][k] *
35                    layer1[i + I][j + J][K];
36        }
37
38    ... // layer 3 - 8
39
40    // layer 9: activation
41    int ret = 0;
42    double res = -100000;
43    for (int i = 0; i < 10; i++) {
44      if (layer8[i] > res) {
45        res = layer8[i];
46        ret = i;
47      }
48    }
49    return ret;
50 }
```

However, it is also possible to update the analysis to perform a more realistic scenario. If the original input is kept and the process searches only the pixel locations and values, then the result can be used as adversarial inputs. This analysis would be much harder because there are not so many ways to change an existing image. Figure 10 shows an exemplary result of performing such an analysis with differential fuzzing. The left side shows the original image that is classified as 6. The right side shows an image with 50% changed pixel that is classified as 8. In the experiment, differential fuzzing needed more than 60 h to generate the adversarial input.

classified as 6

classified as 5

Fig. 9 Inputs identified by DF after 1375 s by fuzzing two images that differ in up to 1% of the pixels. The learned model classifies the left image as a 6, while it classifies the right image as a 5. The images differ only in 7 pixels

classified as 6

classified as 8

Fig. 10 Adversarial changes identified by DF after 60.89 h by fuzzing up to 50% pixel changes for a fixed image. The learned model classifies the left (original) image as a 6, while it classifies the right image as an 8. The images differ in 314 pixels

Summary of Evaluation The results for this experimental setup show the different benefits of the two different approaches (fuzzing and symbolic execution) and why it is important to combine them! HYDIFF leverages its differential symbolic execution component to quickly generate a first output difference and further leverages differential fuzzing to identify even more output differences. HYDIFF does not only combine the results of both components, but the components can benefit from each other's inputs to further improve the outcome. Overall, the evaluation for the neural network subjects has shown that all three techniques (DF, DDSE, and their hybrid combination HYDIFF) can be used to find adversarial inputs for neural networks. Although this scenario shows the limitation of all approaches, output differences have been generated.

7 Conclusion and Future Work

This work contributes the concept of hybrid differential software testing (HYDIFF) as a combination of differential fuzzing (DF) and differential dynamic symbolic execution (DDSE). HYDIFF's fuzzing component employs a search-based differential exploration implemented by a genetic algorithm. Its benefit is the inexpensive generation of inputs as well as the generation of unexpected inputs due to the random mutation strategies. HYDIFF's symbolic execution component performs a systematic exploration guided by several differential heuristics. Because it can incorporate concrete inputs at runtime, it also can be driven by the inputs of the fuzzing component. It further can overcome specific constraints due to its constraint-solving capabilities. This supports fuzzing, which might not reach deep program behaviors due to its random nature. Overall, HYDIFF strengthens the presented differential fuzzing technique by combining it with the heuristic-based, systematic exploration in symbolic execution. As combination this supports a wide spectrum of differential testing applications and contributes a generally usable testing technique.

For evaluation purpose, this work showed its applicability on several application scenarios: regression analysis, worst-case complexity analysis, side-channel analysis, and robustness analysis of neural networks. This multifaceted evaluation shows that HYDIFF can be applied in numerous testing disciplines, and so, contributes to the overall research interest of software testing. Additionally, the application of fuzzing for side-channel vulnerability detection already had a direct impact outside of the research community, namely on the development of more fuzzing tools with SIDEFUZZ [49]. HYDIFF complements the existing work on hybrid testing and provides a baseline for future research. In summary, the contributions made by this work (especially the technical abilities to reveal behavioral differences) represent an important step in the direction of better (i.e., more secure and more reliable) software, and hence, support the overall goal of software engineering.

The conducted research also has revealed interesting future research directions. First of all, the application section mentioned the parallel variant HYDIFF's fuzzing component. It would be interesting to further analyze its performance, which could lead to corresponding parallel fuzzing guidelines, and furthermore, it would be interesting to develop a parallel symbolic execution variant. Additionally, the research around HYDIFF aims at the generation of test inputs, which can be continued to perform actual debugging and repair of the identified errors and vulnerabilities. Therefore, an interesting future work could be the automated repair in the areas of software evolution and security vulnerabilities and their combination with the techniques proposed in this work.

Acknowledgments I want to thank my family and friends for supporting me during my PhD. My great appreciation goes to all my co-authors and my particular gratitude to Lars Grunske and Corina Păsăreanu for their great support.

References

1. Noller, Y.: Hybrid differential software testing. Ph.D. Thesis, Humboldt-Universität zu Berlin, Mathematisch-Naturwissenschaftliche Fakultät (2020) https://doi.org/10.18452/21694

2. Nilizadeh, S., Noller, Y., Păsăreanu, C.S.: Diffuzz: differential fuzzing for side-channel analysis. In: Proceedings of the 41st International Conference on Software Engineering, ICSE '19, pp. 176–187. IEEE Press, Piscataway (2019). https://doi.org/10.1109/ICSE.2019.00034

3. Noller, Y.: Differential program analysis with fuzzing and symbolic execution. In: Proceedings of the 33rd ACM/IEEE International Conference on Automated Software Engineering, ASE 2018, pp. 944–947. ACM, New York (2018). https://doi.org/10.1145/3238147.3241537

4. Noller, Y., Kersten, R., Păsăreanu, C.S.: Badger: complexity analysis with fuzzing and symbolic execution. In: Proceedings of the 27th ACM SIGSOFT International Symposium on Software Testing and Analysis, ISSTA 2018, pp. 322–332. ACM, New York (2018). https://doi.org/10.1145/3213846.3213868

5. Noller, Y., Nguyen, H.L., Tang, M., Kehrer, T.: Shadow symbolic execution with java pathfinder. SIGSOFT Softw. Eng. Notes 42(4), 1–5 (2018). https://doi.org/10.1145/3149485.3149492

6. Noller, Y., Nguyen, H.L., Tang, M., Kehrer, T., Grunske, L.: Complete shadow symbolic execution with java pathfinder. SIGSOFT Softw. Eng. Notes 44(4), 15–16 (2019). https://doi.org/10.1145/3364452.33644558

7. Noller, Y., Păsăreanu, C.S., Böhme, M., Sun, Y., Nguyen, H.L., Grunske, L.: Hydiff: Hybrid differential software analysis. In: Will appear in: Proceedings of the 42nd International Conference on Software Engineering, ICSE '20 (2020)

8. ISO/IEC/IEEE International Standard—Systems and software engineering–Vocabulary. ISO/IEC/IEEE 24765:2017(E), pp. 1–541 (2017). https://doi.org/10.1109/IEEESTD.2017.8016712

9. DeRemer, F., Kron, H.H.: Programming-in-the-large versus programming-in-the-small. IEEE Trans. Softw. Eng. 2(2), 80–86 (1976). https://doi.org/10.1109/TSE.1976.233534

10. Vliet, H.V.: Software Engineering: Principles and Practice, 3rd edn. Wiley, London (2008)

11. Orso, A., Rothermel, G.: Software testing: A research travelogue (2000–2014). In: Proceedings of the on Future of Software Engineering, FOSE 2014, pp. 117–132. Association for Computing Machinery, New York (2014). https://doi.org/10.1145/2593882.2593885

12. Fraser, G., Arcuri, A.: A large-scale evaluation of automated unit test generation using evosuite. ACM Trans. Softw. Eng. Methodol. 24(2) (2014). https://doi.org/10.1145/2685612

13. Palikareva, H., Kuchta, T., Cadar, C.: Shadow of a doubt: testing for divergences between software versions. In: 2016 IEEE/ACM 38th International Conference on Software Engineering (ICSE), pp. 1181–1192 (2016). https://doi.org/10.1145/2884781.2884845

14. Person, S., Dwyer, M.B., Elbaum, S., Păsăreanu, C.S.: Differential symbolic execution. In: Proceedings of the 16th ACM SIGSOFT International Symposium on Foundations of Software Engineering, SIGSOFT '08/FSE-16, pp. 226–237. ACM, New York (2008). https://doi.org/10.1145/1453101.1453131

15. Luckow, K., Kersten, R., Păsăreanu, C.S.: Symbolic complexity analysis using context-preserving histories. In: 2017 IEEE International Conference on Software Testing, Verification and Validation (ICST), pp. 58–68 (2017). https://doi.org/10.1109/ICST.2017.13

16. Petsios, T., Zhao, J., Keromytis, A.D., Jana, S.: Slowfuzz: Automated domain-independent detection of algorithmic complexity vulnerabilities. In: Proceedings of the 2017 ACM SIGSAC Conference on Computer and Communications Security, CCS '17, pp. 2155–2168. ACM, New York (2017). https://doi.org/10.1145/3133956.3134073

17. Antonopoulos, T., Gazzillo, P., Hicks, M., Koskinen, E., Terauchi, T., Wei, S.: Decomposition instead of self-composition for proving the absence of timing channels. SIGPLAN Not. 52(6), 362–375 (2017). https://doi.org/10.1145/3140587.3062378

18. Chen, J., Feng, Y., Dillig, I.: Precise detection of side-channel vulnerabilities using quantitative Cartesian Hoare logic. In: Proceedings of the 2017 ACM SIGSAC Conference on Computer

and Communications Security, CCS '17, pp. 875–890. Association for Computing Machinery, New York (2017). https://doi.org/10.1145/3133956.3134058

19. Păsăreanu, C.S., Phan, Q.S., Malacaria, P.: Multi-run side-channel analysis using symbolic execution and Max-SMT. In: 2016 IEEE 29th Computer Security Foundations Symposium (CSF), pp. 387–400 (2016). https://doi.org/10.1109/CSF.2016.34

20. Sun, Y., Wu, M., Ruan, W., Huang, X., Kwiatkowska, M., Kroening, D.: Concolic testing for deep neural networks. In: Proceedings of the 33rd ACM/IEEE International Conference on Automated Software Engineering, ASE 2018, pp. 109–119. Association for Computing Machinery, New York (2018). https://doi.org/10.1145/3238147.3238172

21. Tramer, F., Boneh, D.: Adversarial training and robustness for multiple perturbations. In: Wallach, H., Larochelle, H., Beygelzimer, A., d'Alché-Buc, F., Fox, E., Garnett, R. (eds.) Advances in Neural Information Processing Systems, vol. 32, pp. 5858–5868. Curran Associates, Red Hook (2019)

22. Goodfellow, I.J., Shlens, J., Szegedy, C.: Explaining and harnessing adversarial examples (2014). arXiv preprint arXiv:1412.6572

23. Cha, S.K., Avgerinos, T., Rebert, A., Brumley, D.: Unleashing mayhem on binary code. In: 2012 IEEE Symposium on Security and Privacy, pp. 380–394 (2012). https://doi.org/10.1109/SP.2012.31

24. Stephens, N., Grosen, J., Salls, C., Dutcher, A., Wang, R., Corbetta, J., Shoshitaishvili, Y., Kruegel, C., Vigna,' G.: Driller: augmenting fuzzing through selective symbolic execution. In: 23nd Annual Network and Distributed System Security Symposium, NDSS 2016, San Diego, California, USA, February 21–24, 2016 (2016). https://doi.org/10.14722/ndss.2016.23368

25. Harrold, M.J.: Testing evolving software. J. Syst. Softw. **47**(2), 173–181 (1999). https://doi.org/10.1016/S0164-1212(99)00037-0

26. Yoo, S., Harman, M.: Regression testing minimization, selection and prioritization: a survey. Softw. Testing Verif. Reliab. **22**(2), 67–120 (2012). https://doi.org/10.1002/stvr.430

27. Brennan, T., Saha, S., Bultan, T., Păsăreanu, C.S.: Symbolic path cost analysis for side-channel detection. In: Proceedings of the 27th ACM SIGSOFT International Symposium on Software Testing and Analysis, ISSTA 2018, pp. 27–37. ACM, New York (2018). https://doi.org/10.1145/3213846.3213867

28. Miller, B.P., Fredriksen, L., So, B.: An empirical study of the reliability of Unix utilities. Commun. ACM **33**(12), 32–44 (1990). https://doi.org/10.1145/96267.96279

29. Godefroid, P., Klarlund, N., Sen, K.: Dart: Directed automated random testing. In: Proceedings of the 2005 ACM SIGPLAN Conference on Programming Language Design and Implementation, PLDI '05, pp. 213–223. Association for Computing Machinery, New York (2005). https://doi.org/10.1145/1065010.1065036

30. King, J.C.: Symbolic execution and program testing. Commun. ACM **19**(7), 385–394 (1976). https://doi.org/10.1145/360248.360252

31. Böhme, M., Pham, V.T., Roychoudhury, A.: Coverage-based greybox fuzzing as Markov chain. In: Proceedings of the 2016 ACM SIGSAC Conference on Computer and Communications Security, CCS '16, pp. 1032–1043. ACM, New York (2016). https://doi.org/10.1145/2976749.2978428

32. Pham, V.T., Böhme, M., Santosa, A.E., Căciulescu, A.R., Roychoudhury, A.: Smart greybox fuzzing. IEEE Trans. Softw. Eng. 1–17 (2019)

33. Böhme, M., Pham, V.T., Nguyen, M.D., Roychoudhury, A.: Directed greybox fuzzing. In: Proceedings of the 2017 ACM SIGSAC Conference on Computer and Communications Security, CCS '17, pp. 2329–2344. ACM, New York (2017). https://doi.org/10.1145/3133956.3134020

34. Website: American fuzzy lop (AFL)—a security-oriented fuzzer (2014). http://lcamtuf.coredump.cx/afl/

35. Zeller, A., Gopinath, R., Böhme, M., Fraser, G., Holler, C.: The fuzzing book. In: The Fuzzing Book. Saarland University (2019). https://www.fuzzingbook.org/

36. Person, S., Yang, G., Rungta, N., Khurshid, S.: Directed incremental symbolic execution. In: Proceedings of the 32Nd ACM SIGPLAN Conference on Programming Language Design and

Implementation, PLDI '11, pp. 504–515. ACM, New York (2011). https://doi.org/10.1145/1993498.1993558

37. Yang, G., Păsăreanu, C.S., Khurshid, S.: Memoized symbolic execution. In: Proceedings of the 2012 International Symposium on Software Testing and Analysis, ISSTA 2012, pp. 144–154, ACM, New York (2012). https://doi.org/10.1145/2338965.2336771

38. Majumdar, R., Sen, K.: Hybrid concolic testing. In: 29th International Conference on Software Engineering (ICSE'07), pp. 416–426. IEEE Computer Society, Los Alamitos (2007). https://doi.org/10.1109/ICSE.2007.41

39. Website: Software-artifact infrastructure repository (2019). http://sir.unl.edu

40. Just, R., Jalali, D., Ernst, M.D.: Defects4j: A database of existing faults to enable controlled testing studies for java programs. In: Proceedings of the 2014 International Symposium on Software Testing and Analysis, ISSTA 2014, pp. 437–440. ACM, New York (2014). https://doi.org/10.1145/2610384.2628055

41. Website: Commons CLI (2019). https://commons.apache.org/proper/commons-cli/

42. Website: DARPA's Space/Time Analysis for Cybersecurity (STAC) program (2015). https://www.darpa.mil/program/space-time-analysis-for-cybersecurity

43. Website: Debian bug report log 800564—php5: trivial hash complexity DoS attack (2015). https://bugs.debian.org/cgi-bin/bugreport.cgi?bug=800564

44. Lipp, M., Schwarz, M., Gruss, D., Prescher, T., Haas, W., Fogh, A., Horn, J., Mangard, S., Kocher, P., Genkin, D., Yarom, Y., Hamburg, M.: Meltdown: reading kernel memory from user space. In: 27th USENIX Security Symposium (USENIX Security 18), pp. 973–990. USENIX Association, Baltimore (2018)

45. Kocher, P., Horn, J., Fogh, A., Genkin, D., Gruss, D., Haas, W., Hamburg, M., Lipp, M., Mangard, S., Prescher, T., Schwarz, M., Yarom, Y.: Spectre attacks: exploiting speculative execution. In: 2019 IEEE Symposium on Security and Privacy (SP), pp. 1–19 (2019). https://doi.org/10.1109/SP.2019.00002

46. Barthe, G., D'Argenio, P.R., Rezk, T.: Secure information flow by self-composition. In: Proceedings. 17th IEEE Computer Security Foundations Workshop, 2004, pp. 100–114 (2004). https://doi.org/10.1109/CSFW.2004.1310735

47. Kocher, P.C.: Timing attacks on implementations of Diffie-Hellman, RSA, DSS, and other systems. In: Koblitz, N. (ed.) Advances in Cryptology—CRYPTO '96, pp. 104–113. Springer, Berlin, Heidelberg (1996)

48. Website: Deep learning test toolset (2020). https://github.com/theyoucheng/DLTT

49. Website: SideFuzz: Fuzzing for side-channel vulnerabilities (2018). https://github.com/phayes/sidefuzz

Ever Change a Running System: Structured Software Reengineering Using Automatically Proven-Correct Transformation Rules

Dominic Steinhöfel

Abstract Legacy systems are business-critical software systems whose failure can have a significant impact on the business. Yet, their maintenance and adaption to changed requirements consume a considerable amount of the total software development costs. Frequently, domain experts and developers involved in the original development are not available anymore, making it difficult to adapt a legacy system without introducing bugs or unwanted behavior. This results in a dilemma: businesses are reluctant to change a working system, while at the same time struggling with its high maintenance costs. We propose the concept of *Structured Software Reengineering* replacing the ad hoc forward engineering part of a reengineering process with the application of behavior-preserving, proven-correct transformations improving nonfunctional program properties. Such transformations preserve valuable business logic while improving properties such as maintainability, performance, or portability to new platforms. Manually encoding and proving such transformations for industrial programming languages, for example, in interactive proof assistants, is a major challenge requiring deep expert knowledge. Existing frameworks for automatically proving transformation rules have limited expressiveness and are restricted to particular target applications such as compilation or peep-hole optimizations. We present *Abstract Execution*, a specification and verification framework for statement-based program transformation rules on JAVA programs building on symbolic execution. Abstract Execution supports *universal quantification* over statements or expressions and addresses properties about the (big-step) *behavior* of programs. Since this class of properties is useful for a plethora of applications, Abstract Execution bridges the gap between expressiveness and automation. In many cases, fully automatic proofs are in possible. We explain REFINITY, a workbench for modeling and proving statement-level JAVA transformation rules, and discuss our applications of Abstract Execution to code refactoring,

D. Steinhöfel (✉)
CISPA Helmholtz Center for Information Security, Saarbrücken, Germany

Software Engineering Group, TU Darmstadt, Darmstadt, Germany
e-mail: dominic.steinhoefel@cispa.de

M. Felderer et al. (eds.), *Ernst Denert Award for Software Engineering 2020*,
https://doi.org/10.1007/978-3-030-83128-8_10

cost analysis of program transformations, and transformations reshaping programs for the application of parallel design patterns.

1 Introduction

"When Companies Become Prisoners of Legacy Systems": this title of a *Wall Street Journal* article [41] well describes the predominant perception of legacy software systems in academia. Indeed, legacy systems are often associated with *high maintenance costs* [12, 13, 40], ranging between 67% and 90% of the total software costs [13]. In a more recent case study [12], an amount of 75% was reported for a financial services company. Interestingly, this perception is not always shared in industry. In an interview with 26 industry practitioners [26], they describe their legacy systems as businesses-critical, reliable, and proven systems. The same survey names the loss of expert knowledge about the software, high maintenance costs, and the desire to increase flexibility as main drivers for *modernization* of legacy systems.

Practitioners are facing a dilemma: they are reluctant to "change a running system" encoding valuable domain knowledge and representing high business value, while struggling with the costs to keep it running. The stakes are high, and the risks to introduce bugs or unwanted behavior during legacy system modernization are considerable [19]. A major challenge is that the original source code has been evolving substantially, documentation might be missing, and domain experts as well as developers involved in past developments might not be available any more [19, 52]. Therefore, even minor modifications present high risk [52].

Software Reengineering is the "examination and alteration of a subject system to reconstitute it in a new form" [11]. The goal is to preserve domain knowledge encoded in existing software, while improving desirable nonfunctional properties like maintainability, performance, and flexibility. In the case of business-critical legacy systems, reengineering efforts must be especially careful to maintain the essential semantics of the subject system, for example, through the introduction of automated tests [16]. While automated testing should be part of any serious software development, it bears two problems: first, writing meaningful, fine-granular tests for legacy systems is nontrivial in presence of missing documentation and domain experts. Second, post hoc verification only informs about a failure *after* its introduction.

Regression Verification [20] allows automatically verifying the equivalence of closely related versions of the same program. If the changes applied during reengineering are small enough, regressions can in principle be excluded using this methodology. However, this requires analyzing whole methods after each change, and side effects or irregular completion (e.g., exceptions) are not considered.

We propose *structured* software reengineering as an alternative. Following Chikofsky and Cross [11], reengineering (1) starts with a *reverse engineering* phase to achieve a more abstract description of the system, followed by (2) a *forward engineering* or *restructuring* phase. Structured reengineering does not impose requirements on phase (1), which aims to carve out reengineering goals and concrete suggestions for code modifications. Instead of then proceeding with the usual process (then interleaving manual changes and post hoc verification (using testing or more heavyweight techniques), structured reengineering consists of applying sequences of *proven-correct program transformation rules* to the legacy system. Such rules consist of a schematic description of code fragments on which they are applicable and of a set of preconditions. Each rule has been *certified* in advance to guarantee that *for all applicable input programs*, an application of the rule results in a semantically equivalent program. Such proofs only have to be conducted *once* per rule; whenever applying it to a concrete program matching the schematic description, one merely has to show that the preconditions are satisfied. Additionally, a rule can be equipped with nonfunctional guarantees, for instance, on the execution time of the transformed result or with an informal description of its intention.

This approach has the following advantages:

1. It guarantees the preservation of the business logic contained in the original legacy system, even in the absence of domain experts and documentation.
2. The preconditions which have to be checked prior to the execution of the transformation are local to the transformed piece of code. This is especially beneficial during applications in huge (method/class/module) contexts.
3. If the applied rules guarantee additional (nonfunctional) properties on top of semantic preservation, such properties of the resulting system are obtained on the fly. This also helps to assure that the transformation process proceeds toward the reengineering goals, and to select rules accordingly.

To be practical, structured reengineering requires *catalogs of transformation rules* as well as *tool support*, such as the integration into an IDE. While this seems to be an obstacle, it turns out that documentation and tool support already exist for a popular class of code transformations, namely *refactoring* rules. Refactoring aims to improve the internal structure of code while maintaining its semantics [18]; the goal is to make the code better to read and maintain by humans. Fowler published a well-organized catalog of refactoring techniques [17, 18]. Many of them, such as *Extract Method* and *Slide Statements*, are implemented in major IDEs (e.g., Eclipse or IntelliJ IDEA). The intention of each refactoring technique is thoroughly documented and motivated along examples. However, the set of preconditions necessary for semantic preservation is almost always incomplete, and naively using refactorings offered by an IDE can easily *break the input program* [14, 44]. We discuss this in Sect. 4.

To illustrate the application of structured reengineering, we consider an example from [18] computing the total salary and average age of the employees of a company. The corresponding code is depicted in Fig. 1, Listing 1. Observe that the loop in Lines 4–7 performs two different tasks: it (1) computes the average age, operating on the variable avgAge and reading the age field of the elements in the people array, and (2) computes the total salary, operating on the variable totalSalary and reading the salary field of the elements in the people array. The *Split Loop*

Listing 1 Original program.

```
1 People[] people = employees();
2 float avgAge = .0;
3 int totalSalary = 0;
4 for (People person: people) {
5   avgAge += person.age;
6   totalSalary += person.salary;
7 }
8 avgAge = avgAge / people.length;
```

Listing 2 After *Split Loop* and *Slide Statements*.

```
1 People[] people = employees();
2 float avgAge = .0;
3 int totalSalary = 0;
4 for (People person: people)
5   avgAge += person.age;
6 avgAge = avgAge / people.length;
7 for (People person: people)
8   totalSalary += person.salary;
```

Fig. 1 Computing average age and total salary for a list of employees

refactoring technique [18] suggests to split a loop doing two different things into two loops (see Fig. 1, Listing 2). If code readability is a chosen reengineering goal, it makes sense to apply this technique. Additionally, this makes it easier to apply further optimizations, such as converting the loops to map-reduce transformations using (parallel) streams.

Program transformations can be expressed as input-output pairs of programs containing placeholders representing arbitrary expressions or statements. After instantiating the placeholders s.t. the input program matches the program fragment to transform, the original fragment is replaced by the output program with the same instantiations. Thus, the *Split Loop* transformation can be expressed as

$$\textbf{for } (itExpr) \{ P \, Q \} \rightsquigarrow \textbf{for } (itExpr) \{ P \} \quad \textbf{for } (itExpr) \{ Q \}$$

However, this simple rule comes with strings attached. The most common obstacle is that locations written and accessed by statements P and Q are overlapping; in this case, the loop must not be split. Apart from preconditions on written and accessed locations, abrupt completion has to be regarded: P and Q might complete abruptly because of a (labeled) **break** and **continue**, a **return**, or because of a thrown exception. The latter also applies for *itExpr*. In Sect. 4, we present certified preconditions for refactoring techniques which we derived using a refinement loop based on feedback from failed proof attempts. For our example, Listing 2 shows the result of the application of *Split Loop* on Listing 1. In addition, we also moved the division in Line 8 from Listing 1 to before the second loop using a *Slide Statements* refactoring. This keeps together the code concerned with the computation of the average age, which one could now extract into a new method using an *Extract Method* refactoring. Those techniques are also discussed in Sect. 4.

A critical part in the development of transformation rule catalogs is the effort that needs to be invested to prove the desired properties of the rules. Formalizing and proving the rules in interactive proof assistants like Isabelle [37] or Coq [8] requires substantial effort for manually writing proof scripts, as can be observed in the work on verified compilers [29, 31, 51]. Previously proposed approaches for proving program transformations *automatically* (e.g., [9, 20, 33, 49]) are tailored to a particular target application (e.g., symbolic execution rules or peephole optimizations) and have a limited expressiveness (e.g., only abstract statements *or* expressions, no loops, no specification of written and accessed locations).

We developed *Abstract Execution (AE)* [47, 50], a specification and verification framework based on Symbolic Execution (SE). AE trades off the flexibility of interactive proof assistants with the automation offered by specialized techniques: it restricts the properties of transformations that can be proved to *universal, behavioral* properties on statement level (no existential quantifiers, no reasoning about internal structure of placeholders, no transformations on class level), and offers an *expressive specification language* for describing represented concrete programs. The result is a system in which *many meaningful transformations* (such as all refactoring rules in Sect. 4) can be proven *fully automatically.*

We implemented AE for the JAVA language as an extension of the KeY program prover [2]. As KeY allows manual inspection of generated proof trees, we can draw feedback from failed proof attempts that lets us further refine our transformation models in an iterative manner. To further increase the usability of our approach, we developed REFINITY [48] (available at http://www.key-project.org/REFINITY), presented in Sect. 3. REFINITY offers editor support dedicated to developing transformation rules in AE and greatly simplifies the interaction with the KeY system.

To kick-start the creation of a catalog of transformation rules suitable for structured reengineering, we formalized and proved three types of transformation rules:

1. We prove nine statement-level *refactoring rules* from Fowler's textbooks [17, 18], including two with loops (Sect. 4). In all cases, full semantic equivalence of programs before and after the transformation is proved.
2. Three rules for *restructuring sequential code for subsequent parallelization* [22] are discussed in Sect. 5. This comprises two complex loop transformations, for which we still achieve more than 99.7% proof automation. We prove semantic equivalence and further properties needed for parallel execution of the code.
3. In Sect. 6, we derive results about the *cost impact* of seven loop transformation rules, interacting with an external cost analysis tool. The resulting *Quantitative AE* framework [4] is the first approach to—fully automatically—analyze and certify the cost of schematic programs, and the first to reason about the cost impact of transformation *rules.*

Structure of This Chapter

We explain our Abstract Execution framework in Sect. 2. The REFINITY workbench for modeling and proving JAVA code transformation rules is presented in Sect. 3. Our applications on refactoring rules, restructuring for parallelization, and cost analysis of transformations are presented in Sects. 4–6. We conclude and mention promising future work in Sect. 7.

The contents of this chapter are derived from two main chapters of the PhD thesis of the author [47, Chapters 4 and 6], the original publication on Abstract Execution [50], and from three follow-up publications [4, 22, 48].

2   Abstract Execution

Abstract programs contain schematic placeholders representing many concrete statements or expressions. They naturally occur in many areas of computer science. Program synthesis [42, 46], for example, can be phrased as "show that there *exists* an instantiation of a *scaffold* satisfying my desired property." The scaffold is an abstract program, and the instantiation the result of the synthesis process. Consider, for example, the abstract program

$$\texttt{int f(int[] a) \{ } \boxed{P} \texttt{ return a[0]; \}}$$

containing an abstract statement *P*. To synthesize a version of method f returning the smallest element of array a (assuming that a is non-empty), we can *instantiate* *P* with "`Arrays.sort(a);`", and thus prove that there is a concrete program matching the scaffold and satisfying the desired specification.

Universal properties quantifying over programs are traditionally proven by *structural induction* [10]. Early work relied on pen-and-paper proofs [32, 36]. Recently, interactive theorem provers are used to mechanize correctness proofs, for example, in the CompCert verified compiler [31] or in the verification of the seL4 microkernel [28]. To prove, for example, that after executing "`int x=1; ` *P*" the value of x is 1, one should differentiate the cases of *P* being an assignment, conditional statement, loop, etc. In the case of industrial programming languages like JAVA, this approach quickly gets out of hand. The core idea of Abstract Execution [47, 50] is that it does not matter what *kind of statement P* is instantiated with, as long as it *does not write to variable* x and *completes normally* (e.g., does not throw an exception). In other words, we are concerned with the observable *behavior* of the possible instantiations.

We implemented this kind of reasoning as an extension of *Symbolic Execution* [6, 10, 27]. The principle of SE is to explore *all paths in a program* by replacing concrete inputs by symbols. Whenever the execution depends on the concrete value of an input (as for an `if` statement with symbolic guard), SE performs a case distinction and follows each path separately. During the execution, assignments are tracked in a *symbolic store*, while case distinctions update the *path condition*. A *symbolic state* is a pair (*PC*, *Store*) consisting of a path condition *PC* and a symbolic store *Store*. For example, executing an `if` statement with condition "`a>=0`" creates two successor states, one where $a \geq 0$ is added to the path condition, and one where $a < 0$ is added. A symbolic store is, in the simplest case, a sequence of assignments such as $(a := b, b := -b)$. This represents all (infinitely many) states where a attains the initial value of b, and b attains its negated initial value. In a state (*PC*, *Store*), all right-hand sides in *Store* are constrained by the conditions in *PC*: the state $(\{b < 0\}, (a := b, b := -b))$ represents all concrete states where a attains the initial, *negative* value of b, and b the *positive* inverted value. For example, the concrete states $a \mapsto -1, b \mapsto 1$ and $a \mapsto -17, b \mapsto 17$ are elements of this set of *concretizations*. We refer to [47, Chapter 3] for a discussion of SE and its semantics.

But how can we symbolically execute an *abstract* statement or expression? Our solution (1) reflects the abstractness on the level of symbolic stores and path conditions, and (2) performs a case distinction for all completion modes (normal completion, abrupt completion due to a thrown exception, **break**, etc.) in separate SE branches.

The central concept are abstract (state) updates. If the abstract statement P depends on a set of locations *footprintP* and may write to a set of locations *frameP*,[1] executing P in a state $(PC, Store)$ leads, for the case of normal completion, to a state

$$(PC, Store \circ \mathcal{U}_P(frameP :\approx \texttt{\textbackslash value}(footprintP)))$$

where $\mathcal{U}_P(frameP :\approx \texttt{\textbackslash value}(footprintP))$ is the abstract update and $\circ$ a *concatenation operator* for symbolic stores. The semantics of the abstract update is a collection of nonabstract updates with left-hand sides in *frameP*, and all right-hand sides depend at most on the values of locations in *footprintP*. Thus, an abstract store containing abstract updates represents up to infinitely many nonabstract stores, each representing up to infinitely many concrete assignments. The concatenation is resolved by interpreting the locations in *footprintP* in the context of *Store*; assignments by the abstract update of locations in *frameP* overwrite already existing ones in *Store*.

Abstract Execution provides a versatile specification framework allowing to precisely and, at the same time, abstractly specify assigned and read locations, and conditions for abrupt completion. Moreover, one can define functional assertions on the resulting symbolic state. Subsequently, we expound our specification language in Sect. 2.1. In Sect. 2.2, we show how to symbolically execute abstract programs.

2.1 Specifying Abstract Programs

AE extends the JAVA language with two keywords: "**abstract_statement** P;" and "**abstract_expression** *Type* e;" for declaring an *abstract statement* with identifier P and an *abstract expression* of type *Type* with identifier e, respectively. *We use the term Abstract Program Element (APE) to refer to both abstract statements and expressions.* If two APEs with the *same identifier* appear in a program (or a context of two programs), they are assumed to have the same semantics. This is especially useful for expressing transformations: two APEs on the left- and right-hand sides of a transformation rule represent the same concrete programs.

To specify frame, footprint, and abrupt completion behavior of APEs, we use JAVA Modeling Language (JML) [2, 30] specification comments starting with "@". For example, the abstract statement

```
//@ assignable x, y;
//@ accessible \nothing;
\abstract_statement P;
```

---

[1] We adopt the convention to call locations changed by a program its *frame* and locations that may be read by a program its *footprint* (see, e.g., [2, 25]).

Table 1 Problematic cases for *Slide Statements*

	Statement 1	Statement 2	Counterexample		
			Inputs	Result before	Result after
(1)	x++;	y = 2*z;			
(2)	x++;	y = 2*x;	$x = 1, y = 1$	$x = 2$, $y = 4$	$x = 2$, $y = 2$
(3)	x++;	x = y;	$x = 1, y = 1$	$x = 1$, $y = 1$	$x = 2$, $y = 1$
(4)	x = 20 / y;	y = 5;	$x = 1, y = 0$	$x = 1$, $y = 0$, **Exc.**	$x = 4$, $y = 5$
(5)	x = 20 / 0;	y = 5;	$x = 1, y = 0$	$x = 1$, $y = 0$, **Exc.**	$x = 1$, $y = 5$, **Exc.**

represents all concrete statements assigning *at most* variables x and y, while having no access to the state at all. Thus, "x=17;" is an instance of P, while "x=y;" is not (it reads y). There also exists the option to *enforce* some assignment of a location: "**assignable** x, **hasTo**(y);" specifies that y *has to* be assigned. Then "x=17;" would no longer be an instance of P (but, e.g., "x=17; y=17;" is).

When modeling transformation rules, *concrete* frames and footprints (such as x and y) are usually insufficient: a transformation should be applicable regardless of the names (and numbers) of variables and fields available in a particular context. We leverage the *theory of dynamic frames* [25] to that end. A dynamic frame is a set-valued specification variable representing an *unknown set of concrete locations*. Instead of enumerating variables in a frame as we did above, a placeholder symbol is used, for example, *frameP* or *footprintP*. If needed, the meaning of these symbols can be refined in specifications using usual set operations. For example, one can specify $x \in frameP$, or $frameP \subseteq frameQ$. These operations have corresponding representatives in JML; for simplicity, we continue using the mathematical notation.

We explain how to express constraints about frames and footprints along a refactoring technique from Sect. 4: *Slide Statements*, which we already mentioned in the introduction. The purpose of this refactoring is to bring statements closer together which participate in a common task, contributing to better understandability and preparing for subsequent refactorings like *Extract Method*.

To motivate the constraints which we are going to define, we present some example cases with counterexamples in Table 1. The two statements in Line 1 of the table can be swapped without problems: Their behavior is fully independent. In Line 2, the frame of the first statement intersects with the footprint of the second statement. Thus, applying *Slide Statements* leads to different results for variable y before and after the application: *frames and footprints of both statements must be disjoint*. This is not enough: a later occurring statement can overwrite changes of an earlier one. An example for this is shown in Line 3, where the overall result equals the result of the statement occurring last: *the frames of both statements must be disjoint*.

Figure 2 depicts an abstract program model for the *Slide Statements* refactoring including the two constraints on frames and footprints. The abstract statements A and B from the input model (Listing 3) occur in reverse order in the output

Listing 3 Input Model	Listing 4 Output Model
1 *//@* ~~ae_constraint~~	/*@ ae_constraint
2 @ *frameA ∩ footprintB = ∅ &&*	@ *frameA ∩ footprintB = ∅* &&
3 @ *frameB ∩ footprintA = ∅* &&	@ *frameB ∩ footprintA = ∅* &&
4 @ *frameA ∩ frameB = ∅;* */	@ *frameA ∩ frameB = ∅;* */
5	
6 //@ **assignable** *frameA*;	//@ **assignable** *frameB*;
7 //@ **accessible** *footprintA*;	//@ **accessible** *footprintB*;
8 \abstract_statement A;	\abstract_statement B;
9	
0 //@ **assignable** *frameB*;	//@ **assignable** *frameA*;
1 //@ **accessible** *footprintB*;	//@ **accessible** *footprintA*;
2 \abstract_statement B;	\abstract_statement A;

Fig. 2 Abstract program model for *Slide Statements* ignoring abrupt completion

model (Listing 4). Both abstract statements are annotated with dynamic frame symbols *frameA/footprintA* and *frameB/footprintB*, respectively, for their frames and footprints. Our constraints on them are implemented using an **ae_constraint** declaration in Lines 1–4: the constraints in Lines 2 and 3 enforce disjointness of frames and footprints, while the constraint in Line 4 enforces disjointness of the frames. Assuming normal completion, AE can prove these constraints sufficient.

In the JAVA language, we however have to take abrupt completion (here, exceptions and **return**s) into account. Line 4 in Table 1 shows an example where the order of the statements determines not only the result values of the considered variables but also the resulting *completion mode* (exception vs. normal completion) for the shown test case. These statements would, though, anyway not be amenable for *Slide Statements* since the requirement on the disjointness of frames and footprints is not met. In the scenario shown in Line 5, frames and footprints *are* disjoint; the outcome is still different before and after transformation, since early exceptional termination of the first statements impedes the assignment of 5 to y before, but not after the swap. This leads us to the additional requirement for semantic preservation in the presence of abrupt completion: *if one statement completes abruptly, the assignments by the other statement must not be "relevant."* If we are not concerned about the final value of variable y, we may reorder these statements. Furthermore, *abrupt completion must be mutually exclusive*, because otherwise (1) the assignments by *both* statements would have to be irrelevant, and (2) there could be different *reasons* for abrupt completion (**return** vs. thrown exception, different thrown exception types/objects).

Figure 3 shows the extension of the *Slide Statements* transformation model considering exceptions. For space reasons, we ignore **return**s here; the full model is available in [47, Appendix E]. If no conditions on abrupt completion behavior of APEs is provided, as in Fig. 2, AE automatically explores all paths corresponding to each possible completion mode. In Fig. 3, we bind exceptional behavior, using the "**exceptional_behavior requires** ...;" keyword, to uninterpreted predicates *throwsExcA/throwsExcB* (Lines 15–16 and 21–22). The

Listing 5 Input Model	Listing 6 Output Model

```
1  /*@ ae_constraint                      /*@ ae_constraint
2  @    frameA ∩ footprintB = ∅ &&         @    frameA ∩ footprintB = ∅ &&
3  @    frameB ∩ footprintA = ∅ &&         @    frameB ∩ footprintA = ∅ &&
4  @    frameA ∩ frameB = ∅ &&             @    frameA ∩ frameB = ∅ &&
5  @    \mutex(                            @    \mutex(
6  @       throwsExcA(\value(footprintA)), @       throwsExcA(\value(footprintA)),
7  @       throwsExcB(\value(footprintB))) && @     throwsExcB(\value(footprintB))) &&
8  @    (throwsExcA(\value(footprintA))     @    (throwsExcA(\value(footprintA))
9  @       ⟹ frameB ∩ relevant = ∅) &&     @       ⟹ frameB ∩ relevant = ∅) &&
10 @    (throwsExcB(\value(footprintB))     @    (throwsExcB(\value(footprintB))
11 @       ⟹ frameA ∩ relevant = ∅); */    @       ⟹ frameA ∩ relevant = ∅); */
12
13 //@ assignable frameA;                  //@ assignable frameB;
14 //@ accessible footprintA;              //@ accessible footprintB;
15 /*@ exceptional_behavior requires       /*@ exceptional_behavior requires
16 @    throwsExcA(\value(footprintA)); */ @    throwsExcB(\value(footprintB)); */
17 \abstract_statement A;                  \abstract_statement B;
18
19 //@ assignable frameB;                  //@ assignable frameA;
20 //@ accessible footprintB;              //@ accessible footprintA;
21 /*@ exceptional_behavior requires       /*@ exceptional_behavior requires
22 @    throwsExcB(\value(footprintB)); */ @    throwsExcA(\value(footprintA)); */
23 \abstract_statement B;                  \abstract_statement A;
```

Fig. 3 Model for *Slide Statements* with exceptions, extensions highlighted in gray

intended meaning is "the abstract statement A/B throws an exception *if, and only if*, the predicate *throwsExcA/throwsExcB* holds." Since whether or not a statement throws an exception is usually determined by its footprint (e.g., "x/y" throws an arithmetic exception iff y is zero), we define these predicates parametric in the values of the footprints: the dynamic frame *footprintA* represents a set of *locations*, while the expression **\value**(*footprintA*) represents the *values* of this set. Analogously to our usage of dynamic frame specification variables, we can now use these predicates in constraints (Lines 5–11 in Fig. 3). In Lines 5–7, we stipulate that *either* statement A *or* statement B may throw an exception (but not both) using the "**\mutex**" keyword. Assuming an abstract location set *relevant* representing relevant locations, we subsequently impose that if one statement completes abruptly due to a thrown exception, the frame of the other statement only contains *irrelevant* locations (Lines 8–11).

Our implementation of AE automatically *proves* semantic equivalence of the full model (including the specifications for **return**s, which work similarly to the ones for exception) in less than 20 s—*once and for all*, for all input programs satisfying the specified constraints. Given such a proof, we can be sure that our specified constraints are *sufficient for a safe application of the refactoring rule*.

In addition to "**exceptional_behavior**", the keywords "**return_behavior**" for abrupt completion due to a **return** and, for loop bodies, "**break_behavior**" for **break**s and "**continue_behavior**" for **continue**s are supported. For labeled **break**s, one writes "**break_behavior** (*lbl*)" (similarly for labeled **continue**s). Moreover, "**requires**" can be replaced by "**ensures**" to specify a *post*condition on the resulting state. While this is rarely needed for transformation rules, it can be useful, for example, in incremental, "correct-by-construction" program development.[2]

The specification framework we have just presented is designed with real applications *and* automatic proofs in mind. In Sects. 4–6, we demonstrate that it is strong enough to model interesting transformations from different areas of code optimization. Next, we introduce our Symbolic Execution rules for AE.

2.2   Symbolic Execution of Abstract Program Elements

Symbolic execution of an APE results in separate execution branches for each possible abrupt completion mode. Figure 4a visualizes the relevant part of the execution tree for an abstract statement (we omitted labeled **break**s and **continue**s). Assuming that we start in a symbolic state $(PC, Store)$, we produce symbolic output states s_{normal} for normal completion, s_{exc} for abrupt completion due to a thrown exception, and so on. In the figure, symbolic states are input states for the execution of the annotated statement. The variables res and exc of types Object and Throwable, respectively, are created fresh, that is, they are not declared anywhere else in the context program. The execution tree for an abstract expression (Fig. 4b) looks similarly, but as expressions can only complete normally or due to a thrown exception, an abstract expression node only has two successors. We point out that also expressions can have a non-empty frame, as in "x > y++".

In the remainder of this section, we show how the states s_{normal}, s_{exc} etc. are formally constructed. This is an important part of our framework, but not required for understanding the sections that follow. Readers not interested in the formalism can therefore safely skip to Sect. 3, where we describe how to use AE in practice.

Our central concept is the *abstract update*: for an APE P with frame *frameP* and footprint *footprintP*, an abstract update $\mathcal{U}_P(frameP :\approx \mathtt{\backslash value}(footprintP))$ has the same effect on the state as P. However, while P may complete abruptly (e.g., throw an exception), the abstract update *always completes normally*.

To express the symbolic input states for successors of APEs in the execution tree, we need to *apply* symbolic stores to formulas: we write $[\![Store]\!]formula$ for the transformation of *formula* according to *Store*. For example, $[\![x := 17]\!]x \geq 0$ is equivalent to $17 \geq 0$ and thus to true.

Subsequently, we define the symbolic states resulting from the execution of an abstract statement "**\abstract_statement P;**" in the symbolic state $(PC, Store)$. We write *normalPost*, *excPre*, *excPost*, etc., for the pre- and postconditions specified using JML "**requires**" and "**ensures**" clauses in the scope of the respective behavior ("**normal_behavior**", "**exceptional_behavior**", etc.).

---

[2] The use of AE for Correctness-by-Construction has been explored in a Master's thesis [53].

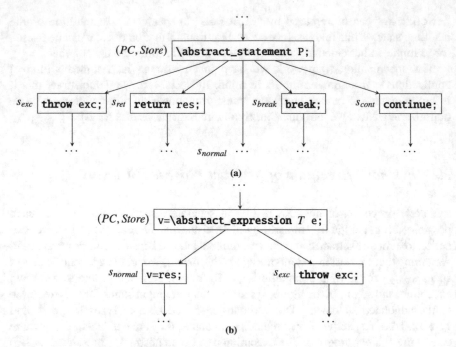

(a)

(b)

Fig. 4 Execution tree fragments for abstract statements and abstract expressions. Symbolic input states for tree nodes ((PC, $Store$), s_{exc}, etc.) are annotated on the left-hand side of the nodes. (**a**) Execution tree fragment for an abstract statement. (**b**) Execution tree fragment for an abstract expression

Normal Completion

We use the abbreviation *completesNormally* to denote the negated disjunction of the preconditions for all other completion modes: *completesNormally* $\iff$ $\neg(excPre \vee returnPre \vee breakPre \vee continuePre)$. This precondition is evaluated in the initial store *Store*, while the postcondition *normalPost* is evaluated in the resulting store after the application of the abstract update (and can thus represent constraints on the resulting state). In case the abstract statement is specified to *always complete abruptly* in *Store*, the precondition $[\![Store]\!](completesNormally)$ evaluates to false. Then, this symbolic execution branch becomes infeasible and is not followed any further. This holds similarly for all other branches discussed below.

Formally, we define the symbolic state s_{normal} as

$$s_{normal} := (PC \cup \{[\![Store]\!](completesNormally),$$

$$[\![Store \circ \mathcal{U}_{\mathrm{P}}(frameP :\approx \mathbf{\backslash value}(footprintP))]\!](normalPost)\},$$

$$Store \circ \mathcal{U}_{\mathrm{P}}(frameP :\approx \mathbf{\backslash value}(footprintP)))$$

Abrupt Completion Due to a Thrown Exception

The state s_{exc} for completion due to a thrown exception is constructed similarly to s_{normal}, just with the appropriate pre- and postconditions. There is one addition: we initialize the exception variable exc (see Fig. 4a) to a value $exc^P(\mathbf{\backslash value}(footprint))$, where "$exc^P$" is a unary function symbol exclusively introduced in symbolic execution of the abstract statement P: it is generated *fresh* when first encountering P, but is *re-used* whenever another occurrence of P is executed. We follow the same procedure for abstract update symbols $\mathcal{U}_P$. This is especially useful for equivalence proofs, since abstract statements with the same identifiers exhibit the same behavior—*when executed in the same state*. It is thus essential to pass the current value of P's footprint to the exc^P function, since P might throw different exception objects for different initial execution states. The variable exc can be referred to in the postcondition *excPost* to constrain the values of the thrown exception object.

$$s_{exc} := \big(PC \cup \{[\![Store]\!](\ excPre\ ),$$

$$[\![Store \circ \mathcal{U}_P(frameP :\approx \mathbf{\backslash value}(footprintP)) \circ$$

$$(\texttt{exc} := exc^P(\mathbf{\backslash value}(footprint)))\ ]\!](\ excPost\ )\},$$

$$Store \circ \mathcal{U}_P(frameP :\approx \mathbf{\backslash value}(footprintP)) \circ$$

$$(\texttt{exc} := exc^P(\mathbf{\backslash value}(footprint)))\ \big)$$

Abrupt Completion Due to a Returned Result

The symbolic state s_{ret} for a **return** statement of a result is constructed exactly the same way as s_{exc} for a thrown exception. If the abstract statement is executed in the context of a **void** method, the initialization of the res variable is omitted (and the execution tree contains a "**return;**" instead of a "**return res;**" node). As in the exceptional case, the postcondition *returnPost* can refer to the res variable to characterize the returned result (in the context of a non-**void** method).

$$s_{ret} := \big(PC \cup \{[\![Store]\!](returnPre),$$

$$[\![Store \circ \mathcal{U}_P(frameP :\approx \mathbf{\backslash value}(footprintP)) \circ$$

$$(\texttt{res} := result^P(\mathbf{\backslash value}(footprint)))]\!](returnPost)\},$$

$$Store \circ \mathcal{U}_P(frameP :\approx \mathbf{\backslash value}(footprintP)) \circ$$

$$(\texttt{res} := result^P(\mathbf{\backslash value}(footprint))))$$

Abrupt Completion Due to a Break or Continue Statement

The state s_{break} for abrupt completion due to a **break** looks exactly like s_{normal} for normal completion with different pre- and postconditions, as initialization of a returned or thrown object is not required. If the abstract statement occurs outside any loop, we omit this state and the corresponding node in the execution tree.

$$s_{break} := \big(PC \cup \{ [\![Store]\!](breakPre),$$

$$[\![Store \circ \mathcal{U}_P(frameP :\approx \texttt{\textbackslash value}(footprintP))]\!](breakPost) \},$$

$$Store \circ \mathcal{U}_P(frameP :\approx \texttt{\textbackslash value}(footprintP)) \big)$$

The **continue** case is analogous. For *abstract expressions*, s_{normal} has a simpler *completesNormally* condition (i.e., $\neg excPre$) and contains an initialization of the res variable similar to s_{ret} for abstract statements; s_{exc} is identical.

To reason about the symbolic states arising from the execution of APEs, we provide a number of simplification and normalization rules for symbolic stores with abstract updates. We refer to [47, Sec. 4.3.2] for their full definitions. We demonstrate some of these rules in the following example.

Example 1 (Execution of the Slide Statements Model) We investigate the "normal completion" case of the *output* model for the *Slide Statements* refactoring from Listing 6, Fig. 3 on Page 206. The final state after executing the abstract statements is

$$(\{frameA \cap footprintB = \emptyset,\ frameB \cap footprintA = \emptyset,\ frameA \cap frameB = \emptyset,$$

$$mutexFormula,$$

$$\neg throwsExcB(\texttt{\textbackslash value}(footprintB)),$$

$$\neg [\![\mathcal{U}_B(frameB :\approx \texttt{\textbackslash value}(footprintB))]\!]throwsExcA(\texttt{\textbackslash value}(footprintA))\},$$

$$(\mathcal{U}_B(frameB :\approx \texttt{\textbackslash value}(footprintB)) \circ \mathcal{U}_A(frameA :\approx \texttt{\textbackslash value}(footprintA))))$$

For simplicity, we omit conditions on abrupt completion due to other reasons than a thrown exception. The first four elements in the path condition stem from the **ae_constraint** specification in Lines 1–11 in Listing 6, where *mutexFormula* abbreviates the condition on mutual exclusion of abrupt completion (Lines 5–11).

First, we apply the abstract update $\mathcal{U}_B(\ldots)$ to the *throwsExcA* expression in the path condition and resolve the update concatenation in the store by the rule transforming $(Store_1 \circ Store_2)$ to $(Store_1, [\![Store_1]\!]Store_2)$, resulting in

$$(\{frameA \cap footprintB = \emptyset,\ frameB \cap footprintA = \emptyset,\ frameA \cap frameB = \emptyset,$$

$$mutexFormula,$$

$$\neg throwsExcB(\texttt{\textbackslash value}(footprintB)),$$

$$\neg throwsExcA([\![\mathcal{U}_B(frameB :\approx \texttt{\textbackslash value}(footprintB))]\!]\texttt{\textbackslash value}(footprintA))\},$$

$(\mathcal{U}_{\mathrm{B}}(frameB :\approx \backslash\texttt{value}(footprintB)),$

$\|\mathcal{U}_{\mathrm{B}}(\textit{frameB} :\approx \backslash\texttt{value}(footprintB))\|(\mathcal{U}_{\mathrm{A}}(frameA :\approx \backslash\texttt{value}(footprintA)))))$

Next, we simplify the application $[\![\mathcal{U}_{\mathrm{B}}(\dots)]\!]\mathcal{U}_{\mathrm{A}}(\dots)$ in the store to

$\mathcal{U}_{\mathrm{A}}(frameA :\approx [\![\mathcal{U}_{\mathrm{B}}(frameB :\approx \backslash\texttt{value}(footprintB))]\!](\backslash\texttt{value}(footprintA))).$

The expression $[\![\mathcal{U}_{\mathrm{B}}(frameB :\approx \backslash\texttt{value}(footprintB))]\!](\backslash\texttt{value}(footprintA))$ occurs two times in the resulting state: once in the path condition and once in the symbolic store. Since the path condition contains the assumption $frameB \cap footprintA = \emptyset$, we know that the assignments due to $\mathcal{U}_{\mathrm{B}}(\dots)$ are irrelevant for $\backslash\texttt{value}(footprintA)$; we deduce that we can drop $[\![\mathcal{U}_{\mathrm{B}}(\dots)]\!]$ and obtain the much simpler state

$(\{frameA \cap footprintB = \emptyset, frameB \cap footprintA = \emptyset, frameA \cap frameB = \emptyset,$

$\quad mutexFormula,$

$\quad \neg throwsExcB(\backslash\texttt{value}(footprintB)), \neg throwsExcA(\backslash\texttt{value}(footprintA))\},$

$(\mathcal{U}_{\mathrm{B}}(frameB :\approx \backslash\texttt{value}(footprintB)), \mathcal{U}_{\mathrm{A}}(frameA :\approx \backslash\texttt{value}(footprintA))))$

There is one more rule we are going to apply; this time, it is not a simplification but a *normalization* rule. The state we obtain by executing the *input* model for *Slide Statements* in Listing 5 equals the one from above for the output model, with one exception: the order of the abstract updates in the store. Indeed, we cannot simply swap elements of a store, since a later element might overwrite assignments by an earlier one. However, we know from the path condition that $frameA \cap frameB = \emptyset$. Therefore, we can apply a normalization rule reordering abstract updates according to the lexicographic order of their identifiers. Our final result is

$(\{frameA \cap footprintB = \emptyset, frameB \cap footprintA = \emptyset, frameA \cap frameB = \emptyset,$

$\quad mutexFormula,$

$\quad \neg throwsExcB(\backslash\texttt{value}(footprintB)), \neg throwsExcA(\backslash\texttt{value}(footprintA))\},$

$(\mathcal{U}_{\mathrm{A}}(frameA :\approx \backslash\texttt{value}(footprintA)), \mathcal{U}_{\mathrm{B}}(frameB :\approx \backslash\texttt{value}(footprintB))))$

This state is equivalent to the final state for the input model (as the path condition is a set, the order of path constraints is irrelevant). Assuming that this also holds for the abrupt completion cases, we conclude the equivalence of the input and output models for *Slide Statements*, and follow that applying this transformation is semantics-preserving for all concrete instantiations satisfying the constraints we formalized.

3   The REFINITY Workbench

We implemented AE by extending the KeY [2] program prover. The extension consists of ~5.5k lines of JAVA and ~400 lines of *Taclet* code. Taclets are KeY's language for SE rules, which we had to significantly extend for our AE taclets. More implementation details are available in [47, Sec. 4.4].

Using this implementation, one can reason about programs containing APEs. However, symbols such as dynamic frames and abstract predicates have to be declared in KeY input files separately from the JAVA code. Proof obligations for showing the equivalence of two abstract program fragments (which is the prime application of AE and needed for our case studies described in Sects. 4 and 5) have to be manually defined. Those proof obligations are all structurally similar, but tedious to write from scratch. Additionally, there is no editing support for abstract programs, which require a significant amount of JML specification lines.

Addressing these issues, we developed REFINITY [48], a workbench for specifying and proving properties of statement-level JAVA code transformation rules. A major driver for the development of REFINITY was an invited talk in a tutorial session at iFM'19,[3] where participants without any background in using KeY successfully applied REFINITY to prove the correctness of two refactoring techniques.

Figure 5 shows the REFINITY GUI. Input and output models for a transformation rule are written to the two text fields at marker ①. When editing, one can

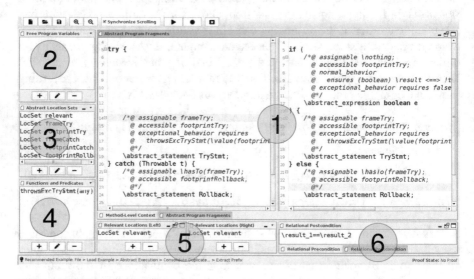

Fig. 5 The REFINITY window

---

[3] https://ifm2019.hvl.no/refa/#pcrr.

use a number of keyboard shortcuts for creating stubs for APEs and transformation constraint. Field ② contains global program variables which can be referred to in the input and output model. In the compartment labeled ③ , we declare dynamic frame variables used in the model ("LocSet" is the sort for abstract location sets, i.e., dynamic frames). REFINITY models include by default an additional location set *"relevant"* representing all relevant locations. If we do not impose further constraints, for example, exclude some locations from *relevant*, correctness has to be proven under the assumption that *all* locations are in this set. Abstract predicates (like *throwsExcA*(...) in the previous section) and functions are declared in input field ④ .

Fields ⑤ and ⑥ specify global assumptions and proof objectives. The effects of the abstract programs specified in field ① are recorded in two *sequences* \result_1 and \result_2 for the input and output model. Their elements can be accessed using array syntax, for example, \result_1[0]. Positions 0 and 1 are reserved for returned results and thrown exceptions. Starting from position 2, the final values of "relevant locations" declared in fields ⑤ (with the dynamic frame *relevant* being the default) are stored. The standard postcondition, which we see in field ⑥ , is \result_1==\result_2. Without constraints about *relevant*, this specifies that returned values, thrown exceptions, and the whole memory after termination have to be identical. More fine-grained postconditions can also be specified: for example, if the first relevant location is an integer variable, "\result_1[2]>2*\result_2[2]" is admissible. The global "Relational Precondition" (⑥) has access to the *initial* values of free program variables (field ②) and abstract location sets (field ③).

Pressing ▶ transforms the model into a KeY proof obligation and starts the automatic proof search. If KeY reports success, the specified model is correct. Saved proof certificates can be validated against the loaded model using the ✸ button.

During development of a new model, KeY will usually finish unsuccessfully, leaving one or more proof goals open. In rare cases and for highly complicated models, the reason could be that KeY needs more time or is not able to close the proof although the model is valid—we hit a *prover incapacity*. In the latter case, one can try to close the proof by interacting with the prover. More likely, though, are problems in the model. Inspecting the open goals provides feedback on how to refine the model to make it sound. Possible *refinements* include (1) declaring the disjointness of dynamic frames, (2) imposing mutual exclusion on abrupt completion behavior, (3) declaring a functional postcondition for APEs, and (4) refining the relational *post*condition or (4) adding a relational *pre*condition.

The proof obligation REFINITY generates for KeY consists of a JAVA class with two methods left(...) and right(...) containing the abstract program fragments, and a problem description file containing proof strategy settings, declarations of variable, function, predicate, and abstract location set symbols and the proof goal (expressed in KeY's program logic "JAVA Dynamic Logic" [2]). Such proof goals easily span around 40 lines in concrete syntax.

REFINITY spares the user from having to deal with such technicalities, simplifying the modeling process. It automatically creates the mentioned files, starts a KeY proof with reasonable presets, and displays proof status information in its status bar. Additionally, it supports syntactic extensions unsupported by KeY.

Execution of Abstract Loops

Symbolic execution of loops requires advanced techniques: when loop guards are symbolic, we cannot know the number of iterations after which the loop will terminate. Frequently, *loop invariants* are employed to abstract loop behavior. A loop invariant is a specification respected *by every loop iteration*, which can be used to abstract away from the concrete loop regardless of the number of iterations. It is generally hard to come up with suitable invariants; indeed, *specifications* have been identified as the "new bottleneck" of formal verification (see, e.g., [2]). In program equivalence proofs using functional verification techniques, one even needs the *strongest* possible invariant for each occurring loop ([7], [47, Sec. 5.4.2]).

Luckily, there is a way to *generically* specify *abstract* strongest loop invariants which we can use in AE. Assume a loop with guard $g(x)$ operating on a single variable x. The formula $Inv(x)$ is a strongest loop invariant for that loop if it is (1) preserved by every run, and (2) there is *exactly one* value v s.t. $Inv(v)$ holds and $g(v)$ does *not* hold. Condition (2) means that there remains no degree of freedom in the choice of the value of x after loop termination: *Inv* describes the *exact*, final value. We can rewrite the condition to $\exists v; \forall x; ((Inv(x) \land \neg g(x)) \rightarrow x = v)$.

Generalizing this to a loop with an abstract expression as guard and dynamic frame specification variables as frame and footprint yields a condition constraining instantiations of abstract invariant formulas to abstract *strongest* ones. We can add this condition as a precondition in REFINITY and use the abstract invariant formula in our program. We refer to [47, Sec. 6.2] for a full account.

REFINITY can be downloaded at `key-project.org/REFINITY/`. It comes with a number of examples to get started with modeling transformation rules. The next three sections are devoted to particular applications of REFINITY and AE.

4   Correctness of Refactoring Rules

Refactoring aims to change code in a way that does *not alter its external behavior*, yet improves its *internal structure* [18]. In the context of software reengineering, refactoring can contribute to better understandability, and thus to the maintainability of a legacy system. Generally, refactoring is a risky process, especially for poorly understood legacy systems. It has been shown that common refactorings can easily, and accidentally, change a program's behavior [15]. Most refactorings come with preconditions. If those are not met, the transformed program might not compile, or—which is worse—compile, but behave in a different way. Testing contributes to safe refactoring, but can do much in line for insufficiently robust test suites [5].

In contrast to other code transformations, code refactoring is well supported in modern IDEs. Unfortunately, relying on refactoring tools does not automatically guarantee the preservation of program behavior [14, 44], as these tools typically do not implement *all* preconditions [45]. Indeed, documentation of preconditions for safe refactoring in literature is vastly incomplete, as we discovered in our case study.

Using REFINITY [48], we modeled nine statement-level refactoring techniques from [17, 18], including two with loops. In an iterative process, we refined the models by adding additional constraints, until we could prove them semantically equivalent.

Most *practically applied* refactorings are confined to method bodies [43]. However, existing work on correctness of code refactoring almost exclusively regards high-level techniques such as "move field" or "pull up method." AE and REFINITY thus focus on a significant blind spot by addressing *statement-level* transformations.

By documenting precise preconditions for safe, statement-level refactoring, we contribute insights useful for building more robust refactoring tools. Those can eventually be adopted for structured reengineering of legacy systems.

In the remainder of this section, we outline our derived preconditions for safe applications of the nine considered refactoring techniques. Note that since we prove *equivalence* of input and output models, we simultaneously consider *dual refactoring techniques* (such as *Inline Method* for *Extract Method*). A more detailed account and full abstract program models are provided in [47, Sec. 6.3 and Appendix E].

Slide Statements
We already discussed *Slide Statements* in Sect. 2.1. The idea of this technique is to reorder statements to keep those together which fulfill a common purpose [18]. Let *frameA/frameB* and *footprintA/footprintB* be the frames and footprints of the participating statements A and B, respectively. We derived the following preconditions (only the first three of which are documented in [18]):

1. *frameA* and *frameB* have to be disjoint.
2. *frameA* and *footprintB* have to be disjoint.
3. *frameB* and *footprintA* have to be disjoint.
4. A may only complete abruptly if B completes normally, and vice Versa.
5. if A completes abruptly, B performs no assignments relevant to the outside, and vice versa.

Consolidate Duplicate Conditional Fragments
This variation of *Slide Statements* consists in moving code that is executed in all branches of a conditional statement to outside that conditional. We modeled four variants: extracting (1) a common *prefix* from an **if** statement, (2) a common

postfix from an `if` statement, (3) a common postfix from a `try-catch` statement to after the `try-catch`, (4) a common postfix from a `try-catch` statement to the `finally` branch of the `try- catch`. The two variants (3) and (4) are distinguished due to an ambiguity in the refactoring's description ("(moving) to the final block" [17]).

Variant (1) comes with the very same preconditions as *Slide Statements*. Variant (2) can be applied without preconditions. The extraction of a postfix from a `try` statement (variant (3)) to after that statement can be applied under the assumption that P does not throw an exception, which also can be deduced from the description in [17]. Furthermore, P must not access the caught exception object. Those restrictions also apply for variant (4). For this variant of the refactoring, schematically

$$\text{try} \{ Q_1 \, P \} \text{ catch } (T \ e) \{ Q_2 \, P \}$$
$$\rightsquigarrow \quad \text{try} \{ Q_1 \} \text{ catch } (T \ e) \{ Q_2 \} \text{ finally } \{ P \}$$

we derived the additional, unmentioned precondition that Q_1 must not complete due to a `return`. Otherwise, P would be executed after, but not before the refactoring.

Consolidate Conditional Expression

For the case of sequential or nested conditionals with "the same result" [17], this refactoring proposes to merge these into a single check to improve clarity. The two variants of this technique are schematically represented as

$$\text{if } (expr_1) \{ P \} \text{ if } (expr_2) \{ P \} \quad \Big| \quad \text{if } (expr_1) \{ \text{if } (expr_2) \{ P \} \}$$
$$\rightsquigarrow \quad \text{if } (expr_1 \parallel expr_2) \{ P \} \quad \Big| \quad \rightsquigarrow \quad \text{if } (expr_1 \ \&\& \ expr_2) \{ P \}$$

Our interpretation of "have the same result" is that P *always* returns or throws an exception (as in all examples in [17]). Thus, P is never executed twice in the sequential case. In the case of nested `if` statements, P can complete *arbitrarily*.

Both variants can be applied *without additional preconditions*. Fowler mentions that conditionals *must not have any side effects*, which is, however, *only* necessary for logical connectors *without short-circuit evaluation* (i.e., "$|$" and not "$||$", etc.).

Extract Method, Decompose Conditional, and Move Statements to Callers

Method extraction is a well-known refactoring technique implemented in many IDEs. According to [17], it may be applied if the extracted code does not assign more than one local variable referenced in the outside context. We discovered two additional, unmentioned constraints: (1) The extracted fragment must not return, since this changes control flow. (2) If the newly created method is a *query* and the extracted fragment throws an exception, it must not change the value of the returned query result variable before. For the second precondition, consider the following example:

```
1  int avg = ????;             int avg = ERROR;
2  try {                       try {
3    avg = sumOfElems(intList);     avg = average(intList);
4    avg /= intList.size();
5  } catch (ArithmeticException ae) {}   } catch (ArithmeticException ae) {}
6  averages.add(avg);          averages.add(avg);
```

When presented with an empty list, the computation of the average in Line 4 will complete abruptly because of a division by 0. Thus, the value of avg will be 0 (the sum of no elements) at Line 6 before the refactoring, while its value *after* the transformation is that of the constant ERROR: The method average completes abruptly and avg is not assigned in Line 3. One might argue that this is an improvement; still, it is not semantics-preserving. What is more, as we always prove semantic *equivalence*, the reverse direction *Inline Method* is also covered. In the example, one would introduce a bug when following the reverse direction and inlining method average.

Decompose Conditional [17] is a variant where condition and both branches of an **if** statement are extracted to individual methods. For the branches, this is identical to *Extract Method*; there is no precondition for the extracted *condition*.

Move Statements to Callers [18] is a variant of *Inline Method* where a prefix (and not the whole body) of a method is moved to the callers. Conversely, *Move Statements into Method* moves statements before an invocation to inside the called method. The same restrictions as for *Extract Method/Inline Method* apply.

Replace Exception with Test

In our example for *Extract Method* above, we used a **try** statement to react to the *expected* behavior that a list can be empty. Instead, we could have *tested* the list for emptiness, and reserved exceptions for *unexpected* behavior. Observe that then, method extraction of the two statements computing the list's average would even have been safe. This observation, on the other hand, suggests that the *Replace Exception with Test* is not generally semantics-preserving, though no restrictions are mentioned in literature. Assume a statement P throws an exception if the condition *cond* holds. *Replace Exception with Test* transforms "**try** { P } **catch** (...) { Q }" to "**if** (!(*cond*)) { P } **else** { Q }". In our first proof attempt, we found the problem that if P throws an exception, it might change the relevant state before completing. After the refactoring, this is no longer the case (cf. the change to the variable avg above). We derived four scenarios under which this refactoring *is* safe:

One can safely apply *Replace Exception with Test* if it either holds that (1) the frame of P is disjoint from the set of relevant locations *and* from the frame of Q (it may still influence Q's behavior by writing to its *footprint*), or (2) the frames of P and of Q are disjoint from the set of relevant locations, and Q always completes normally, or (3) the frame of P is disjoint from the footprint of Q, and Q *has to* assign *all* locations assigned by P, or (4) statement Q starts with a "rollback" resetting all locations in the frame of P to independent values. None of these conditions have been mentioned before.

Split Loop

Loop splitting is a common optimization technique which we also address in Sect. 5 and 6. Apart from being useful for, for example, code parallelization, it contributes to readability by dividing loops with separate concerns, and by clearing the way for subsequent optimizations such as the replacement by stream operations. Schematically, "`while` (g) $\{ P\ Q \}$" gets "`while` (g) $\{ P \}$ `while` (g) $\{ Q \}$". We isolated the following sufficient preconditions: (1) The frames of P and Q have to be disjoint from the footprint of g, and the frame of g is empty, (2) the frames of P and Q have to be disjoint, (3) the frame of P must be disjoint from the footprint of Q, and vice versa, (4) the guard g and statement P must not complete abruptly, and (5) Q must not complete abruptly before g and P committed their final results (or, established their invariants). None of these have been documented in [17, 18].

Observe that loops over an iterator (with a guard like "`it.hasNext()`") do not satisfy these preconditions: a call to "`it.next()`" in P or Q changes the state on which the evaluation of g depends, which is not allowed due to condition (1). Therefore, it is not safe to apply *Split Loop* to such loops.

Remove Control Flag

Instead of using a "control flag" for deciding when to terminate a loop, this refactoring suggests to resort to **break** or **continue** statements to better communicate the intended control flow. The shortcut associated by the introduction of abrupt completion, however, generally breaks semantic equivalence. Any code that would have been executed after setting the control flag (which is skipped by the shortcut) must not have effects visible outside the loop. Otherwise, it has to be duplicated:

$$\text{while } (!\text{done } \&\& \ g) \{ \text{ if } (cond) \{ P \quad \text{done=\textbf{true}; } \} \ Q \}$$
$$\rightsquigarrow \text{while } (g) \{ \text{ if } (cond) \{ P \ \boxed{Q} \text{ break; } \} \ Q \}$$

Relying on the mechanics described in [17] likely produces incorrect results.

We proved both *Slide Statements* and *Remove Control Flag* using abstract strongest invariants. For *Remove Control Flag*, we apply an even stronger type of loop invariant also considering abrupt completion (standard invariants only have to hold at loop *entry*, and not after (abruptly) leaving the loop).

In the subsequent two sections, we regard code transformations from an optimization point of view: how can we transform code such that it can be *better parallelized* (Sect. 5), and what is the effect of a transformation on *execution cost* (Sect. 6)?

5 Restructuring for Parallelization

Legacy systems were typically developed before the widespread use of modern software engineering techniques [40] like parallel programming interfaces such as OpenMP. *Adapting* existing sequential legacy software to *parallel environments* can save time and money, while avoiding the loss of domain knowledge. One powerful method to parallelize programs are *parallel design patterns* [24, 34] embodying best practices and correct as well as efficient usage of parallelization interfaces. This even yields a *semi-automatic* approach [38] for migrating sequential to parallel code.

As legacy code was not written with parallel patterns in mind, it often does not allow immediate application of a pattern: a certain amount of prior *code restructuring* is unavoidable in most cases. The DiscoPoP [38] framework implements a small number of *sequential* code transformation schemata that frequently suffice to bring sequential code into the form required for the application of a parallel pattern. To ensure that the parallelized program retains the functionality of the original legacy code, it is essential to ensure the correctness of the sequential restructuring rules.

In [22], we focused on three representative restructuring techniques, isolated conditions under which they are safe to apply, and proved—using Abstract Execution and REFINITY—that these conditions are sufficiently strong. Those schemata, previously developed within the DiscoPoP framework, are (1) *Computational Unit (CU) Repositioning*, (2) *Loop Splitting*, and (3) *Geometric Decomposition*. The latter two are loop transformations using an advanced memory layout specification mechanism. The corresponding proofs are, for a change, not fully automatic but require a small number of manual rule applications (<0.3% of all applications). We brief the most relevant aspects of the formalizations and proofs for these three schemata.

CU Repositioning

A CU is a piece of code with little to no internal parallelism, and the basic unit of dependence graphs generated by DiscoPoP. *CU Repositioning* prepares code for an application of the *pipeline pattern*. In a pipeline, each unit can depend on units in prior stages, but *not* in later stages [35]. To enable this pattern, it is sometimes required to *reposition* a later occurring CU to the first CU, merging those into a single CU. In practice, this usually means to move statements occurring after a loop or call to before that loop/call. *CU Repositioning* is an instance of *Slide Statements* (cf. Sect. 4) with *the same preconditions*. This is a notable connection between refactoring and parallelization: the same transformation can serve different purposes.

Loop Splitting

Loop Splitting is an optimization splitting one into several loops. Here, it is used to enable the *Do-All* parallel design pattern, which requires that there are no data dependences between different loop iterations. When an initial segment of iterations *does* have external dependences, we can factor out this segment and apply *Do-All* to

Fig. 6 Abstract memory layout for *Loop Splitting* of a loop with t iterations at index D

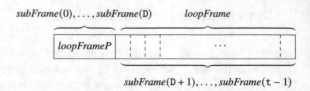

$subFrame(0), \ldots, subFrame(D)$ $loopFrame$

$loopFrameP$

$subFrame(D + 1), \ldots, subFrame(t - 1)$

the remaining iterations. *Loop Splitting* is a special case of the *Split Loop* refactoring additionally requiring that the parts that are to be parallelized are independent.

Our REFINITY model thus sets up a more advanced memory layout, as depicted in Fig. 6. Each of the t loop iterations operate on their own set of memory locations *subFrame(i)*. Assuming that we factor out the first $D + 1$ iterations, the precondition on the correctness of the restructured *sequential* code is that *subFrame*(0) to *subFrame*(D) (the part pulled out) are disjoint from *subFrame*(D + 1) to *subFrame*(t − 1) (the subjects to *Do-All*). In addition, the location sets *subFrame*(D + 1) to *subFrame*(t − 1) have to be disjoint from each other, which is a prerequisite for *Do-All*.

This modeling technique using a *family* of location sets required extensions of AE and REFINITY. The existing proof strategies are yet lacking dedicated support for the arising constraints, which is why we had to perform 7 simple and 16 non-trivial proof steps (out of a total of 15,600 steps) manually, which amounts to 0.1%.

Geometric Decomposition

If a program can be understood as a *sequence of operations* on a *main data structure*, often the best way of parallelization is to decompose this structure. Lists, for example, can be *decomposed* into substructures in a similar manner as dividing a *geometric* region into subregions—hence the name. We focused on the decomposition of a loop with t iterations into N loops of size t/N. These N loops can then be run in parallel.

Geometric Decomposition is a *generalization* of *Loop Splitting*: instead of dividing a loop into *two* parts, it is split into N > 1 parts. Our model uses a similar abstract memory setup as for *Loop Splitting*. The essential correctness precondition is that each bundle of iterations of size t/N has to operate on a separate memory region.

This transformation is the most complex one proven with AE up to now. The proof consists of ~84k rule applications, of which 215 are manual (0.26%).

6 Cost Analysis of Transformation Rules

Apart from running previously sequential code in parallel, one can aim at reducing the *execution cost of sequential code* by applying optimizing transformations, as exercised by many compilers [1]. What is more, when transforming code for *different* reasons (e.g., during code refactoring), one may be concerned about the impact on execution cost. A good example is *Split Loop*: naively, one could use performance as an argument against dividing one loop into two, disregarding understandability of the resulting code. However, the overhead attached to loop splitting merely consists in double evaluations of the loop guard, which is often negligible.

Cost analysis for *individual* programs has been addressed by a plethora of tools (e.g., [3, 21, 23]). The relative cost of *different concrete* programs has been subject to formal analyses (e.g., [39]). However, the cost impact of program *transformations*, which can be coined as the relative cost of two *schematic* programs, has not been studied before. We proposed *Quantitative Abstract Execution (QAE)* [4], the first approach to analyze the cost of schematic programs and thus of transformations.

Our technique combines a new frontend to the COSTA cost analyzer [3] and an extension of the AE framework implemented in KeY to a *fully automatic* toolchain. Its workflow is visualized in Fig. 7. One starts with an abstract program and a cost model (number of instructions, allocated memory, etc.) which are input to the cost analyzer ①. Each cost model comes in three flavors differing in their *strength*. Those are, in descending order, *exact*, *upper bound*, and *asymptotic cost*. Generally, we try to derive exact bounds first. The output of the analyzer is a *cost bound* w.r.t. the chosen cost model and a set of *cost invariants* and *ranking functions* for each loop in the program. We enrich the initial transformation model by translating this *quantitative information* to the QAE specification framework. The result of this is given to the QAE implementation on top of KeY ②. We use a proof strategy specifically tailored to the kinds of constraints arising in QAE to obtain a *certificate* for the correctness of the cost bounds in the chosen strength. If the certification process succeeds, we save the certificate and output the bounds ③. Otherwise, we *weaken* the strength of the cost model: from exact cost we descend to upper bound and later to asymptotic cost. Then, we continue at ①. Alternatively, one can inspect the failed proof attempt to obtain feedback for improving components ① or ②.

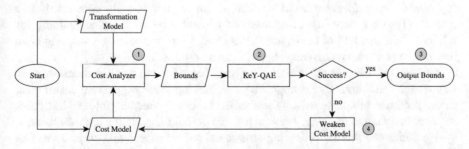

Fig. 7 Workflow of our approach to cost analysis of transformation rules

We implemented our toolchain as a command-line application. Excluding the libraries, and not counting blank lines and comments, it consists of 1,803 lines of PYTHON code (the extension of the cost analyzer), 703 lines of JAVA code (the conversion tool transforming the output of the cost analyzer to input files for KeY), and a 389-line bash script implementing the overall workflow.

We evaluated our approach for seven typical code optimization rules. In six cases, we used the number of executed instructions as a cost model, and in one case the heap consumption. The result consists of *abstract* cost bounds parametric in the concrete cost of the schematic elements from the transformation model. For the case of *Split Loop*, for example, we obtain a bound like $(\#it + 1) \cdot \left(2 \cdot cost_g(fp_g) + cost_P(fp_P) + cost_Q(fp_Q)\right)$ *after* the transformation, where $\#it$ is the number of iterations, and $cost_x/fp_x$ the abstract cost placeholder symbol and cost footprint for APE x, respectively.

Cost analysis took about 50 ms for each problem, while performing the proofs took between 13 s and 30 s. All proofs worked fully automatically and *did not require manual auxiliary specifications*, which was possible for three reasons: (1) We focused exclusively on *quantitative aspects*, leaving aside semantic equivalence (which can be verified separately). Dynamic frames are replaced by representative sets of *program variables* that can be handled by the cost analyzer. (2) The cost analyzer automatically produced *cost invariants* for loops and *ranking functions* needed to show termination. (3) Our new *proof strategy*, integrating external SMT solvers and different strategies for handling arithmetic problems, proved to be *effective for all problems at hand*.

7   Conclusion and Future Work

Legacy software systems are challenging both researchers and practitioners with an intricate problem: Transform *substantial code bases* of *high value*, but *poorly performing*, *insufficiently documented*, and *abandoned* by most of their original developers, into a system implementing the *same functionality*, but making use of *modern software engineering techniques* and *best practices*.

Software reengineering addresses this problem. It generally consists of two phases: (1) A *requirements extraction* and *reverse engineering* phase aiming for a better understanding of the legacy system and the reengineering goals; and (2) a *forward engineering* phase carrying out the actual transformation.

Phase (2) constitutes the critical step: here, behavior can be altered, and domain knowledge and ultimately *money* can be lost. Testing alone is generally insufficient in the presence of sparse existing test suits, as writing meaningful *new* test cases requires insight into the legacy system and the domain knowledge it implements.

We addressed this by proposing *structured* software reengineering: instead of changing code *arbitrarily* and relying on tests (or good luck), we suggest to use *proven-correct* code transformations from a predefined catalog for incrementally changing a legacy system. Correctly applied, this approach guarantees the preservation of *all* functional behavior of the input system. Furthermore, transformations can have clear nonfunctional *objectives*, such as improving readability, runtime performance, or amenability to parallelization.

To kick-start a catalog of proven transformation techniques, we developed *Abstract Execution* (Sect. 2), the first *general-purpose framework* for *automatic* reasoning about statement-level JAVA code transformations, and REFINITY (Sect. 3), a workbench for encoding and proving transformations. We used these tools to (1) derive preconditions for safe code refactoring and prove them sufficient (Sect. 4), (2) prove the safety of transformations used by code parallelization tools to prepare sequential code for the application of parallel design patterns (Sect. 5), and (3) develop an automatic approach to assess the cost impact of program transformations (Sect. 6).

There are many directions for future work on structured software reengineering: (i) Extending the catalog of proven-correct transformation techniques. For transformations *above* statement level, other techniques could be leveraged. (ii) Efficient checks for whether a transformation specified in AE is applicable for a program remain to be implemented (a prototypical demonstrator is contained in REFINITY). (iii) The AE approach could be adapted to different programming languages, or even to differing languages for source and target of a transformation, to address, for example, Cobol programs which the financial industry still relies on. The feasibility of this is demonstrated by an earlier work addressing the translation of JAVA to LLVM IR using a simple version of abstract statements and updates [49]. (iv) To find its way into industrial practice, structured software reengineering needs robust, usable tool support. We envision an IDE with drag'n'drop support of transformations from a catalog (including documentation) onto the code, with automatic sanity checks, or, where this is not possible, automatically generated test cases or at least appropriate warnings. One could even think of automating the process by automatically matching and applying transformations contributing to a selected optimization goal.

Software has come to stay. Structured software reengineering contributes to sustainable software life cycles whenever it stays longer than expected.

References

1. Aho, A.V., Sethi, R., Ullman, J.D.: Compilers: Principles, Techniques, and Tools. Addison-Wesley, Reading (1986)
2. Ahrendt, W., Beckert, B., Bubel, R., Hähnle, R., Schmitt, P.H., Ulbrich, M. (eds.): Deductive Software Verification—The KeY Book. LNCS, vol. 10001. Springer, Berlin (2016). https://doi.org/10.1007/978-3-319-49812-6
3. Albert, E., Arenas, P., Genaim, S., Puebla, G., Zanardini, D.: Cost analysis of object-oriented bytecode programs. Theor. Comput. Sci. **413**(1), 142–159 (2012). https://doi.org/10.1016/j.tcs.2011.07.009

4. Albert, E., Hähnle, R., Merayo, A., Steinhöfel, D.: Certified abstract cost analysis. In: E. Guerra, M. Stoelinga (eds.) Proc. 24th Intern. Conf. on Fundamental Approaches to Software Engineering (FASE). LNCS, vol. 12649, pp. 24–45. Springer, Berlin (2021). https://doi.org/10.1007/978-3-030-71500-7_2
5. Alves, E.L.G., Massoni, T., de Lima Machado, P.D.: Test coverage of impacted code elements for detecting refactoring faults: an exploratory study. J. Syst. Softw. **123**, 223–238 (2017). https://doi.org/10.1016/j.jss.2016.02.001
6. Baldoni, R., Coppa, E., D'Elia, D.C., Demetrescu, C., Finocchi, I.: A survey of symbolic execution techniques. ACM Comput. Surv. **51**(3), 50:1–50:39 (2018). https://doi.org/10.1145/3182657
7. Beckert, B., Ulbrich, M.: Trends in relational program verification. In: Principled Software Development—Essays Dedicated to Arnd Poetzsch-Heffter on the Occasion of his 60th Birthday, pp. 41–58 (2018). https://doi.org/10.1007/978-3-319-98047-8_3
8. Bertot, Y., Castéran, P.: Interactive theorem proving and program development—Coq'Art: the calculus of inductive constructions. Texts in Theoretical Computer Science. An EATCS Series. Springer, Berlin (2004). https://doi.org/10.1007/978-3-662-07964-5
9. Bubel, R., Roth, A., Rümmer, P.: Ensuring the correctness of lightweight tactics for JavaCard dynamic logic. Electr. Notes Theor. Comput. Sci. **199**, 107–128 (2008). https://doi.org/10.1016/j.entcs.2007.11.015
10. Burstall, R.M.: Program proving as hand simulation with a little induction. In: Information Processing, pp. 308–312. Elsevier, Amsterdam (1974)
11. Chikofsky, E.J., Cross, J.H.II..: Reverse engineering and design recovery: a taxonomy. IEEE Softw. **7**(1), 13–17 (1990). https://doi.org/10.1109/52.43044
12. Crotty, J., Horrocks, I.: Managing legacy system costs: a case study of a meta-assessment model to identify solutions in a large financial services company. Appl. Comput. Inform. **13**(2), 175–183 (2017). https://doi.org/10.1016/j.aci.2016.12.001
13. Cuadrado, F., García, B., Dueñas, J.C., G., H.A.P.: A case study on software evolution towards service-oriented architecture. In: Proc. 22nd Inter. Conf. on Advanced Information Networking and Applications (AINA), pp. 1399–1404. IEEE Computer Society, Silver Spring (2008). https://doi.org/10.1109/WAINA.2008.296
14. Daniel, B., Dig, D., Garcia, K., Marinov, D.: Automated testing of refactoring engines. In: 6th Joint Meeting of the European Software Engineering Conference and the ACM SIGSOFT International Symposium on Foundations of Software Engineering, pp. 185–194 (2007)
15. Eilertsen, A.M., Bagge, A.H., Stolz, V.: Safer refactorings. In: Margaria, T., Steffen, B. (eds.) Proc. 7th ISoLA. LNCS, vol. 9952 (2016). https://doi.org/10.1007/978-3-319-47166-2_36
16. Feathers, M.C.: Working effectively with legacy code. In: Zannier, C., Erdogmus, H., Lindstrom, L. (eds.) Proc. 4th Conf. on Extreme Programming and Agile Methods. LNCS, vol. 3134, p. 217. Springer, Berlin (2004). https://doi.org/10.1007/978-3-540-27777-4_42
17. Fowler, M.: Refactoring: Improving the Design of Existing Code. Object Technology Series. Addison-Wesley, Reading (1999)
18. Fowler, M.: Refactoring: Improving the Design of Existing Code, 2nd edn. Addison-Wesley Signature Series. Addison-Wesley, Reading (2018)
19. Fürnweger, A., Auer, M., Biffl, S.: Software evolution of legacy systems—a case study of soft-migration. In: Hammoudi, S., Maciaszek, L.A., Missikoff, M., Camp, O., Cordeiro, J. (eds.) Proc. 18th Intern. Conf. on Enterprise Information Systems (ICEIS), pp. 413–424. SciTePress, Setúbal (2016). https://doi.org/10.5220/0005771104130424
20. Godlin, B., Strichman, O.: Regression verification: proving the equivalence of similar programs. Softw. Test., Verif. Reliab. **23**(3), 241–258 (2013). https://doi.org/10.1002/stvr.1472
21. Gulwani, S., Mehra, K.K., Chilimbi, T.M.: SPEED: precise and efficient static estimation of program computational complexity. In: Shao, Z., Pierce, B.C. (eds.) Proc. 36th POPL. ACM (2009). https://doi.org/10.1145/1480881.1480898

22. Hähnle, R., Heydari Tabar, A., Mazaheri, A., Norouzi, M., Steinhöfel, D., Wolf, F.: Safer parallelization. In: Margaria, T., Steffen, B. (eds.) Proc. 9th Intern. Symposium on Leveraging Applications of Formal Methods, Verification and Validation (ISoLA): Engineering Principles, Part II. LNCS, vol. 12477. Springer, Berlin (2020). https://doi.org/10.1007/978-3-030-61470-6_8

23. Hoffmann, J., Hofmann, M.: Amortized resource analysis with polynomial potential. In: Gordon, A.D. (ed.) 19th European Symposium Programming Languages and Systems (ESOP). LNCS, vol. 6012. Springer, Berlin (2010). https://doi.org/10.1007/978-3-642-11957-6_16

24. Huda, Z.U., Jannesari, A., Wolf, F.: Using template matching to infer parallel design patterns. TACO 11(4), 64:1–64:21 (2014). https://doi.org/10.1145/2688905

25. Kassios, I.T.: The dynamic frames theory. Formal Asp. Comput. 23(3) (2011). https://doi.org/10.1007/s00165-010-0152-5

26. Khadka, R., Batlajery, B.V., Saeidi, A., Jansen, S., Hage, J.: How do professionals perceive legacy systems and software modernization? In: Jalote, P., Briand, L.C., van der Hoek, A. (eds.) 36th Intern. Conf. on Software Engineering (ICSE), pp. 36–47. ACM, New York (2014). https://doi.org/10.1145/2568225.2568318

27. King, J.C.: Symbolic execution and program testing. Commun. ACM 19(7), 385–394 (1976)

28. Klein, G., Andronick, J., Elphinstone, K., Heiser, G., Cock, D., Derrin, P., Elkaduwe, D., Engelhardt, K., Kolanski, R., Norrish, M., Sewell, T., Tuch, H., Winwood, S.: seL4: formal verification of an operating-system kernel. Commun. ACM 53(6), 107–115 (2010). https://doi.org/10.1145/1743546.1743574

29. Klein, G., Nipkow, T.: A machine-checked model for a java-like language, virtual machine, and compiler. ACM Trans. PLS 28(4), 619–695 (2006)

30. Leavens, G.T., Poll, E., Clifton, C., Cheon, Y., Ruby, C., Cok, D., Müller, P., Kiniry, J., Chalin, P., Zimmerman, D.M., Dietl, W.: JML Reference Manual (2013). http://www.eecs.ucf.edu/~leavens/JML//OldReleases/jmlrefman.pdf. Draft revision 2344

31. Leroy, X.: Formal verification of a realistic compiler. Commun. ACM 52(7), 107–115 (2009)

32. London, R.L.: Correctness of a compiler for a lisp subset. In: Proc. ACM Conf. on Proving Assertions About Programs, pp. 121–127. ACM, New York (1972). https://doi.org/10.1145/800235.807080

33. Lopes, N.P., Menendez, D., Nagarakatte, S., Regehr, J.: Practical verification of peephole optimizations with alive. Commun. ACM 61(2), 84–91 (2018). https://doi.org/10.1145/3166064

34. Massingill, B.L., Mattson, T.G., Sanders, B.A.: Parallel programming with a pattern language. Int. J. Softw. Tools Technol. Transf. 3(2), 217–234 (2001). https://doi.org/10.1007/s100090100045

35. Mattson, T.G., Sanders, B., Massingill, B.: Patterns for parallel programming. Pearson Education, London (2004)

36. McCarthy, J., Painter, J.: Correctness of a compiler for arithmetic expressions. Mathematical Aspects of Computer Science, vol. 1 (1967)

37. Nipkow, T., Paulson, L.C., Wenzel, M.: Isabelle/HOL—A Proof Assistant for Higher-Order Logic. LNCS, vol. 2283. Springer, Berlin (2002). https://doi.org/10.1007/3-540-45949-9

38. Norouzi, M.A., Wolf, F., Jannesari, A.: Automatic construct selection and variable classification in OpenMP. In: Eigenmann, R., Ding, C., McKee, S.A. (eds.) Proc. ACM Intern. Conf. on Supercomputing (ICS). ACM, New York (2019). https://doi.org/10.1145/3330345.3330375

39. Radicek, I., Barthe, G., Gaboardi, M., Garg, D., Zuleger, F.: Monadic refinements for relational cost analysis. Proc. ACM Program. Lang. 2(POPL), 36:1–36:32 (2018). https://doi.org/10.1145/3158124

40. Ransom, J., Sommerville, I., Warren, I.: A method for assessing legacy systems for evolution. In: Proc. 2nd Euromicro Conference on Software Maintenance and Reengineering (CSMR), pp. 128–134. IEEE Computer Society, Silver Spring (1998). https://doi.org/10.1109/CSMR.1998.665778

41. Schneider, A.: When companies become prisoners of legacy systems. Wall Street J. (2013). https://deloitte.wsj.com/cio/2013/10/01/when-companies-become-prisoners/

42. Smith, D.R.: KIDS: a semiautomatic program development system. IEEE Trans. Softw. Eng. **16**(9), 1024–1043 (1990). https://doi.org/10.1109/32.58788
43. Soares, G., Catao, B., Varjao, C., Aguiar, S., Gheyi, R., Massoni, T.: Analyzing refactorings on software repositories. In: Proc. 25th Brazilian Symposium on Software Engineering (SBES), pp. 164–173. IEEE Computer Society, Silver Spring (2011). https://doi.org/10.1109/SBES.2011.21
44. Soares, G., Gheyi, R., Massoni, T.: Automated behavioral testing of refactoring engines. IEEE Trans. Software Eng. **39**(2), 147–162 (2013). https://doi.org/10.1109/TSE.2012.19
45. Soares, G., Gheyi, R., Serey, D., Massoni, T.: Making program refactoring safer. IEEE Softw. **27**(4), 52–57 (2010). https://doi.org/10.1109/MS.2010.63
46. Srivastava, S., Gulwani, S., Foster, J.S.: From program verification to program synthesis. In: Proc. 37th POPL, pp. 313–326 (2010). https://doi.org/10.1145/1706299.1706337
47. Steinhöfel, D.: Abstract execution: automatically proving infinitely many programs. Ph.D. Thesis, TU Darmstadt, Dept. of Computer Science, Darmstadt, Germany (2020). https://doi.org/10.25534/tuprints-00008540. http://tuprints.ulb.tu-darmstadt.de/8540/
48. Steinhöfel, D.: REFINITY to model and prove program transformation rules. In: Oliveira, B.C.D.S. (ed.) Proc. 18th Asian Symposium on Programming Languages and Systems (APLAS). LNCS, vol. 12470. Springer, Berlin (2020). https://doi.org/10.1007/978-3-030-64437-6_16
49. Steinhöfel, D., Hähnle, R.: Modular, correct compilation with automatic soundness proofs. In: Margaria, T., Steffen, B. (eds.) Proc. 8th ISoLA. LNCS, vol. 11244, pp. 424–447. Springer, Berlin (2018). https://doi.org/10.1007/978-3-030-03418-4_25
50. Steinhöfel, D., Hähnle, R.: Abstract execution. In: Proc. Third World Congress on Formal Methods—The Next 30 Years (FM) (2019). https://doi.org/10.1007/978-3-030-30942-8_20
51. Tan, Y.K., Myreen, M.O., Kumar, R., Fox, A., Owens, S., Norrish, M.: A new verified compiler backend for CakeML. In: Proc. 21st ICFP. ACM, New York (2016). https://doi.org/10.1145/2951913.2951924
52. Vijaya, A., Venkataraman, N.: Modernizing legacy systems: a re-engineering approach. Int. J. Web Portals **10**(2), 50–60 (2018). https://doi.org/10.4018/IJWP.2018070104
53. Winterland, D.: Abstract Execution for Correctness-by-Construction. Master's thesis, Technische Universität Braunschweig (2020)

Static Worst-Case Analyses and Their Validation Techniques for Safety-Critical Systems

Peter Wägemann

Abstract The reliable operation of systems with both timing and energy requirements is a fundamental challenge in the area of safety-critical embedded systems. In order to provide guarantees for the execution of tasks within given resource budgets, these systems demand bounds of the worst-case execution time (WCET) and the worst-case energy consumption (WCEC). While static WCET analysis techniques are well established in the software development process of real-time systems nowadays, these program analysis techniques are not directly applicable to the fundamentally different behavior of energy consumption and the determination of the WCEC. Besides the missing approaches for WCEC bounds, the domain of worst-case analyses generally faces the problem that the accuracy and validity of reported analysis bounds are unknown: Since the actual worst-case resource consumption of existing benchmark programs cannot be automatically determined, a comprehensive validation of these program analysis tools is not possible.

This summary of my dissertation addresses these problems by first describing a novel program analysis approach for WCEC bounds, which accounts for temporarily power-consuming devices, scheduling with fixed real-time priorities, synchronous task activations, and asynchronous interrupt service routines. Regarding the fundamental problem of validating worst-case tools, this dissertation presents a technique for automatically generating benchmark programs. The generator combines program patterns so that the worst-case resource consumption is available along with the generated benchmark. Knowledge about the actual worst-case resource demand then serves as the baseline for evaluating and validating program analysis tools. The fact the benchmark generator helped to reveal previously undiscovered software bugs in a widespread WCET tool for safety-critical systems underlines the relevance of such a structured testing technique.

P. Wägemann (✉)
Friedrich-Alexander University Erlangen-Nürnberg (FAU), Chair in Distributed Systems and Operating Systems, Erlangen, Germany
e-mail: wagemann@cs.fau.de

© The Author(s) 2022
M. Felderer et al. (eds.), *Ernst Denert Award for Software Engineering 2020*,
https://doi.org/10.1007/978-3-030-83128-8_11

227

1   Introduction

One central challenge of the 2020s in the domain of embedded computing systems is the reliable operation of systems that face energy constraints due to harvesting energy from the environment [4]. Additional to the existence of energy constraints, applications increasingly come up with both energy and timing constraints, such as medical devices (like implantable defibrillators) with harvesting mechanisms [16]. Such systems have to meet real-time guarantees on the timely execution of tasks, and additionally, tasks have to be executed within given energy budgets due to being battery-operated and dependent on energy-harvesting techniques. In order to enable safe scheduling under consideration of available time and energy resources, developers require the values of the *worst-case execution time (WCET)* as well as the *worst-case energy consumption (WCEC)* of each task.

Static program analysis tools of the system's program code are the fundamental means in the domain of real-time systems to determine the tasks' bound of the WCET [32]. While practical analyses for the timing-related problem exist for systems with fixed real-time priorities [1, 5], these techniques are not directly applicable to the fundamentally different problem of energy consumption and the assessment of WCEC values. For example, for the WCEC-related problem, analyses that only consider the real-time priorities of tasks are insufficient: Tasks with a low real-time priority have the possibility to temporarily activate power-consuming devices (e.g., transceivers). The activation of a device, in turn, influences the power demand (and likewise the energy demand over time) of each task in the system irrespective of their priority. Thus, worst-case energy-consumption analyses need to consider such *mutual influences* between tasks in the whole system.

Besides the missing approaches for WCEC values, static worst-case analysis tools generally face the fundamental problem of missing evaluations and validations of the reported worst-case bounds: Based on sound abstraction, analysis tools yield safe resource-consumption bounds. However, the actual WCET and likewise the actual WCEC of arbitrary (benchmark) programs are unknown since such nontrivial properties cannot be automatically extracted from existing programs [12, 20]. Due to this missing knowledge, the assessment of the analysis tool's accuracy (i.e., the distance between reported bound and actual worst case) is not possible, and the analysis pessimism remains unknown. Furthermore, the lack of the actual worst case leaves the question unanswered whether the implemented analysis contains software bugs since the actual baseline is not available.

The dissertation [33] addresses the mentioned problems of (1) determining WCEC bounds, (2) validating static worst-case analyzer, and (3) operating energy- and time-constrained embedded systems. Figure 1 illustrates the conceptual structure of the dissertation. The following three solutions are the main contributions of the dissertation:

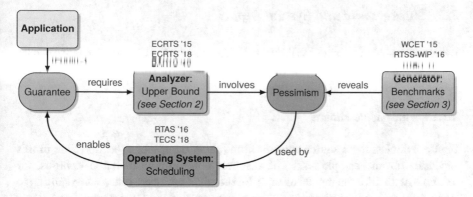

Fig. 1 Conceptual structure of the dissertation: Runtime guarantees demand upper resource-consumption bounds, which are determined by static worst-case tools. A benchmark-generation technique reveals the expected degree of analysis pessimism and thereby validates the reported results of the analysis tools. An operating-system kernel, which makes use of resource bounds, eventually enables applications to operate safely

1. The WCEC analyzer *SysWCEC* determines upper bounds of the energy consumption of tasks in systems that are scheduled with fixed priorities [24, 25, 27] (see Sect. 2).
2. The benchmark generator *GenE* allows for the first time comprehensive evaluations and validations of static worst-case tools based on automatically generated benchmarks, whose actual worst case is known [26, 28, 31] (see Sect. 3).
3. The operating-system kernel *EnOS* supports the reliable operation of systems with both timing and energy constraints based on a priori knowledge of WCET and WCEC bounds [29, 30].

While this chapter gives insight into the first two main contributions with the focus on system-software engineering, the third aspect goes beyond the scope of this chapter. The chapter is structured as follows: Sect. 2 first presents background information on the problem of WCEC analyses and gives insight into the analyzer *SysWCEC*. The fundamental problem of validating worst-case tools is discussed in Sect. 3, along with the solution of *GenE* for this problem. Sect. 4 concludes this chapter.

2 Worst-Case Analyses

The following Sect. 2.1 presents background information on static worst-case analyses and the system model of the dissertation. The main problem statement for WCEC analyses is discussed in Sect. 2.2. Section 2.3 introduces *SysWCEC*, an analyzer for system-wide WCEC analyses.

2.1 Background and System Model

Besides the analysis results' validity, analysis pessimism is a core problem of static
worst-case analyses. The causes of this problem are outlined as follows.

2.1.1 Analysis Pessimism

Figure 2 depicts the resource consumption (either energy or execution time in this
scenario) for an example task. The resource consumption of the task varies, for
example, with different input data or different initial hardware states when starting to
execute the task. Static worst-case tools rely on pessimistic assumptions during their
analyses that eventually yield safe, however, overestimating bounds. The distance
between the actual worst case and the reported upper bound describes the analyzer's
pessimism for a safe execution of the task. Static worst-case analysis techniques are
subdivided into the phase of (1) program-flow analysis and (2) hardware analysis.
The first phase, which also known as path analysis, explores the possible program
paths, determines value constraints of variables, and assigns loop bounds in order
to yield upper bounds on executed paths. For example, a mediocre path analysis
without the ability to precisely model path constraints is forced to pessimistically
include all branches with the highest resource demand, irrespective of whether the
combination of these branches is an actually feasible program path. The second
phase of hardware analysis uses the executable machine code of the application and
determines (under consideration of the target's caching and pipelining behavior) the
actual cost (e.g., in mJ for WCEC or in ms for WCET) of each executed basic block.
Both the path- and hardware-analysis phase contribute to the overall pessimism of
this analysis. Section 3 gives further details on how to isolate and assess the factors
that contribute to an analyzer's pessimism. Both analyses phases model the runtime
behavior of the executed program on the target platform; thus, analyses demand
detailed knowledge about the targeted system model, which is outlined as follows.

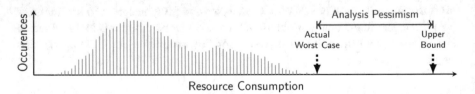

Fig. 2 Histogram of an example task's resource consumptions

2.1.2 System Model

All executed code of the application is available for the analysis. As usual for
embedded systems, the number of tasks is statically known. Due to the economics
of resource-constrained embedded systems, the systems execute the (single) application on one processing core as part of a microcontroller unit. In contrast to desktop
machines, these processing cores have limited complexity, which is a beneficial
property for static worst-case analyses and allows determining precise hardware
models. All tasks in the system are handled by the scheduler according to their fixed
priorities. The tasks have the possibility to acquire operating-system resources (e.g.,
mutexes) for synchronization purposes. These resources as well as their associated
users are statically known. Asynchronous interrupts are common in the targeted
systems, for example, in the case of timer interrupts for deadline monitoring. For
static worst-case analyses, these interrupts pose a considerable challenge since
analysis techniques have to encompass the possible dynamic behavior by static
means. A requirement for bounding the occurrence of interrupts is that their arrival
is bounded by a minimum inter-arrival time (i.e., the minimum timespan between
two successive interrupts). For the power consumption of the system (and thus
the energy demand over time), software-controlled devices play an essential role.
Devices are not necessarily external to the microcontroller unit, such as transceiver
devices for communication. Instead, numerous internal devices, such as timer
subsystems or analog-to-digital converters, are usually available. Both internal and
external devices have the same power-consumption behavior in view of a static
analysis tool: The activation of a device leads to an increase of the whole system's
power demand and the deactivation, in turn, reduces the power, which is further
discussed as follows.

2.2 Problem Statement of WCEC Analysis

For the purpose of energy savings, devices are kept active only for the duration while
their service is required. Figure 3 illustrates such a temporary device activation,
for example, for sending out a packet via a transceiver device. This temporary
device activation is executed by the task τ_{LOW} with low priority in contrast to
the second task with higher priority τ_{HIGH}. The task τ_{HIGH} is, in turn, activated
through an interrupt service routine (ISR). ISRs generally preempt running tasks,
regardless of the tasks' real-time priority. In the example, the low-priority task's
device activation leads to an increase of the systems power demand from 5 mW to
35 mW. As illustrated on the right part of Fig. 3, two possible runtime scenarios
exist in view of the energy demand from the start until the completion of τ_{LOW}:
In scenario a (see t_a in Fig. 3), the interrupt occurs in the system state of lower
power demand (i.e.,5 mW). In contrast, the ISR is serviced in scenario b (t_b) in the
state of the higher power demand. This second scenario is the worst case in terms
of the energy demand (i.e., area under the power demand). This worst-case scenario

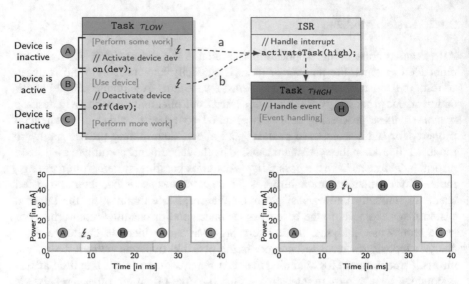

Fig. 3 The system-state–dependent power demand of the whole system influences the energy demand of each task

is indeed the worst case for both τ_{LOW} (whole area) as well as for τ_{HIGH} (red area below ⒣). The worst case of τ_{HIGH} is initiated by the fact that the task starts executing with a higher initial power demand (caused by τ_{LOW}). For the analysis of the WCET, these context-sensitive power states are irrelevant, and only the unilateral influence of lower- tasks by higher-priority tasks is of interest. In contrast, WCEC analyses must account for system-wide de-/activations of devices as well as the system's total power state. When reconsidering the example, τ_{HIGH} influences the energy demand of τ_{LOW} by a prolonged execution time. However, also τ_{LOW} influences τ_{HIGH} due to τ_{LOW}'s responsibility for τ_{HIGH}'s higher power state. To summarize the observations: WCEC analyses have to consider all device de-/activations along the system-wide program paths in order to account for the mutual influences between all tasks in the system.

2.3 SysWCEC: Whole-System WCEC Analysis

The dissertation proposes the *SysWCEC* approach [25] for solving the problems mentioned above. In a nutshell, *SysWCEC* consists of four steps:

1. *Decomposition*: The code of the application is decomposed into blocks with a common set of active devices and, thereby, a common power state.
2. *Path Exploration*: Based on the result of the decomposition, *SysWCEC* conducts an explicit enumeration of all possible system-wide program paths.

3. *Problem Formulation*: The knowledge about the program paths is the foundation for the formulation of an integer linear program (ILP).

4. ILP Formulation: Solving the ILP with its objective of the worst-case behavior, eventually yields a WCEC bound of the analyzed task.

The following section gives further insight into *SysWCEC*'s working principle, based on the example illustrated in Fig. 3.

2.3.1 Decomposition: Power Atomic Basic Blocks

The left part of Fig. 4 illustrates the original system with the three components of τ_{LOW}, τ_{HIGH}, and the ISR. The step of the decomposition relies on the existing technique of *atomic basic blocks (ABBs)* [21, 22]. The core concept of ABBs is to split up the application's code at a system-call location (e.g., task activation, acquisition of mutex). In other words, each system call forms a terminator in the atomic–basic-block graph. Each ABB thereby forms an atomically schedulable unit from the perspective of the system's real-time scheduler, whereas each ABB may be executed inside a different system state. The *SysWCEC* approach extends this notion of atomic basic blocks to support power-aware considerations. That is, *SysWCEC* uses the device-related system calls (i.e., the calls that change the system's active device configuration) as additional terminators, which results in the graph of *power atomic basic blocks*, or *PABBs* for short. As a result, the PABB graph holds blocks with a common set of active devices and, thus, a common state of the power demand. When considering the result of this decomposition in the running example (see right

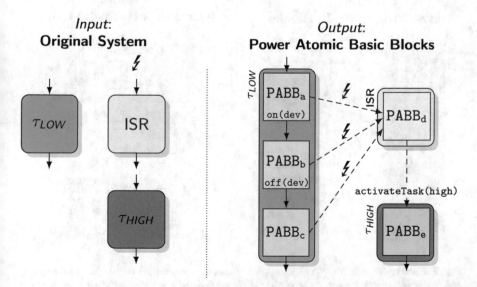

Fig. 4 Decomposition into PABB Graph: The original system is decomposed into blocks with a common set of active devices

part in Fig. 4), the low-priority task τ_{LOW} now consists of three parts: the PABB_a with the code prior to the device activation, PABB_b with the code with the active device, and PABB_c with the code after the device deactivation.

2.3.2 Path Exploration: Power-State–Transition Graph

The subsequent step after the decomposition of the original system into the PABB graph is the path exploration. The input of this analysis step is the PABB graph, and the output is a power-state–aware graph, named *power-state–transition graph (PSTG)*. Figure 5 illustrates the working principle of this path exploration based on the running example: The algorithm starts with the initial power state of the lower power consumption of 5 mW. The path-exploration algorithm accounts for the operating-system semantics (e.g., the fixed-priority scheduling strategy) and the potentially occurring interrupts. For each possible state transition, the PSTG inserts an edge to a corresponding PSTG node that describes the system state. Regarding the handling of varying power demands, the algorithm accounts for device-state changes and for the associated power-demand changes. If no power-state change happens alongside a transition, the path exploration propagates the current power state. The algorithm terminates when all possible states are visited, which is possible due to the bounded number of system states in embedded systems with their fixed number of tasks. As illustrated on the right side of Fig. 5, the PSTG finally holds all context-sensitive program paths with their power consumptions. The knowledge

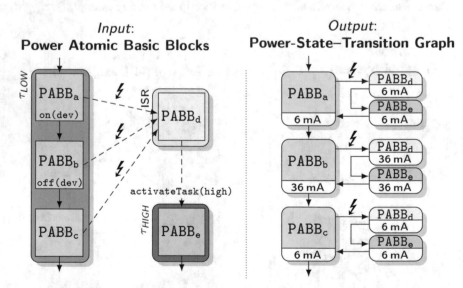

Fig. 5 Path Exploration: The *SysWCEC* approach uses the decomposed system (i.e., PABB graph) and conducts an explicit enumeration of all possible system paths, which results in the power-state–transition graph

about these possible system-wide program paths enables *SysWCEC* to tackle the problem of mutual influences between tasks.

2.3.3 ILP Formulation

The PSTG is the main input for the third analysis step in *SysWCEC*, the formulation of an integer linear program. *SysWCEC* exploits the main technique for formulating maximum flow problems from the well-established approach of the *implicit path enumeration technique (IPET)* [14]. The IPET targets single-threaded executions and uses the program's control-flow graph as input. Based on the control-flow graph's branches, the IPET inserts constraints from the program's flow into an ILP formulation. With the same purpose of finding an upper bound of the cost through a flow graph, the *SysWCEC* approach leverages the IPET's single-threaded approach to the system-state level. *SysWCEC* now uses the PSTG's paths as constraints for an ILP formulation. The objective function of the ILP is shown in the following Eq. 1, which determines the maximum flow through the system's state graph of the analyzed task with its nodes ($v \in \mathcal{V}$) and transitions in between ($\varepsilon \in \mathcal{E}$):

$$max\left(\left(\underbrace{\sum_{v \in \mathcal{V}} WCEC(v) \cdot f(v) \right) + \left(\underbrace{\sum_{\varepsilon \in \mathcal{E}} WCEC(\varepsilon) \cdot f(\varepsilon) \right) \right)}_{\text{nodes}} \quad \underbrace{}_{\text{edges}} \tag{1}$$

The variables $f(v)$ and $f(\varepsilon)$ denote the execution frequencies of the corresponding nodes and edges. Finally, *SysWCEC* directs this problem formulation to an optimizing solver (e.g., `gurobi`, `lp_solve`), which determines bounds on these execution frequencies and yields the final WCEC bound for the analyzed task.

2.3.4 Cost Modeling

As shown in Eq. 1, the *SysWCEC* approach demands for the context-sensitive costs of each node and each edge in the PSTG. Edge costs are often known from documentation, such as the time and energy demand for the activation of an analog-to-digital converter or transceiver. For the nodes $\mathcal{V}$, *SysWCEC* extracts the costs from the executed code within the PSTG node. For this cost modeling of executed code, *SysWCEC* benefits from a synergy between WCET and WCEC analysis: The multiplication of the maximum (context-sensitive) power demand, which is available for each PSTG node, with the worst-case execution time of the respective node results in an energy-consumption bound for the node. That is, the cost modeling relies on the subsequent Eq. 2:

$$WCEC(v) = P_{max}(v) \cdot WCET(v) \tag{2}$$

That way, the $WCEC(v)$ value is *indirectly* determined by means of the max-imum power, instead of a direct instruction-level energy-consumption modeling technique [17, 23]. For the determination of $WCET(v)$, existing timing-analysis approaches are applied, which also account for the microarchitectural temporal behavior (i.e., caching and pipelining behavior) on the target machine [19].

By employing these techniques, *SysWCEC* determines upper bounds on the energy consumption of a task while considering all other tasks and power-related activities. However, the question on the accuracy of these resource-consumption estimates, from the view of the actual worst case, is left unanswered. The following Sect. 3 focuses on the problem of the analysis accuracy of $WCET(v)$ values, which, in turn, contribute to the overall energy-related analysis pessimism according to Eq. 2.

3   Validation of Worst-Case Analyses

The following Sect. 3.1 outlines the main problems of assessing the accuracy of static worst-case analysis tools. One solution for these problems is *GenE*, which is presented in Sect. 3.2.

3.1   Problem Statement of Validating Worst-Case Analyses

As previously illustrated in Fig. 2, the bound reported by the worst-case analysis tool overestimates the actual worst-case resource consumption of the analyzed task. This overestimating scenario assumes a bug-free implementation of the analysis algorithm, which employs abstractions that make pessimistic assumptions on the dynamic runtime behavior. Existing approaches for assessing the degree of analysis pessimism use benchmark suites, which are written on the level of source code (e.g., C). The fundamental problem with this type of evaluation is that the actual baseline is missing, which is the actual worst case serving as ground truth. This problem of missing baselines also prevails when trying to validate if the reported bound actually overestimates the actual worst case.

Unfortunately, the actual worst case as well as all relevant program facts, such as loop bounds or mutually exclusive program paths, cannot be automatically extracted from existing benchmark programs [12, 20]. Moreover, the manual extraction of these program facts is labor-intensive and error-prone. Due to the lack of knowledge on the actual baseline, existing evaluation and validation techniques have limited significance since the absolute degree of over- or—in the presence of software bugs—underestimation on a global scale is unknown.

A further problem when conducting evaluations based on existing benchmark suites is that these programs usually consist of numerous challenges for the static analyzer. The task τ_{sort} in the following Listing 1 serves as an example to illustrate this problem. This task's code sorts the numbers held in the array `values`.

Listing 1 Listing with several program components that cause the analyzer to potentially overestimate the actual worst-case resource consumption

```
1  const size_t N = 1024;
2  int32_t values[N];
3
4  TASK(τsort){
5    ...
6    for(i = 0; i < N-1; i++){
7      for(j = 0; j < N-1-i; j++){
8        if(compare(values[j], values[j+1]))
9          swap(&values[j], &values[j+1]);
10
11     }
12   }
13 }
```

The outer loop in Line 6 has a constant iteration bound, while the inner loop's bound in Line 7 is decremented with each iteration of the outer loop. Thereby, this nested loop has a rectangular loop shape (i.e., N-1·N-1). If analyzers are not able to precisely bound this type of loop, a pessimistic assumption is a rectangular loop shape, which overestimates the actual worst case. Furthermore, input-dependent computations (as outlined in Line 8) cause overestimations if the analyzer cannot automatically determine value constraints. Eventually, the task τ_{sort} is executed on a hardware platform. Thus, the analyzer has to model the dynamic hardware behavior (i.e., pipelining, caching) in order to report an accurate bound. All these factors contribute to the overall analysis pessimism. When having a poor analysis result, system developers face the problem that the individual causes for the high degree of overestimation are unknown.

3.2 GenE: Benchmark Generator for WCET Tools

The *GenE* benchmark [26, 28] is one possible solution for the problem of conducting comprehensive evaluations and validations of worst-case tools. *GenE* generates benchmarks in a way that all program facts are known. Based on this knowledge about these facts, *GenE* is able to determine the actual WCET, which, in turn, serves as ground truth for the validation of static analyzers.

The basic principle of *GenE* is explained best by using a metaphor: Benchmarks are like mazes for analyzers, which need to find a way possible through the maze. However, even if an analyzer finds a way (i.e., solution), it is still unknown if this way is the optimal path. *GenE* follows a different approach: First, *GenE* predefines a path and then successively inserts branches around this path. Thereby, *GenE* builds the maze around this path. Due to *GenE*'s generative approach, the optimal (i.e., actual worst-case) path is known by construction.

3.2.1 Program Pattern

For the process of benchmark generation, *GenE* relies on numerous *program patterns*. These patterns are implemented inside the generator and have the following properties and objectives:

- *Worst-Case–Aware*: The patterns have awareness of their worst-case path and all relevant program facts, such as possible value constraints on introduced variables.
- *Composable*: Patterns have so-called *insertion points* that offer the possibility to insert further program patterns in order to generate new, complex benchmarks.
- *Realistic*: Although *GenE* produces synthetic benchmarks, it aims to output realistic benchmark scenarios that pose realistic challenges for worst-case tools. To solve this problem, *GenE* uses patterns from existing WCET benchmarking suites [8, 9]. Other patterns originate from industry applications or from patterns that are documented in literature to be challenging [3].
- *Resilient*: Compilers have the possibility to decisively change the programs' structure when conducting aggressive optimizations. In order to account for such optimizations, *GenE* uses patterns that already resemble optimized code.

GenE implements these patterns on the level of the LLVM intermediate representation [13]. However, for the sake of readability, the following Listing 2 illustrates a pattern of *GenE* using the C programming language. This pattern, named `init-once`, mimics a lazy initialization of components, which is often found in embedded systems to initialize hardware components.

Listing 2 Pseudo code of *GenE* pattern with insertion points. The actual implementation of program patterns relies on a lower abstraction level (i.e., LLVM intermediate representation).

```
1  static bool initialized = false;
2  void use_hardware(){
3    if (!initialized){
4      // init hardware
5      init(); // insertion point I₁
6      initialized = true;
7    }
8    // use hardware:
9    ... // insertion point I₂
10 }
```

The worst-case analyzer faces the challenge to model the global variable `initialized`. If the analysis is not able to handle such value constraints, it has to pessimistically include the (expensive) call of the function `init()`, which, in turn, causes an overestimating WCET estimate.

Line 5 and 9 in this pattern highlight the two insertion points I_1 and I_2. At these points in the benchmark, further possible patterns are inserted, which are summarized in the following enumeration:

- *Atomic Patterns*: This class of patterns includes arithmetic operations and assignments of constant or computed values.

- *Loop Patterns*: *GenE* implements several shapes of loops, such as nested loops or loops with an input-dependent/constant iteration count.
- *Path Patterns*: The pattern of Listing 2 is part of the path-pattern class. Additionally, this class contains patterns with mutually exclusive paths (due to the value constraints or infeasible paths (i.e., dead code).

The fact that *GenE* implements these patterns on the low abstraction level of LLVM intermediate representation gives *GenE* reasonable control over the generated code on the machine-code level without the need to implement patterns directly with a target-specific assembly language. For the mapping between the machine-code representation and the LLVM representation, *GenE* relies on the technique of control-flow–relation graphs [10], which are implemented in the `Platin` toolkit for static analyses [18].

3.2.2   Pattern Suites

In order to tackle the problem of monolithic benchmarks, *GenE* has the notion of *pattern suites*. These suites consist of a subset of all available patterns in *GenE*'s pattern library. For example, the pattern suite `hardware analysis` voids the influence of overestimations due to challenging loops or path constraints. Specifically, *GenE* produces here a single program path with the available patterns (i.e., introduction of variables, arithmetic operations) in the benchmark. This benchmark then challenges the analyzers' ability to model the target's hardware behavior (i.e., caching, pipelining). Regarding the analysis stage of value analysis, *GenE* supports a dedicated suite that inserts variables, arithmetic operations on these variables, and branches based on the value constraints of the computed variables. This suite targets the analyzers' performance in view of the value-range–modeling problem. The main benefit of the pattern suites is the possibility to have benchmarks that are tailored toward a specific scenario (i.e., hardware or path analysis). These scenarios then help developers to reveal individual strengths and weaknesses of analyzers.

3.2.3   Inputs and Outputs of *GenE*

The configuration of the pattern-suite type is one input to the *GenE* generator, as shown in Fig. 6. Besides the suites, *GenE* demands a *path budget*, which approximates the number of instructions (on level of the LLVM intermediate representation) along the generated worst-case path. Increasing the value of the path budget leads to an increase of the benchmark's complexity since a higher budget allows *GenE* to insert more and longer patterns. A further input is the value for the worst-case input value. This value is especially important for the generator because using this value as input for the generated benchmark leads to an execution of the designated worst-case path. This worst-case input value is an integer and also fulfills the purpose of the generator's seed value. That is, varying the worst-case input value

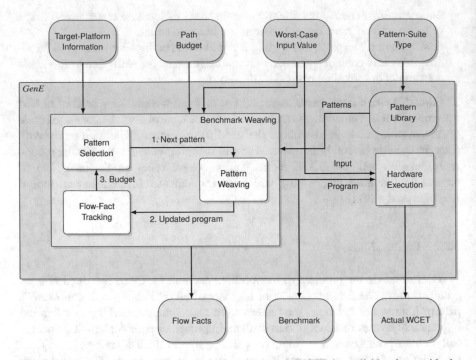

Fig. 6 *GenE* generates benchmarks such that the actual WCET is available along with the generated benchmark. This actual WCET value is necessary for comprehensive evaluations and validations of static analysis tools

also changes the selection of the patterns in a pseudo-random way. By measuring the execution of the worst-case path (either on the target platform or by means of a cycle-accurate simulator), *GenE* determines the actual WCET for the generated benchmark. Thus, *GenE* requires information about the selected target-hardware platform. Besides this actual WCET value, *GenE* provides the generated program along with the relevant flow facts (e.g., loop bounds).

3.3   Benchmark Weaving

As illustrated in Fig. 6, the benchmark-weaving algorithm selects a pattern from the available subset of *GenE*'s pattern library. After inserting the next pattern into the benchmark under construction, the algorithm updates the related flow facts.

An important aspect of the benchmark-weaving algorithm is the mechanism for guaranteeing that the designated worst-case path is—in any case—longer than other (non–worst-case) program paths through the benchmark. Specifically, *GenE* uses a substantially larger path budget for the worst-case path when inserting a branch in the control flow. For example, along the worst-case path, *GenE* uses a factor of 25 more instructions compared to any other non-worst-case path. With that approach of overweighting the branches of the worst-case path, *GenE* also compensates for varying instruction times due to the target processor and pipelining behavior. *GenE* supports the configuration of this overweighting factor as a target-specific parameter.

3.4   *Metrics^{WCA}: Validation of GenE's Benchmarks*

The generation of synthetic benchmarks brings up the question of whether the benchmarks are realistic and comparable, for example, with existing benchmark suites in the context of WCET-analysis research. In order to assess the complexity of *GenE*'s benchmarks with other benchmarks, the dissertation presents *Metrics^{WCA}* [31], code metrics for worst-case analyses. *Metrics^{WCA}* relies on several existing complexity measures ($\mathcal{CM}$), which have partly been used in the context of WCET analysis [9]. Some examples of these complexity measures are the number of loops (including their nesting depths) $\mathcal{CM}_{loops}$, the depth of the longest call chain $\mathcal{CM}_{call}$, or McCabe's cyclomatic complexity $\mathcal{CM}_{cc}$ [15]. A novelty of *Metrics^{WCA}* is their property of accounting for the impact of compiler optimizations on the benchmark under evaluation. That is, *Metrics^{WCA}* compare the complexity measures of an optimized version of the benchmark with its original (unoptimized) variant. The result of this comparison is a *resilience factor* $\mathcal{R}$ for a specific complexity measure $\mathcal{CM}$:

$$\mathcal{R}_{\mathcal{CM}} = \frac{\mathcal{CM}_{\text{after optimization}}}{\mathcal{CM}_{\text{before optimization}}} \tag{3}$$

As an example, a benchmark has 12 loops ($\mathcal{CM}_{loops} = 12$) and all loops are optimized out due to the compiler's loop-unrolling optimization (i.e., $\mathcal{CM}_{loops} = 0$ in the optimized variant). As a consequence, this benchmark has a resilience of $\mathcal{R}_{loops} = 0\%$ against the loop-unrolling optimization. From the perspective of assessing an analyzer's performance for determining loop bounds, this benchmark with zero resilience is unsuited since the problem of loop bounds is already straightforward to solve for optimizing compilers. The main observations [26] when applying *Metrics^{WCA}* to *GenE*'s benchmarks are (1) a high resilience against compiler optimizations and (2) comparable complexities with respect to a benchmark suite for WCET analysis [8]. These experiments used the standard configuration of *GenE*'s path budget. A benefit of *GenE*'s generative approach is that an increase of this configuration value leads to benchmarks with larger complexity measures. Thus, the automatically generated benchmark's complexity can be tuned in contrast to existing benchmarks.

Table 1 *GenE* detects individual strengths and weaknesses of the tools' loop-bound analyses

	`constant loop`	`input-dependent loop`	`down-sampling loop`	`triangular loop`
Analyzer `aiT`	✓	✓	✓	✗
Analyzer `Platin`	✓	✓	✗	✓

3.5 Determining Individual Strengths and Weaknesses of Analyzers with GenE

GenE's notion of pattern suites enables developers to identify the individual strengths and weaknesses of analyzers. Table 1 shows results of *GenE*'s loop-related suites. The symbol ✓ expresses a successful solution to the respective loop-bound challenge and ✗ indicates that the analyzer reported unbounded loops.

The `constant loop` suite inserts the patterns of variables, arithmetic expressions, and loops with a constant iteration bound. Both WCET analyzers `Platin` [18] and `aiT` [1] can solve this challenge. In the `input-dependent loop` suite, the iteration bound is computed based on the benchmark's input value, and both analyzers find value constraints to bound these loops. The `down-sampling loop` is a loop that decrements the iteration variable in the loop's body in addition to the loop's header. That way, the iteration variable can no longer be described as a closed-form expression. `aiT` solves this challenge while `Platin` fails. The situation is inverted in the `triangular loop` suite: `Platin` internally makes use of the LLVM compiler infrastructure, which supports scalar-evolution expressions [2]. Due to the scalar-evolution analysis, `Platin` is able to solve the challenge of the `triangular loop` suite.

3.6 Validation of the *aiT* WCET Analyzer

With knowledge of the ground truth, the actual WCET, *GenE* evaluates the overestimation of analyzers and likewise validates that the reported estimate indeed bounds the worst case. In order to conduct such evaluations, *GenE* generated 10,000 benchmarks for an ARM Cortex-M4 platform (Infineon XMC4500) and compared the actual WCET with the value reported by the commercial analyzer `aiT`. Figure 7 shows a histogram of the occurrences of the overestimations. In these experiments, the geometric mean of all overestimations is 23%. An overestimation of 0% would indicate that all reported bound are equal to the respective actual worst case. However, these experiments also revealed reported values where `aiT` erroneously underestimated the actual WCET. Based on these benchmarks, AbsInt, the company behind `aiT`, could confirm these underestimations. According to AbsInt, these bugs were caused by an erroneous hardware model for memory accesses and the pipelining behavior. Subsequently, AbsInt released a revised version of `aiT`, where

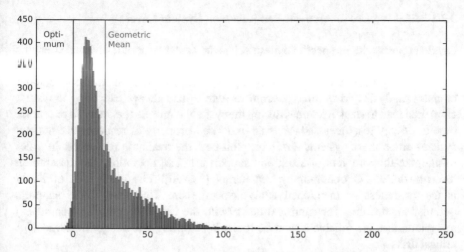

Fig. 7 Histogram of over- and underestimations reported by aiT based on 10,000 automatically generated benchmark programs. A value of 0% indicates the optimum (i.e., no analysis pessimism). All (red) values smaller than 0% are underestimations and, consequently, show erroneous analysis reports

no underestimation could be found with the help of *GenE*. With regard to the fact that developers use static WCET analyses for highly safety-critical systems, the benchmark generator *GenE* is a suitable software tool for testing analyzers and increasing their quality.

3.7   Related Work and Generators in the GenE Family

The original idea for the development of the *GenE* benchmark generator is based on the Csmith tool [34]: Csmith generates programs in the C programming language (i.e., C99) for the purpose of stress-testing compilers. Using the benchmarks generated by Csmith, 325 previously unknown bugs were revealed in both open-source and commercial C compilers. These results emphasize the relevance of such structured testing tools. With the same intention and the focus on evaluating bug-detection tools, the program Bug-Injector [11] produces benchmarks by relying on bug templates. In contrast to these tools, *GenE* targets comprehensive evaluations of static WCET analyzers.

Besides the original *GenE* tool for the main aim of WCET analysis, we developed *GenEE*, a benchmark generator that specifically targets WCEC analyses [7]. Furthermore, we proposed *Taskers*, a generator for whole real-time systems with multiple tasks [6].

3.7.1 Making Use of Analysis Pessimism on System Level

GenE supports with its specific pattern suites the assessment of individual strengths and weaknesses of WCET analyzers. Although this assessment shows the specific optimization potential of analysis techniques, pessimism remains in the safe upper bounds. Analysis and runtime pessimism (due to not always executing the worst case) then lead to slack resources during the system's runtime (i.e., unused execution time or energy resources). Slack is an undesired property of resource-constrained systems since these systems aim to exploit best the available resources. In order to mitigate this problem of slack and support efficient operation, the dissertation presents the *EnOS* operating-system kernel [29, 30]. The basic idea of *EnOS* is the awareness of mentioned analysis pessimism. That way, *EnOS* supports optimistic scheduling for uncritical tasks (with the use of monitoring techniques) and guarantees the reliable execution under both timing and energy constraints of critical tasks.

4 Conclusion

The dissertation [33] targets the reliable operation of safety-critical systems with both timing and energy constraints. The first main contribution is the program analyzer *SysWCEC* that determines upper energy-consumption bounds of tasks. *SysWCEC* implements an analysis technique for the modeling of temporarily active power consumers. Furthermore, the analyzer accounts for the scheduling semantics with fixed priorities, the tasks' use of operating-system resources (e.g., mutexes), synchronous task activations, and asynchronous interrupts.

Determining the degree of analysis pessimism is a fundamental problem in the domain of worst-case analyses. The dissertation solves the problem of evaluating and validating WCET analysis tools by means of the *GenE* benchmark generator. *GenE* combines small program patterns while keeping track of program-flow facts and, thereby, generates new complex benchmarks, whose worst-case behavior is known. The fact that *GenE*'s generated benchmarks helped to discover previously undetected software bugs in a commercial WCET analysis tool emphasizes the relevance of such structured analysis-testing tools.

The source-code repositories of *SysWCEC*, *GenE*, *Metrics*^{WCA}, and *EnOS* are available online:
https://gitlab.cs.fau.de/syswcec
https://gitlab.cs.fau.de/gene
https://gitlab.cs.fau.de/enos

(continued)

Dataset that helped to reveal software bugs in the `aiT` tool:
https://www4.cs.fau.de/Research/GenE/

References

1. AbsInt: aiT WCET analyzers. https://www.absint.com/ait/
2. Bachmann, O., Wang, P.S., Zima, E.V.: Chains of recurrences—a method to expedite the evaluation of closed-form functions. In: Proceedings of the International Symposium on Symbolic and Algebraic Computation (ISSAC '94), pp. 1–8 (1994)
3. Chu, D.H., Jaffar, J.: Symbolic simulation on complicated loops for WCET path analysis. In: Proceedings of the 9th International Conference on Embedded Software (EMSOFT '11), pp. 319–328 (2011)
4. Cohen, A. et al.: Inter-disciplinary research challenges in computer systems for the 2020s. Tech. rep., USA (2018)
5. Dietrich, C., Wägemann, P., Ulbrich, P., Lohmann, D.: SysWCET: Whole-system response-time analysis for fixed-priority real-time systems. In: Proceedings of the 23nd Real-Time and Embedded Technology and Applications Symposium (RTAS '17), pp. 37–48 (2017)
6. Eichler, C., Distler, T., Ulbrich, P., Wägemann, P., Schröder-Preikschat, W.: TASKers: A whole-system generator for benchmarking real-time-system analyses. In: Proceedings of the 18th International Workshop on Worst-Case Execution Time Analysis (WCET '18), pp. 6:1–6:12 (2018)
7. Eichler, C., Wägemann, P., Schröder-Preikschat, W.: GenEE: a benchmark generator for static analysis tools of energy-constrained cyber-physical systems. In: Proceedings of the 2nd Workshop on Benchmarking Cyber-Physical Systems and Internet of Things (CPS-IoTBench '19) (2019)
8. Falk, H., Altmeyer, S., Hellinckx, P., Lisper, B., Puffitsch, W., Rochange, C., Schoeberl, M., Sørensen, R., Wägemann, P., Wegener, S.: TACLeBench: a benchmark collection to support worst-case execution time research. In: Proceedings of the 16th International Workshop on Worst-Case Execution Time Analysis (WCET '16), pp. 1–10 (2016)
9. Gustafsson, J., Betts, A., Ermedahl, A., Lisper, B.: The Mälardalen WCET benchmarks: Past, present and future. In: Proceedings of the 10th International Workshop on Worst-Case Execution Time Analysis (WCET '10), pp. 137–147 (2010)
10. Huber, B., Prokesch, D., Puschner, P.: Combined WCET analysis of bitcode and machine code using control-flow relation graphs. In: Proceedings of the 14th Conference on Languages, Compilers and Tools for Embedded Systems (LCTES '13), pp. 163–172 (2013)
11. Kashyap, V., Ruchti, J., Kot, L., Turetsky, E., Swords, R., Pan, S.A., Henry, J., Melski, D., Schulte, E.: Automated customized bug-benchmark generation. In: Proceedings of the 19th International Working Conference on Source Code Analysis and Manipulation (SCAM '19), pp. 103–114 (2019)
12. Knoop, J., Kovács, L., Zwirchmayr, J.: WCET squeezing: On-demand feasibility refinement for proven precise WCET-bounds. In: Proceedings of the 21st Conference on Real-Time Networks and Systems (RTNS '13), pp. 161–170 (2013)
13. Lattner, C., Adve, V.: LLVM: A compilation framework for lifelong program analysis & transformation. In: Proceedings of the International Symposium on Code Generation and Optimization (CGO '04), pp. 75–86 (2004)
14. Li, Y.T.S., Malik, S.: Performance analysis of embedded software using implicit path enumeration. In: ACM SIGPLAN Notices, vol. 30, pp. 88–98 (1995)
15. McCabe, T.J.: A complexity measure. IEEE Trans. Softw. Eng. **4**, 308–320 (1976)

16. Ouyang, H., Liu, Z., Li, N., Shi, B., Zou, Y., Xie, F., Ma, Y., Li, Z., Li, H., Zheng, Q., Qu, X., Fan, Y., Wang, Z.L., Zhang, H., Li, Z.: Symbiotic cardiac pacemaker. Nat. Commun. **10**, 1821 (2019)
17. Pallister, J., Kerrison, S., Morse, J., Eder, K.: Data dependent energy modeling for worst case energy consumption analysis. In: Proceedings of the 20th International Workshop on Software and Compilers for Embedded Systems (SCOPES '17), pp. 51–59 (2017)
18. Puschner, P., Prokesch, D., Huber, B., Knoop, J., Hepp, S., Gebhard, G.: The T-CREST approach of compiler and WCET-analysis integration. In: Proceedings of the 9th Workshop on Software Technologies for Future Embedded and Ubiquitous Systems (SEUS '13), pp. 33–40 (2013)
19. Raffeck, P., Eichler, C., Wägemann, P., Schröder-Preikschat, W.: Worst-case energy-consumption analysis by microarchitecture-aware timing analysis for device-driven cyber-physical systems. In: Proceedings of the 19th International Workshop on Worst-Case Execution Time Analysis (WCET '19), pp. 6:1–6:12 (2019)
20. Rice, H.G.: Classes of recursively enumerable sets and their decision problems. Trans. Am. Math. Soc. **74**(2), 358–366 (1953)
21. Scheler, F.: Atomic Basic Blocks: Eine Abstraktion für die gezielte Manipulation der Echtzeitsystemarchitektur. Ph.D. Thesis, Friedrich-Alexander-Universität Erlangen-Nürnberg, Technische Fakultät (2011)
22. Scheler, F., Schröder-Preikschat, W.: The real-time systems compiler: migrating event-triggered systems to time-triggered systems. Softw. Practice Exp. **41**(12), 1491–1515 (2011)
23. Sieh, V., Burlacu, R., Hönig, T., Janker, H., Raffeck, P., Wägemann, P., Schröder-Preikschat, W.: An end-to-end toolchain: from automated cost modeling to static WCET and WCEC analysis. In: Proceedings of the 20th International Symposium on Real-Time Distributed Computing (ISORC '17), pp. 1–10 (2017)
24. Wägemann, P., Dietrich, C., Distler, T., Ulbrich, P., Schröder-Preikschat, W.: Whole-system WCEC analysis for energy-constrained real-time systems (artifact). Dagstuhl Artifacts Series **4**(2), 7:1–7:4 (2018)
25. Wägemann, P., Dietrich, C., Distler, T., Ulbrich, P., Schröder-Preikschat, W.: Whole-system worst-case energy-consumption analysis for energy-constrained real-time systems. In: Proceedings of the 30th Euromicro Conference on Real-Time Systems (ECRTS '18), vol. 106, pp. 24:1–24:25. Dagstuhl (2018)
26. Wägemann, P., Distler, T., Eichler, C., Schröder-Preikschat, W.: Benchmark generation for timing analysis. In: Proceedings of the 23rd Real-Time and Embedded Technology and Applications Symposium (RTAS '17), pp. 319–330 (2017)
27. Wägemann, P., Distler, T., Hönig, T., Janker, H., Kapitza, R., Schröder-Preikschat, W.: Worst-case energy consumption analysis for energy-constrained embedded systems. In: Proceedings of the 27th Euromicro Conference on Real-Time Systems (ECRTS '15), pp. 105–114. IEEE, Piscataway (2015)
28. Wägemann, P., Distler, T., Hönig, T., Sieh, V., Schröder-Preikschat, W.: GenE: A benchmark generator for WCET analysis. In: Proceedings of the 15th International Workshop on Worst-Case Execution Time Analysis (WCET '15), vol. 47, pp. 33–43 (2015)
29. Wägemann, P., Distler, T., Janker, H., Raffeck, P., Sieh, V.: A kernel for energy-neutral real-time systems with mixed criticalities. In: Proceedings of the 22nd Real-Time and Embedded Technology and Applications Symposium (RTAS '16), pp. 25–36 (2016)
30. Wägemann, P., Distler, T., Janker, H., Raffeck, P., Sieh, V., Schröder-Preikschat, W.: Operating energy-neutral real-time systems. ACM Trans. Embedded Comput. Syst. **17**(1), 11:1–11:25 (2018)
31. Wägemann, P., Distler, T., Raffeck, P., Schröder-Preikschat, W.: Towards code metrics for benchmarking timing analysis. In: Proceedings of the 37th Real-Time Systems Symposium Work-in-Progress Session (RTSS WiP '16) (2016)
32. Wilhelm, R. et al.: The worst-case execution-time problem—overview of methods and survey of tools. ACM Trans. Embedded Comput. Syst. **7**(3), 1–53 (2008)

33. Wägemann, P.: Energy-constrained real-time systems and their worst-case analyses. Ph.D. Thesis, Friedrich-Alexander-Universität Erlangen-Nürnberg (FAU) (2020). https://nbn-resolving. org/urn:nbn:de:bvb:29-opus4-146935
34. Yang, X., Chen, Y., Eide, E., Regehr, J.: Finding and understanding bugs in C compilers. In: Proceedings of the 32nd Conference on Programming Language Design and Implementation (PLDI '11), pp. 283–294 (2011)

Improving the Model-Based Systems Engineering Process

Michael von Wenckstern

Abstract Modern embedded software systems are becoming more and more complex. Engineering embedded systems raise specific challenges that are rarely present in other software engineering disciplines due to the systems' steady interactions with their environment. Research and industry often describe embedded systems as component and connector models (C&C). C&C models describe the logical architecture by focusing on software features and their logical communications. In C&C models, hierarchical decomposed components encapsulate features, and connectors model the data flow between components via typed ports. As extra-functional properties, for example, safety and security, are also key features of embedded systems, C&C models are mostly enriched with them. However, the process to develop, understand, validate, and maintain large C&C models for complex embedded software is onerous, time consuming, and cost intensive. Hence, the aim of this chapter is to support the automotive software engineer with: (i) automatic consistency checks of large C&C models, (ii) automatic verification of C&C models against design decisions, (iii) tracing and navigating between design and implementation models, (iv) finding structural inconsistencies during model evolution, (v) presenting a flexible approach to define different extra-functional properties for C&C models, and (vi) providing a framework to formalize constraints on C&C models for extra-functional properties for automatic consistency checks.

1 Introduction

The industry area of embedded and cyber-physical systems is one of the largest and it influences our daily life. The global embedded systems marked are getting up to 225 billion US dollar by end of 2021 [24]. Example domains of embedded systems

M. von Wenckstern (✉)
Software Engineering, RWTH Aachen University, Aachen, Germany
e-mail: vonwenckstern@se-rwth.de

are automotive, avionics, robotics, railway, production industry, telecommunication, consumer electronics, and much more.

Model-based engineering, especially component and connector (C&C) models to describe logical architectures, is one common approach to handle the large complexity of embedded systems. Components encapsulate software features; the hierarchical decomposition of components enables formulating logical architectures in a top-down approach. Connectors in C&C models describe the information exchange via typed ports; they model black-box communication between software features.

The current development of complex C&C-based embedded systems in industry mostly involves the following steps [1, 6]: (1) formulating functional and extra-functional requirements as text in *IBM Rational DOORS*; (2) creating a design model of the software architecture including its environment interactions in *SysML*; (3) developing a complete functional/logical model to simulate the embedded system in *Simulink*; and (4) system implementation based on available hardware in C/C++ satisfying all extra-functional properties.

This current development process has the following disadvantages [9]: (a) *SysML* models do not follow a formalized approach leading to misunderstandings; (b) the check between the informal *SysML* architecture design and the *Simulink* model is done manually, and thus, error prone and time consuming; (c) refactoring of *Simulink* models (e.g., dividing a subsystem) needs manual effort in updating the design model; and (d) most tools do not support a generic approach for different extra-functional property kinds, and thus, these properties are modeled as comments or stereotypes where consistency checks can only be done manually.

My research [23] aims to improve the development process of large and complex C&C models for embedded systems by providing model-based methodologies to develop, understand, validate, and maintain these C&C models. Concretely, my concepts support the embedded software engineer with: (i) automatic consistency checks of C&C models; (ii) automatic verification of logical C&C models against their design decisions; (iii) automatic addition of traceability links between design and implementation models; (iv) finding structural inconsistencies during model evolution; (v) providing a flexible framework to define different extra-functional property types; (vi) presenting an *OCL* framework to specify (company-specific) constraints about structural or extra-functional properties for C&C models; and (vii) generation of positive or negative witnesses to explain why a C&C model satisfies or violates its extra-functional or structural constraints or its design decisions.

Prototype implementations of above-mentioned concepts and an industrial case study in cooperation with Daimler AG show promising results in improving the model-based development process of embedded and cyber-physical systems in industry.

This chapter is a summary of the PhD thesis *Verification of Structural and Extra Functional Properties in Component and Connector Models for Embedded and Cyber Physical Systems* [23]. This chapter focuses on examples how the development process for the left part of the V-model can be improved. Detailed related work analyses comparing different tools and concepts like *Mentor Capital*,

Polarsys Arcadia, *PREEvision* [23, Section 2.3], as well as related C&C (modeling) languages such as *AADL*, *ACME*, *Ada*, *AutoFOCUS*, *AUTOSAR*, *LabView*, *MARTE*, *Modelica*, *SysML*, *SystemC*, *Verilog*, and more [23, Section 3.2 and Section 5.2] are discussed in the PhD thesis.

2   Systems Engineering Process at Daimler AG

This section presents results of our case study with Daimler AG in 2017 [1]. The case study included several interviews with an employee at Daimler AG to understand the current model-based and component-based development process as well as the challenges engineers are facing.

2.1   Current Development Process at Daimler AG

Both ISO 26262 *Road vehicles—Functional safety* and ISO/SAE 21434 *Road vehicles—Cybersecurity engineering* follow the V-model and are the international standards for automotive industry. The steps on the left side of the V-model from top to bottom are *system design, specification of software safety/security requirements, software architectural design*, and *software unit design and implementation*; the steps on the right side from bottom to top are *software unit testing, software integration testing, verification of software safety/security requirements*, and *item integration and testing* [3].

The design of a system is mostly described as textual requirements with links to each other; one famous requirement management tool is *IBM Rational DOORS* (short *DOORS*). Later extra-functional requirements for safety or security of a system's design are identified; examples for safety (security process is based on the safety one) are functional safety concept, technical safety concept, system safety, and hardware failures. These extra-functional and stakeholder requirements are integrated into existing requirements of a system's design.

The design of a software architecture is mostly modeled in *SysML* block diagram definitions. Common *SysML* tools in industry are *Enterprise Architect*, *ArchiMate*, *Metropolis*, *Cameo Systems Modeler*, and *PTC Integrity Modeler*. The requirements are modeled separately in these tools and are linked to the corresponding modeling elements, so that traceability is always given [19].

After the design (high-level interaction between components themselves and their environment) is modeled in *SysML*, engineers at Daimler AG create manually an executable model in *Simulink* regarding to the previously defined design decisions. To have the traceability between requirements, *SysML* design models, and *Simulink* implementation models, engineers at Daimler AG add to every subsystem in *SysML* and in *Simulink* an information block containing a link to the requirement specification in *DOORS* [1]. Adding and maintaining these links manually is time consuming and error prone.

This development process has the following disadvantages:

- The check between the informal *SysML* architecture design and the *Simulink* model is done manually.
- The requirement links must be created manually for architectural design model and for the *Simulink* model.
- There exists no automatic check in finding outdated *Simulink* subsystems after updating *SysML* design models (e.g., due to model evolution).
- If *Simulink* models are refactored (e.g., subsystem is split into several ones), it may occur that the *SysML* design model is not updated, and then the architecture model becomes obsolete.
- Early inconsistencies in the *SysML* software architecture design, created by different persons or even different teams in large companies, must be detected manually.

2.2 Improving the Development Process at Daimler AG

To mitigate most of these above-mentioned disadvantages, this subsection presents a slightly modified development process and verification tools, as shown in Fig. 1. The advantage of this new process is that it is completely compatible to existing tools (cf. right side of Fig. 1). The general workflow of this new process including existing tools is:

1. *DOORS* requirements are automatically extracted to a set of textual requirements.
2. Engineers create manually for each requirement a C&C high-level design model.
3. C&C design models are automatically transferred to graphical *SysML* diagrams.
4. The links between *DOORS* requirement IDs and C&C design models enable to automatically derive tracing information between *DOORS* and *SysML* diagrams.
5. Synthesis algorithms automatically check against structural inconsistencies in high-level C&C design models.
6. Engineers add manually extra-functional properties to the C&C high-level design model based on the textual requirements.
7. The *OCL* (Object Constraint Language) framework checks automatically the consistence of the added extra-functional requirements of the high-level design.
8. Engineers create manually the functional C&C model based on textual requirements and the C&C high-level design models.
9. Verification automatically checks whether the functional C&C model satisfies all C&C high-level design models.

10. The functional C&C model is automatically transformed to a *Simulink* model.
11. The result of step 9 enables to automatically derive tracing information between all *SysML* diagrams and the one *Simulink* model as well as tracing information between all *DOORS* requirements and the one *Simulink* model.[1]
12. The *Simulink* model is executed. Measured runtime information (e.g., timing) automatically enriches the C&C model via extra-functional properties.
13. Engineers enrich manually the C&C model with extra-functional properties based on user manuals of software or hardware components, for example, price or ASIL.
14. The *OCL* framework checks automatically the consistency of the extra-functional properties added in steps 12 and 13 to the functional C&C model.
15. The *OCL* framework in combination with the verification in step 9 validates automatically whether all extra-functional properties in the functional C&C model satisfy all extra-functional requirements in all C&C design models.

Even though the new toolchain is larger, there are less manual steps needed due to the higher automation of the steps in this new toolchain. Creating *SysML* diagrams

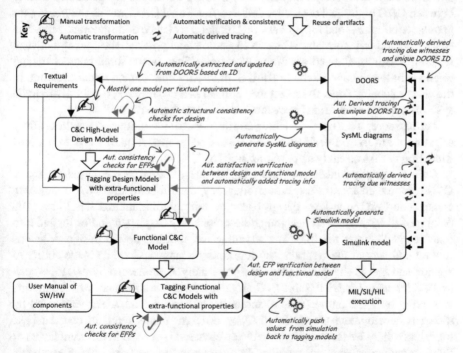

Fig. 1 Modified development process, compatible to V-model (only left side of V-model is shown here)

---

[1] Due to existing tracing information between *SysML* and *DOORS* due to steps 2 and 3.

based on textual requirements needs one manual step in the existing approach: $DOORS \rightarrow^2 SysML$ diagrams. The improved toolchain also needs only one manual step to translate textual requirements to C&C high-level design models as shown in Fig. 1: $DOORS \Rightarrow$ Textual Requirements $\rightarrow$ C&C High-Level Design Models $\Rightarrow SysML$ diagrams. The same holds to create *Simulink* models based on *DOORS* requirements and *SysML* diagrams, where the additional manual step in the existing approach is to create *Simulink* models manually, whereas in the new toolchain the functional C&C models are created manually: $DOORS \rightarrow SysML$ diagrams $\rightarrow$ *Simulink* model $\equiv DOORS \Rightarrow$ Textual Requirements $\rightarrow$ C&C High-Level Design Models $\rightarrow$ Functional C&C Model $\Rightarrow$ *Simulink* model.

In the existing approach, the tracing between *DOORS* and *SysML* diagrams, between *DOORS* and *Simulink* model, as well as between *SysML* diagrams and *Simulink* model is done manually. In contrast, **the new toolchain does the tracing between C&C high-level design models and functional C&C model automatically**. Thus, only the tracing between textual requirements and C&C high-level design models is done implicitly manually as each C&C design model belongs to one requirement. Based on this implicit relation between textual requirements and C&C high-level design models as well as the automatically generated tracing between C&C high-level design models and functional C&C model, the tracing for textual requirements and functional C&C model can also be done automatically. The two automatic transformations enable to automatically derive the tracing between *DOORS* requirements and the *Simulink* model. This means three manual tracing relations in the old approach are equivalent to only one manual tracing relation in the new toolchain. **Thus, the new toolchain saves a lot of work, especially in agile systems engineering, and it prevents manual tracing errors.**

Furthermore, **the new toolchain adds** due to its unique semantics **many additional automatic verifications** to ensure better model quality and **to prevent modeling errors as early as possible**: steps 5, 7, 9, 14, and 15.

C/C++ compiler/linker toolchains create one executable file based on many C/C++ source code text files. In a similar way, the EmbeddedMontiArc toolchain creates one C&C high-level design based on multiple textual text input files. The combined C&C high-level design can be graphically displayed and/or logged into one "merged" larger text file. The advantage of splitting up the design decisions into several textual files (similar as programming languages do it) is the ability to version and merge changes in these files separately. Commercial *SysML* tools such as *PTC Integrity Modeler* (short *PTC IM*) use a database approach, which supports to version only the entire (design) model including all *SysML* elements used by different development teams. In *PTC IM* different teams work in one database model, as otherwise (tracing) links between elements—created in different layers or by different teams—are not possible. In contrast to the database linking approach, the presented textual C&C modeling language family (cf. Sect. 4) to specify C&C high-level designs as well as functional C&C models uses readable full qualified

---

$^2 \Rightarrow$: automatic transformation; $\rightarrow$: manual transformation.

names (instead of generated encrypted IDs by *PTC IM*) to establish the linking process.

The synthesis algorithm enables to check the C&C high-level design against inconsistencies [10, 12]. If this algorithm generates a functional C&C model that is not on the specified high-level design, then the design is consistent; otherwise the specified design is inconsistent. For inconsistent designs, the synthesis algorithm generates user-friendly error messages, which include a natural text of the problem description, and a minimal C&C witness containing the involved components causing the conflict. Since these checks are completely automatic, they can be integrated in a commit-based or nightly continuous integration process. These algorithms are described by Maoz and Ringert [15].

The high-level design can be enriched with extra-functional properties such as safety, performance, or security ones. The strong typed tagging mechanism allows to tag only correct elements which reduces human errors (e.g., shifting a line lower). An example of a check for the tagging mechanism is unit correctness: A velocity tag of a car cannot be 9 kg. Since for each extra-functional property consistency constraints can be defined, the validation framework (cf. Sect. 7) can check full-automatically (no further user action is required) the correctness of the design model with its enriched extra-functional properties. For example, the tool can check whether the price of a component is larger than the sum of the prices of its subcomponents.

EmbeddedMontiArc (cf. Sect. 6) is a textual modeling language extending *Simulink* with new features such as complete unit support as well as component and port arrays. These extensions facilitate an easier description of functional C&C models: (1) Model references must not be copied to be used multiple times, and (2) stronger types with units prevent inconsistencies when connecting ports. Additionally, our textual approach is based on the modular Java class concept that supports to split one model into several textual files to be modified and versioned by different teams.

Furthermore, the layout algorithm [23, Subsection 8.5.1.] creates nice graphical representations with boxes and lines of the textual model. These graphical representations enable an easier navigation between different components. Furthermore, the layout algorithm avoids manually (and time-consuming) adaptions of the graphical model when adding new ports.[3] Based on the automatically calculated layout of the textual model, a *MATLAB* script file containing *Simulink* API calls with x and y coordinates of subsystems creates the *Simulink* model. Hence, the here presented workflow can be easily integrated into the existing workflow of Daimler AG being based on *SysML* and *Simulink* tools.

Additionally, my PhD thesis [23, Section 7.4f] also defines formally when a functional model satisfies all its design models. If the design verification was successful, then the tooling infers automatically all tracing information/links. In

---

[3] *Simulink* does not have a layout algorithm, yet [7]. But other modeling tools such as *Ptolemy* II [4] and *LabView* [18] have one.

case the functional model does not satisfy the design model, then non-satisfaction witnesses with user-friendly error messages pointing directly to the error locations are generated.

Besides the case study focusing on structural consistency checks which is explained in this chapter, there exist also case studies with Daimler AG [21], BMW Group [9], and FEV GmbH [20] with focus on behavioral parts of C&C and *Simulink* models. All these case studies in the automotive domain helped to understand the model-based systems engineering process in detail and how to improve it.

3 Creating C&C High-Level Designs Based on Requirements

In step 2 in Sect. 2.2 the engineer creates for each textual requirement, a C&C high-level design model. The top part of Fig. 2 shows one requirement of the ADAS (advanced driver assistant system) requirement FA-6 based on our case study with Daimler AG. The prefix FA is an abbreviation of Fahrerassistenzsystem which is the German word for ADAS. The requirement FA-6 is part of the functions describing the Distronic feature.

The bottom part of Fig. 2 shows the manual created C&C view. The word C&C view is used as synonym for C&C high-level design in this chapter. This view views

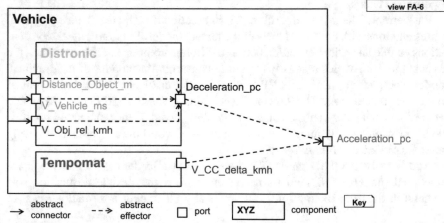

Fig. 2 Requirement FA-6 of unit Distronic of ADASv4 (top) and the view created for this requirement by the domain experts (bottom); copied from [1, Fig. 5].

the high-level architectural design model for this specific requirement, for example, how the dataflow between different C&C model should be. The colors in the text and in the C&C view illustrate the mapping between both. The names in the if condition phrase are mapped to input ports as the Distronic component needs to read those values to produce the correct reaction.

The solid arrows in Fig. 2 represent abstract connectors. The left top abstract connector going from Vehicle to the Distance_Object_m abstract port of the Distronic components states that the Vehicle component has an input port which delegates its value without modifying it to an input port of the Distronic subsystem having the signal name Distance_Object_m. As the view shows only an abstraction (one viewpoint), the hierarchy between Vehicle and Distronic is not direct; thus, in the *Functional C&C Model* the vehicle may have the subcomponent AdaptiveCruiseControl, and AdaptiveCruiseControl has as one subcomponent Distronic.

The dashed arrows in Fig. 2 represent abstract effectors. The top right abstract effector going from the abstract port Deceleration_pc of the Distronic component to Acceleration_pc of the Vehicle component states that the output port with the signal name Deceleration_pc of the Distronic component influences the value of the output port with the signal name Acceleration_pc of the Vehicle component. Influence means that value of Deceleration_pc may be modified by other components.

The abstract port Deceleration_pc is not mentioned in the FA-6 requirement. However, the domain experts[4] included this abstract port in the C&C view as the deceleration value (100% deceleration means the car is not accelerating at all, 0% deceleration means that the car accelerates with its maximal acceleration) is a limiting factor of the vehicle's acceleration, and the domain experts meant that this port is crucial to understand the implementation of this requirement.

4 Automatic Structural Consistency Checks for Design Models

An advantage of the improved development process is the automatic consistency check in step 5 between two C&C high-level design models.

Figure 3 shows two further created C&C design models by two different engineers. The synthesis algorithm [16] throws an exception as it cannot generate a valid functional C&C model based on the given three views: view FA-6 in Fig. 2 as well as view FA-31 and view FA-32 in Fig. 3. The exception message would be similar to *Design conflict between view FA-31 and view FA-32: The*

---

[4] The word domain expert in this chapter refers to the domain expert (an employee at Daimler AG in 2017) who created the C&C high-level designs based on the textual requirements in the industrial case study together with Daimler AG.

2.2.5   Speed Limiter

FA-31: The current vehicle speed is adapted as speed limit.

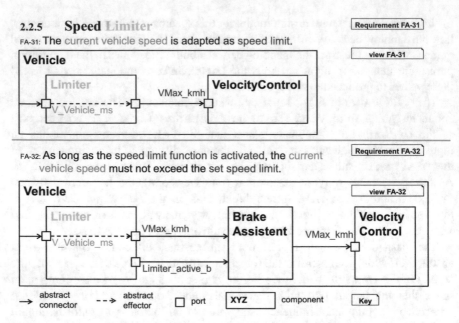

Fig. 3   Conflict in C&C high-level design models view FA-31 and view FA-32

port VMax_kmh of VelocityControl component can only progress a single value for each time step. However it receives two different values: (1) one value from the Limiter component in view FA-31 and (2) another value from the BrakeAssistent component in view FA-32.

These precise exception messages of the synthesis algorithm help the architects who are creating the C&C high-level design models to resolve inconsistencies in the architecture while they are creating their view design models for each requirement.

5   Satisfaction Verification Between Design and Functional Model

In step 8 in Sect. 2.2 the engineer creates the functional C&C model based on all textual requirements and based on all C&C high-level design models. In our case study with Daimler AG, the ADAS part contained of 68 requirements [1, Table 1] and the corresponding C&C model had over 1 000 C&C components and over 3 500 C&C ports [23, Table 8.17]. For such a large functional model it is very time consuming to verify manually whether it satisfies the previously in step 2 defined architecture containing of many C&C high-level design models. Therefore, the Software Engineering chair including the author of this chapter developed a verification tool to automatically check the satisfaction verification between all C&C design models and the one C&C functional model. To increase the trust of the result provided by the verification tool, the tool generates for each C&C design model one satisfaction witness illustrating why the functional model satisfies this C&C design model.

Figure 4 presents the generated satisfaction witness reasoning why the "FAS" functional model satisfies the C&C design model in Fig. 2. The verification algorithm only creates textual output of witnesses; the layout tool, which also transforms the textual C&C functional models to graphical *Simulink* models in step 10, generates good understandable graphical witnesses such as the one shown in Fig. 4.[6]

The blue highlighted connectors in the bottom left part of Fig. 4 belong to the connector chain of the witness representing the abstract connector going from Vehicle (unknown port) to Distronic's V_Obj_rel_kmh port in the C&C high-level design. Additionally, Fig. 4 highlights the witness elements (i.e., upper colored atomic blocks and signal lines in the C&C functional model) belonging to the abstract effector starting at the Distance_Object_m port and ending at Deceleration_pc port of the Distronic subsystem.

Figure 4 shows all elements of the generated satisfaction witness, that is, it contains all components, ports, and connectors so that all elements of the C&C high-level design in Fig. 2 are matched at least once. Note that the satisfaction witness shows for each abstract connector and abstract effector only the shortest path in the C&C functional model. In contrast, the tracing witness contains ALL paths of the C&C functional model which match any element described in the C&C high-level design. The verification witness is used as argument to reason why or also why not a functional model satisfies a specific design model.

The purpose of a tracing witness[7] is to trace down to all components, ports and connectors in the functional model based on a design model. A practical use case for the tracing witness is the following: Due to a product update some requirements and, thus also, some high-level design models are updated. The generated tracing witness identifies all elements in the functional C&C model which are affected by the design and requirement updates. The size and complexity of the generated tracing witness enables a first effort and price estimation for the product update. Furthermore, the

---

[5] The complete graphical C&C model is available from:https://embeddedmontiarc.github. io/webspace2/svg/vis/v4/daimler.v4.oeffentlicher_Demonstrator_FAS_v04.dEMO_FAS. dEMO_FAS.subsystem.dEMO_FAS.dEMO_FAS_Funktion_extended.html.

[6] The generated graphical output of the layout tool is available from https://embeddedmontiarc.github.io/webspace2/svg/vis/v4/FA6_Witness/daimler.v4. oeffentlicher_Demonstrator_FAS_v04FA6.dEMO_FAS.dEMO_FAS.subsystem.dEMO_FAS. dEMO_FAS_Funktion_extended.html. Figure 4 shows a manually and slightly modified layout which is space and color optimized for this chapter.

[7] The generated layout of the tracing witness for requirement FA-6 is available from https://embeddedmontiarc.github.io/webspace2/svg/vis/v4/FA6_TracingWitness/daimler. v4.oeffentlicher_Demonstrator_FAS_v04FA6Tracing.dEMO_FAS.dEMO_FAS.subsystem. dEMO_FAS.dEMO_FAS_Funktion_extended.html.

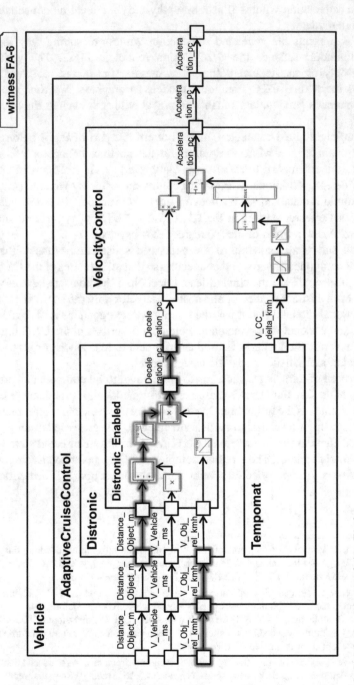

Fig. 4 Satisfaction witness of view FA-6

components inside the generated tracing witness supports management in booking the needed teams for this product update.[8]

6 Creating C&C Functional Models Efficiently with *EmbeddedMontiArc*

EmbeddedMontiArc is a textual domain-specific language to create functional C&C models for cyber-physical systems in an efficient way. Therefore, *EmbeddedMontiArc* supports the international systems of units, generics, component libraries, configuration parameters, as well as arrays of ports and component instantiations to facilitate modular and reusable functional architectures.

EmbeddedMontiArc is a textual modeling family to describe both structural (as already shown in the previous sections) and also behavior models. Behavioral languages part of *EmbeddedMontiArc* family are: automata, *MontiMath* (typed version of *MATLAB*), *MontiMathOpt* (math plus nonlinear optimization problems), *CNNArch* (convolutional networks for deep learning), and *OCL* (object constraint language for logical declarative description of components). This chapter does not focus on the behavioral languages. However, the publications of Kusmenko and von Wenckstern [8, 9, 11–13] contain behavioral models describing the logic of self-driving cars created with *EmbeddedMontiArc*. A complete behavioral *EmbeddedMontiArc* model for the logic of PacMan to escape four ghosts including a simulator and a debugger exists as online demonstrator.[9]

The functional C&C model in Fig. 4 shows the OEM perspective, where the Vehicle component receives the distance to the preceding vehicle as number input directly from a smart sensor doing already the image capturing as well as the object recognition. The smart sensor (developed by an automotive tier-1 supplier for different OEMs) receives as input an image matrix of the front car camera, performs spectral clustering to divide the images into segments, the object detector can separate the objects to identify the car in front and to measure the distance to it.

This section explains the features and the syntax of *EmbeddedMontiArc* on an image spectral cluster component [14] which could be part of the smart sensor.

The basic idea is depicted as a functional C&C model in Fig. 5 and can be summarized as follows. Let $x_{ij} \in [0, 255]^3$ be the three-dimensional pixel value of an image at position (i, j) encoding a point in the HSV (hue, saturation, value) color space. For better handling, an $N \times M$ image is represented as a vector, mapping a position (i, j) to the vector index $M \cdot i + j$, where N and M are

---

[8] Mostly subcomponents can be matched to teams; for example, team one is responsible for Tempomat and VelocityControl, and team two works on Distronic, Distancewarner, and EmergencyBrake.

[9] The online demonstrator is available from: https://embeddedmontiarc.github.io/webspace/InteractiveSimulator/indexPacman.html.

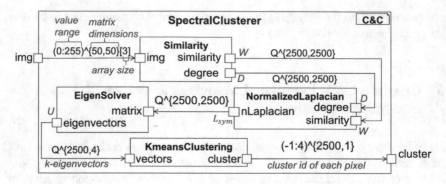

Fig. 5 C&C architecture of the SpectralClusterer

the height and the width of the image, respectively. First, a symmetric similarity matrix $W \in \mathbb{R}^{NM \times NM}$ is computed. Consequently, the entry of W at position (h, k) provides information on the similarity of the two pixels corresponding to the indexes h and k. Pixel similarity may be defined in terms of distance, color, gradients, etc. Second, the so-called graph Laplacian is computed as $L = D - W$ where D is the so-called degree matrix defined as $D = \text{diag}(W \mathbb{1}_{N \times M})$ with $\mathbb{1}_{NM}$ being an $N \cdot M$ dimensional column vector full of ones. Often it is advantageous to use the symmetric Laplacian

$$L_{sym} = D^{-\frac{1}{2}} L D^{-\frac{1}{2}} = \text{diag}(\mathbb{1}_{NM}) - D^{-\frac{1}{2}} W D^{-\frac{1}{2}} \tag{1}$$

as outlined in [22]. For efficiency reasons, as they do not carry valuable cluster information the identity matrix and the minus depicted in red are often dropped in concrete implementations obtaining the simplified term highlighted in blue. Note that computing L_{sym} requires a matrix inversion on the diagonal matrix D as well as two matrix multiplications. Now the eigenvectors corresponding to the k smallest eigenvalues of L_{sym} have to be computed where k is the number of clusters we want to detect. If this number is unknown, an index can be used to estimate it [5]. Furthermore, let U be an $NM \times k$ matrix with the k eigenvectors as its columns. Each row of this matrix represents one pixel in a feature space which should be easier to cluster by the standard k-means algorithm.

EmbeddedMontiArc is a textual domain-specific language to model logical functions in a C&C based manner. *EmbeddedMontiArc* places emphasis on the needs of the embedded, cyber-physical systems, as well as the automotive domains and is particularly used for controller design [9]. As an example, the elaborate numeric type system allows declarations of variable ranges as well as accuracies. Furthermore, units are an inherent part of signal types, and hence tedious and error-prone tasks like checking the physical compatibility of signals (weights cannot be added to lengths) as well as unit or prefix conversion (feet to meters, km to m) are delegated to the *EmbeddedMontiArc* compiler.

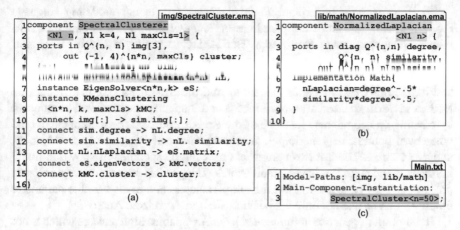

Fig. 6 Textual *EmbeddedMontiArc* code of the graphical C&C SpectralClusterer component shown in Fig. 5. (**a**) EmbeddedMontiArc model of SpectralClusterer. (**b**) EmbeddedMontiArc model of atomic component NormalizedLaplacian. (**c**) Main component instantiation

Figure 6 shows how the spectral cluster in Figure 5 is modeled in *Embedded-MontiArc*. Figure 6b represents one subcomponent of (a). As *EmbeddedMontiArc* is inherent to C&C languages, the main language elements of *EmbeddedMontiArc* are component and connect. While the former defines a new component followed by its name, for example, in line 1 of Fig. 6a, the latter connects two ports of subcomponents with each other, for example, in lines 10–15 in Fig. 6a.

The behavior of a component can be either defined by a hierarchical decomposition into subcomponents as in the case of Fig. 6a or using an embedded behavior description language.

The behavioral language shown in this code example is a matrix-based math language, used in lines 6–8 of Fig. 6b respectively. As *EmbeddedMontiArc* is strongly typed, errors like wrong matrix dimensions are caught at compile-time, in contrast to *MATLAB/Simulink* where this is a runtime exception. A matrix property system leverages performance optimizations as well as further compatibility checks in the compilation phase. If a matrix is declared to be diagonal, both memory and computational complexity of the generated code can be reduced dramatically. If furthermore, the domain of the matrix is constrained to non-negative entries, it can be inferred that the matrix is positive-semidefinite allowing the inversion function to be used on it and guaranteeing that the result will be positive-semidefinite again [2].

As this spectral clustering example shows each *EmbeddedMontiArc* component resides in its own text file so that multiple users or teams can work on one large C&C modeling project simultaneously. Compared to other C&C languages where models are stored in a proprietary binary format in one single file, such as Simulink's slx format, this facilitates the usage of version control systems, merging, and conflict solving but also textual searching in model repositories.

The next paragraphs explain *EmbeddedMontiArc* textual modeling language more in detail. The modeling paradigm of *EmbeddedMontiArc* is based on Java with language elements from Ada. The `Main.txt` file in Fig. 6c is similar to Java's manifest file. Line 1 defines model paths where the parser looks for component type definitions; in this example it includes the `img` (for image) and the `library/mathamatics` folders to find the `SpectralCluster` and the `NormalizedLaplacian` type. Lines 2 and 3 specify the top level component by creating one component instance of the `SpectralCluster` component type whereby it bounds the generic parameters with the following values n=50, k=4, and maxCls=1. The last two parameters may not be specified as shown in line 3 in (c), as k and maxCls have default values. The general generic concept is based on Java, and the concepts to have default parameters and to also enable parameter binding by name and not only via position are borrowed from Ada.

The support of generics in *EmbeddedMontiArc* enables high reusage which is not possible in *Simulink* yet. For example, for applying the same clustering algorithm on a 100×100 image instead of the small 50×50, one requires only to replace the expression n=50 to n=100 in line 3 in (c).

Lines 1 and 2 in Fig. 6a define the `SpectralClusterer` component type which has three input and one output ports as well as three generic parameters. The three generic parameters are of type N1 representing the mathematical type $\mathbb{N}_1$ accepting values $1, 2, 3, \ldots$.

Line 3 defines the three input ports by applying port array notation. The names of the input ports are img[1], ..., img[3] for the three color channels HSV. All three ports accept as values $n \times n$ (which is in our example 50×50) rational matrices which is defined as Q^{n, n} in *EmbeddedMontiArc*; Q represents the math type $\mathbb{Q}$. All three ports could be used independently, for example, by connecting each of them to different subcomponents. The `SpectralClusterer` produces as output a $n \cdot n \times maxCls$ matrix (which is in this example a vector with 2 500 elements) with the cluster id of the pixel; all elements of the `cluster` matrix are in the interval from -1 to $+4$ (including both end points).

Line 5 instantiates one `Similarity` subcomponent instance which accepts as input a 50×50 ($n = 50$) matrix and produces as output the similarity and the degree matrix of type $\mathbb{Q}^{2\,500 \times 2\,500}$.

Line 6 instantiates the `NormalizedLaplacian` subcomponent instance and bounds the value `NormalizedLaplacian.n` to 2500 (`SpectralClusterer.n` $= 50$) which is defined in Fig. 6b.

Lines 7 and 8 instantiate the two further subcomponents. Lines 10 to 15 connect the ports of the defined subcomponents as shown in Fig. 5.

EmbeddedMontiArc also supports to add algebraic information for matrix types as shown in line 3 in Fig. 6b with the keyword `diagonal`.

Additionally, *EmbeddedMontiArc* supports units. For example, port in (0 km/h : 250 km/h) V_Obj_rel_km defines the input port V_Obj_rel_kmh of the `Distronic` component as shown in Fig. 4. The strong type system with units prevents errors like connecting ports with incompatible units such as Distance_Object_m having port type (0m : 500m) with port V_Obj_rel_kmh.

The textual syntax for C&C design models for step 2 in Sect. 2.2 is very similar to the textual syntax of *EmbeddedMontiArc* shown in Fig. 6a. For example, the port definition in design models support a question mark as port type to express underspecification: port out ? velocity. Detailed information about the concrete and abstract syntax of the textual C&C high-level design and functional modeling languages is available in my PhD thesis [23, Chapters 3, 4, 7].

7 Enriching C&C Functional Models with Extra-Functional Properties in a Consistent Way

Section 6 showed the textual modeling languages for C&C high-level design models and for C&C functional models. Section 3 presented the concept how to derive the high-level design models from textual requirements and how to create one functional C&C model based on the high-level designs and the requirements. These both sections covered the steps 1–11 of Sect. 2.2.

This section continues with step 13 how the engineer enriches the functional C&C model with extra-functional properties. Therefore, this section shows first how to define a new tag schema to enrich C&C components with ASIL (automotive safety integrity level) information. Later, this section presents a tag model which is to conform to the previously defined tag schema to tag the Vehicle subcomponents of Fig. 4 with concrete ASIL levels. At the end this section explains how to formulate the extra-functional constraint for ASIL in *OCL*: A composed component cannot have higher ASIL than its subcomponents.

Figure 7 shows how to define a new tag schema and how to enrich it with functional C&C models. Line 1 in (a) gives the tag schema a name so that it can be used in tag models. Line 2 in (a) creates the new tag type asil which accepts as

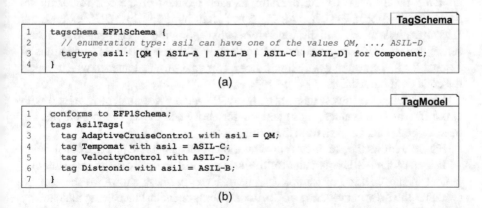

TagSchema

```
1   tagschema EFP1Schema {
2       // enumeration type: asil can have one of the values QM, ..., ASIL-D
3       tagtype asil: [QM | ASIL-A | ASIL-B | ASIL-C | ASIL-D] for Component;
4   }
```

(a)

TagModel

```
1   conforms to EFP1Schema;
2   tags AsilTags{
3       tag AdaptiveCruiseControl with asil = QM;
4       tag Tempomat with asil = ASIL-C;
5       tag VelocityControl with ASIL-D;
6       tag Distronic with asil = ASIL-B;
7   }
```

(b)

Fig. 7 ASIL tag schema and tag model example. (**a**) Tag schema definition of extra-functional property asil. (**b**) Tag model enriching components with extra-functional property asil

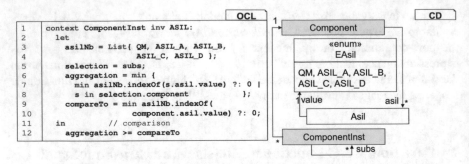

```
                                                              OCL                                            CD
1    context ComponentInst inv ASIL:              1        Component
2      let
3        asilNb = List{ QM, ASIL_A, ASIL_B,               «enum»
4                       ASIL_C, ASIL_D };                  EAsil
5        selection = subs;
6        aggregation = min {                              QM, ASIL_A, ASIL_B,
7          min asilNb.indexOf(s.asil.value) ?: 0 |        ASIL_C, ASIL_D
8          s in selection.component        };     1 value                      asil *
9        compareTo = min asilNb.indexOf(
10                       component.asil.value) ?: 0;                 Asil
11     in          // comparison
12       aggregation >= compareTo                 *   ComponentInst
                                                            * ↑ subs
```

Fig. 8 *OCL* code to force that composed component cannot have higher ASIL than its subcomponents. The right part shows the class diagram of the abstract syntax of *EmbeddedMontiArc* with gray background merged with the abstract syntax defined by the tag schema in Fig. 7a with white background. Detailed information about the abstract syntax is available in my PhD thesis [23, Chapter 4]

values QM (not safety relevant), ASIL-A, ..., ASIL-D (highest safety level). One tag schema can contain multiple tag types to build up tag libraries. For example, a tag schema *SafetySecurity* could contain the tag types *asil*, *reliability*, *encryption*, and *firewallConfig*.

Figure 7b presents how to tag the components AdaptiveCruise, Tempomat, and VelocityControl in Fig. 4 with the asil levels QM, ASIL-B, ASIL-C, and ASIL-D.

Figure 8 shows the *OCL* code checking that the ASIL of all subcomponents must be higher or equal than the ASIL of the composed component. Lines 3 and 4 define the asilNb helper list. This list maps each ASIL to a number so that a comparison of ASILs is possible. The expression asilNb.indexOf(x) returns 0 for QM, 1 for ASIL_A, 2 for ASIL_B, 3 for ASIL_C, and 4 for ASIL_D.

The indexOf[10] function is extended to accept a set as parameter by applying the Java indexOf operator to each element of the set; for example, asilNb.indexOf({QM, ASIL_C}) returns {0, 3}. *OCL* extends all Java operators to set and list operators when applying it element-wise makes sense; this way *OCL* expressions—often dealing with sets due to its navigations of associations—come along with less forall or exists statements, which makes the code easier to read.

Line 7 takes the lowest number of an ASIL when a component is tagged with two different ASIL values, and it takes 0 for QM when the subcomponent has not been tagged at all. Line 12 does the comparison.

Figure 9 shows the graphical representation of the generated positive consistency witnesses of the ASIL constraint for the AdaptiveCruiseControl subcomponent in the Vehicle example in Fig. 4. Every witness shows (a) the context (which is the AdaptiveCruiseControl component instance being matched by

---

[10] cf. http://mbse.se-rwth.de/book2/index.php?c=chapter3-2.

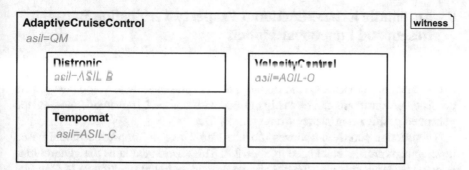

Fig. 9 Positive consistency witness of `asil` constraint for `AdaptiveCruiseControl` example in Fig. 4 enriched with the values shown in Fig. 7b.

line 1 in Fig. 8), (b) all elements stored in the `selection` variable (which are the three subcomponents `Distronic`, `Tempomat`, and `VelocityControl` being matched by line 5 in Fig. 8), (c) filling elements to understand the witness (e.g., if a port is part of (a) or (b), then also the corresponding component to which this port belongs to is shown in the witness), and (d) all extra-functional properties being addressed in the *OCL* constraint (which is in this case only the `asil` one being used in lines 7 and 10 in Fig. 8).

The generated positive (or negative) consistency witnesses are as minimal as possible. Thus, it is very easy for the engineer to understand why (or also why not) a large functional C&C model satisfies a specific consistency constraint rule as the ASIL one in this example.

This section presented a model-driven approach for adding extra-functional properties to functional C&C models. The here shown tagging mechanism enables noninvasive extensions of functional C&C models and also C&C high-level design models (shown in the next section) with attributes for extra-functional properties. Importantly, this concept provides means for integrated formal analyses of the consistency of tagged values. Consistency ranges from type-safety and units of quantitative measures to complex dependencies across component hierarchies as well as between component definitions and their instances. The *OCL* framework provides a way to define and to check rich consistency rules of extra-functional property values based on selection (line 5 in Fig. 8), aggregation (lines 6–8), and comparison (line 12) operators. This work allows for independent definition and organization of tagged properties to support reuse across models and development stages.

More *OCL* consistency examples for real-life problems are available in my PhD thesis [23, Chapter 6] and in the paper [17].[11]

---

[11] The *OCL* verification tool is available under https://git.rwth-aachen.de/monticore/publications-additional-material/-/tree/master/OCLVerifyTool.

8 Automatic Extra-Functional Property Verification Between Design and Functional Models

The previous section illustrated how easy it is to enrich functional C&C models with extra-functional properties. Additionally, Sect. 3 presented how company specific consistency constraints can be easily defined with our *OCL* framework and how the generated positive consistency witness looks like.

This section shortly introduces the last step 15 of the improved model-based development process elucidated in Sect. 2.2. This section explains the general idea how to check whether all extra-functional properties in the functional C&C model satisfies all extra-functional requirements specified in all C&C high-level design models.

The top part of Fig. 10 presents an extra-functional requirement about the worst case execution time for the critical path inside the Distronic component: *If the distance to the preceding vehicle decreases, distronic decelerates within* 20 *ms.*

The bottom left part shows the corresponding graphical C&C high-level design model; the effector from the Distance_Object_m port to the Deceleration_pc port has been tagged with the extra-functional requirement: wcet ≤ 20ms

The bottom right part reprints the Distronic component of Fig. 4. Based on the measured runtime information (cf. step item 12), the atomic subcomponents of Distronic have been enriched with the extra-functional property execution time values: (i) both multiplication blocks mult1 and mul2 need 7 ms; (ii) the linear and saturate need 10 ms, as well as the sum block needs only 5 ms.

Figure 11 defines the tag types et (execution time) for Components and wcet (worst case execution time) for Effectors. Both the tag schema and the model language support all SI units completely as shown in lines 4 and 7: the execution time of a component can only have a value between 0 ms and 1 min.

2.2.1 Distronic

FA-146: **(k) If the** distance to the preceding vehicle **decreases, distronic** decelerates within 20ms.

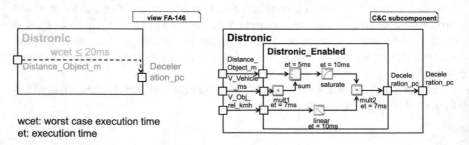

wcet: worst case execution time
et: execution time

Fig. 10 ASIL tag schema and tag model example

```
                                                          TagSchema
1   tagschema ExecutionTime {
2      // number type of unit time: et (execution time) can be b/w 0 ms and 1 min
3      // only components in the functional C&C model can be tagged with et
4      tagtype et: (0ms : 1 min) for Component;
5      // ONLY effectors in C&C high-level desing model can be tagged with wcet
6      // (worst case execution time)
7      tagtype wcet: <= (0ms : 1 min) for Effector;
8   }
```

Tag schema definition of extra-functional properties et and wcet.

Fig. 11 ASIL tag schema and tag model example

```
                                                          TagModel
1   conforms to ExecutionTime;
2   tags WcetTags{
3     within Distronic {
4        tag effector Distance_Object_m -> Deceleration_pc with wcet <= 20ms;
5     }
6   }
```

(a)

```
                                                          TagModel
1   conforms to ExecutionTime;
2   tags EtTags{
3     within Distronic_Enabled {
4        tag sum with et = 5ms;
5        tag saturate, linear with et = 10ms;
6        tag mult1, mult2 with et = 7ms;
7     }
8   }
```

(b)

Fig. 12 ASIL tag schema and tag model example. (**a**) Tag model enriching C&C high-level design view FA-146 with extra-functional property wcet. (**b**) Tag model enriching C&C high-level design view FA-146 with extra-functional property wcet

Tag types to enrich the functional C&C model, as already presented in Sect. 3, represent concrete extra-functional property values. Therefore, these always have an assignment operator (=), which can be skipped as shown in line 4.

Tag types to enrich the C&C high-level design model represent underspecified extra-functional requirements expressing a Boolean constraint. For this reason the Boolean comparison operator (such as $<, \leq, \subseteq, \in, \supset, \geq, >$) must be specified as shown with <= in line 7.

Figure 12a shows that C&C high-level design models can be enriched with extra-functional requirements nearly in the same way as functional C&C models with extra-functional properties. Ports are identified via their component name and their port name, because different components may have the same port name. The within keyword in line 3 is syntactic sugar to express that all expressions inside it refer to the component specified. Line 4 enriches the effector with the extra-functional requirement as illustrated in the bottom left part of Fig. 10. An equivalent notation of lines 3–5 is the following: `tag effector Distronic.Distance_Object_m -> Distronic.Deceleration_pc with wcet <= 20ms;`.

Figure 12b displays the textual code how to enrich the functional C&C model with the measured execution times as illustrated in the bottom right part of Fig. 10. The tag model language supports to enrich multiple C&C elements at once with the same value as shown in lines 5 and 6.

In our example, we assume that the (here not shown *OCL*) constraint does the following: First, it selects all components of the C&C subcomponent which are matched by effector shown in `view FA-146` in Fig. 10. These are the components `Distronic, Distronic_Enabled, sum, saturate`, and `mult2`. Second, it aggregates all the execution time values of these components whereby a missing `et` tag is interpreted as 0 ms. The aggregation result is $22ms = 0ms + 0ms + 5ms + 10ms + 7ms$. Third, it compares whether the aggregation result of the functional C&C model is smaller or equal to the wcet (worst case execution time) requirement of the enriched effector. In this example, the aggregation result is $22ms$ and is NOT smaller or equal to the requested worst case execution time of $20ms$ of the enriched effector in the `view FA-146`. Thus, the functional C&C model in the bottom right part of Fig. 10 does not satisfy the view as well as it violates the `FA-146` requirement.

The verification tool does not only automatically check whether all extra-functional properties of the functional C&C model satisfy all extra-functional requirements specified in all C&C high-level designs, it also generates useful witnesses directly pointing to the mismatch. Figure 13 shows the graphical representation provided by the verification algorithm for this concrete example. The satisfaction witness creation algorithm for extra-functional properties is similar to the consistency witness creation algorithm presented in the previous section.

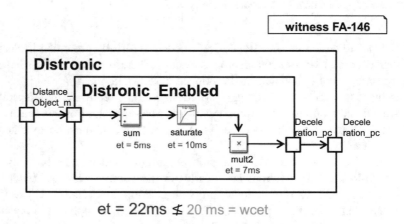

Fig. 13 ASIL tag schema and tag model example

9 Conclusion

This chapter showed the developed methodology to improve the model-based systems engineering process of large and complex C&C models for embedded and cyber-physical systems, especially in the automotive domain. The here presented approach extends the current model-based development process of large car manufactures identified during common case studies.

The main achievements of this work are concepts and tools for automatic consistency checks between requirements, high-level design models, functional C&C models, and extra-functional properties. These automatic checks with its user-friendly witness generations prevent errors at design and implementation phase, and thus, provide a way to improve quality, to increase development speed, and to save money.

This chapter demonstrated the capabilities and benefits of the proposed model-based process improvements on a running example of an advanced driver assistant system.

References

1. Bertram, V., Maoz, S., Ringert, J.O., Rumpe, B., von Wenckstern, M.: Component and connector views in practice: an experience report. In: Conference on Model Driven Engineering Languages and Systems (MODELS'17), pp. 167–177. IEEE, Piscataway (2017). http://www.se-rwth.de/publications/Component-and-Connector-Views-in-Practice-An-Experience-Report.pdf
2. Borgmann, M.: Matrix taxonomy (2006). https://www.nari.ee.ethz.ch/teaching/ha/handouts/linalg3p.pdf
3. Brenner, C.: How to ensure functional safety, according to ISO 26262 (2013). https://blogs.itemis.com/en/how-to-ensure-functional-safety-according-to-iso-26262. Accessed 29 April 2021
4. Cheng, C.H.: autoCode4 integrated inside Ptolemy II (ver. 11.0.devel) (2016). https://youtu.be/ImSHmsnUyeA?t=34s. Accessed 31 July 2018
5. Desgraupes, B.: Clustering indices. Univ. Paris Ouest-Lab Modal'X 1, 34 (2013)
6. Drave, I., Greifenberg, T., Hillemacher, S., Kriebel, S., Kusmenko, E., Markthaler, M., Orth, P., Salman, K.S., Richenhagen, J., Rumpe, B., Schulze, C., Wenckstern, M., Wortmann, A.: SMArDT modeling for automotive software testing. Softw. Practice Exp. 49(2), 301–328 (2019)
7. Goser, A.: MATLAB Answers: Clean up Simulink block diagram (2012). https://de.mathworks.com/matlabcentral/answers/30016-clean-up-simulink-block-diagram. Accessed 31 July 2018
8. Grazioli, F., Kusmenko, E., Roth, A., Rumpe, B., von Wenckstern, M.: Simulation framework for executing component and connector models of self-driving vehicles. In: Proceedings of MODELS 2017. Workshop EXE, CEUR 2019 (2017). http://www.se-rwth.de/publications/Simulation-Framework-for-Executing-Component-and-Connector-Models-of-Self-Driving-Vehicles.pdf
9. Hillemacher, S., Kriebel, S., Kusmenko, E., Lorang, M., Rumpe, B., Sema, A., Strobl, G., von Wenckstern, M.: Model-based development of self-adaptive autonomous vehicles using the SMARDT methodology. In: Proceedings of the 6th International Conference on Model-Driven

Engineering and Software Development (MODELSWARD'18), pp. 163–178. SciTePress, Setúbal (2018)

10. Kriebel, S., Kusmenko, E., Rumpe, B., von Wenckstern, M.: Finding inconsistencies in design models and requirements by applying the SMARDT process. In: Tagungsband des Dagstuhl-Workshop MBEES: Modellbasierte Entwicklung eingebetteter Systeme XIV (MBEES'18). Univ. Hamburg (2018). http://www.se-rwth.de/publications/Finding-Inconsistencies-in-Design-Models-and-Requirements-by-Applying-the-SMARDT-Process.pdf

11. Kusmenko, E., Pavlitskaya, S., Rumpe, B., Stüber, S.: On the engineering of AI-powered systems. In: O'Conner, L. (ed.) ASEW19. Software Engineering Intelligence Workshop (SEIW19), pp. 126–133. IEEE, Piscataway (2019). http://www.se-rwth.de/publications/On-the-Engineering-of-AI-Powered-Systems.pdf

12. Kusmenko, E., Ronck, J.M., Rumpe, B., von Wenckstern, M.: EmbeddedMontiArc: textual modeling alternative to simulink. In: Proceedings of MODELS 2018. Workshop EXE (2018)

13. Kusmenko, E., Rumpe, B., Schneiders, S., von Wenckstern, M.: Highly-optimizing and multi-target compiler for embedded system models: C++ compiler toolchain for the component and connector language EmbeddedMontiArc. In: Conference on Model Driven Engineering Languages and Systems (MODELS'18). IEEE, Piscataway (2018)

14. Kusmenko, E., Rumpe, B., Strepkov, I., von Wenckstern, M.: Teaching playground for C&C language EmbeddedMontiArc. In: Proceedings of MODELS 2018. Workshop ModComp (2018). http://www.se-rwth.de/publications/Teaching-Playground-for-C-and-C-Language-EmbeddedMontiArc.pdf

15. Maoz, S., Pomerantz, N., Ringert, J.O., Shalom, R.: Why is my component and connector views specification unsatisfiable? In: 2017 ACM/IEEE 20th International Conference on Model Driven Engineering Languages and Systems (MODELS), pp. 134–144 (2017). https://doi.org/10.1109/MODELS.2017.26

16. Maoz, S., Ringert, J.O., Rumpe, B.: Synthesis of component and connector models from crosscutting structural views. In: Meyer, B., Baresi, L., Mezini, M. (eds.) Joint Meeting of the European Software Engineering Conference and the ACM SIGSOFT Symposium on the Foundations of Software Engineering (ESEC/FSE'13), pp. 444–454. ACM, New York (2013). http://www.se-rwth.de/publications/Synthesis-of-Component-and-Connector-Models-from-Crosscutting-Structural-Views.pdf

17. Maoz, S., Ringert, J.O., Rumpe, B., von Wenckstern, M.: Consistent extra-functional properties tagging for component and connector models. In: Workshop on Model-Driven Engineering for Component-Based Software Systems (ModComp'16), CEUR Workshop Proceedings, vol. 1723, pp. 19–24 (2016). http://www.se-rwth.de/publications/Consistent-Extra-Functional-Properties-Tagging-for-Component-and-Connector-Models.pdf

18. National Instruments: Automatische Bereinigung von LabVIEW-Blockdiagrammen (2009). http://www.ni.com/tutorial/7386/de/. Accessed 31 July 2018

19. Plataniotis, G., Ma, Q., Proper, E., de Kinderen, S.: Traceability and modeling of requirements in enterprise architecture from a design rationale perspective. In: Research Challenges in Information Science (RCIS), 2015 IEEE 9th International Conference on, pp. 518–519. IEEE, Piscataway (2015)

20. Richenhagen, J., Rumpe, B., Schloßer, A., Schulze, C., Thissen, K., von Wenckstern, M.: Test-driven semantical similarity analysis for software product line extraction. In: International Systems and Software Product Line Conference (SPLC '16), pp. 174–183. ACM, New York (2016). http://www.se-rwth.de/publications/Test-Driven-Semantical-Similarity-Analysis-for-Software-Product-Line-Extraction.pdf

21. Rumpe, B., Schulze, C., von Wenckstern, M., Ringert, J.O., Manhart, P.: Behavioral compatibility of simulink models for product line maintenance and evolution. In: Software Product Line Conference (SPLC'15), pp. 141–150. ACM, New York (2015). http://www.se-rwth.de/publications/Behavioral-Compatibility-of-Simulink-Models-for-Product-Line-Maintenance-and-Evolution.pdf

22. Von Luxburg, U.: A tutorial on spectral clustering. Stat. Comput. **17**(4), 395–416 (2007)

23. von Wenckstern, M.: Verification of Structural and Extra Functional Properties in Component and Connector Models for Embedded and Cyber Physical Systems. Aachener Informatik-Berichte, Software Engineering, Band 44. Shaker Verlag (2020). http://www.se-rwth.de/phdtheses/Diss-von-Wenckstern-Verification-of-Structural-and-Extra-Functional-Properties-in-Component-and-Connector-Models-for-Embedded-and-Cyber-Physical-Systems.pdf
24. Zion Market Research: Global Embedded Systems Market Will Reach USD 225.34 billion by 2021 (2017). https://tinyurl.com/ofetbpzw. Accessed 14 February 2021

Understanding How Pair Programming Actually Works in Industry: Mechanisms, Patterns, and Dynamics

Franz Zieris

Abstract During pair programming (PP), two software developers work closely together on a technical task on one computer. Practitioners expect a number of benefits, such as faster progress, higher quality, and knowledge transfer. Much of prior research focused on directly measurable effects from laboratory settings, but could not explain the large variations observed. My research follows the Grounded Theory Methodology and is aimed at understanding how PP actually works by uncovering the underlying mechanisms to ultimately formulate practical advice for developers. The main findings from my qualitative analysis of recordings of 27 industrial PP sessions are: Task-specific *knowledge about the software system* is crucial for pair programming. Pairs first make sure they have a shared understanding of the relevant parts before they acquire lacking knowledge together. The transfer of *general software development knowledge* plays a rather small role and only occurs *after* the pair dealt with its need for system knowledge. Pairs who maintain a shared understanding may have short, but highly-productive *Focus Phases*; if their *Togetherness* gets too low, however, a *Breakdown* of the pair process may occur.

1 Introduction

The idea of *pair programming* (PP) is probably as old as programming itself: Instead of dealing with a technical problem alone, two software developers sit down on one machine and work on the task together. In the 1990s, Coplien described this idea with his *Pair Design* pattern [6, p. 294], and it has become widely known under its current name in the context of Beck's agile development method *eXtreme Programming* [2], where it is one of the twelve core practices.

As Beck puts it, "*pair programming is a dialog [...] a conversation at many levels*" [2, p. 100]. It is a universal development practice that can be applied

---

F. Zieris (✉)
Freie Universität Berlin, Berlin, Germany
e-mail: zieris@inf.fu-berlin.de

M. Felderer et al. (eds.), *Ernst Denert Award for Software Engineering 2020*,
https://doi.org/10.1007/978-3-030-83128-8_13

to technical tasks beyond mere implementation, such as specifying requirements, architectural and lower-level design, debugging, and testing. It is independent of software domains and technology stacks. With screensharing or dedicated tools, the pair members do not even need to share the same physical workspace [11]. Consequentially, PP is widely used: Estimated conservatively, about 30% of all developers pair-program at least sometimes [13]. Surveys show that practitioners expect a range of benefits [3]:

- Two developers combine their knowledge to produce more ideas and work on more complicated tasks than either pair member could alone and produce better designs in less time.
- They build up lacking knowledge for debugging or system understanding faster and more reliably, which also helps them catch defects in the making.
- They may learn from each other or acquire new knowledge together, which helps them with future tasks and avoids knowledge silos in the team.

In industrial contexts, the transfer of knowledge is particularly important, which is why companies such as Pivotal (now part of VMware) use *"continuous pair programming"* and *"overlapping pair rotation"* for its long-term effects [12].

Although pair programming has been a research subject since the 1990s, it is still not clear to which degree and under which conditions it holds up to these expectations. Through my research, I want to provide actionable advice for practitioners by understanding how PP actually works, which prior research mostly failed to explain (see Sect. 2): Laboratory experiments disregard the complex process that is the pairs' interactions and rely on unrealistically small and simple tasks which do not come close to the knowledge demands of industrial software development. To close that gap, I collected data in industry—mostly video-recordings of everyday PP sessions, along with field observations and interviews—and analyzed it qualitatively (see Sect. 3). I provide a short overview of parts of my findings and how I validated them with practitioners in Sect. 4 before I conclude in Sect. 5. This chapter is based on four peer-reviewed publications [20–22, 24] and my PhD thesis [19].

2 Overview of Pair Programming Research

There are two main categories of pair programming studies. On the one hand are quantitative studies that compare, under controlled conditions, the results of developers working in pairs to those working alone (Sect. 2.1). Here, the pairs are often formed by researchers and work on carefully chosen tasks. On the other hand are qualitative analyses of natural situations where developers form pairs in a self-decided, often spontaneous manner to work on complex issues (Sect. 2.2).

In the following discussion, I exclude the plethora of studies on pair programming in educational settings where the worked-on tasks are merely a means to an end such as homework assignments or small student projects. I also exclude

PP studies that are based solely on questionnaires and interviews, as the subjects' reports do not necessarily reflect real events accurately and in detail.

2.1 Quantitative Pair Programming Studies: Findings and Problems

There has been a number of controlled experiments in which the quality and speed of programming pairs is compared to solos. The meta-analysis by Hannay et al. [7] covers 18 such experiments and finds small and medium positive PP effects on *quality* and (wall-clock) *time*,[1] but no significant effect on *effort*:[2] Pairs appear to be faster, but *not twice* as fast to outweigh the immediate cost of paying two developers. More noteworthy, however, is the large between-study variance, or *heterogeneity*, which indicates that the experiments actually measured *different* effects rather than the *same* effect with some added random noise. Future work should thus focus "*on untangling the moderating factors*" such as task complexity, developer experience (in programming and in pair-programming), motivation, and team climate [7].

The large experiment by Arisholm et al. [1] attempted to understand the influence of two of these factors on *quality* and *time* by hiring 295 professional software developers to work either alone or in pairs on a set of corrective maintenance tasks. To test the impact of developer experience, the groups were split according to their level of *expertise* (junior, intermediate, senior). Additionally, half of the subjects worked in either a "simple system" or a "complex" one in order to investigate the role of *task complexity*. The researchers identified a few tendencies (such as *simple tasks get done faster with PP* and *juniors appear to produce higher quality with PP*), but could not explain the moderating effect of either *task complexity* or *experience* because many differences between the respective subgroups were not statistically significant or even contradictory. In the words of the authors: "*we are still far from being able to explain why we observe the given effects.*"

The recurring problems of many, even high-profile quantitative PP studies are:

1. There are simply too many potential moderator variables to be tested in controlled experiments with reasonable effort. The above experiment by Arisholm et al. [1] failed to understand just *two* and failed despite tremendous effort and cost.
2. The experimental situations differ from industrial practice in a number of relevant ways, including the following (illustrated with aspects of Arisholm et al.'s experiment): The subjects have little prior experience with the practice of working in pairs (93 out of 98 pairs had *no prior PP experience*); the systems

---

[1] Note that the 95% confidence intervals of the standardized effect sizes are quite large: Hedge's $g = [0.07, 0.60]$ for the effect on *quality* and $g = [0.13, 0.94]$ for *time*.

[2] The 95% confidence interval accordingly spans negative and positive values: $g = [-1.18, 0.13]$

are rather small (even the "complex system" comprised merely 12 classes and 287 lines of code); the tasks are small, too, and span only short time periods (the average pair completed all their three tasks in 1 h); developers have no say in with whom to pair or whether to pair at all for the given task (researchers formed only pairs with the *same* level of expertise); common *quality* metrics only account for short-term effects (e.g., number of passed test cases, or just a single binary *correctness* value). Additionally, the subjects work in systems completely unknown to them, which does not at all represent everyday practice where developers usually build up a mental model of their system over months or even years.

All these constraints are in service of keeping measurements comparable between subjects and the extent of the experiments manageable. At the same time, they reduce the complexity of software development to mere programming contests—and are still not able to explain the observed effects.

3. In effect, *pair programming* is considered to be something canonical which developers simply *do* when told to do so. But how to pair-program "right"? Do the pair members discuss several ideas upfront and carefully select the best? Do they assume the often proposed roles of active "driver" who writes the code, and "navigator" who watches out for defects and larger implications (e.g., Williams and Kessler [17])? Or do they follow the idea of one partner until they hit a dead-end and then switch places? Or does one partner remain silent until she notices a problem? Different pairs will probably follow different approaches.

Overall, quantitative comparisons of solo and pair programming in contrived settings based solely on summative metrics and short-term outcomes are of limited scientific value. To gain a deeper understanding of how and when PP actually works, the underlying *process* needs to be studied using *qualitative* research approaches that observe and analyze the practice under natural conditions in real industrial contexts.

2.2 Qualitative Pair Programming Studies: Findings and Problems

A few qualitative-quantitative studies recorded PP sessions in industrial contexts (e.g., [5]) or at least involved professional developers (e.g., [16]), transcribed and labeled the pairs' dialogs following some coding scheme, and then calculated different statistics. These studies show that there is constant communication during pair programming and that there are no systematic differences between the type of utterances of supposed "drivers" and "navigators"—at least for developers with more than 6 months of pair programming experience [4]. However, these studies use cumulative metrics which only reflect the *total number* of occurrences of certain events, but not their temporal and causal order. Whether a pair member does X twice in the middle of the session, or once in the beginning and once again in the end—

it is counted as two Xs either way. Without considering the *process*, such research approaches are also not well suited to explain pair programming.

Purely qualitative studies focus on building theories rather than testing hypothe-ses. They elaborate on how PP proceeds on a more typical level and show how pairs follow certain communication patterns (e.g., explicit and implicit teaching [8], or *Restarting, Planning, Action* [18]). A central problem of many such studies is that they often result in loose collections of labels concerning some PP aspect, rather than aiming for an integrated theory of PP as a whole. To give one example, Plonka et al. [8] list six *"teaching strategies"* but do not investigate their relationships, e.g., how developers decide which one to use, whether there are preferred ones, or whether they are a matter of conscious decision at all. These studies do not provide obvious starting points for further research. Furthermore, a practitioner perspective—which would at least hint at possible applications in industry—is often missing.

3 Research Goal, Data, and Method

The goal of my research is to understand how pair programming, and in particular, *knowledge transfer* in pair programming, actually works. This is not about deciding whether pair programming is "better." Rather, I want to provide actionable advice for practitioners who want to pair-program, allowing them to avoid problems and reap the potential benefits.

My qualitative research follows the *Grounded Theory Methodology* (GTM) as formulated by Strauss and Corbin [14] and builds on the groundwork of Salinger and Prechelt [10], who developed a "vocabulary" of base activities to characterize the fundamental building blocks of a PP process.

The basis for my analyses is data which colleagues and myself have been collecting in industry since 2007. So far, we recorded 67 sessions of professional software developers in 13 companies working on their everyday tasks in pairs (sometimes also in groups of three or four). The recordings consist of a screencast, webcam video, and audio of the pair's dialog (see Fig. 1). We also conducted reflective interviews with the developers the day after their recording and organized group discussions and workshops to achieve a better understanding of the teams' contexts and to evaluate our findings. All data collection activities are detailed in a technical report [23].

In the manner of *theoretical sampling* [14], I iteratively selected material from the already available repository and established new contacts with three companies to collect additional data. For my analysis, I selected sessions with different contexts (e.g., application domains and technology stacks) and with developers at varying experience levels in both homogenous and heterogenous pair constellations. In total, I analyzed 27 sessions from 10 companies with 29 developers (see Table 1).

I did not perform my analyses on transcripts, but directly on the video material. Notes from field observations and reflective developer interviews provided

Table 1 Analyzed sessions, some of which continue earlier ones (↳). Sessions JA1 and JA2 were distributed, all others colocated; MA1, OA1, OA2, OA5, and OA8 are in English, all others in German. Developers C4, C6, and O3 are female, all others are male. See [23] for more details

ID	Length	Developers	Session content
\multicolumn{4}{l}{Company A: Content Management System (*Java, Objective-C, SQL*)}			
AA1	2 h 22 min	A1 A2	Fix five similar bugs touching both frontend and backend
\multicolumn{4}{l}{Company B: Social Media (*PHP, JavaScript, SQL, HTML, CSS*)}			
BA1	1 h 46 min	B1 B2	Read foreign code, implement cache, discuss specification
BB1	1 h 21 min	B1 B2	New feature from scratch (template); discuss requirements
BB2	1 h 51 min	B1 B2	↳ impl. model, controller, template; discuss requirements
BB3	1 h 32 min	B1 B2	↳ implement template, controller; discuss requirements
\multicolumn{4}{l}{Company C: Graphical Geo Information System (*Java*)}			
CA1	1 h 18 min	C1 C2	Implement new form in GUI (C1 already started)
CA2	1 h 24 min	C2 C5	Architecture discussion (C5 already started), refactoring
CA3	2 h 10 min	C6 C7	Implement context menu entry, incl. test case & refactoring
CA4	1 h 34 min	C4 C7	Implement selection feature w/ special key-binding
CA5	1 h 23 min	C3 C4	Implement feature to split graphical elements
\multicolumn{4}{l}{Company D: Estate Customer Relationship Management (*Java, XML*)}			
DA2	2 h 24 min	D3 D4	Planned feature impl., turned to widespread refactoring
\multicolumn{4}{l}{Company E: Logistics and Routing (*C++, XML*)}			
EA1	1 h 17 min	E1 E2	Step-by-step debugging of display error in the GUI
\multicolumn{4}{l}{Company J: Data Management for Public Radio Broadcast (*Java*)}			
JA1	1 h 7 min	J1 J2	Walkthrough of J2's code, discuss possible refactorings
JA2	1 h 15 min	J1 J2	Review of J2's new API, define requirements
\multicolumn{4}{l}{Company K: Real Estate Platform (*Java, SQL, CoffeeScript*)}			
KA1	1 h 59 min	K1 K2	Set up dev. env. discuss inter-system API design, 1st impl.
KB1	53 min	K2 K3	Add new class to model, write and debug database migration
KC1	59 min	K2 K3	Set up test env., discuss test approaches for GUI feature
KC2	2 h 1 min	K2 K3	↳ trying diff. test approaches, struggling w/ debugger

(continued)

Table 1 (continued)

ID	Length	Developers	Session content
Company M: Data Analysis in Energy and Transportation Sector (*SQL*)			
MA1	2 h	M1 M2	Explanation of table model
Company O: Online Project Planning (*CoffeeScript*)			
OA1	1 h 24 min	O3 O4	Understand foreign component, try to read state for testing
OA2	1 h 32 min	O3 O4	↳ try to set up (parts of) the component for testing
OA5	1 h 9 min	O1 O3	Bug fix: amend test cases, refactor prod. code, fix the bug
OA8	1 h 16 min	O3 O4	Failing test: Investigate prod. and test code, correct mocks
Company P: Online Car Part Resale (*PHP, SQL*)			
PA1	58 min	P1 P2	Walkthrough of DB migration (written by P1), discuss req.
PA2	1 h 30 min	P1 P2	↳ test of migration, debugging, refactor test cases
PA3	1 h 31 min	P1 P3	Implement new API endpoint w/ tests (P3 already started)
PA4	1 h 42 min	P1 P3	↳ implement DB access with OR-mapper

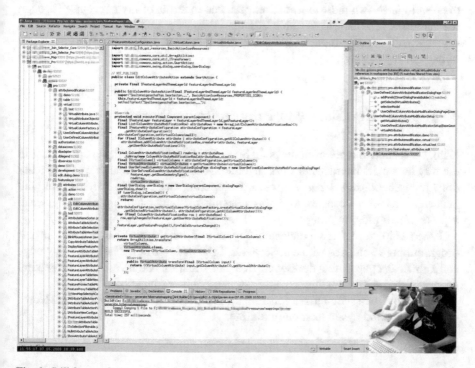

Fig. 1 Still frame of a recorded pair programming session (webcam video in bottom right corner)

Table 2 Member reflection activities with their format and roles of participants (SM—Scrum Master, PO—Product Owner, TM—Technical Manager, D—Developer)

Context	Format	Participants
Company K	Presentation and discussion	~50 (div. roles)
Company O	Workshop	2×SM, 1×PO
Company P	1-on-1 interview	1×SM
Company P	Workshop	6×D, 1×SM, 1×PO
Company P	Post-recording interview (3×)	2×D per interview (3×D in total)
Company Q	1-on-1 interview	1× TM
Company R	Workshop	10×D, 2×TM, 1×SM

additional context information. I applied the GTM practices of *open*, *axial*, and *selective coding* [14] by starting at the level of thousands of individual utterances, and working my way up over hundreds of knowledge transfer episodes (running between a couple of seconds and a few minutes), to clusters of episodes, and to the overall dynamic of whole sessions, until my concepts reached *theoretical saturation* [14].

I evaluated my findings through different *member reflection* activities [15]: 1-on-1 interviews with Scrum Masters and workshops consisted of a short presentation of my research findings followed by reflections on the participants' personal experiences; post-recording interviews were more concrete, as I framed the developers' own most recent PP experience in terms of my concepts. Through the activities summarized in Table 2, I made sure my concepts and observations resonate with the practitioners. In the following section, I provide a brief overview of parts of my findings.

4 Results: How *Does* Pair Programming Work?

Here, I present two types of findings. In Sect. 4.1, I describe low-level differences in the way how pairs interact and work together. Although my research was originally only focused on *knowledge transfer*, deciphering these basic mechanisms and behavioral patterns occurred to me as relevant for understanding all higher-level aspects of pair programming.

I then skip over a few conceptual layers and take a bird's-eye view on pair programming sessions as whole in Sect. 4.2. I characterize how available knowledge and knowledge gaps affect developers in a pair situation and investigate the general dynamics that arise from this.

Section 4.3 then summarizes concrete ideas for how software development teams can apply my findings in their daily routine.

4.1   Fluency and Togetherness

Among the analyzed pairs, I noticed considerable differences in how *fluent* their respective processes were. Most pairs have a continuous flow of conversation where they introduce new topics (which I mark with a ★), refer back to these topics to evaluate or extend them (marked with either ▲ or ◀, in case the partner has yet to "arrive" at the same topic), and clear up the occasional misunderstanding through meta-communication (●)—just like in any normal conversation. But a pair's **Fluency** can also take one of two extreme forms.

On the one hand, some pairs have high-paced **Focus Phases** during which there are practically no speech pauses and where the partners complete each other's thoughts, sentences, and even code lines: There is a quick succession of ★s and ▲s. The developers may speak *at the same time* and in incomplete sentences, but nevertheless understand each other perfectly, such that corrective ●s are rare. It is impossible to grasp the dynamic of a Focus Phase by reading a transcript alone. As an approximation, I compiled all the activities of one Focus Phase in Fig. 2: Within 60 seconds, the pair discusses 11 (!) different topics, constantly talking and editing.

On the other hand, the pair process may also suffer from a **Breakdown**, where the developers do not evaluate each other's ideas and proposals (more self-referential ◀s than pair-referential ▲s) or may even fall into embarrassed silence (a communicative defect, marked with ◆):

O3: *"Ah, it expects a number, but we pass an object."*   ★
O4: [looks puzzled at O3]   ◆
O3: *"It's an object, it's a key-value pair."*   ◀
O4: [silently moves mouse cursor aimlessly across the screen for 30 seconds]   ◆

The Fluency of a PP process comes from the ease with which the two developers can understand the content and intentions of each other's actions and utterances. I call this a pair's momentary **Togetherness**. Through analyzing situations of both high and low Fluency, of close and little Togetherness, I identified the following five contributing factors:

1. A **shared understanding of the software system** allows for efficient communication (e.g., by speaking of "*Factory*" instead of "*FeatureLayerAttributeTable-CellRendererFactory*" and still be perfectly understood by the partner). Where such shared understanding is lacking, more wordy explanations are necessary or more misunderstandings need to be cleared up.
2. A **shared understanding of software development in general** has a similar influence. Knowing about common architectural styles, design patterns, and typical ways to approach certain problems allows for efficient communication and discussion of ideas. Otherwise, it is more difficult to evaluate the partner's proposals which puts a strain on a pair's Togetherness (e.g., "*Erm, okay? Go on then. I'm quite out of my depths here.*").
3. **One shared plan**, e.g., in the form of a strategic decision made earlier, provides a backdrop for quickly understanding and amending tactical proposals:

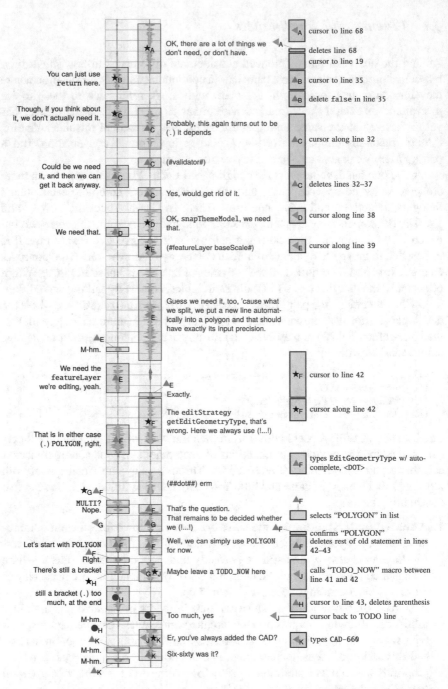

Fig. 2 A Focus Phase of 60 seconds (time runs from top to bottom; columns 1 and 2 contain the pair's utterances, and column 3 the editing activities). The pair starts new topics, furthers them, and repairs potential misunderstandings in quick succession. Overall, they discuss eleven topics (indices A–K), while one partner performs code changes on-the-fly

C3: *"Shall we copy the code and check line-by-line whether it makes sense?"*
C4: *"OK, let's see what we need."*
[... two minutes later ...]
C3: *"[opens file] Ok, there are lot of things we don't need."*
C4: *[pointing at existing code] "That can just not ... ..."*

Without such an understanding, misunderstandings are more common because one developer may have difficulties understanding how their partner's actions fit in the big picture.

O3: *"Maybe* durationInDays *is not defined."*
O4: *"It is defined. Here."*
O3: *"Can we debug this?"*
O4: *"We already did!"*

4. **Workspace awareness** is reduced in distributed pair programming due to the spatial separation of the two developers, but can also be a problem in colocated settings, e.g., with too-small font sizes (*"Where are you right now, which class?"*).
5. A **language barrier** can come from using a foreign language (e.g., in a discussion of two non-native English speakers: *"An 'offset' is a duration?"*) and from idiosyncrasies in one's way of speaking (e.g., saying *"Wait a second"* while meaning *"I'm now going to take mouse and keyboard."*).

The following short exchange illustrates how several of these factors come together.

A Pair's Moment of High Togetherness
The pair agreed on changing the signature of an interface method, and developer C5 asks his partner C2:

C5: *"Erm, do you know the–"* [right-clicks on method name to open context menu]
"How I access the feature to change a method?"
C2: *"That doesn't get you anywhere."*

While C2 does not answer C5's question, his reaction reveals that he very well understood what his partner intends to do. In particular, four factors help C2 understand the following aspects, allowing him to react so promptly:

- **No language barrier**: C5's utterance is a question to which he expects an answer.
- **Workspace awareness**: C5 wants to apply a refactoring (opened context menu) on some method (cursor position).
- **Shared understanding of software development**: C5 refers to the refactoring "Change Method Signature," which is known to both developers for changing a method's signature in all places where it is declared, implemented, or called.

(continued)

- **One shared plan**: C5 wants to apply this particular refactoring probably with the expectation to save some manual editing on their way to change the interface.

This exchange also illustrates that high Togetherness is not the same as agreeing with the partner: C2 apparently disagrees with the C5's assessment of how much time and effort can be saved by applying the automatic refactoring.

The five factors are not independent from another and problems from one factor may also add to the difficulties of another (e.g., a language barrier *and* reduced workspace awareness). Good pairs become aware of their shortcomings and find ways to cope with them, e.g., compensating reduced workspace awareness by more verbose commentary of their editing activities (factor 4), or taking the time to explain some programming idiom which puzzled the partner (factor 2). A pair's Togetherness may change over the course of a session. The partners may (inadvertently or consciously) reduce their Togetherness (*"You go on. I say when I'm back on track."*) or maintain their Togetherness through ● repair activities (*"Why did you just do this?"*).

The not-explained variance of the effects measured in PP experiments (see Sect. 2.1) could be due to differences in Togetherness among the subject pairs *and* different competencies to deal with them. Factors 2 and 3 (shared understanding of software development and one shared plan) may play an important role even in contrived experimental situations. But there is no telling in hindsight. This observation emphasizes the importance of understanding the underlying processes rather than just reducing PP to *time spent* and *lines of code produced*. With such a narrow perspective, pair properties such as Fluency and Togetherness remain hidden.

4.2   Knowledge Wants, Knowledge Needs, and Prototypical Dynamics

At the heart of my research is the question of how pair programmers transfer and acquire knowledge. A central observation is that knowledge transfer happens in **every session**—be it as the decided *goal* to introduce the partner to a part of the system she has never seen before, or as a *side-effect* of closing a gap in each other's system or programming understanding (maintaining Togetherness, see Sect. 4.1).

In the course of a pair programming session, a developer will sooner or later perceive a **Knowledge Want**, which could be paraphrased as *I want to know this* (internal Knowledge Want), *I want you to know this* (external), or *We want to know this* (collective). This is what motivates episodes of knowledge transfer during

Fig. 3 Initial constellations of Knowledge Needs in the analyzed pair programming sessions. *One-sided S gap* and *Two-sided S gap* are quite common ("normal" software development); *No relevant gaps* and *Too-large, two-fold gap* are rare (greenfield development, and impossible task); *Complementary gaps* can lead to a mutually satisfying teaching and learning experience

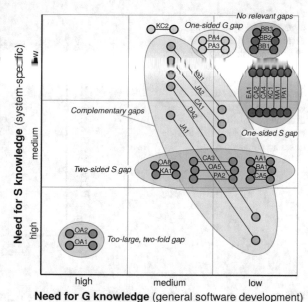

which she asks her partner, provides her with explanations, or involves her in the acquisition of new knowledge through reading source code until her Knowledge Want is satisfied.

In contrast to local Knowledge Wants, a developer is not necessarily aware of the extent of her global **Knowledge Need**, which are her knowledge gaps regarding to the specific demands of the task. The same task may be *easy* for someone with all the relevant knowledge available (low Knowledge Need), or rather *difficult* if the system or technology are unfamiliar (high Knowledge Need). Conversely, the same developer will have to deal with different Knowledge Needs for different tasks.

Based on the analysis of hundreds of knowledge transfer episodes, I distinguish two types of knowledge that are relevant in industrial pair programming sessions: System-specific **S knowledge**, which includes knowledge about requirements, the architecture and low-level design, concrete usage of technologies, and behavior of the system and defects; and generic **G knowledge** about software development as such, which covers design patterns, programming languages, tools, and libraries.

Pair programming sessions can now be characterized by the extent of the partners' initial Knowledge Needs regarding the S- and the G-dimension and the trajectory they take by pursuing their Knowledge Wants. I identified six recurring initial pair constellations (Fig. 3), including pairs with *Complementary Gaps*, where one partner possesses more task-relevant G knowledge (e.g., about design patterns and refactorings) while the other has more task-relevant S knowledge (e.g., because she originally implemented that part of the system). Others may have a *One-Sided S Gap*, which occurs often when one partner built up an S advantage through prior work.

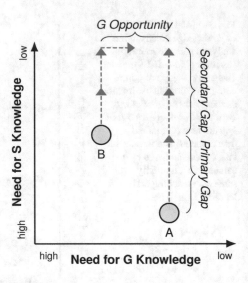

Fig. 4 Three session dynamic prototypes. Pairs first address differences in system understanding (*Primary Gap*) before acquiring lacking system understanding together (*Secondary Gap*). A difference in software development knowledge then poses an *Opportunity*

Considering the knowledge trajectories taken by the pairs in *all* sessions, I discovered the following three **prototypical session dynamics** (see also Fig. 4):

1. **Closing the Primary Gap**, which is the difference in task-specific system understanding between the pair members. There might be no such gap, if both developers worked on the task before. Quite often, however, a developer joins another who already worked on the task. This is the case in this example, where one developer has a fresh mental model of the system and his partner does not:

    C1: *"I already started and programmed for an hour. I started with the GUI. I'll show you quickly"* [opens overview of recent changes]

    In another scenario, one partner's last encounter with a piece of software was several months ago, but he still has an S knowledge advantage because his partner has never seen it:

    J2: *"Do you know the plugin, or don't you know it?"*
    J1: [exhales audibly] *"Just show to it me again."*
    J2: *"OK, I can give you the big picture of what this plugin does, overall."*

    If there is a Primary Gap, pairs address it early in their session. Not dealing with this gap properly is an impediment to the pair's Togetherness (factor 1, shared system understanding, see Sect. 4.1).

2. **Closing the Secondary Gap**, which consists of acquiring task-relevant system knowledge which neither developer possesses. This is common in debugging scenarios but can also happen in the context of feature implementations where the pair needs to find the right spot to add new logic. Pair programmers may acquire such understanding together by reading source code or using a debugger. Good pairs make sure to maintain their Togetherness in this phase, too: If one partner pulls ahead, she helps her partner take the ental steps. Note that in some

situations, it may not be necessary for both partners to understand the system to the same degree, e.g., if only one of them is expected to continue working on it in the future.

3. *G Opportunity* arises when one partner possesses more *G* knowledge than the other. Unlike a difference in S knowledge, a G knowledge difference was never a problem in the analyzed sessions. In all instances, however, pairs only seized this opportunity *after* closing their Primary and Secondary Gaps. Even if the *Knowledge Need* was already there, pairs do not appear to develop a *Knowledge Want* regarding G knowledge until their S Knowledge Wants are satisfied. Therefore, exchanges like this one tend to happen only late in the session:

> [... 1:30 hours into session DA2 ...]
> D4: *"Do you know about OSGi class loading?"*
> D3: *"Class-what? Not really, no."*
> D4: *"Should I tell you?"*
> D3: *"Sure."*

These three dynamics characterize the majority of all analyzed PP sessions: Pairs first address their Primary Gap, then their Secondary Gap, before potentially seizing their G Opportunity.

The special case are pairs where *both partners* lack relevant G knowledge. A moderate deficit is not problematic, as the developers simply try to complete their task with the means available. If the pairs lack a lot of G knowledge, however, their task gets much more difficult because they cannot build up the necessary system understanding, as one developer exclaims after an hour of trying to understand a single source file:

> O3: *"Type? Function? I don't even know what this is!"*

Such situations should be rare, though, as practitioners appear to avoid such massive overtaxation by choosing partners and tasks that match their existing knowledge.

Overall, knowledge transfer in pair programming in industry is mostly about *system understanding*. Not only does the vast majority of knowledge transfer episodes pertain to system-specific *S knowledge* rather than generic *G knowledge*; pair programmers also deal with their S knowledge gaps *first*, before they may look for *G Opportunities* to explain general software development concepts.

4.3 Practical Applications

I developed the following three practices for software development teams to make use of my findings in their everyday practice:

1. **Pair Forming**: Teams can use the G-S chart (Fig. 3) to discuss the Knowledge Needs of all team members for an upcoming task and find a favorable constellation, e.g., one with a *G Opportunity*.

2. **Set Session Goal**: Do both pair members need to understand the task-relevant system parts enough to continue the work, or is some *Primary Gap* tolerable? Is there a G Opportunity that could be seized?
3. **Reflect on Session**: After the session, the pair may consider questions like: Did we underestimate our Knowledge Needs, i.e., are there lacking pieces of S or G knowledge whose relevance we were not aware of? Should we discuss these with the rest of the team?

I evaluated my findings and the practice ideas in four companies through workshops and interviews. Overall, concepts presented in this chapter were well received by the practitioners. Due to practical constraints such as team size, developer availability, and tasks with a rigid scope, I was only able to test the third practice *Reflect on Session* in the field. It helped the developers remember and appreciate pieces of knowledge that they transferred or acquired in their session:

> P1: *"I guess that [P3] learned in both dimensions, even technologically [G knowledge] since we now use more PHP7–"*
> P3: *"Right! I totally forgot about that. That was actually really cool."*

Although I had no chance to observe it, the practitioners also expected the other two practices (*Pair Forming* and *Set Session Goal*) to have positive effects, if their context allowed them more degrees of freedom.

5 Summary and Outlook

Pair programming is a way of developing software that is amendable to every aspect of software development in all application domains, regardless of concrete technology. It is widely used in industry with the expectation to speed up development, lead to higher quality, and spread knowledge in development teams. Prior research focused too much on directly measurable effects and too little on the processes and mechanisms that are at work when two software developers tackle a complex problem together in a real environment. My qualitative analysis of 27 industrial pair programming sessions from 10 companies lead to the following central observations:

- Despite what has been proclaimed for many years, the typical programmer pair in industry does *not* consist of an active "driver" and a strategically thinking and defect-hunting "navigator," but of two software developers who are engaged in a dialog, discussing ideas and building up a shared understanding of task and system. Admittedly, one of them usually does happen to use keyboard and mouse to interact with the computer for some time span, but that is not what makes pair programming work.
- What allows pairs to a have *fluent* process is a high degree of *Togetherness* which enables them to understand each other's ideas and arguments. In particular, pairs need to maintain a shared understanding of their software system and of

software development in general. Having one shared plan also helps a long way. Additionally, pairs may need to cope with reduced workspace awareness or language barriers of sorts. Doing all of the above may lead to short, but highly productive issues in their Togetherness drops too low, a Breakdown of their process may ensue.

- Two main types of knowledge are relevant in industrial pair programming sessions: Pairs mostly deal with (lacks of) specific knowledge about their software system (*S knowledge*) and to a lesser degree with (lacks of) generic knowledge about software development general (*G knowledge*). Transfer of S knowledge practically happens in *all* pair programming sessions.
- There is a number of recurring pair constellations which result from the individually different levels of applicable pre-existing knowledge. A pair's constellation is highly *task-dependent*: The same two developers may have their supposed "expert" and "novice" labels reversed when they work in different parts of the system or happen to need certain technology skills. Amending the task's scope therefore can put both developers in the position to teach the other something new.

My work focused primarily on two of the five factors that influence a pair's Togetherness: Their shared understanding of the software system and of software development in general (factors 1 and 2, see Sect. 4.1). Other research by Schenk et al. [11] already looked at how good pairs deal with reduced *workspace awareness* (factor 4). This leaves an in-depth analysis of *decision making*, i.e., how pairs come up with *one shared plan* (factor 3), as important future work. Although I did not encounter it in my data, practitioner literature suggests that they are also more ways for a pair's process to have a *Breakdown*, e.g., due to *power dynamics* [9].

I was personally involved in collecting primary data in four companies (K, M, O, and P; see also Table 1) and evaluated the above findings in five contexts (Table 2), where they were met with great resonance, which is an important quality criterion of qualitative research besides the rigorous analysis of rich data [15]. Beyond the "scientific" results already discussed, my interactions with the practitioners were fruitful, because it made the teams aware of how little thought they had previously put into what *their* implementation of the pair programming practice actually entails:

- Company O, for example, considered themselves an "all-PP company." They could not organize a structured onboarding process and mandated pair programming and regular team rotations instead. However, during my 4-week observation period, there were only a few PP sessions, but a widespread lack of technology knowledge, which the Scrum Masters only became aware of through my research activities.
- The product owner and developers in company P expected pair programming to yield "all the benefits," but had no priority: Better design, fewer defects, faster progress, transfer of knowledge, and enjoyable work were all equally important, and each PP session was expected to have these effects. My workshop made them reconsider their priorities.

It is my impression that my discussions with the practitioners made them reflect on their work, motivated discussions on which PP effects they actually care about, and made them see forming pairs considerately, setting sessions goals, and reflecting on recent PP sessions as opportunities to achieve these effects.

I try to keep in touch with the companies even years after the initial data collection (in particular through their Scrum Masters) and continue to seek the exchange with more practitioners to make my findings more widely known.

References

1. Arisholm, E., Gallis, H., Dybå, T., Sjøberg, D.I.: Evaluating pair programming with respect to system complexity and programmer expertise. IEEE Trans. Softw. Eng. **33**(2), 65–86 (2007). https://doi.org/10.1109/TSE.2007.17
2. Beck, K.: Extreme Programming Explained: Embrace Change. Addison-Wesley, Reading (1999)
3. Begel, A., Nagappan, N.: Pair programming: What's in it for me? In: Proceedings of the Second ACM-IEEE International Symposium on Empirical Software Engineering and Measurement, pp. 120–128. ACM, New York (2008). https://doi.org/10.1145/1414004.1414026
4. Bryant, S.: Double trouble: Mixing qualitative and quantitative methods in the study of extreme programmers. In: IEEE Symposium on Visual Languages and Human Centric Computing, VL/HCC '04, pp. 55–61. IEEE, Piscataway (2004). https://doi.org/10.1109/VLHCC.2004.20
5. Bryant, S., Romero, P., du Boulay, B.: Pair programming and the mysterious role of the navigator. International Journal of Human-Computer Studies **66**(7), 519–529 (2008). https://doi.org/10.1016/j.ijhcs.2007.03.005
6. Coplien, J.: A generative development-process pattern language. In: Rising, L. (ed.) The Patterns Handbook: Techniques, Strategies, and Applications, pp. 243–300. Cambridge University Press, Cambridge (1998)
7. Hannay, J.E., Dybå, T., Arisholm, E., Sjøberg, D.I.: The effectiveness of pair programming: a meta-analysis. Inform. Softw. Technol. **51**(7), 1110–1122 (2009). https://doi.org/10.1016/j.infsof.2009.02.001
8. Plonka, L., Sharp, H., van der Linden, J., Dittrich, Y.: Knowledge transfer in pair programming: an in-depth analysis. International Journal of Human-Computer Studies **73**, 66–78 (2015). https://doi.org/10.1016/j.ijhcs.2014.09.001
9. Pyhäjärvi, M.: Power dynamics in pairs and mobs (2018). https://visible-quality.blogspot.com/2018/05/power-dynamics-in-pairs-and-mobs.html
10. Salinger, S., Prechelt, L.: Understanding Pair Programming: The Base Layer. Books on Demand (2013). http://www.inf.fu-berlin.de/inst/ag-se/pubs/SalPre13-baseconbook.pdf
11. Schenk, J., Prechelt, L., Salinger, S.: Distributed-pair programming can work well and is not just distributed pair-programming. In: Proceedings of the 36th International Conference on Software Engineering, ICSE '14, pp. 74–83. ACM Press, New York (2014). https://doi.org/10.1145/2591062.2591188
12. Sedano, T., Ralph, P., Péraire, C.: Sustainable software development through overlapping pair rotation. In: Proceedings of the 10th ACM/IEEE International Symposium on Empirical Software Engineering and Measurement, ESEM '16, pp. 19:1–19:10. ACM Press, New York (2016). https://doi.org/10.1145/2961111.2962590
13. StackOverflow: 2018 stack overflow developer survey (2018). https://insights.stackoverflow.com/survey/2018
14. Strauss, A., Corbin, J.: Basics of Qualitative Research. Grounded Theory Procedure and Techniques. Sage Publications, New York (1990)

15. Tracy, S.J.: Qualitative quality: eight "big-tent" criteria for excellent qualitative research. Qual. Inq. **16**(10), 837–851 (2010). https://doi.org/10.1177/1077800410383121
16. Walle, T., Hannay, J.E.: Personality and the nature of collaboration in pair programming. In: Proceedings of the 3rd International Symposium on Empirical Software Engineering and Measurement, pp. 203–213. IEEE, Piscataway (2009). https://doi.org/10.1109/ESEM.2009.5315996
17. Williams, L., Kessler, R.R.: Pair Programming Illuminated. Addison-Wesley, Reading (2002)
18. Zarb, M., Hughes, J., Richards, J.: Industry-inspired guidelines improve students' pair programming communication. In: Proceedings of the 18th ACM Conference on Innovation and Technology in Computer Science Education, pp. 135–140 (2013). https://doi.org/10.1145/2462476.2462504
19. Zieris, F.: Qualitative analysis of knowledge transfer in pair programming. Ph.D. Thesis, Fachbereich Mathematik und Informatik, Freie Universität Berlin (2020). https://doi.org/10.17169/refubium-28718
20. Zieris, F., Prechelt, L.: On knowledge transfer skill in pair programming. In: Proceedings of the 8th ACM/IEEE International Symposium on Empirical Software Engineering and Measurement, ESEM '14, pp. 11:1–11:10. ACM, New York (2014). https://doi.org/10.1145/2652524.2652529
21. Zieris, F., Prechelt, L.: Observations on knowledge transfer of professional software developers during pair programming. In: Proceedings of the 38th International Conference on Software Engineering Companion, ICSE '16 (SEIP), pp. 242–250. ACM, New York (2016). https://doi.org/10.1145/2889160.2889249
22. Zieris, F., Prechelt, L.: Explaining pair programming session dynamics from knowledge gaps. In: Proceedings of the 42nd International Conference on Software Engineering, ICSE '20, pp. 421–432. ACM, New York (2020). https://doi.org/10.1145/3377811.3380925
23. Zieris, F., Prechelt, L.: PP-ind: Description of a repository of industrial pair programming research data (2020). https://arxiv.org/abs/2002.03121v5
24. Zieris, F., Prechelt, L.: Two elements of pair programming skill. In: Proceedings of the 43rd International Conference on Software Engineering, ICSE '21 (NIER). IEEE, Piscataway (2021). https://arxiv.org/abs/2102.06460

Printed in the United States
by Baker & Taylor Publisher Services